BOGART
A Life in Hollywood

◆ ◆ ◆

BIOGRAPHIES BY JEFFREY MEYERS

A Fever at the Core: The Idealist in Politics

Married to Genius

Katherine Mansfield

The Enemy: A Biography of Wyndham Lewis

Hemingway

Manic Power: Robert Lowell and His Circle

D. H. Lawrence

Joseph Conrad

Edgar Allan Poe: His Life and Legacy

Scott Fitzgerald

Edmund Wilson

Robert Frost

Bogart: A Life in Hollywood

BOGART

A Life in Hollywood

◆ ◆ ◆

JEFFREY MEYERS

FROMM INTERNATIONAL
NEW YORK

Contents

Illustrations   *vii*

Acknowledgments   *ix*

Prologue: Bogart and Hemingway   *1*

1 ✦ Childhood, Andover and the Navy, 1899–1919   5

2 ✦ Broadway and Failure in Hollywood, 1920–1934   23

3 ✦ *The Petrified Forest* and Warner Bros., 1935–1937   48

4 ✦ Strife with Mayo, 1937–1942   78

5 ✦ Professional Gangster, 1938–1940   95

6 ✦ John Huston and *The Maltese Falcon*, 1941–1942   *114*

7 ✦ War Movies and *Casablanca*, 1943   *132*

8 ✦ Warner, Bacall and Howard Hawks, 1944–1946   *159*

9 ✦ Fourth Marriage, 1945–1950   *184*

10 ✦ A Celebrity in Politics, 1947–1951   *196*

11 ✦ Mexico and the Florida Keys, 1948–1950   *218*

12 ✦ Africa and the Academy Award, 1951–1953   *244*

13 ✦ A Versatile Actor, 1954   *270*

Contents

14 ✦ The Desperate Hours, 1954–1956   287

15 ✦ A Respectable Disease, 1956–1957   304

    Epilogue: The Bogart Cult   318

    Notes   327

    Bogart's Plays and Films   352

    Bibliography   354

    Index   359

Illustrations

Dr. Belmont DeForest Bogart, c. 1900
Maud Bogart with baby Humphrey, 1900 (*Courtesy of Joe Hyams*)
Maud's sketch of baby Humphrey, 1900
Humphrey, 1901 (*Courtesy of Kobal Collection*)
Humphrey, 1907 (*AP/Wide World Photos*)
Bogart at Andover, 1917
Bogart in naval uniform, 1918 (*AP/Wide World Photos*)
Stuart Rose, 1918
William A. Brady, 1928
Cradle Snatchers, with Mary Boland (center), 1925
Helen Menken, 1923
Mary Philips, 1936 (*Culver Pictures*)
I Loved You Wednesday, with Rose Hobart, 1932
The Petrified Forest, with Bette Davis and Leslie Howard, 1936 (© *1936 Turner Entertainment Co. All rights reserved*)
Jack Warner and his studio, 1940s (*Courtesy Warner Bros.*)
Marked Woman, 1937, with Bette Davis and Mayo Methot (© *1937 Turner Entertainment Co. All rights reserved*)
Angels with Dirty Faces, with James Cagney, 1938 (© *1938 Turner Entertainment Co. All rights reserved*)
Dead End, with Marjorie Main, 1937
Bogart and Mayo, drunk and kicking, early 1940s
King of the Underworld, 1939 (*Courtesy of Kobal Collection*)
Horn Avenue house, with Bogart and Mayo, 1942
Virginia City, 1940 (*Culver Pictures*)
Putting on make-up for *The Return of Doctor X*, 1939 (*Courtesy of Eastman House*)

Illustrations

High Sierra, with Ida Lupino, 1941

The Maltese Falcon, with Peter Lorre and John Huston, 1941 *(Courtesy of Eastman House)*

The Big Shot, with Irene Manning, 1942 *(Courtesy of Irene Manning)*

Verita Peterson, 1943 *(Courtesy of Verita Peterson Thompson)*

Casablanca, with Claude Raines, Paul Henreid and Ingrid Bergman, 1943

Slim and Howard Hawks, 1940s *(Courtesy of the Estate of Nancy Kieth)*

To Have and Have Not, with Lauren Bacall and Marcel Dalio, 1945

Bogart and Bacall, with her gold whistle, late 1940s *(Courtesy Warner Bros.)*

The *Santana*, 1940s *(Culver Pictures)*

The Big Sleep, with Bacall, John Ridgely and Howard Hawks, 1946 *(Courtesy of Eastman House)*

Dark Passage, with Bacall, 1947 *(Courtesy of Kobal Collection)*

Bogart signing the Warners contract, with Morgan Maree, Sam Jaffe, Bacall and Mary Baker, December 1946 *(Courtesy Warner Bros.)*

Committee for the First Amendment, flying to Washington: Geraldine Brooks, Paul Henreid, June Havoc, Bogart, Marsha Hunt, Bacall, Gene Kelly, Danny Kaye, Richard Conte and Evelyn Keyes, October 1947 *(Courtesy of Marsha Hunt and Evelyn Keyes)*

The Treasure of the Sierra Madre, with John Huston and Walter Huston, 1948 *(Culver Pictures)*

Key Largo, with Bacall and John Huston, 1948 *(Courtesy Warner Bros.)*

Richard Brooks, 1950s

Bogart drinking with Bacall and Mike Romanoff, late 1940s *(Courtesy of Gloria Romanoff)*

Bogart with his panda, 1949 *(Bettmann)*

In a Lonely Place, with Nicholas Ray and Gloria Grahame, 1950 *(Columbia Pictures)*

The *African Queen* tows the actors and crew up the Ruiki River, 1951

232 South Mapleton Drive, 1950s *(AP/Wide World Photos)*

Bogart with Stephen, Leslie and Bacall, 1954

Nunnally Johnson, 1959 *(Courtesy of Dorris Johnson)*

Beat the Devil, with Peter Lorre, 1954

The Caine Mutiny, with Van Johnson and Todd Karns, 1954 *(Columbia Pictures)*

The Barefoot Contessa, with Ava Gardner, 1954

Acknowledgments

It is a pleasure to acknowledge the generous assistance I received while writing this book. Many friends provided books, photocopies and clippings, addresses and phone numbers, tips and leads, medical explanations, encouragement and sound advice: Morris Brownell, Jackson Bryer, Quentin Curtis, Ronald Hayman, Richard Hertz, Francis King, Phillip Knightley, John Martin, Arthur Miller, Ellen Nims, Dr. Mario Papagni, David and Janet Peoples, and Dr. Joseph Perloff. I am grateful to Paul and Dr. Ellen Alkon for warm hospitality in Los Angeles.

For personal interviews I would like to thank Angela Allen, Clarence Bruner-Smith, Jack Cardiff, Edward Dmytryk, Amanda Dunne, Ted Eden, Dr. Michael Flynn, Frank Hamlin, Marsha Hunt, Kim Hunter, Joe Hyams, Dorris Johnson, Evelyn Keyes, Ernest Lehman, Joan Leslie, Cynthia Lindsay, Delbert Mann, Irene Manning, Jess Morgan, Sheridan Morley, Richard Morse, Marvin Paige, Gloria Romanoff, Lizabeth Scott, Vincent Sherman, Jeanie Sims, Warren Stevens, John Strauss, Gloria Stuart, Sylvia Sheekman Thompson, Verita Peterson Thompson, David Thomson, Sir Peter Ustinov, Malvin Wald, Billy Wilder and Sir John Woolf. I also had phone conversations with Dr. William Beck, Leslie Bogart, Julius Epstein and Katharine Hepburn.

For letters about Bogart I am grateful to Eddie Albert, Matthew Bernstein, Theodore Bikel, Travis Bogard, Anne Brewer, Karen Choppa, Jonathan Coe, Alistair Cooke, Aljean Harmetz, Bruce Kawin, Harrison Kinney, Leonid Kinskey, Ring Lardner, Jr., Leslie Huston Marple, Susan Ray, Frank Sinatra, Robert Sklar, Peter Viertel and Victoria Wilson; and to various institutions: American Red Cross, British Film Institute, Columbia Pictures, Columbia University College of Physicians and Sur-

Acknowledgments

geons, Curtis Management, Directors Guild of America, Federal Bureau of Investigation and Senator Barbara Boxer, Greenwood Publishers, IATSE (Local 706), Medical Society of the State of New York, Museum of the City of New York, National Personnel Records Center (Naval Personnel Records), New York Academy of Medicine, Ontario County (New York) Records and Archives Center, Screen Actors Guild, Shapiro-Lichtman Agency, Steuben County (New York) Historian, University of California Medical School, USO: United Service Organizations, Warner Bros., Writers Guild of America and Yale University Alumni Records.

The main sources of unpublished material, clippings and rare films on Bogart are at the Doheny Library of the University of Southern California, which has the Warner Bros. Archive (contracts, memos, correspondence, scripts, daily production logs and publicity material) as well as the papers of Edgar Bergen, Philip Dunne, Mark Hellinger, Louella Parsons and Jack Warner (curators: Stuart Ng and the extraordinarily helpful Ned Comstock); and the Margaret Herrick Library of the Academy of Motion Picture Arts and Sciences, which has the papers of the magazine writer Gladys Hall, Hedda Hopper, John Huston, the publicist Marty Weiser, and oral histories of Philip Dunne, Gene and Marjorie Fowler, and Sam Jaffe (curator: Sam Gill).

I also did research at the American Film Institute, the Pacific Film Archive, UCLA (curator: Lou Ellen Kramer), the University of California at Berkeley and Berkeley Public Library; and received additional material from many other libraries: Boston University (Eric Hatch and Nunnally Johnson papers; curator: Howard Gotlieb), Brigham Young University (Howard Hawks papers), Burbank Public Library, Columbia University (Ronald Grele, Oral History Research Office), Cornell University, Harvard University, Multnomah County Library (Portland, Oregon), New York Public Library for the Performing Arts, Ohio State University (Louis Bromfield papers), Phillips Academy, Andover (curator: Ruth Quattlebaum), Princeton University, Southern Methodist University, Trinity School (curator: Barbara Lutz), United States Naval Academy, University of Texas, Vanderbilt University, Wesleyan University, Wisconsin Center for Film and Theater Research, Wisconsin State Historical Society and University of Wyoming.

Peter Davison gave me shrewd editorial advice. As always, my wife, Valerie Meyers, scrutinized each chapter, improved the book and compiled the index.

The ice does not break until someone mentions the movies. Suddenly, everyone is alert and adept.

Gore Vidal, *Screening History*

BOGART
A Life in Hollywood

✦ ✦ ✦

PROLOGUE

Bogart and Hemingway

BOGART AND HEMINGWAY never met, but their personal lives and creative work were strikingly similar. As an actor Bogart was the greatest exponent of the romantic Hemingway hero, who dominated American literature from the 1920s until the 1960s. Both acted out in real life the persona—Bogie and Papa—they had established in their work. Expert at inventing a fascinating public image, they knew the satisfactions of celebrity and the perils of fame. Both succumbed to the temptations of drink and women, and had uneasy relations with the critics and the press.

They were born in 1899, and Hemingway died four years after Bogart. They belonged to prominent, upper-class families that had come from northern Europe to America in the seventeeth century and grew up with servants in large luxurious houses. They loved their weak fathers, who were doctors and had their offices on the first floor of the family residence, and disliked their domineering mothers. Maud Bogart was a nationally-known illustrator who specialized in portraits of children; Grace Hemingway was an opera singer who later exhibited her paintings. In the summers the families migrated to country houses, the Bogarts to upstate New York, the Hemingways to northern Michigan, where the fathers taught the sons to hunt and to fish. Late in life, the fathers lost a great deal of money in bad investments. Belmont Bogart became a morphine addict; Clarence Hemingway committed suicide.

In photographs taken during early childhood the handsome, well-groomed little boys look remarkably alike. They disliked their sissy-sounding first names: Humphrey and Ernest. Their distant mothers, substituting sentimentality for genuine affection, sometimes drowned their sons in saccharine effusions. Maud wrote a story in which "Baby Dimple had a good cry in the 'comfiest' of all places, Mother's arms." Hemingway sati-

1

rized his Mom in "Soldier's Home": "'Don't you love your mother, dear boy? . . . I'm your mother,' she said. 'I held you next to my heart when you were a tiny baby.' Krebs felt sick and vaguely nauseated." Bogart explained, in a frank confessional article, why he had never loved his mother. John Dos Passos, shocked by Hemingway's condemnation of Grace, said he was "the only man I ever knew who really hated his mother."[1] Both men learned to detect phonies at an early age, and developed what Hemingway called a "built-in shit detector." They refused to attend college and set out to learn from direct experience in the world. Both were politically active and became liberal Democrats.

Bogart and Hemingway, heavy drinkers, were suspicious of men who did not drink. But they started late in the day and never let drinking interfere with their work. Alcohol loosened their tongues, and they were fond of obscene language, affectionately insulting nicknames, witty wise-cracks and cruel mockery of friends and enemies, which Bogart called "needling" and Hemingway called "talking rough." They developed, in both life and art, a sceptical, stoic and belligerently masculine style, with speech and gestures cut down to a stark minimum. Men would often pick fights with them in bars to test their tough-guy image, which they maintained with reckless bravado. Bogart ate glass till his mouth bled; the accident-prone Hemingway ran with the bulls and hunted big game.

Hemingway was as handsome as a film star, Bogart as sophisticated as a writer. Both had four wives, one for each phase of their careers, and usually married the women with whom they slept. They adhered to an old-fashioned and somewhat puritanical morality, and criticized their friend Ingrid Bergman for destroying her film career by having an illegitimate child with Roberto Rossellini. They followed a repetitive pattern in marriages. Bogart married actresses, Hemingway married midwestern journalists. They usually had an affair with their future wives while still married to their current ones. Lauren Bacall and Martha Gellhorn both advanced their careers by marrying famous men in their profession. Mayo Methot and Mary Welsh became alcoholics while trying to keep up with their husbands' drinking.

Howard Hawks and John Huston, Bogart's two best directors, were both friends of Hemingway. While Bogart played the Hemingway hero in films like *To Have and Have Not,* Huston became the Hemingway hero by boxing, racing horses, going to war and killing elephants. Bogart, more interested in the man than in his work, questioned Peter Viertel, another mutual friend, about Hemingway and included the novelist on his list of favorite drinkers. Both men had a passion for their boats (the *Santana* and the *Pilar*), loved to escape to the quiet and solitude of the ocean, and went on submarine-hunting expeditions in World War II. Bogart read all of Hemingway's books, and was fond of attributing to the writer a phrase that expressed his own feelings: "The sea is the last free place on earth."[2]

One critic maintained that gangsters did not "know how they were supposed to behave. So Hollywood taught them." But Hemingway—who had covered the crime scene in Kansas City and emphasized the dramatic and visual aspects of gangsters—actually created the natty dress, menacing wisecracks and unrestrained violence of the movie racketeers. One of the criminals in Hemingway's "The Killers" (1925) "wore a derby hat and a black overcoat buttoned across the chest. His face was small and white and he had tight lips. He wore a silk muffler and gloves. . . . [The hoods] ate with their gloves on . . . [and] were dressed like twins. Both wore overcoats too tight for them. . . . The cut off barrels of the shotguns made a slight bulge under the waist." Hemingway's precise description clearly foreshadows Bogart's smart attire in all his gangster roles from the early 1930s to "Gloves" Donahue in *All Through the Night* (1942). As Bogart says, in Huston's *Across the Pacific* (1942), of the Japanese villains who are trying to hide their weapons: "tight clothes don't go with guns."

In Hemingway's story (which reads like a screenplay) the killers, awaiting the arrival of their victim, taunt and intimidate workers in a diner with a series of threatening insults that require immediate assent:

> "You're a pretty bright boy, aren't you?"
> "Sure," said George.
> "Well, you're not," said the other little man. "Is he, Al?"
> "He's dumb."

One of the killers, giving orders to his captives, is compared to a member of a vaudeville team and to "a photographer arranging for a group picture." He tells George: "Ever go to the movies? . . . You ought to go to the movies more. The movies are fine for a bright boy like you." Eight years later, after the Prohibition era had inspired a series of gangster films like *Little Caesar* (1930) and *Public Enemy* (1931), Hemingway's detective in "The Gambler, the Nun, and the Radio" warns the wounded Mexican about confusing art and life: "Listen. This isn't Chicago. You're not a gangster. You don't have to act like a moving picture. It's all right to tell who shot you."[3]

Raymond Chandler's *The Big Sleep*, strongly influenced by Hemingway, inspired one of Bogart's greatest films. Chandler emphasized the connection between real, fictional and cinematic gangsters when he remarked of Joe Brody: "His voice was the elaborately casual voice of the [Hemingwayesque] tough guy in pictures. Pictures have made them all like that."[4] As Bogart's cynical Harry Dawes observes in *The Barefoot Contessa* (1954): "Life, every now and then, behaves as though it had seen too many bad movies."

Bogart, who played a Fitzgerald hero in his romantic roles on stage in the 1920s, was transformed into a Hemingway hero in his gangster films of the 1930s. He starred in *To Have and Have Not* (Lauren Bacall's first film) in the 1940s. In the 1950s he and Bacall played in a radio series called *Bold Venture* that was (like Hemingway's novel) set in a seedy Havana hotel. Bogart also appeared with Joan Fontaine in a radio version of *A Farewell to Arms*. The burning of the missionary outpost in *The African Queen* (1951) was filmed in Butiaba, near Lake Albert and Murchison Falls in Uganda, where Hemingway had two plane crashes (and was reported dead) in January 1954. The following year Bogart, an expert sailor, wanted and was well suited to play the gaunt Cuban fisherman in the film version of *The Old Man and the Sea*. But the ruddy, rotund and absurdly miscast Spencer Tracy, who had bought the rights and was co-producer, got the part.

Hemingway tapped into the national consciousness to create his laconic gangsters and vulnerable tough guys; Bogart gave these American archetypes enduring life on the screen. Their best work, *The Sun Also Rises* and *Casablanca,* remains as fresh and alive now as the day it first appeared. Bogart embodied Hemingway's hardened hero, torn between ironic fatalism and despairing courage, who seeks authenticity and adheres to a strict code of honor. The most popular actor of the twentieth century remains a vivid presence in our imagination, still widely imitated and instantly recognized throughout the world. In the 1960s he became a cult figure whose reputation is even greater now than in his lifetime.

❖ 1 ❖

Childhood, Andover and the Navy

1899-1919

⟨ I ⟩

HUMPHREY BOGART, whose surname means "orchard," came from a long line of solid Dutch burghers and was a direct descendant of the original Dutch settlers in New York. In later life the reckless tough guy rarely mentioned his upper-class background, but he belonged to the Holland Society and proudly displayed the family coat of arms on his wall. His paternal grandfather had invented a commercially successful process that used tin for offset lithography and the family—who invested its money in Michigan timberland—was very well off. Though not listed in the *Social Register*, the Bogarts appeared in *Who's Who in New York* and in Dau's *New York Blue Book* from 1907 until 1933.

Humphrey's genial, easy-going father achieved considerable success in medicine. He provided a striking contrast to Humphrey's manically driven mother, a well-known commercial artist. Both were socially ambitious and had great hopes for their oldest child and only son. Belmont DeForest Bogart was born in upstate New York in 1868. He graduated in 1888 from Phillips Academy in Andover, Massachusetts, where he played on the baseball and football teams. Handsome, sturdily built and nearly six feet tall, he was a natural athlete, a keen sailor and a superb wing shot. He loved to track deer in Canada and owned a rustic hunting lodge. In a photograph taken in the late 1890s, the Victorian paterfamilias wears a three-piece suit with a high collar and tiepin, parts his dark hair in the middle and has a full moustache. Though he looks severe, he was a witty, charming and convivial man. A heavy drinker, he liked the company of bartenders, mechanics and truck drivers, and preferred outdoor sports to medicine. Each summer he took several months off to indulge his passion for hunting and sailing.

Belmont's three years at Andover qualified him to study medicine. He earned his degree at Columbia University's College of Physicians and Surgeons in 1896 and was licensed to practice the following year. While he was working as an intern a horse-drawn ambulance turned over, fell on him, and broke his ribs and leg. Improperly set, his leg had to be broken again, and after this accident he never fully recovered his health.

Dr. Bogart nevertheless built up a prominent practice as a surgeon and heart and lung specialist. He was associated with Presbyterian Hospital, Bellevue and the Sloane Hospital for Women, and had many wealthy and influential patients. After his marriage in 1898, he set up his thickly-carpeted, mahogany-paneled office on the first floor of the family town house at 245 West 103rd Street (then a fashionable part of the city), between Broadway and West End Avenue, where Humphrey would see the patients lined up in the waiting room.

The three-story brownstone town house had bay windows, carved bas reliefs and a pigeon coop on the roof. In keeping with Dr. Bogart's social position, the grand interior boasted high ceilings, wide stairways, crystal chandeliers, heavy tapestries, classical statues, parquet floors and Oriental rugs. Two Irish maids, supplemented by a laundress and cook, maintained the house and served the family. Together they cost only seventeen dollars a week. At a time when taxes were low, Dr. Bogart earned, in addition to the income from his inheritance, $20,000 a year. "When I was born," Bogart later said, "the family was worth a tremendous amount of money. We had a country place and a house in New York. My father had an excellent practice. When I was fifteen, my father made bad investments and lost a good deal of money. . . . But we were never in any financial straits."

Bogart's mother, Maud Humphrey, was descended from a judge and from a wealthy manufacturer. Her father, John Perkins Humphrey, had a prosperous shoe store on Main Street in Rochester, New York, where she was born (three years before Belmont) on March 30, 1865. As a child, she could see mules pulling the barges through the Erie Canal. Talented and precocious, she studied at the Art Students League in New York from 1886 to 1894, and for some years in Paris at the Académie Julian and with the American painter James McNeill Whistler. The Académie had been founded in 1860 by Rodolphe Julian, a former prizefighter and model, who knew nothing about painting. It was segregated, and had a section for men, with nude models, in the Latin Quarter; and another for women, without nude models, just off the Champs-Elysées. William Rothenstein described the Académie as a "congeries of studios crowded with students, the walls thick with palette scrapings, hot, airless and extremely noisy."

Maud, an attractive and impressive woman, had red frizzy hair, a strong nose and firm jaw. In a turn-of-the-century photograph, she holds her baby son and is elaborately attired in a large beribboned hat, high silk scarf, velvety dress and wide belt around her narrow waist. The stately, fastidious woman — with caustic wit and imperious manner — was known as "Lady Maud." A militant suffragette, she would also stand on street corners and sell balloons with the printed slogan "Votes for Women."

Trained in the bohemian art world, Maud also developed a shrewd sense of business. Her long career as an illustrator of calendars, greeting cards, fashion magazines and more than twenty story books (two with her sister Mabel), and as a portrait painter of socialite children, flourished from the 1890s through the 1920s. In 1894, for example, Frederick Stokes published her *Treasury of Stories, Jingles and Rhymes: With 140 Vignette Illustrations in Half Tone.* She worked in the sentimental Victorian tradition, painting stylized cherubic children with round faces, chipmunk cheeks, curly blond ringlets, large eyes, button noses, rosy lips, frilly collars and long white dresses. Her work promoted Prudential Insurance and Ivory soap, appeared on the covers of *Harper's* and *Century* magazines, and was exhibited in New York and Boston.

In 1910, when Humphrey was ten years old, Maud became artistic director of the *Delineator,* a women's fashion magazine, and kept the job for twenty years. Theodore Dreiser had been the editor from 1907 to 1910, publishing essays and stories by H. L. Mencken, Edgar Wallace and A. A. Milne, and articles on topical issues like divorce and women's suffrage. During the war it was violently anti-German, and later carried pieces on postwar morality and radical politics. After 1926 it became less serious, emphasized fashions and built up a circulation of two million.

Maud was in charge of all layouts, covers, drawings and illustrations. The magazine, published by Butterick, was chiefly a means of selling the immensely profitable patterns manufactured by the company. Dreiser's biographer wrote that "you read the magazine, you saw the dress, you bought the pattern. . . . In the July, 1907, *Delineator,* 148 pages long, the first seven features . . . were devoted to fashions and contained 150 careful drawings of dresses, nightgowns, underwear, bathing suits and other garments for which Butterick would supply the patterns. Thirty-six more pages were devoted to such allied subjects as cookery, homemaking, society and children, leaving only 21 pages for fiction and eight for articles."[1] In the Butterick Building two thousand poorly paid workers turned out the patterns, and its underground floors contained one of the biggest printing plants in the world.

Maud loved her job and was obsessed by her work. She had a studio on the third floor of the brownstone, tended to ignore her family and gave up almost everything else in life. But she earned a great deal more than Belmont and received the enormous salary of $50,000 a year. Bogart portrayed her as a narrow, joyless creature and said: "I doubt that she read very much. I know that she never played any games. She went to no parties, gave none. And I can't remember that she even had any friends." When the pressure became too intense, she suffered agonizing migraine headaches and had to retire to her darkened room.

‹ II ›

WHEN BELMONT was still a medical student and Maud was living at the Hotel San Remo in New York, they met at a party in an artist's studio, and married in 1898. Their first child, Humphrey DeForest Bogart, was born in Sloane's Hospital in New York, weighing eight pounds seven ounces, on December 25, 1899.[2] Bogart—who called himself a "nine-teenth-century man" and believed in traditional values—came into a world of gaslights and hansom cabs. McKinley was president, Victoria was queen and the Boer War was raging in South Africa. Charles Laughton, Noel Coward, Alfred Hitchcock and James Cagney were all born that year. Thorsten Veblen described the kind of luxurious life enjoyed by the Bogarts in *The Theory of the Leisure Class* and inventors made the first magnetic recording of sound, a crucial step in the evolution of talking pictures.

Dr. Bogart carefully tested the newborn child's grip and proudly announced that he had just produced a surgeon. Maud made drawings of her chubby-cheeked, sparsely-thatched infant, who became famous when he appeared in a national advertising campaign for Mellin's baby food. A celebrity soon after his birth as "the original Maud Humphrey baby," Bogart said, "there was a period in American history when you couldn't pick up a goddamned magazine without seeing my kisser in it." But he had to pay a penalty for fame: "When I was a kid, it gave me a kind of complex. I was always getting the razz from friends."

Humphrey's sister Frances (called Pat) was delivered by Dr. Bogart in 1901 and Katherine (called Kay) appeared in 1903. Soon after Pat's birth, Humphrey became seriously ill with pneumonia. The overprotective Maud observed: "He is a manly lad, but too delicate in health." In a photograph taken the following year, however, he appears as a robust, chubby-cheeked two-year-old, with neatly combed hair, a billowing shirt and side-buttoned overalls with rolled-up cuffs. Maud preferred to dress her son in Little Lord Fauntleroy suits that she had made herself, and used him as an in-house model for her drawings. When Belmont tried to discipline the boy by hitting him, Maud defended her son and screamed: "If you ever touch him again, I'll kill you."[3]

Burdened by his famous portrait and a name that seemed both effeminate and absurd, Humphrey was mocked by his schoolmates and got into many fights. His sissy image was intensified during his early teens when, dressed in white kid gloves and patent-leather pumps, he danced with young ladies (including Ira Gershwin's future wife) at formal cotillions. Attempting to be more manly, he shot out the red lanterns placed around building sites with his new air rifle. He also liked to swagger into Broadway matinées with his close friend and neighbor Bill Brady. Encouraged to follow his father's profession, he performed an operation at the age of eight. Exaggerating the incident, Bogart recalled: "I had put together a first aid kit filled with iodine, bandages, scalpels, scissors, pocket knives, butcher knives, needles and cotton. Kay had a boil on her arm and I opened it. She nearly bled to death."

Humphrey called Dr. Bogart "Father," but addressed his regal and reserved mother as "Maud." Both parents were politically conservative: Belmont was Presbyterian and Republican, Maud Episcopalian and High Tory. A snob and anti-Semite, Maud had a sharp tongue and savage wit that terrified the servants. Her intense jealousy of other women made it difficult for her handsome younger husband to keep a nurse for very long. Belmont, constantly nagged by his wife, expressed his frustration and anger by needling the servants, who were always complaining to Maud and giving notice. When the parents fought, as they frequently did, Humphrey and his sisters would pull the bedclothes over their heads to muffle the bitter words. The marriage was maintained more for the sake of propriety than for the children.

Obsessed by her work, suffering from migraines and quarreling with her husband, Maud found it impossible to express affection and love for her son, and left him to be brought up by the maids. After Bogart achieved great fame, he offered a remarkably frank and perceptive analysis of the sharp contrast between his mother's saccharine portraits and her hard-boiled character: "I was brought up very unsentimentally but very straightforwardly. A kiss, in our family, was an event. Our mother and father didn't glug over my two sisters and me. They had too many things to do, and so did we. Anyway, we were mainly the responsibility of the servants. I can't say that I loved my mother, but I respected her. Ours was not the kind of affection that spills over or makes pretty pictures. If, when I was grown up, I [had] sent my mother one of those Mother's Day telegrams or said it with flowers, she would have returned the wire and flowers to me, collect."[4]

The happiest time of Humphrey's childhood was undoubtedly the long summers he spent at the family's house at Seneca Point on Lake Canandaigua, near Rochester, in the Finger Lakes. Maud had bought the ten-year-old lakefront property from the widow of a wealthy brewer when she was pregnant with Humphrey in June 1899. Willow Brook—which had a high turret, mansard roof, large front porch and two-hundred-foot shoreline—"more closely resembled an estate. The fifty-five acres included a working farm, ice house, stretches of manicured lawns, and a dock with a sailboat." Maud brought her servants from New York, and did portraits of the local girls. Since there was no church nearby, Belmont took his turn holding divine service in his home. Peaceful Seneca Point, which had no electricity or cars, resembled the lake in Minnesota described by Bogart's contemporary Zelda Fitzgerald: "When summer came, all the people who liked the summertime moved out to the huge, clear lake not far from town, and lived there in long, flat cottages surrounded with . . . pine trees, and covered by screened verandas."

Frank Hamlin, the son of a local banker, who spent many summers with Humphrey, recalled that he was in his element at the lake. A hero and leader, he was always thinking up things for the boys to do and showed for the first time a serious interest in the theater:

> The leader of our Seneca Point gang was Hump Bogart, who was destined to distinguish himself as an actor. He lived on the other side of the Adams and became something of a local hero when he rescued my three-year-old brother, Arthur, who had fallen off the end of the dock. Being a little older than the rest of us, Hump was able to run things much his own way—and did. He was the leader when we played follow-the-leader. He decided when to slide down the first falls of Seneca Glen and whether to watch the butchering of a steer up in Bert Johnson's barn—a gory business. On rainy days we would roll up our living room rug and under General Bogart's direction, refight the Crimean War with our correctly uniformed lead soldiers from F. A. O. Schwarz. Hump wrote the script, se-

lected the casts and directed the plays we produced for our nickel-a-seat audiences. The plots were usually suggested by the splendid, if somewhat worn and smelly costumes sent up from New York by Mr. [William] Brady, a leading Broadway theatrical producer and friend of the Bogarts. Especially wonderful were the real chaps from *The Girl of the Golden West.* Hump's sister Caddy [Kay] was allowed to play the girl but was not a regular member of our gang. That was before boys played with girls at Seneca Point.

Humphrey—glad to escape from school and the city—loved boats and water, and would row out on the lake, towing a little raft with a pet mouse on it. When he was ten years old, he said, "my father gave me a one-cylinder motorboat and I used to putt-putt around the lake all day, exploring every watery inch of it. I determined then that I'd have a 'real' boat. I believe my ideas went way beyond the yacht class. I had something in mind like a private ocean liner."[5] Later on, he had his own sloop on the lake and became an expert sailor. In 1916, after Belmont had lost a lot of money, Maud sold the house at Seneca Point. The family then spent two months on Fire Island, New York, where they were quarantined during an outbreak of infantile paralysis.

‹ III ›

HUMPHREY ATTENDED the private De Lancey School, on the upper West Side, from the 1st through 4th grades. In September 1909 he entered the elite and socially impeccable Trinity School. It was founded in 1709 by William Huddleston, a lawyer and schoolmaster, who deplored the "want of a publick school in the city of New York where . . . poor children . . . might be taught gratis" and wished to educate the poor in the new English colony in order to combat the "abundance of irreligion."

By Humphrey's day Trinity provided education for the rich rather than the poor. In 1895 the school had moved to a large, gray stone building at 139 West 91st Street, between Columbus and Amsterdam Avenues, about half a mile from the Bogarts' town house. In 1913 the annual school fees were $213; three years later they went up to $256. The twenty-five boys in each grade were formally dressed in blue Eton suits and vests, white shirts with brass-buttoned detachable collars and, in cold weather, a velvet-collared Chesterfield overcoat. From 1903 to 1937 the Rector of the High Episcopal School—which still exists at the same address—was the Reverend Dr. Lawrence "Bunny" Cole.

Trinity's motto was *Fides Labore et Virtute* (faith through work and virtue). According to the *Yearbook* of 1917–18, the "School naturally lays emphasis on the moral and religious as well as on the intellectual and physical development of its pupils. . . . Each day's session is begun with prayers in the chapel." The boys knelt for the litany on Fridays and celebrated Communion on Holy Days. The "curriculum was determined by the admission requirements of Columbia College," which included Greek, Latin, mathematics and modern languages. The school had football, baseball, tennis and track teams, but Humphrey did not play on any of them. He did, however, use the rifle range in the basement of the school.

Humphrey's eight years at Trinity were marked by poor grades and many absences. He would be (along with Truman Capote, who later completed the screenplay of *Beat the Devil*) the most famous graduate of the school. But he left a very faint trail and showed no interest in Trinity after leaving it. One fellow student remembered him as "a timid, mousy little guy who never opened his trap. . . . Bogart never came out for *anything*. He wasn't a very good student. . . . He added up to nothing in our class."

From the 5th through 8th grades (1909–13) Humphrey took English, Spelling, Arithmetic, Geography and History, and had a 67.5 percent average. From the 9th through 11th grades (1913–16) he followed the scientific course, took Religion (in which he got the highest marks), English, Algebra and Geometry, English and American History, French and German, Drawing and (in his last year) Physics, and had an even worse 64.3 percent average. A prolonged attack of scarlet fever forced Humphrey to repeat his third year of high school, which he found humiliating and boring. When he repeated courses, his grades went up only one percent. Despite the strict discipline, he later remembered his German teacher, unpopular during the war, glaring furiously as the boys hurled erasers and books at him.

Humphrey, whose unusual name continued to plague him (though he did not change it when he became an actor), was scorned for never taking part in after-school activities. Instead, he was picked up by a nursemaid in a starched uniform and obediently went home to model for his mother. Learning to pose for an indulgent yet hard-to-please artist was his first experience as an "actor." Like Jack Warner later on, Maud put him into a stereotyped role and forced him to play it. This duty reinforced his sissy image, curtailed his freedom and emphasized Maud's power over him. He resented and disliked his mother, who exploited but ignored him and gave him no affection. Her obsession with work cut him off from normal social life both in school and in the family. His classmates also thought he was strange and sullen, and gave "the impression that he was a very spoiled boy. When things didn't go his way, he didn't like it a bit."[6] Though he was an extremely poor student, his parents sent him to the intensely competitive Andover to complete his final year of high school.

‹ IV ›

PHILLIPS ACADEMY in Andover, Massachusetts—twenty miles north of Boston—is the oldest and one of the finest prep schools in America. Founded by Calvinists in April 1778, during the American Revolution, it was dedicated "to enlarging the minds and forming the morals of the youths committed to its care," and to guarding boys "against the first dawnings of depraved nature." But it seemed to encourage Humphrey's ability to evade school work and have a good time. Like the equally high-minded Trinity School, Andover taught Life as well as Knowledge and instructed "Youth, not only in English and Latin grammar, Writing, Arithmetic, and those Sciences, wherein they are commonly taught, but more especially to learn them the *Great End and Real Business of Living*."[7]

Many distinguished figures had been associated with the Academy. "John Hancock signed the articles of incorporation, Paul Revere designed its seal in silver"; George Washington addressed the school in 1798, John Adams was the fourth principal and Charles Bulfinch built its three handsome buildings in the Georgian style. Its alumni included the inventor Samuel Morse, the judge Oliver Wendell Holmes, the statesman Henry Stimson, the writer Edgar Rice Burroughs and, later on, the photographer Walker Evans, the painter Frank Stella—and George Bush. A great many boys went from Andover to Yale, and Dr. Bogart expected his son to go there as well. In preparation for college, Humphrey read Owen Johnson's popular rah-rah novel *Stover at Yale* (1911), which ignored the realities of academic study and painted a rosy picture of college life.

On January 30, 1917, during Humphrey's last year at Trinity, Dr. Bogart wrote Alfred Stearns, the headmaster at Andover, reminding him that they had been baseball and football teammates in the class of 1888 and explaining that he planned to send his son there. Humphrey was obviously admitted more for family connections than for scholastic merit. In early February he followed his father's overture with his own rather stilted letter, probably dictated by his parents. Mindful of his family's recent financial losses, he expressed concern about the cost yet wanted to maintain his comfort. He reminded Dr. Stearns that they had been introduced by Dr. Bogart during the Christmas vacation and then got down to business: "My object in writing this letter is to reserve a room in 'commons.' I should like a suitable roommate selected by you. I should also like a personal estimate of my expenses at Andover to show my father, including Tuition, Board and other necessary expenses. I wish to reduce my expenses as much as possible and still be comfortable. I would like to know the date at which I am expected to report to the Academy. Thanking you in advance for this courtesy, Yours respectfully."

On August 18 an Andover official sternly noted that Humphrey had not secured college credit at Columbia because of low grades in English, French and German, though he had studied these subjects for three years and had repeated them once. A month later, in a letter to Stearns of September 13, Dr. Bogart responded to this criticism, announced Humphrey's arrival, and tried to allay the Headmaster's doubts by praising his son's character and desire to succeed:

> My son Humphrey will take his examination in English at Columbia on the 21st and arrive at Andover on the 23rd. . . . May I ask if Humphrey is to have a roommate and, with your approval, that he be placed with a boy in his Class, i.e., Senior Scientific.—We expect Humphrey to graduate this year and to go to college.—I have the assurance of Dr. Cole of Trinity School that he can do this.—Humphrey is a splendid fellow and very popular with every one—he will do good work if placed with a boy who will not take his attention from the regular study periods.—He has expressed a desire to go to Andover alone and meet you again personally.—As Mrs. Bogart is quite ill it will be impossible for me to go with him.—May I ask that you take a personal interest in the boy so that he will get started on the right path which will I am sure lead to a successful year.[8]

Despite two reminders about the need for proper guidance and a suitable roommate, Humphrey—immature and away from home, an outsider in a high-powered school and close-knit group of boys—was given a small, spartan, single room. Number 5, Taylor Hall, had a fireplace, a steel cot, an oak desk and chair, a chest of drawers and a closet. The bathroom, shared with six other boys on the floor, was next to his room.

Frederick Boyce, the physics teacher and housemaster, lived on the first floor with his wife and children.

A photograph of Humphrey at Andover shows him lounging on the floor of the dormitory during a party with seven friends. Another portrays him in front of a classy open car. Dressed in white, with high canvas shoes and a bow tie, hair slicked down and parted in the middle, he holds a pipe and fuzzy dog, and has a somewhat surly expression on his handsome face. By the time he reached Andover, he was pretty tired of trying to live up to his parents' expectations. He was noted for his shooting and his wrestling ability, went out with girls, took part in student pranks and had a good time.

As at Trinity, he neglected his studies, was "entirely uninterested in his work and . . . by Christmas time had failed three out of five courses." The defiant Humphrey later criticized the teaching methods and blamed his incompetent teachers for failing to arouse his interest in the Bible, English, French, Chemistry and Geometry: "The problem was the way I was taught. They made you learn dates and that was all. They'd say, 'A war was fought in 1812.' So what? They never told you why people decided to kill each other at just that moment. And I hated the smugness of people in authority. I can't show reverence when I don't feel it. I was always testing my instructors to see if they were as bright or godlike as they seemed to be." He finally decided that they didn't have much to offer and that he could learn much more outside of school.

There was no place in Andover for the conspicuously idle student and the school, threatening rather than helping the boy, soon took the appropriate disciplinary action. The white-thatched, eagle-beaked Dr. Stearns, who ruled from 1903 until 1933, had closely scrutinized Humphrey's academic progress (or lack thereof), and during the second half of his senior year issued a carefully calibrated series of warnings that were meant to focus his mind on his studies. When he recklessly ignored them, the Headmaster lost patience and (in contrast to the more tolerant Trinity) promptly expelled him.

On December 22, 1917, after Humphrey's poor performance during the first term, Stearns told Dr. Bogart that Humphrey had the ability to do the work but had not tried very hard. He then withdrew some of his privileges in order to spur him on to greater seriousness: "I am enclosing herewith Humphrey's report for the term just closed. The record is not so good as it ought to be and the deficiencies recorded must be attributed largely to indifference and lack of effort. Humphrey's instructors seem to be unanimous upon this point, and in consequence we have felt it necessary to withdraw . . . the privilege of out-of-town and evening excuses. I trust that this may be all that is necessary to induce him to put forth more earnest efforts in the future."

Two months later, on February 19, 1918, with no improvement in sight, Stearns wrote Dr. Bogart that he had put the delinquent on probation and demoted him to a lower-level English class. He spoke of an impending catastrophe if there was no radical change in attitude and warned of the danger of expulsion:

> Last week your boy's case came up for consideration in connection with the recent scholarship rating; and because of the poor record which he has made this term the faculty voted to place him on probation. . . . I have taken pains to make inquiries since, and find that all his teachers agree that he has good ability but that he has not exerted himself at all seriously during the current term; and that his low standing . . . is largely due to that fact. It was also decided that his work in English should be readjusted, as he seems wholly unable at this time to meet the requirements. . . .
>
> Under the circumstances we shall, of course, watch Humphrey's record for the balance of the term with the greatest care; for unless there is an all-round improvement during that time, we shall, of course, be compelled to require his withdrawal. I earnestly hope that such a catastrophe as this may be avoided; and I am sure that it can be if the boy will only do his part. I shall have a talk with him at the earliest opportunity, and shall do my best to impress upon him the seriousness of the situation.

By return post, on February 23, Dr. Bogart, while agreeing with the Headmaster about Humphrey's indolent habits, revealed that he did not fully understand Humphrey's problems and loyally defended his son. He portrayed Humphrey as an essentially good boy who loved Andover (perhaps for the wrong reasons), but had been led astray by girls and sports. He also offered the traditional alternative for the hedonistic schoolboy — the threat of a job:

> Both his mother and myself will do everything in our power to have the boy "find himself."—I am much pleased that you are to have a personal interview, which I feel will have the desired effect.—Humphrey is a good boy, with no bad habits, who

simply has lost his head temporarily.—He is very fond of Andover and loved to talk of you while home for the Christmas holidays. The whole problem to my mind seems to be that the boy has given up his mind to sports and a continuous correspondence with his girl friends.—I had before your letter came written Humphrey a sharp letter, stating that if he did not adhere closely to the requirements that you demand, I would immediately request his dismissal from Andover and put him to work. May I request Dr. Stearns that every effort be used to impress upon my son the necessity of a complete change in his habits and his outlook on life.[9]

Six weeks later, on April 2, Stearns reported that Humphrey's slight improvement (stirred by dire threats from school and home) justified "extending the period of his probation in the hope and belief that the gains already noted will become even more pronounced as the new term gets under way."

Finally, as Humphrey failed to sustain his illusory improvement, Stearns announced his doom. Writing to Dr. Bogart on May 18, only a month before graduation, citing the view of his teachers, and wanting to avoid an embarrassing last-minute failure, Stearns dealt with the matter by expelling the boy. He admitted that the school bore some responsibility for the situation, and tried to make the best of it by stating that Humphrey, who had not even appeared to make an effort, would ultimately benefit from this disaster:

> To my great regret I am forced to advise you that Humphrey has failed to meet the terms of his probation and that it becomes necessary therefore for us to require his withdrawal. . . . I have learned from the boy's instructors that it was the unanimous opinion of those who are familiar with the situation that it would be unwise for Humphrey to remain here longer. I cannot tell you how deeply I regret our inability to make the boy realize the seriousness of the situation and to put forth the effort required to avert this disaster.
>
> My experience, covering a good many years now, leads me to believe that Humphrey will profit greatly from this seemingly unfortunate occurrence, and that it will tend to bring him to his senses as nothing else could do. I only express the sincere hope that this will prove the turning point in the boy's life, and

that from now on he will develop that serious purpose which
he appears to have lacked thus far.

Propelled by his parents' ambitions and completely unprepared for the
rigorous curriculum, Humphrey received discipline rather than guidance,
encouragement and the "personal interest" Dr. Bogart had asked for at
Andover. Trinity had nurtured him, but Andover failed to keep him on
track. If he had stayed at Trinity instead of transferring to a more demanding school, he might have graduated and gone to college.

The Bogarts were upset when the Headmaster offered no hope of
Humphrey's return the following year. They were also deeply disappointed
that Humphrey had deliberately destroyed his chances for a diploma from
Andover, an education at Yale and a career as a surgeon. Writing in her
husband's absence and clearly furious with both her son and the school,
Maud told Stearns she had already arranged for Humphrey's employment
with an eminent shipbuilder: "I am sending Humphrey $25.00 with in-
structions to come home at once, packing up his belongings and shipping
them home. I believe that is what you ask. Mr. Frank E. Kirby, a very
prominent Naval Architect, and now building ships for the Government,
has promised to give Humphrey a 'job' in the ship yard at once. I trust the
boy will come to his senses and work. As Mr. Kirby has both brains and
influence . . . I hope he can help Humphrey."

After Bogart became famous he wanted to be remembered as a hell-
raiser rather than an academic failure at Andover. By his own account, he
was expelled for ducking an unpopular teacher in a pond. In a letter of
May 1949 to George Frazier, who was doing research on Bogart for an
article in *Life* magazine, an Andover official retrospectively recognized
Bogart's great talent and recalled a prank that he would later use in his
escape-from-prison films: "he appeared to be having quite a bit of trouble
with a sizeable majority of his courses, and apparently the faculty felt that
here was a man who could do great things if he sets his mind to it. . . .
[There is a] vague off-the-record recollection of once having found a
dummy in Bogie's bed one evening, which would indicate that Bogie was
somewhere he shouldn't have been."[10]

In other reports of his expulsion Bogart swung from huffy outrage, "I'm
leaving this place, and for good. It's a waste of time here," to the frank
admission that "the bastards threw me out." He also gave his mistress
Verita Peterson a more sober and accurate view of the episode by confessing his academic limitations: "I was a dumb son of a bitch, and if I hadn't
got kicked out for drinking, I would have flunked out anyway. I left
Andover under duress."

Bogart had no fond memories of Trinity, but remained attached to Andover. Despite his disgraceful exit at the end of his senior year, he told a reporter, soon after his son was born: "I hope he goes to Andover, my old school." (In fact, his son went to Milton Academy and failed out of school as his father had done.) When criticized, while playing Captain Queeg in *The Caine Mutiny*, for not acting as a naval officer should, Bogart indignantly defended his behavior and replied: "I went to school at Andover. Are you trying to tell me that Annapolis turns out better gentlemen than Phillips Academy?" Yet a residue of bitterness inevitably remained. When the secretary of the Alumni Fund later "asked him for a contribution, he sent back one dollar, which [he felt was] what he owed Andover."[11] Though Bogart never graduated from high school, he received an excellent education at Trinity and Andover and profited by what he had learned. Articulate and quick-witted, he had a good mind and could hold his own with intellectual friends.

< **V** >

HUMPHREY RETURNED home to face the wrath of his parents and hear their tediously familiar recriminations. "You've had every chance that could be given to you, and you have failed," Maud rather unctuously declared, "—not only yourself but your parents. We don't intend to support you for the rest of your life. You're on your own from now on." Instead of building ships with Frank Kirby, Humphrey decided to sail in them. Following his love of the sea, he joined the navy (six weeks after leaving school) on July 2, 1918. Eager for fun and oblivious to danger, he recalled his mood at the time: "At eighteen war was great stuff. Paris! French girls! Hot damn! . . . The war was a big joke. Death? What does death mean to a kid of seventeen? The idea of death starts getting through to you when you're older." Trying to see Humphrey's rash act in a positive way, on July 6 Dr. Bogart proudly told the Andover Registrar: "The boy on his arrival home at once enlisted in the Naval Reserve Corps and is now at Pelham Bay" on Long Island Sound. "Please bring this to Dr. Stearns' attention and give Humphrey due credit for his patriotic spirit."[12]

Seaman number 1123062 went to boot camp at the Naval Reserve Training Station in Pelham Bay and emerged as coxswain. In a contemporary photograph he stands stiffly at attention, with fists clenched, and wears a sailor's dress uniform with white puttees, long knotted cravat and white cap low on his forehead. On October 2 Dr. Bogart told Stearns that

Humphrey had applied for a transfer to Naval Aviation and asked for a letter of recommendation. Making the best of a bad case, Stearns wrote two days later to the commanding officer: "Bogart was a member of our student body last year; and while not a brilliant scholar . . . he is a boy of good character, full of enthusiasm, and when once he has familiarized himself with your requirements, I feel confident he will go fast and far."

Humphrey's poor grades and lack of a high school degree obviously hurt his chances. Rejected by the glamorous air arm of the navy, on November 27 — sixteen days after the Armistice was signed and the war ended — he joined the troopship USS *Leviathan*. He spent the next eight months as a helmsman in the peacetime navy, ferrying troops back and forth between Hoboken, Liverpool and Brest, and made about twelve crossings in the North Atlantic. Confined to routine duties, he never saw the French girls in Paris.

The *Leviathan* had three huge funnels, masts fore and aft, and zebra-like camouflage stripes. In the summer of 1918 it had carried Franklin Roosevelt, Assistant Secretary of the Navy, from France back to the United States. Originally commissioned as the *Vaterland* and built by the Germans for transporting troops, it was seized, along with all German merchant ships in American ports, when the United States declared war in April 1917. After repairs were made, the ship was pressed into service by the navy.

The navy transports had a distinguished record during the war and, Roosevelt wrote, successfully escorted all American "troops, munitions, and supplies in safety to the shores of France." Convoys of four or five large troopships, each carrying four to five thousand soldiers, zig-zagged through the submarine zone and across the Atlantic. They were escorted by ten or twelve destroyers, which used guns, torpedoes and depth charges against the German U-boats. Steaming "without lights while continuously maneuvering in close formation," the troopships, traveling at twelve to twenty knots, took about three weeks to cross the ocean. Westbound ships sailed south along the coast of France to the Bay of Biscay before recrossing the Atlantic. A naval historian wrote that "no troopship coming to the coast of France by an American escort was ever successfully attacked," and the navy transported more than two million troops without losing a single man.[13]

Humphrey did the same duty, but without the danger of enemy attack. In February 1919 he was transferred to the USS *Santa Olivia,* but (perhaps while drunk) missed the boat when it sailed for Europe on April 14. He turned himself in, had the offense commuted from Deserter to Absent Without Leave, and served three days' solitary confinement on bread and water. Despite this dereliction, he seemed to have matured and his fitness reports were good. On a scale of 1 to 4, he got 3 or more in proficiency, and 4 in sobriety and obedience. He later summarized his naval career by recalling: "I enlisted on the *Granite State,* a training ship. Then I went to boot camp and then on the *Leviathan.* Then on the *Santa Olivia,* both troopships. I was helmsman on both, striking for quartermaster. The *Leviathan* was a big bastard, a [three] stacker with forty-eight coal burners. As helmsman I stood two hours on and two hours off."

The only extraordinary event during Humphrey's naval service was the mysterious accident that left a scar on the right side of his upper lip. There are two accounts, equally implausible, of how it happened. In one version, he was wounded in the lower lip by a flying wood splinter during the shelling of the *Leviathan.* But since the war was over by the time he joined the ship, it is unlikely that it was ever shelled. His brother-in-law rejected this story (invented perhaps by Bogart himself or by the publicity department at Warner Bros.) and said he was wounded in Boston's South Station while escorting a prisoner to the Portsmouth Naval Prison in New Hampshire. In this version, he acted out one of his heroic film roles: "The man was handcuffed, though not to him, and when they changed trains in Boston he asked Humphrey for a cigarette. Humphrey cheerfully complied, and while he was producing a match the man raised his manacled hands and smashed him across the mouth, and fled. Humphrey, his lip almost torn off, whipped out his .45 and dropped the man as he ran."

When the actress Louise Brooks met Bogart in 1924, she noticed that "at one corner of his upper lip a scarred, quilted piece hung down in a tiny scallop. When Humphrey went into films [in 1930], a surgeon [his father] sewed up the scallop, and only a small scar remained." The wound provided his characteristic tough-guy scar and — by supposedly damaging the nerve — his lisp, grimace and distinctive stiff-lipped speech.

Humphrey was honorably discharged from active service on June 18, 1919 in Brooklyn, New York. He reached the rank of seaman second class (but never made quartermaster) and was decorated with a modest Victory medal with clasp. When he returned home from the navy his mother, though proud of his war service, merely said, with her usual restraint: "Good job, Humphrey." In the summer of 1919 he found his sisters still in school, his mother as cold and self-absorbed as ever, his father in poor health and financial trouble. He had to find something to do, but had no idea what it would be.

Though he was not deeply affected by the war, his year of active service threw the teenager into contact with a very different class of men from the wealthy boys he had known at Trinity and Andover, and gave him much greater experience and responsibility than he could have had as a college freshman. His summers at Seneca Point inspired a lifelong passion for sailing; the navy strengthened his ties to the sea and gave him valuable expertise. He put this to good use when he raced his own yacht, served as a coast guard volunteer in World War II and commanded many ships in his nautical roles—from *Action in the North Atlantic* to *The Caine Mutiny.*

Alistair Cooke observed that Humphrey rebelled "against the gentility of his parents and the life they had expected him to lead."[14] Liberal rather than conservative in politics, he defied authority, mocked conventional behavior, punctured pretensions, attacked phonies and hated snobs. But his family life and education determined his character and values. His upper-class background gave him an aristocratic self-assurance and his early renown as a Mellin's baby accustomed him to fame. He inherited his parents' high ambitions and social standards, but not their wealth and property. He lacked their drive for success and could not meet their high expectations. Like his father, he married strong-willed women, developed a taste for domestic quarrels and used his caustic wit to needle both friends and enemies.

As a child Bogart was pampered and given all the social advantages, but he was constrained and repressed, and lacked both affection and love. Despite his sissy image and privileged origins, he would play rebellious, criminal characters in the movies. His style of acting, which evolved from his character, was severe and restrained, and he had to break down his emotional reserve in order to reach his full potential as a performer.

⟡ 2 ⟡

Broadway and
Failure in Hollywood
1920-1954

⟨ I ⟩

AFTER THE WAR Bogart, like most unqualified veterans, had difficulty finding work. His experience at sea got him a job as inspector with the Pennsylvania Tug and Lighterage Company, tracing lost shipments and reporting on damage to tugs and barges. But it was hard to settle down after the war and he got fed up with the routine after only three months. Seeking guidance, he went to see the boss, who gave him some stale advice: "Work hard and some day you'll be president." When Bogart learned there were fifty thousand employees between himself and the president, he immediately resigned. In his next, equally tedious and ephemeral job, he was a runner (who never actually runs, but delivers securities to brokerage houses and banks), then a bond salesman, for his father's Wall Street brokers, S. W. Straus.

Bogart found his vocation accidentally, through the father of his boyhood friend Bill Brady. Though Humphrey had put on plays at Seneca Point (with costumes sent by Mr. Brady), he had never shown any interest in the theater while at school. But, with no other prospects, he eagerly seized the chance to enter a glamorous profession. "I was born to be indolent," he later said, "and this was the softest of rackets."

The colorful and dynamic William A. Brady—Dr. Bogart's neighbor, friend and patient—was the son of a Dublin immigrant who had come to California in the Gold Rush. His father, an ardent Secessionist during the Civil War, edited a newspaper in San Francisco, where William was born in 1862. After the family moved to New York, he began his Horatio Alger career by shining shoes and selling newspapers on the street. The hard-drinking, cigar-smoking Brady, a big man with a wide florid face

23

and shock of fair hair, dressed impeccably and displayed a gold watch chain across his expansive belly. A born gambler with a shrewd instinct for drama, he was a film pioneer, produced 260 plays during his long professional life and also managed two heavyweight boxing champions, Gentleman Jim Corbett and Jim Jeffries. In his autobiography, *Showman,* Brady described one of his many successes and revealed how he had made his fortune. Elmer Rice's *Street Scene* (1929) "cost me $6,000 to produce, the profits came to a cool half-million and the movie rights sold for $165,000 more."[1]

William's wife Grace George and daughter Alice Brady, who appeared in plays with Bogart, were both successful actresses. The fair-haired, blue-eyed Grace was educated in a convent and had studied at the American Academy of Dramatic Art. She made her debut as a schoolgirl and appeared in more than fifty plays — including *The School for Scandal* and *Captain Brassbound's Conversion* — in the half-century between 1894 and 1951. William described her style as "the fast-building, vivacious, chin-up and tongue-sparkling sort of thing, with wit and tears mingled." Alice Brady (seven years older than Bogart) had studied voice and begun her career in operettas. She then moved to romantic leads and became one of the highest paid silent film stars. She appeared in many pictures in the 1930s and won an Academy Award for best supporting actress in *In Old Chicago* (1938). When a broken ankle forced her to remain at home on the night of the ceremony, a "representative" accepted on her behalf and then disappeared with her Oscar. Alice, protesting that she never received it, got another one. The imposter was never seen again. Bogart's friend Bill, Jr., overshadowed by his flamboyant father, became an unsuccessful producer. In 1935 he died in a fire in Colts Neck, New Jersey.

In 1920 Bogart successively became Brady's office boy, assistant company manager and, at fifty dollars a week, production manager at his Peerless Film Studios in Fort Lee, New Jersey. His job was to rent the furniture, take care of the money and pay the actors. When Brady fired the director of a film called *Life,* starring Arlene Pretty and Rod La Rocque, Bogart got his first break and was told to finish it. "I did a fine job," he recalled, with his usual self-deprecating irony. "There were some beautiful shots of people walking along the streets, with me in the window making wild gestures. There was an automobile chase scene in which a car ran into itself. So Mr. Brady stepped in and directed the rest of it himself." Brady also tried to help Bogart by encouraging him to write stories and send them to the producer Jesse Lasky. Bogart took his advice, but nothing ever came of them.

In 1920 Bogart toured for six months with *A Ruined Lady,* starring Grace George, and lived out of his suitcase in a series of seedy but lively theatrical hotels. As stage manager—responsible for baggage, props and scenery—he kept the show on schedule, collected the tickets, pulled up the curtain, prompted actors, rang down the curtain and counted the take. When the juvenile lead became ill, Bogart took his place. Throughout his career he faithfully followed Grace George's professional advice: "Always keep working. Never be available. By constant working, you learn the business"—and also give the impression that you're always in demand.

⟨ **II** ⟩

THE NUMBER OF Broadway productions increased steadily throughout the 1920s (157 in 1920–21, 200 in 1922–23, 280 in 1927–28) and then fell sharply during the Depression. From 1922 through 1935 Bogart appeared in twenty-one different plays. He never took acting lessons or studied the basic techniques of stage deportment, speech, dialects, singing, dancing, fencing and gymnastics. He constantly had to look for work, scanning the pages of *Billboard* and *Variety,* auditioning on a bare stage in a dark theater as the producer and director, sated by scores of other applicants, hissed out curt dismissals from the stalls. He had to "live" his part and act in character, master and interpret new roles, working with the other actors for four weeks before the play opened. He would read his lines with the cast as they sat around a table, then learn his entrances and cues, and observe the chalk marks that indicated his positions on the stage. He would have to adjust to the scenery, lighting, costumes, props and make-up. Finally, in the full dress rehearsals, the actors struggled to put it all together and achieve a convincing dramatic performance. In the try-outs in Philadelphia, New Haven and Boston, he would have to learn new lines during the rewrites. After opening on Broadway, he waited nervously with the cast for the crucial reviews that would make or break the play, justify or destroy all their hard work. After the show closed in New York, he went on the road with the touring company.

He hoped each play would succeed, trying to remain optimistic despite some clear signs of disaster, and was often disappointed. Though he had three hits in his first eight plays, most of them ran for less than seventeen weeks and only five lasted for more than twenty-two. Bogart never adopted the flamboyant, pretentious manners of theater people or spoke of acting as an art. To him, it was just a job, which was more pleasant than working in an office and left plenty of time to pursue his other interests. He ignored poverty, uncertainty, scorn and rejection in the hope or illusion that one day he would find a part that would make him a star.

He remained steadily employed, in a long string of rather foolish comedies, by acting lightweight romantic heroes who came from his own class and background. These entertaining commercial plays, in which he usually got good notices, were very different from the revivals of Ibsen and Chekhov and the serious theater of the time. In 1923–24, for example, when Bogart was playing stereotypical characters in *Meet the Wife* and *Nerves,* John Barrymore's *Hamlet* and Eugene O'Neill's *Desire Under the Elms* brought tragic themes to Broadway. Though Bogart took more serious roles in the 1930s, after two brief failures in Hollywood, he did not appear in a first-rate play until he established his reputation and achieved fame in *The Petrified Forest* (1935). Immediately after that long-awaited success, he acted in three summer-stock shows before starting his main career in films.

Bogart made his Broadway debut on January 2, 1922 in *Drifting,* starring Alice Brady, produced by William Brady and directed by John Cromwell. The plot and Bogart's role were equally absurd. A deacon's daughter, cast out for an innocent prank by her stern father, becomes a femme fatale in a cabaret in China. Caught up in a revolution, she is rescued by an American soldier. The tallish Bogart, who had a minor role as a Japanese butler, tried to look humbly Oriental and sort of crouched when he came on stage. He was also terribly nervous: "I had one line of dialogue. I gave a beautiful performance as the houseboy on opening night. As I carried out a tray of dishes, I dropped them and the audience howled."[2] Dr. Bogart, watching his son act for the first time, tried to whip up some enthusiasm by loyally whispering to the audience around him: "The boy is good, isn't he?"

After appearing on tour in *Drifting,* Bogart got the juvenile lead in *Swifty.* Produced by Brady, it starred Frances Howard (who later married Samuel Goldwyn) and opened in October 1922. Bogart played Tom Proctor, a young aristocrat who seduces an innocent country girl and refuses to marry her. Her brother Swifty, a good-hearted boxer, retaliates by eloping with Proctor's sister. Bogart was so inexperienced that he asked the director, John Cromwell: "What do I do? Do I face out to the audience when I speak my lines, or do I talk to the characters?" He later recalled his second disastrous performance: "On opening night I got so scared I had to walk off the stage to get a glass of water, leaving Hale [Hamilton, the leading man] twiddling his thumbs. He was rather upset. So were the critics."

It was a bad play and he was terrible in it. Alexander Woollcott called the comedy "a consistently incredible piece, a little more gauche and artless than the average."[3] The *New York Times* said: "Nobody believes what is happening or cares what the upshot may be." One vitriolic critic noted that Bogart "gave some rather trenchant exhibitions of bad acting." Condemned all round, the play limped on for three weeks and then folded. But to be mentioned at all seemed like praise to Bogart. When the negative reviews were all in, Maud—whose caustic judgment deflated Belmont's heartfelt approbation—pointedly used the past tense and savagely remarked: "So you wanted to be an actor, eh?"[4]

After this inauspicious start Bogart did not appear in another play for more than a year. He made himself useful to William Brady, and was also helped by his parents. During the era of Prohibition and speakeasies, when people drank more than ever, the young Bogart, like one of Scott Fitzgerald's heroes, indulged in the pleasures of dancing, alcohol and sex. He consorted with debutantes and went out with actresses—including Helen Menken, who had replaced Alice Brady in *Drifting*. In "May Day" (1920), Fitzgerald described the dreamy, intoxicating, romantic atmosphere of a formal dance at a fashionable New York restaurant:

> At one o'clock a special orchestra, special even in a day of special orchestras, arrived at Delmonico's, and its members, seating themselves arrogantly around the piano, took up the burden of providing music. . . . During the performance the lights were extinguished except for the spotlight on the flute-player and another roving beam that threw flickering shadows and changing kaleidoscopic colors over the massed dancers.
>
> Edith had danced herself into that tired, dreamy state habitual only with débutantes, a state equivalent to the glow of a noble soul after several long highballs. Her mind floated vaguely on the bosom of the music; her partners changed with the unreality of phantoms under the colorful shifting dusk, and to her present coma it seemed as if days had passed since the dance began.

Fitzgerald's friend and Bogart's contemporary, Edmund Wilson, who called himself "a man of the twenties," said that exciting decade was characterized by Bogart's favorite pastimes, "drinks, animated conversation, gaiety: an uninhibited exchange of ideas. Scott Fitzgerald's idea that somewhere things were 'glimmering.'" In the early 1920s Bogart smoked his Andover pipe, sailed off Long Island, went ice skating and horseback riding in Central Park, attended fashionable jazz parties and spent weekends at country houses. He went to the Lambs Club on West 44th Street and to the Mayfair, another actors' club, which met every Saturday night for dancing at the Ritz-Carlton Hotel. He also hung around "21" and other congenial speakeasies with a popular journalist who later became his producer and partner: "In the old days on Broadway during Prohibition . . . we'd sit around the 'Silver Slipper' with Mark Hellinger, or go over to Tommy Lyman's joint and get him to sing torch songs."[5] He also checked the competition by going to plays and by watching movies in the new theaters that were decorated like Moorish mansions and Venetian palaces.

Though Bogart was a good golfer, he eventually found it too exasperating. After losing his temper and throwing his clubs around, he finally decided to take up more tranquil forms of recreation. His father had taught him chess, which became his favorite game and lifelong pleasure. Later, in Hollywood, he took lessons from Herman Steiner, an American grand master and chess editor of the *Los Angeles Times,* and played whenever he could. The screenwriter Curt Siodmak was a frequent partner, but claimed he could not afford to continue because his opponent, at every sitting, would drink a whole bottle of his Scotch. Bogart explained that he "enjoyed chess because there is no luck to it. I don't like games based on luck. Chess is an intellectual exercise. Also a companionable game. I play it very well." His ability to master the chess board was probably connected to his ability to master his lines almost as soon as he read them.

Bogart had his first Broadway success in a comedy *Meet the Wife,* starring Clifton Webb and the fluttery grande dame Mary Boland. It opened in November 1923, ran for 232 performances, and paid him $150 a week. Bogart, who played a newspaper reporter, smiled a lot, had impeccable manners and pursued the young daughter. Such charming and fatuous roles—in which he was supposed to have said: "Tennis, anyone?"—made few demands on Bogart as an actor, but he seemed to have no higher ambitions. He would appear, with hair slicked back, wearing white flannels and a cable-knit sweater, and carrying tennis racquets. The point of this get-up, Bogart amusingly explained, was not merely to indicate an idle, sporty youth: "The playwright gets five or six characters into a scene and doesn't know how to get them offstage. So what does he do? He drags in the juvenile, who has been waiting in the wings for just such a chance. He comes in, tennis racquet under his arm, and says: 'How about a game of tennis?'" In a lively article of 1940, after he had adopted a tough guy image in Hollywood, Bogart condemned his youthful roles as foolish and effeminate. He called them "glorified stage waits during which I was supposed to model a pinch-back sports coat, one of those pansified neckcloths and the swishiest new model of hair wave. For about six months I was the lion of the lady-finger mob, very much in demand at all the musicales and tea-fights."

Bogart played his first serious role as an aviator in *Nerves,* which opened in September 1924, a month after *Meet the Wife* had closed. In this drama three young men meet at a house party on Long Island, go off to test their courage in war (where one of them shatters his nerves in combat) and are reunited after the war. Bogart's second wife, Mary Philips, also appeared in this play, which was directed by Bill Brady, Jr. Though it closed after only sixteen performances, Bogart, having suddenly become an accomplished actor, got his first favorable notices. The *New York Times,* calling him "dry and fresh," said: "He has rapidly covered the distance that leads from obscurity to the comparative security of a definite place in the knowledge of theatrical managers and observers."[6] Alexander Woollcott, who had superciliously written of Bogart in *Swifty:* "The young man who embodied the aforesaid sprig was what might mercifully be described as inadequate," now changed his mind and confessed: "These words are hereby eaten." Bogart referred to Woollcott's original condemnation when mocking his early roles. But the critics' praise made him believe he could make it as an actor.

The actress Louise Brooks, in the most perceptive essay on Bogart, re-membered him speaking his lines in *Nerves* "with a well-projected baritone and good diction. . . . In 1924, my first impression of Humphrey Bogart was of a slim boy with charming manners, who was unusually quiet for an actor." Brooks was certain that Bogart's "lip wound gave him no speech impediment, either before or after it was mended," and thought he delib-erately cultivated an idiosyncratic way of speaking: "Over the years, Bogey practiced all kinds of lip gymnastics, accompanied by nasal tones, snarls, lisps, and slurs. His painful wince, his leer, his fiendish grin were the most accomplished ever seen on film."

After taking the summer off—riding, sailing, drinking and going to parties—Bogart appeared in September 1925 in the farcical *Cradle Snatchers,* which made the audience laugh hysterically and ran for well over a year. Bogart deftly played José Vallejo, the most cynical of three comically gauche college boys. Paid by three middle-aged wives to behave like ardent lovers, they have a "three day petting party" on Long Island to provoke the husbands' jealousy. José gets carried away and becomes ex-cessively bold. Acting the stereotypical Spanish lover, he hyperbolically claims to have strangled the bulls instead of killing them with a sword: "Am I not Don José Vallejo, the matador, whose two strong arms have choked the breath out of the bulls in the rings in Barcelona? . . . Am I not Don José Vallejo, in *whose veins* flows the blood of Castilian princes, who loved as they fought, fiercely and furiously, so that both their enemies and their women die from sheer exhaustion?" At the end of the play he gives the older husband advice about how to handle a woman: "You don't know how to treat your wife. She is young—too beautiful to be neglected as you have done. She wants romance—music—the sweet lush scent of big red roses—under the moon."

A photograph, catching the essence of the play, shows the older women in glittering diaphanous frocks, drinking heavily with the young men in evening dress. The dashing Bogart, sitting behind Mary Boland, observes the proceedings with a detached and somewhat sardonic expression. His screenwriter friend Nunnally Johnson called it "a disgusting play about three old women who have three gigolos to service them. And naturally it was very popular. Bogie had long sideburns, very sleek, black hair slicked back, and he was the kind of fellow you saw and disliked at once." The grace, style and control of Bogart's performance were enthusiastically commended. The critic Amy Leslie, who saw the road show in Chicago, exclaimed that "Bogart created a furor as one of the hired lovers. He is as young and handsome as Valentino, dextrous and elegant in comedy . . . and as graceful as any of our best romantic actors." Bogart had now acquired the timing, elegance, sophistication and wit to succeed in these shallow roles.

In June 1927, nine months after *Cradle Snatchers* closed, Bogart appeared in Margaret Mayo's *Baby Mine*. Lee Patrick, another member of the cast, later played Bogart's secretary and confidante in *The Maltese Falcon*. The play was a revival of a 1910 farce about a wife, addicted to flirting, who is afraid to confess she had lunched alone with her husband's best friend. The jealous but family-minded husband, played by Bogart, leaves her after this trivial incident. But she lures him back by stealing three babies and trying to pass them off as her own. He discovers the truth after many absurd adventures but, realizing that she loves him, decides to stay married to her.

The husband, a well-dressed young businessman with a brisk self-important manner, has no sense of humor. Most of his speeches express exaggerated indignation and got a lot of laughs: "She had the effrontery, the bad taste, the idiocy, to lunch in a public restaurant with the blackguard. . . . Even if she weren't running around—what have we to look *forward* to? What have we to look backward at? One *eternal* round of wrangles and rows. A childless home." When the wife protests, "I never wanted anybody but you," he indignantly replies: "Until you *got* me, yes; and then, you wanted *everybody* but me. Where you *meet* your gentleman friends is beyond me. *I* don't introduce them to you."[7] The comedy starred the owlish Fatty Arbuckle, who was trying to make a comeback after being charged with manslaughter in a lurid Hollywood scandal of 1921. Arbuckle made a long curtain speech and was given a warm reception, but the play closed after only twelve performances.

<h3 style="text-align:center">‹ III ›</h3>

AT THE START of his theatrical career, when he met his first wife, the slightly-built Bogart was five feet nine inches tall and weighed 155 pounds. He had a wolf-lope walk, and his strong rectangular face and rasping voice made a dynamic impression on stage. Brown-haired, brown-eyed and unconventionally handsome, he had a squared off, slightly cleft chin and the distinctive war scar above his lip. Though smartly dressed in plays, in private life he had no interest in clothes, and usually wore a polo shirt and sports jacket. Later on, both on and off screen, he became fond of colorful bow ties, but was happiest on a boat, in T-shirt, jeans and sneakers.

Bogart, the quintessential modern hero, often referred to himself as an "old-fashioned, last-century boy." Articulate, modest and usually polite, he once prompted a grande dame to exclaim: "What a lovely man! Almost the kind of actor you could have in your home." He had a surprising puritanical streak, disliked dirty stories and was repelled by the word "shit," but deliberately sprinkled his speech with foul words. When a woman told him he was a gentleman, he replied: "Don't let it get around. It could ruin my reputation." His stage friend Clifton Webb emphasized the gentle side of his character and observed: "Why, any woman could walk all over him. The man's a softie and—I might add—a very gallant one." Bogart thought it rude to be late and was especially vehement about punctuality. He disliked being touched, was appalled by gushing people and adopted a defensive manner that seemed impersonal, abrupt and rather curt. Louise Brooks wrote that he was so "supremely confident of his own attractiveness to women, he scorned every form of demonstrativeness."[8]

Bogart and Helen Menken, who appeared with him in *Drifting* in 1922, made an attractive couple. She came from a poor background and had very little education, but was a sophisticated woman with a great deal of energy, worldly knowledge and theatrical experience. Born in New York in 1901, the oldest of three children, she began her stage career as a child dancer in *A Midsummer Night's Dream* and acted from 1906 until 1961.

Helen grew up in a world of silence. Since both her parents were deaf mutes and communicated in sign language, they would end their disputes by turning off the lights. Her mother earned money by sewing identification badges for business conventions.

Helen's first job as a child actress paid $3.50 a week. "When I was only a little past my sixth birthday," she said, "I went into the world alone and learned to take care of myself. I worked every day at a regular job and was responsible for what I did. . . . The work wasn't very hard, but it meant being up so late at night, and traveling around, living on trains and in hotels, with queer food to eat at hours that were also queer." She once interrupted a "special children's number by taking an unexpected and sudden bow when she spotted her parents in the audience," but helped support her family and even managed to send her brother to college. While on the road she had several unpleasant experiences. She often had rooms above saloons, where the sounds of drunken singing, swearing and fighting kept her awake all night. When a fire broke out in a theater, she escaped in her underwear, covered by a huge opera cloak. Helen did not go to school until she was twelve years old, and then attended classes for only a year and a half. "As for education," she remarked, "I got it piecemeal as I went along. . . . In the common sense of the word, I haven't any."[9]

Until her first success in 1922, Helen worked mainly in stock and road companies, selling ladies' hats and modeling clothes between acting jobs. She had the same work ethic as Grace George, and reinforced what the older actress had told Bogart: "For years I have taken any part I could get, whether I liked it or not. . . . All I wanted was a chance to work and a salary I could live on." Though she had performed notably in Austin Strong's *Three Wise Fools* (1918), she first became famous in Strong's *Seventh Heaven* (1922) as a street urchin in the lower depths of Paris. In her greatest scene she turns upon her cruel sister and drives her out with the lash of a whip.

Helen had a thin pale face, large dark eyes, a mop of reddish hair, an expressive mouth, narrow shoulders and delicate hands. She was mad about clothes, had a "perfect mania" for shoes and was as high-strung as a thoroughbred horse. The *New York Times* described her appearance and hot-house acting: "Her cleanly etched English, spoken in a husky voice, and her clarity of acting style won many adherents here and abroad. But the slim, five-feet three-inch star with reddish blond hair could also evoke mild criticism from the reviewers for performances that they felt verged on the flamboyant. Miss Menken inevitably brought to her characterizations—however small or great—an incandescent quality and flowing vigor." Louise Brooks, an acute observer, satirized her histrionic manner: "Helen's white, thin face was always ecstatically lifted up to her vision of the Drama. I never heard her talk about anything except the art of the theatre." Helen became "a sensation in *The Captive* [1926], which was closed by the District Attorney . . . because of its lesbian theme."

Bogart once said: "I had enough women by the time I was twenty-seven to know what I was looking for in a wife."[10] He may have had the women, but he hadn't learned how to choose a compatible wife. Disappointing his family's social ambitions, he publicly announced his intention to marry Helen in the *New York Times* of April 5, 1922. Though he acquired the license in 1922, he did not get around to actually marrying her until May 20, 1926. At the time of his marriage he expressed serious doubts to his friends. He misleadingly told them that Helen was ten years older than he was and had bullied him into the wedding; that he would be dominated by her imperious, Maud-like character and overshadowed by her success. But he also knew that she was an established star and could help his career. He later confessed that he had been living with Helen in a flat at 43 East 25th Street and (like the characters he played on stage) felt a moral obligation to do the right thing. Marriage to this weird, sharp-witted woman strengthened his commitment to the bohemian, insecure theatrical life.

The best man was his brother-in-law, Stuart Rose. Bogart and his sister Pat had met Rose at a Thanksgiving dance in 1917 and she had married him in 1924. He had served in the Cavalry in World War I, and was a keen fox-hunter and steeplechaser. After working for a time at Fox Studios and Little, Brown publishers, he became a senior editor at the *Saturday Evening Post.* Bogart was married, while appearing in *Cradle Snatchers,* in the Menkens' apartment at 52 Gramercy Place. In addition to Helen's parents and Maud Bogart, the guests included Bill and Alice Brady, Grace George, Mary Boland (who had been in two plays with Bogart) and Kenneth MacKenna (who had acted in *Nerves*). The bizarre ceremony was conducted in sign language by the pastor from St. Ann's Church for Deaf Mutes. He insisted on speaking the words for the benefit of the guests, who were startled by the strange, unintelligible gargling sounds that emerged from his throat.

Only ten months later, on April 2, 1927 (between *Cradle Snatchers* and *Baby Mine*), Bogart and Helen, known for her fiery temper, formally separated. They had quarreled about petty things like how to run the house and what to feed the dog, about the separations caused by their work and the conflict between their careers and domestic duties. They had equally explosive temperaments, and Bogart said that "what started out to be just a little difference of opinion would suddenly become a battle royal which ended with one or the other walking out in a fine rage." During the divorce proceedings, Menken charged him with cruelty and desertion, asserting that "her husband regarded his career as of far more importance than married life." Rather surprisingly, the prominent actress said she had assumed the traditional woman's role and had "attempted to make her marriage the paramount thing in her life, even offering to relinquish her career." Emphasizing his cruelty for the sake of the divorce, she stated that Bogart on two occasions had struck her on the face. She did not claim alimony, but said he owed her $2,300, which the court ordered him to pay. After a brief, miserable marriage, they were divorced on November 18, 1927.

In a letter of 1927 to the theatrical agent Lyman Brown, Bogart expressed concern about the connection between his public and private life, and wondered if his career would be harmed by adverse publicity: "By this time you have probably read in the papers about what an old meany I am. I have tried my very best to keep my mouth shut—and be discreet. Any talking has come from my so-called 'friends' and not from me. Do you suppose the publicity and the divorce will hurt me in a business way?—I've tried to do the whole thing as nicely as possible and I don't see why it should, but I want your opinion. . . . When the whole thing is over Helen and I will be good friends. . . . She's a wonderful girl." Bogart later told his fourth wife, Lauren Bacall, that he, not Helen, was responsible for the failure of their marriage. He also expressed some bitterness about Helen to the writer-director Richard Brooks, who portrayed Bogart as Steve Taggart in *The Producer* (1951). In the novel Taggart says: "My first wife made a home for me. She's still got it. Two husbands after me occupied that home. She'll be there when it falls down. I hope it falls on her."

Bogart was attracted to domineering women like his mother, and, like his father, learned to submit to them. Strong women provided a challenging audience, reacted to his taunts and were sexually exciting. He acquired a propensity for domestic quarrels, and would have three unhappy marriages. He felt compelled to pick on and provoke wives, friends and enemies, and said of himself: "I always liked stirring up things, needling authority. Even in my childhood it gave me pleasure. I guess I inherited it from my parents. They needled everyone, including each other." He also inherited his parents' emotional reserve, and found it difficult to express his feelings or show affection. A man's man, he had a misogynistic streak and was not, except for wives and mistresses, close to any women. He could be charming and cultivated, but many people found him, when not aggressive, cold, withdrawn and distant.

The energetic Helen Menken, whose third husband was a partner in a Wall Street firm, played Queen Elizabeth in Maxwell Anderson's *Mary of Scotland* (1933), had a radio show in 1940, organized the Stage Door Canteen in World War II and the Tony Awards in 1947. She left retirement in 1960 to tour fifteen cities in Europe and the Middle East with Helen Hayes, June Havoc and the Theatre Guild Company. In 1966 she died of a heart attack in the Lambs Club in New York.[11]

Bogart's divorce coincided with the dramatic decline of his father's health, medical practice, social position and (after many bad investments) family fortune. Dr. Bogart's illness had originated in the ambulance accident in the 1890s that broke his leg and left him in chronic pain. To alleviate his pain and depression, Dr. Bogart, who had easy access to drugs, began to take morphine and soon became an addict. Frank Hamlin, who knew the family at Seneca Point, has the extraordinary recollection of the respectable Belmont and Maud rolling up their sleeves, taking out their needles and shooting up in front of the children at the cocktail hour: "Belmont Bogart was a physician who had concluded that [there was no need for pain any more and that] the recent introduction of morphine was the long-sought solution to all the many sufferings of mankind. On several occasions I saw Dr. and Mrs. Bogart give each other a shot before dinner." Much later, when a friend's dress caught fire during a dance and she had to take morphine to alleviate the pain of the burns, Bogart told her: "It's lucky you're allergic to morphine, unlike my unfortunate father."[12]

According to Dau's *New York Blue Book* and the *American Medical Directory*, Dr. Bogart sold his house in 1925 and moved downtown and across to the East Side. The Bogarts lived more modestly, in separate apartments and mainly on Maud's earnings, at two different addresses in the East 40s from 1926 to 1930. Belmont then gave up his practice and became a ship's doctor on freighters. From 1932 to 1934 Dr. Bogart's professional address was 25 Prospect Place in University Heights, across the Harlem River in the Bronx. He had originally listed his birth date as 1868; but as he grew older, he made himself younger, and claimed to have been born in 1872.

"There was no formal separation between father and Maud," Bogart recalled, noting their unusual arrangement and Maud's devotion. "There was never even a thought of divorce. But they just couldn't stand being together for long. Still, he was ill and he was *hers*. So she went over and cooked breakfast for him every morning and was with him for dinner every night. She hired nurses during his attacks, provided the money for his every want, and sat with him for hours. Then she went home to her own apartment. I never understood the situation, nor did I ask about it. She stood by him to the end, through the years [in the early 1930s] when he was paralyzed and bedridden. But she did it in her own fashion."[13]

⟨ IV ⟩

IN THE LATE TWENTIES and early thirties Bogart married another actress, appeared in two Broadway hits, and made six movies for Fox and Universal during his first, year-long trip to Hollywood. After being dropped by Fox, he returned to New York in June 1931, during the darkest year of the Depression, and was in a play that quickly closed. He then made a second, six-month trip to Hollywood, and appeared in three more films for Columbia and Warners. After being let go once again in July 1932, this time by Columbia, he resumed his career on Broadway and staggered through five successive flops. By 1934, when his second marriage was falling apart, he had been acting for fifteen years, had failed both personally and professionally in New York and Hollywood, and had become characteristically cynical and embittered.

Though able to tolerate the uncertainty of life as an actor, Bogart disliked solitude, hated to return to an empty house and would eventually marry four times. As he later told Verita Peterson, he depended on his wife for emotional security and always needed to have someone around. He felt he always drank too much, provoked people and got into fights without the salutary restraint of a woman, and told the magazine writer Gladys Hall: "I've always liked the domestic pattern . . . because I'm afraid of what I'd do if I were free. . . . I'd bitch myself up in about three days. I need a wife. *I must have a wife.*" In Richard Brooks' incisive novel, *The Producer,* Steve Taggart alludes to the fact that Bogart's second wife, Mary Philips, later married his actor friend Kenneth MacKenna when he wittily remarks: "Haven't you heard about me? Ethical. I go to bed with a woman, I've got to marry her. Then, after me, they marry someone else in the business. If I live long enough I'll be related to every sonofabitch in town."

The petite, blond, curly-haired, delicate-looking Mary Philips — born in New London, Connecticut, two years after Bogart — came from an Irish background. She made her debut as a chorus girl in 1919, was a stage actress in the 1920s and appeared in many films, from *A Farewell to Arms* (1932), in which she played a nurse, to *Lady in the Dark* and *Leave Her to Heaven* in the mid-1940s. A keen bridge player, she was also a sporty, outdoor girl, interested in tennis and golf. Mary, like Helen Menken, also had a fierce temper and once bit a cop's finger when he tried to arrest her for being drunk. Mary had appeared with Bogart in *Nerves* (1924). When he criticized her for stealing his scene, she won his admiration by boldly exclaiming: "Suppose you try to stop me." Nine months after their wedding they played a husband and wife in *Skyrocket*.

On April 3, 1928 — only four and a half months after his divorce from Menken and while appearing in *Saturday's Children* — Bogart married Philips at her mother's home in Hartford. He had a brief spell of impotence at first, but soon recovered his sexual powers. They took a country house in Fairfield, Connecticut, near his brother-in-law Stuart Rose, where they loved to play games — chess and bridge, Parcheesi and Monopoly — with friends. Mary described Bogart as "something of a Puritan, impeccably polite and careful about his language."[14]

In 1928–29, soon after his marriage to Mary, Bogart appeared in two hits. Maxwell Anderson's *Saturday's Children,* directed by Guthrie McClintic, opened on April 9, ran for 310 performances and then toured the country. The coy, sentimental comedy portrays the way to catch a husband, overcome the problems of newlyweds, and make the transition from passion through disillusionment and back to happiness. After his wife leaves him and retreats to a strict ladies' hotel, the young husband climbs the fire escape to visit her and locks himself into her room until they are reconciled. Bogart played the leading role (Rims O'Neil) opposite Ruth Gordon, whom he calls "kid." The tiny, gravel-voiced Gordon had been a leading actress on Broadway since 1918. In the course of the play Bogart is an eager suitor, a reluctant husband and a passionate lover desperate to recapture his wife. "God, I don't know what's the matter with me!" he tells her. "I used to have a little sense. About girls, anyway. Now I act like a damn dummy. . . . Don't you see I can't get along without you? I can't stand being away from you all the time. I keep waking up in the night *(looks into her eyes)*, wanting you." Ruth Gordon recalled that Bogart was willing to go on tour and got the job, although he "wasn't right for the part."

In August 1929 Bogart appeared in his longest-running play, Laurence Johnson's *It's a Wise Child,* which survived the Wall Street crash, lasted for 378 performances and led to his first Hollywood offer. In this entertaining comedy (produced and directed by David Belasco) an engaged woman falls in love with a young bank clerk and breaks her engagement to an elderly fiancé by falsely announcing that she's pregnant by another man. Though the plan backfires when she loses both suitors, she finally marries a young lawyer. Bogart played the transitional beau between the fiancé she abhors and the man she really loves. The heroine, emphasizing his character and good looks, first describes him as "Not one of those silly, dancing, drinking men. He's earnest. He has an ambition in life and, Steve, he's the best-looking man I ever met; tall, clean-skinned, clear-eyed, with a profile like one of those Greek statues." But after he reveals that he cares more about his career than his girl, she dismisses him as "just a foolish kid, afraid of losing his job."

The *New York Times* praised Bogart's unusual vigor and conviction in the role of the handsome bank clerk. He was also noticed by a scout for Fox Film Corporation, who was looking for experienced stage actors to work in the new and rapidly expanding talking pictures. Stuart Rose, who was then the New York story editor for Fox, arranged a screen test. Bogart recalled that "I took dozens of screen tests, but that [scarred] lower lip held me back. The final test was for the male lead in *The White Sister*. Another fellow got the part—Ronald Colman—and I had my lip operated on by my dad."[15] Bogart tested well and was offered a contract at $400 a week. In the summer of 1930 he and Mary took the long cross-country train ride to the tall palm trees, low Spanish houses and wide, empty streets of Los Angeles, and moved into a place called Hollywoodland.

‹ V ›

BOGART'S twenty-five-year film career spanned the "Depression, World War II, the cold war, and the Hollywood blacklist, in the classic years of the studio system from the arrival of sound to the advent of television." Like James Cagney, Spencer Tracy and Clark Gable, he entered movies after being trained in the theater, and believed "the best way to get into the picture business is to go on the stage first." Under contract with Fox, he would no longer have to search endlessly for work, make the tedious rounds of agents and auditions, travel in wearisome road shows, repeat the same foolish lines eight times a week, endure the disdain of a hostile audience, live precariously from play to play and often spend more time preparing a flop than acting in it.

In return for financial security, the studios extracted their due. Contract players, virtually owned by the studio, were required to act in the films assigned to them or risk being suspended without pay. They could be loaned out to other studios for a higher salary, while the studio that owned them received their fee and pocketed the difference. The studios owned all the movie theaters throughout the country, and profits depended on speedy production schedules. A typical movie was made in a matter of weeks, as the studios juggled actors, technicians and sound stages to maximize their enormous output. Bogart had to submit to the strict discipline, act in many inferior movies and work long hours. He would have to endure the boredom of sitting around while cameras, lights and sound booms were positioned, sets and props arranged, in order to shoot only a few minutes of film each day. The contract, moreover, was secure only as long as the studio wanted the actor. He could be dropped, as most actors (and some stars) were, as soon as it was clear that there were no suitable parts and he would not be a success.

Bogart also had to make the transition from stage to film acting. Stage actors had four weeks of rehearsal to gradually develop their characters and scenes. They performed and perfected the whole two-and-a-half-hour play, night after night. They had to project their voices to the distant balcony, but could get away with a certain amount of faking, posturing and missed cues. Making movies, where the emphasis was on the image rather than the word, was significantly different. Rehearsals were much shorter, direction comparatively brief. To increase efficiency and reduce costs, pictures were shot out of chronological sequence. Actors often appeared in only part of the film. Instead of forming an ensemble, they acted their scenes and left the set. Actors in the same movie sometimes never got to know, or even see, each other. Instead of working to achieve a sustained, polished performance, they would try several variations of a short take. They spoke much faster in film, and Bogart quickly mastered the art of rapid dialogue. Since the intense scrutiny of a close-up registered the slightest change of expression, screen acting had to be more natural, lifelike and spontaneous. It was more difficult than on stage to hide, with make-up and a spirited performance, facial blemishes, lack of sleep or ill-health.

Stage performers have the immediate reaction and responsive applause of a live audience. Movie actors have to wait months to get an audience reaction—or to discover their best work has been altered or cut out completely by the editor. Though the technicians and crew provided some response, Bogart found it "hard to feel emotion when right over [the actress's] shoulder I see a big hairy-chested grip scratching himself."[16] The actual passage of time on stage is closely related to real time. But in movies, a series of close-ups can prolong a moment in time for dramatic emphasis, while swift cuts from one scene to another can make time move faster. If a play flops, it disappears and is forgotten. But a bad movie has a permanent existence; it is retained in archives and can now be revived on television and videotape to haunt its makers.

When working Bogart would wake up at about 6:30, arrive at the studio at eight, and go first to the make-up and wardrobe departments. (In the old days, when male actors had to supply their own clothing, he once had to rush out and buy a pair of pajamas for a bedroom scene.) He would then go to the set on the sound stage (the back lot was used for exterior scenes), which often had a clammy, closed-in smell. He checked with the assistant director who had a list of actors appearing in the film. While waiting to be called for his first scene, he would drink a cup of coffee and catch up on the latest gossip in the *Hollywood Reporter*. He would usually rehearse with the other actors before going on camera and again on the set for the director and crew. When everyone was ready, they would shoot.

While waiting for the new set-ups he would reread the script, touch up his make-up or sit around chatting with his stand-in and friends in the cast. He might also return to his dressing room (elaborately graded according to the status of the star) to play cards and read the newspapers, see studio press agents or Hollywood journalists. He sometimes made his own home movies during the longueurs. The work day could be extended to deal with unexpected problems, finish a set-up or shoot at night, and a six-day week was standard.

The director, having planned the shooting schedule and thought out the camera positions and moves, chose the first scene to be shot. Except for the action scenes, he used only one camera. The master scene, at the beginning of the film, established the setting and characters and made them clear to the audience. The first scene of the day would either complete a previous sequence or start a new one. The actors would have memorized their parts, and with experienced players there was no need for extensive discussion about their roles. They came on the set and, practicing emphasis, revising or discarding lines that did not work, ran through their speeches till the scene came alive.

The director told the actors precisely where to stand, where they had come from and were going to. Striving for pace and tempo, fluidity and energy — for there must always be movement in a movie — he would stage the scene. The director and cameraman aimed for dramatic angles and precise images, and used light and shadow to suggest mood and character. They tried to make the scenes and sequences flow together in one natural continuous movement. They wanted the audience to remain unaware of the director and the mechanics of filming, and to have the illusion that they were looking at reality.

The young Bogart had already acted a ladykiller, with Joan Blondell, in a ten-minute Vitaphone movie *Broadway's Like That,* made in New York in 1930. As in the theater, he played positive, often romantic roles in most of his unmemorable early films. He was a handsome adventurer who gets the girl, a good guy from a respectable family who is sent to prison for accidental manslaughter, an American flyer with the Royal Air Force in France, an adventurous marine, a foreman on a western ranch. He began more promisingly in movies than on stage. The *New York Times* said that in his first full-length film, *A Devil With Women* (1930), "Bogart makes his debut in talking pictures and gives an ingratiating performance. Mr. Bogart is both good-looking and intelligent."

In John Ford's *Up the River*, Bogart appeared for the first and only time with Spencer Tracy, who was making his film debut and later became a close friend. A year younger than Bogart, Tracy had also served in the wartime navy and was the first to call him Bogey. In this convict comedy, which Ford made in two weeks and called "a bunch of junk," prisoners arrive at the pen in a limousine, escape whenever they wish and voluntarily return to jail to win the annual baseball game. Lindsay Anderson found in the film "some recognizable Ford touches of slapstick and sentiment; the handling is fast and loose and the comedy of bad men behaving like naughty boys is artlessly disarming."

Bogart, who did not have a starring role in any of his early movies, slipped from third or fourth billing in his first pictures to eighth or ninth in the later ones. He worked with Joan Blondell and with Bette Davis, who would appear with him in several important films, and with Raoul Walsh, who would direct *The Roaring Twenties* and *High Sierra*. During his first year in Hollywood Bogart gave creditable performances and received good notices, but his series of hopelessly mediocre films never gave him a chance to show his talent. Considered a failure, he was dropped by Fox on May 14, 1931, after his sixth picture in one year, and returned to the East Coast.

The actor Conrad Nagel helped explain Bogart's failure in the early 1930s. The head of Universal, famous for his nepotism, had put his son, Carl Laemmle, Jr., who produced *Bad Sister* (one of Bogart's worst movies), in charge of the studio. After the movie was completed, the son called in Bogart and Bette Davis, "one at a time, and told them they had nothing to offer. They were colorless. No fault of theirs. They just didn't photograph. He suggested they go back to New York."[17] Promising careers could thus be ruined by powerful executives who knew almost nothing about the movies.

The desperate state of the theater scene made it extremely difficult for actors to find work. Just as the number of Broadway plays had increased during the 1920s, so they rapidly declined during the Depression of the 1930s. There were 240 new productions on Broadway in 1929–30,

190 in 1930–31 and only 80 (a decrease of two-thirds from the beginning of the decade) in 1938–39. In 1931 the Shuberts, with all their theaters in New York and throughout the country, had gone into receivership. A theater historian wrote that at the beginning of the Depression "there were fewer hits, profits were reduced, salaries were cut, rentals were trimmed, more and more houses remained dark. . . . The evolution of talking pictures was an almost equally ominous disaster," and many legitimate theaters had been converted into movie houses.

Bogart's salary, when he could find employment, plunged alarmingly from $450 to $50 a week. When he could not get a job on stage he tried broadcasting, but did not do very well: "Radio I heard was paying $8,000 a week to experienced actors. So I went to a radio station and made my little spiel. Success! On the strength of my Hollywood reputation I was hired—to act in laxative playlets at $50 a week. I did one program and got canned—not enough of the old wheedle in my voice. . . . I had survived being a bond salesman and if you can live through that you'll live forever." He and Mary moved into crumbling, peeling lodgings at 434 East 52nd Street and lived for a while on Bogart's skill at games. He played chess for fifty cents a round in sleazy joints on Sixth Avenue, earning a few dollars a day, and made more money at bridge in the Players Club than he did as an actor. Despite considerable hardship, Bogart never seriously considered changing his profession. He didn't have any other skills, hated office work, and loved the freedom and excitement of the theater. He accepted his precarious existence and kept hoping for better times.

Bogart's defiant and embittered personality began to emerge during the failure, humiliation and poverty of the early 1930s. He adopted the same persona as Erich von Stroheim, who had played ruthless German villains in American propaganda films during World War I and had been billed as "The Man You Love to Hate." Bogart's first article, published in 1940 before he became a star, was called "Why Hollywood Hates Me." But it really concerned his own lifelong hatred of Hollywood. It was, along with the essay about why he'd never loved his mother, the most revealing thing he ever wrote.

Remembering the struggles, mortification and sense of doom at the beginning of his film career, he observed "how tough and heartless [Hollywood] can be toward an actor on the skids. I know because it crucified me when I was on the skids. . . . It was the first year of sound pictures and the scouts had signed me and everyone else, it seemed. We all walked the plank arm in arm but I made the biggest splash." In this acid-etched period he felt stigmatized by unemployment. Like thousands of other men during the Depression, he was treated as a leper. Former friends "couldn't see my hand when I stuck it out in greeting; probably fearing I'd clamp on to it and make a touch before they could escape." The intensely vulnerable man, recalling his own disappointments as well as his father's rapid decline, said that "tough, unnecessary jolts just tear your heart out, and leave you with too much suspicion." A decade later, his bitter wounds had not yet healed. No wonder that Rose Hobart, who acted in two plays with Bogart in the early 1930s, remembered him as noticeably depressed and behaving like "an absolute son of a bitch."

In December 1931—after six months of chess, bridge and squalor in New York—Bogart appeared, wearing a moustache, in *After All*. The playwright, John Van Druten, would later achieve great success on Broadway with *The Voice of the Turtle, Bell, Book and Candle* and a stage adaptation of Christopher Isherwood's stories, *I Am a Camera*. But his early play closed after only twenty performances.

Bogart enters toward the end of the second act as Duff Wilson, "a man of about 38, humorous, attractive, and extremely charming." An architect married to an invalid, he can't get divorced and is having a secret affair with the daughter of a respectable family. They think he's a moral monster and refuse to meet him. When his wife finally dies, he is able to remarry and have children. The play concerns generational differences, family bonds, and the conflict between conventional values and bohemian life, restraint and freedom. When courting his future wife Duff Wilson reveals his charming romantic character by telling her: "We had a chandelier at home that I thought was the most thrilling thing in the world. And when I was about six I fell in love with a lady in a pantomime because she wore a dress all made of gold sequins."[18] Bogart was again spotted by a talent scout. He eagerly accepted a six-month contract with Columbia, which quickly leased him out to Warner Bros., at the substantial salary of $750 a week. He and Mary once again traveled across the country and moved into the grandly named Château Elysée, a modest apartment house in the heart of Hollywood.

< VI >

IN BOGART'S first gangster film, *Three on a Match* (1932), he is as slick and handsome as in his lightweight romantic roles. But this part finally gave him some scope as an actor and allowed him to be both seductive and terrifying. It was made, according to Warners' hectic schedule, in June

1932 on a low budget of $163,383. The title recalls the superstition that the third person using a light will be unlucky. The picture takes place from the beginning of Prohibition in 1920 to the early years of the Depression, using newspaper headlines (in Warners' formulaic fashion) to show the rapid passing of time.

In the movie three childhood girlfriends take different paths as adults —into crime, business and a wealthy marriage. The rich woman (Ann Dvorak), bored with her husband, leaves a cruise ship with her lover and small son. Bogart (nattily dressed and called "The Mug") enters three-quarters of the way into the picture and kidnaps the intolerably cute child in order to repay his gambling debts. In a characteristic line, he says the police are "swarming around like alleycats after a fishhead." He terrifies the little boy, who begs him, while Bogart plots her doom, not to hurt his mommy. Filled with remorse, wrecked by drink and dope, and knowing she will be killed as soon as the ransom is paid, Dvorak (the unlucky third girl) lipsticks the kidnapper's address on her nightgown and plunges through a window to her death. Bogart is captured and sent to serve the first of many long sentences in prison.

Bogart's second trip to Hollywood coincided with the worst economic crisis in the history of the film industry: "In the early 1930s Hollywood still had the air of a colony about it. Self-contained, and for the most part self-interested, its social structure was solidly based on its business structure; social strata were defined in terms of weekly paychecks. But even this self-enclosed community was not immune to the Depression. By 1933 one third of the nation's movie theaters had closed." It took several years for the Depression to hit, but its effect was devastating. In January 1933 both Paramount and RKO declared their theater chains bankrupt. The major studios fired a great many people and those who remained were forced to take drastic salary cuts. Bogart, despite his fine performance in *Three on a Match,* was one of the victims. Dropped by Columbia after his six-month contract expired, he returned in July 1932, after his second failure to take root in Hollywood, to bleak prospects in New York.

Bogart had ended the 1920s with the tremendous success of *Saturday's Children* and *It's a Wise Child.* Now, desperate for work and without much choice, he haunted the Equity offices, searched through the ads in *Variety,* and returned to romantic roles in several Broadway flops between October 1932 and May 1934. This meant a lot of long rehearsals and many disappointments. In *Chrysalis,* an "astonishingly insignificant" melodrama about a love affair between rich and poor, Bogart played a flashy idler in his effectively slick style. One critic, quoting the arch dialogue, observed that "Mr. Bogart, an oily insect, gets Miss [Margaret] Sullavan drunk and instructs her, through many long and monotonous kisses, in what he refers to as 'the joys of propinquity.'" Elisha Cook, Jr., who would act brilliantly in *The Maltese Falcon* and *The Big Sleep,* also appeared in the play. Elia Kazan, who had a small part and was assistant stage manager, condemned it as "a dreadful production. There were actors with big reputations in the cast, as well as less known actors like Humphrey Bogart, who was playing a 'patent-leather parlor sheik,' but they didn't know what they were doing and [Theresa Helburn, the executive director of the Theatre Guild] couldn't help them." The director Joshua Logan, who met Bogart in New York in 1934, said "he seemed to accept the fact that he was doomed to play poor parts in bad plays . . . [and] used to entertain his friends by reading them his scrapbook of bad notices."[19]

The Mask and the Face by Luigi Chiarelli, translated by Somerset Maugham, was first performed in 1916 and became an immediate success throughout the world. The cast of the 1933 revival included Judith Anderson and Leo G. Carroll, who would later appear with Bogart in *All Through the Night* and in *We're No Angels.* The grotesque satirical comedy portrays a group of jealous and adulterous Italians in a country house on Lake Como. The husband, after announcing that he will kill his wife if she is unfaithful, catches her in the act, sends her away and pretends he has murdered her. Defended in court by his best friend, the lawyer Spina (Bogart), he is acquitted. His wife, seeking reconciliation, secretly returns. She appears at her own mock funeral, confesses the truth and is reunited with her husband.

Spina is one of Bogart's first roles as a cold, manipulative villain. Adroit with women as he is with juries, he has in fact seduced his friend's wife. When she first rejects him, angrily exclaiming that he ought to be chopped in two, he cynically replies: "a woman *always* opens the game with a *certain* amount of violence — bordering on vulgarity." The play suggests that the husband feels the shame of public humiliation more than the actual adultery. A weak, proud man, he needs "to keep the mask on the face of vanity."

Between his last plays Bogart acted in his tenth film, *Midnight* (1934). Made in New York with a camera that rolled shakily forward in the close-ups, it had, like *Three on a Match,* unusual psychological interest and a villainous role for Bogart. In *Midnight* a woman is convicted of murder when the jury foreman asks her, "Did you take his money after you killed him?" and she admits that she did. Held responsible for sentencing the woman to death, the foreman insists he would do the same to his own daughter — played by the charming, baby-faced Sidney Fox.

Bogart, as the heartless gangster and ladykiller Garboni, meets Fox at the trial. He remarks, after the death sentence is pronounced, "Too bad she didn't have the right lawyer." Bogart flirts with her and Fox falls in love with him. She's distressed when he has to run from the police and tells her: "We're through, see. I'm not the guy for you." The camera cuts back and forth from the troubled lovers to the woman in the death cell, whose midnight execution is described on the radio. Just at that moment Fox, suspecting he has another woman and insisting, "I won't let anyone else love you," kills Bogart with his own gun. She returns home, confesses her crime of passion and exclaims: "I'll go to the chair for it."

The District Attorney, who owes the foreman a favor, concocts the far-fetched theory that Bogart was really shot by gangsters and that Fox merely *imagined* she had committed the crime. The devoted and devastated father accepts this convenient lie, shattering the illusion that "the law is the same for everybody." The year before the Production Code began to dictate a rigid morality, Sidney Fox was allowed to get away with murder.[20] Bogart's sharp dress and cynical talk, his treacherous behavior and violent end defined the character that would make him famous in gangster films throughout the 1930s.

‹ VII ›

BOGART RETURNED to New York in 1932, after his second trip to Hollywood, to discover that his father had lost his health and money, that one sister was an alcoholic and the other was permanently insane. His beautiful younger sister Kay had been a model at the Fifth Avenue department store Bergdorf Goodman. But she was too fond of Scotch, burned herself out during Prohibition and, despite Maud's social ambitions, had never married. In 1937, after an appendicitis operation, Kay would die of peritonitis at the age of thirty-four. Bogart said the self-destructive Kay "was a victim of the speakeasy era. She burned the candle at both ends, then decided to burn it in the middle."

Pat Bogart Rose looked like her brother. Tall and athletic, well built and well bred, quiet and shy, she had been a happily married woman. In 1930, after enduring the agonizing twenty-seven-hour delivery of her second child, Pat became manic depressive and had to be hospitalized for mental illness. At her insistence, Stuart Rose divorced her in 1935 and she moved, with Maud, to Hollywood. According to Richard Brooks, Maud also had some sort of psychological disturbance and suffered mental aberrations. Edward G. Robinson, who acted in many movies with Bogart, said "there had been a history of emotional disturbance in his family."[21] Bogart's experience with insanity gave him unusual insight and compassion when he encountered it in his private and professional life.

✧ 3 ✧

The Petrified Forest and Warner Bros.

1935-1957

⟨ I ⟩

ON SEPTEMBER 8, 1934, shortly before Bogart opened in *The Petrified Forest,* his father died of hypertensive heart disease in the grotesquely named Hospital for the Ruptured and Crippled. Belmont was sixty-six years old and had been paralyzed and bedridden for several years. Humphrey inherited a large debt of $10,000 from bad investments and medical expenses, and eventually repaid it. His main legacy was a gold ring, with two rubies and a diamond, which he always wore and can be seen in his photographs and films. Humphrey's account of the deathbed scene comes right out of a sentimental movie. But it gave him a rare opportunity to express affection for the old man who had such a powerful influence on his character. His father, whom Humphrey had disappointed and perhaps neglected, died "an old-school sport who had been brought down roughly in life. 'It was only at that moment,' Bogart later said, 'that I realized how much I really loved and needed him, and I had never told him. Just before he died, I said, "I love you, Father." He heard me, because he looked up at me and smiled. Then he died.'"

In his mid-thirties Bogart was charming and physically attractive. His well-bred parents, whom he called "gentlefolk," had taught him good manners and influenced his tastes and interests, but not his social attitudes and political opinions. During his fifteen years on stage he had often parodied the self he might have been—an aristocratic young social-ite. His role as Duke Mantee in the stage and film versions of *The Petrified Forest* changed all that. As the hedonistic 1920s gave way to the harsher social climate of the 1930s, his family fortunes deteriorated with

48

the times. During the Depression, Bogart found darker, criminal parts and created an entirely different screen personality: brooding, callous, malevolent.

Bogart's screen image was partly created by the playwright Robert Sherwood, the author of *The Petrified Forest*, who was a powerful presence on Broadway in the 1930s and 1940s. Six feet six inches tall, he was educated at Harvard, served in the Canadian Black Watch in World War I and eventually won three Pulitzer Prizes. Unlike the light comedies and routine thrillers that Bogart had been acting in since 1922, Sherwood's play was serious, dramatic and fresh. Bogart's performance created a menacing image that kept him employed in Hollywood for many years. His account of his leap from an obscure melodrama to a major part in an important play makes it all seem entirely fortuitous: "A job in a gruesome little mishap called *Invitation to a Murder* [May 1934] put me back on the main line. Then a girl I knew heard that Arthur Hopkins was casting a leading lady of her type. I went along with her for the walk. When I entered the theatre somebody assumed that I was trying for a part that was open, that of a football player, another White Pants Willie role. But Hopkins, the producer, and Leslie Howard, the star, visualized me as Duke Mantee, the killer heavy, and I was in."

Arthur Hopkins—a short, plump man with a cherubic face—gave a more convincing account of how he discovered Bogart, recognized his potential and enabled him to achieve, for the first time, real stature as an actor:

> Sometimes the first sound of a voice will tell you what you want to know. When I was casting *Petrified Forest* I could think of no one for the part of Duke Mantee. One day I stopped in the Golden Theatre, where a quick failure was just expiring. Between the ticket door and the stage at the Golden there is a curtain that shuts off the stage. While still behind the curtain I heard a dry, tired voice. Instantly I knew it was the voice of Duke Mantee.
>
> When I saw the actor I was somewhat taken aback, for he was one I had never much admired. He was an antiquated juvenile who had spent most of his stage life in white pants swinging a tennis racket. He seemed as far from the cold-blooded killer as one could get, but the voice persisted, and the voice was Mantee's. So I engaged him, and thus started the catapulting career of Humphrey Bogart.[1]

Bogart's success, in fact, was carefully calculated. Hearing of the audition, he grew a three-day beard, dressed in shabby clothes, and, as Louis Bromfield noted: "sacrificed his good looks by cropping his hair so short that his head appeared to be shaven." The front of his hair stood up stiffly, like a miniature forest, and made him look convincingly evil. Blanche Sweet, who also appeared in the play, recalled that Bogart had to transform himself completely in order to act this part:

> He didn't vary his performance one iota from the first day he rehearsed until the day we closed six months later. . . . He evidently had made up his mind what he would do and it was in an entirely different character from what he had ever played on the stage or in any film he had done before that. It was an entirely different character from what he was himself. But I think that was the beginning of his film career because he played this low key, very silent and very deadly kind of character. You know, "Just sit still girl or I'll blow your head off."

Hopkins shrewdly discovered the latent criminal in Bogart, who later emphasized his gratitude by joking: "I think he should get 10 per cent of everything I have earned since then!"

The real Petrified Forest, near Flagstaff, Arizona, is filled with ancient trees that have turned to rock. Sherwood used the fossils to symbolize a dying society. The hero of his play is the romantic, world-weary intellectual Alan Squier, played by the brilliant English actor Leslie Howard. Diffident, polite and soft-spoken, he arrives on foot and out of cash at a roadside restaurant in the Arizona desert. He strikes up a conversation with Gabby, the dreamy and poetic daughter of the proprietor, and immediately establishes an intuitive rapport with her. She longs to study art in France; he is ashamed of his worthless, parasitic life. At the same time, the notorious killer Duke Mantee, fleeing from the police with his gang and waiting for a rendezvous with his girl, turns up in the same place. He has hijacked the car of a wealthy couple, and holds them and their chauffeur hostage. The action of the play is confined to the restaurant, where the gang and the hostages tensely await the dramatic resolution. Despairing of life and wanting Gabby to fulfill her dreams, Squier decides to sacrifice and redeem himself so that she can fulfill her ambitions. He persuades Duke to kill him before escaping. Gabby can then collect his life insurance and leave her oppressive father and irritating grandfather, her boorish suitor and constricted life in the desert.

The swarthy, unshaven Mantee introduces some reality into this absurd yet moving plot. He provides a brutal yet sympathetic contrast to the blond, high-minded Squier, and his notorious robberies suggest a desperate but effective way to get money during the Depression. The tightly-structured play had "fast-moving action, individual characters, suspense, a little humor, well-contrived crises, and some thought-provoking ideas." It opened on January 7, 1935, was an immediate success and ran for 197 performances. Bogart remarked that it "marked my deliverance from the ranks of the sleek, sybaritic, stiff-shirted, swallow-tailed 'smoothies' to which I had seemed condemned for life." The *New York Times* said Bogart "does the best work of his career as the motorized guerrilla."[2] Sherwood sold the film rights for $110,000, and Warner Bros. offered Bogart a contract at $550 a week.

In September 1935 Bogart and Mary Philips became part of the steady migration of talented theatrical people from New York and Europe, and moved to Hollywood for the third time. They first lived in the Garden of Allah on Sunset Boulevard. Cheap and convenient, it had a bohemian atmosphere and in the 1930s was favored by writers like Scott Fitzgerald, Dorothy Parker and Robert Benchley. Built in 1921 as the residence of the silent film star Alla Nazimova, it had two-story Spanish stucco bungalows surrounding the main house and a swimming pool shaped like the Black Sea to remind the actress of her birthplace in Yalta. The Bogarts paid about $300 a month for half a bungalow with a small but pleasant parlor, bedroom and bath. After a while they rented a small adobe house on Horn Avenue, in West Hollywood, which climbs toward the hills north of Sunset Boulevard.

‹ II ›

BOGART'S MOVIE CAREER was founded on his contract with Warner Bros., a studio that had a special kind of energy and made a distinctive type of film. Jack Warner was quite different in outlook and talent from the more serious theatrical impresarios Bogart had known on Broadway. Lacking education and culture, Warner produced mass entertainment at the cheapest price, and set Bogart to work on the gangster movies the studio turned out in factory fashion. His bitter conflicts with Warner were typical of the strained relations between actors and studios under the contract system.

Warner Bros., one of the five major Hollywood studios, had been founded by four sons of a Jewish immigrant cobbler who had come to America from Poland in 1883. The family moved around a great deal, tried various business enterprises and finally settled in Youngstown, Ohio. In 1904 Harry, Albert, Sam and Jack opened a nickelodeon across the state line in New Castle, Pennsylvania. They had their first success with *My Four Years in Germany* in 1917. Backed by Wall Street money, they founded their studio in Burbank, just north of Hollywood, in 1923.

Warners had a profitable run of Rin Tin Tin movies, written by Darryl Zanuck and starring a German shepherd dog, in the 1920s. They bought First National in 1925 and used the First National shield with "WB" on it as their logo. The following year they acquired Vitaphone (a subsidiary formed to exploit sound movies), launched the sound era with Al Jolson's *The Jazz Singer* in 1927 and bought an additional 110 acres of land in 1929. By 1930 Jack, Harry and Sam (Albert had died) owned, in addition to the vast studio, fifty subsidiary companies and a quarter of all the movie theaters in America. Warners, like all the other studios, was hit hard by the Depression. They lost $8 million in 1931 and $14 million in 1932. But in 1935, the year Bogart arrived, they had reversed their losses and had net earnings of $674,000. Their earnings went up to $3,177,000 in 1936 and leaped to a healthy $5,875,000 in 1937.

Warners was known for its economically-made, fast-paced pictures on topical subjects. A Warners historian has described their controversial themes and crusade for social justice:

> Their studio was as powerful as a major newspaper, dealing vigorously with crooked politics, with the Mafia, with the Prohibition gangs, with the lack of privilege of women in a male-dominated society, with the ugliness of theatrical life. Even their musicals were unlike any others: bitter and acrid portraits of the realities of show business. They exposed the evils of newspaper reporting. By their pioneering efforts they attacked racial prejudice in the Deep South and had the chains struck from the ankles of the prison gangs in Georgia.

They provided biographies of heroes of science and literature — Pasteur, Zola, Juárez, Doctor Ehrlich and Reuter. More adventurous than other studios, Warners even bought the film rights to James Joyce's *Ulysses*. "When asked if the company really intended to make it, the answer was: 'Why not?'"

Jack Warner, head of production at Burbank and Bogart's boss, seemed to fit the stereotypical image of the movie mogul. Born in Ontario, Canada, in 1892, while the family was on the move, the youngest of the four brothers, Jack left school after the 4th grade. He started in the business as a boy soprano, entertaining the audience while the movie reels were changed. According to the film historian Neal Gabler, "Jack was not only crude, vulgar, shallow, flashy, contrary, and galling; unlike the vast majority of Hollywood Jews who coveted respectability, he actively cultivated these qualities." Suntanned, foppish, arrogant, and tough, Jack was notorious for his crude and boorish remarks. "Scanning a table of Oriental guests at a banquet for Madame Chiang Kai-shek, he said, 'Holy cow. I forgot to pick up my laundry.'" Introduced to a distinguished rabbi, he remarked: "'How're ya, rab? I caught your act at the Palace. You were great!'"3

Billy Wilder, who had a soft spot for Jack (partly because he never had to work for him), said Jack always wanted to sing and be a stand-up comedian at parties. The director Delbert Mann found Jack outrageously egoistical. During a "command performance" at a lunch for writers and directors, he made a series of outrageous puns and jokes. Some of them were quite funny, most were terrible flops. Lauren Bacall, who had a number of run-ins with Jack in the late 1940s, thought "he was one of the most ill-at-ease human beings I'd ever encountered. When you'd try to talk to him about the script (which he'd probably never read), he'd crack a joke. When you'd try to reason with him, he'd tell you how hard he worked."

The screenwriter Casey Robinson—who wrote Bogart's *Dark Victory* and *Passage to Marseilles*—noted that Jack's lack of interest in scripts and emphasis on the commercial aspects of film-making were actually advantageous to the writer: "In all my nine years at Warner Brothers, I think he read only one of my scripts. His attention was to the contracts, to the fights with actors—he was always having fights with actors—and to publicity. He watched that like a hawk, and you were fired if you had a publicity agent of your own. He ran budgets, how much you could spend —purely administrative." But the despised writers were lucky. Their work got shot as they wrote it because "Warner would not pay for rewrites and reshooting, and because of the attitude of [Jack's executive producer] Hal Wallis."4

Jack built up and ran a multi-million-dollar business, and was not nearly as stupid, philistine and mercenary as he seemed to be. Behind his childish vanity and disarming joker's mask, he had considerable shrewdness and a clear grasp of public taste. Though colleagues like Darryl Zanuck thought he was in it strictly for the money, Warner's movies had more social impact than the classier films of MGM. Like the other bosses, he treated actors like commodities, and got into fierce legal disputes with several of his leading stars: James Cagney, Bette Davis and Olivia de Havilland. Like other actors, Bogart traded freedom for money and security, and then complained about his contractual bondage. He and John Huston loved to make fun of Jack. They resented him because he ran the studio and ran them. Jack wisecracked that Bogart's lisp made him sound like a fairy. Bogart told the press that Jack was a creep. When his boss angrily protested, Bogart put his mind at rest by explaining that he had spelled it "kreep"—an entirely different word.

The critic Robert Sklar explained that the contracts bound the actors but not the studio, which retained extraordinary control over their private lives: "All important screen players, and many directors and writers as well, were obliged, as a condition of obtaining work, to sign contracts binding them to a studio for seven years. The studio's commitment, however, was for no more than six months; the contract gave it an option to renew at the end of every half-year period or to let the agreement lapse, setting the employee at liberty." The contracts also contained a clause that stated "the artist agrees to conduct himself with due regard to public conventions and morals," and gave studios the legal right to dismiss actors who hurt their public image and commercial value by becoming involved in alcoholic, sexual or criminal scandals. According to the English novelist Anthony Powell, who visited Hollywood in the late 1930s, the studio bosses were grasping and stupid, "procrastinating collectively in their business; the fact that their own morals were rarely to be held up as an ideal standard did not prevent them from being hypocritical, unctuous, Pecksniffian in the highest degree."

Bogart's twenty-page, thirty-two-clause, seven-year contract with Warners was negotiated by his agent Myron Selznick and signed on December 10, 1935. It specified that he would be permitted to perform in the London stage version of *The Petrified Forest* (though he never did so); would get period costumes from the studio but would have to provide his own wardrobe for films in modern dress; would receive first-class transportation and lodging on location; could be "rented" to other studios while Warners pocketed the (often substantial) difference between his salary and the rental fee; would have to pay the cost of any delay, unless he was ill, if he did not show up for work; could be indefinitely suspended without pay if he refused a role; and would agree to retakes of scenes for extra pay after his contract was over. If his options were taken up and his contract renewed, his salary would increase in half-yearly or annual increments over a period of seven years from $550 to $1,750 a week.

Though he now had a secure job, he still had to find good parts and shape the course of his career. Louise Brooks—who despised Hollywood, abandoned her American film career and became an actress in Germany in the 1920s—compared stardom to slavery. She pointed out that "in Bogart's time there was no other occupation in the world that so closely resembled enslavement as the career of a film star. . . . If he signed the contract, he became subject to those who paid his salary and released his films. If he did not sign the contract, he was no film star. . . . Studio contracts were always a joke, as far as actors were concerned. Studios could break them at will; the actors were bound by their fear of impoverishing lawsuits and permanent unemployment."

The Warners actors, who appeared with each other in many films, were like the cast of an intimate and successful repertory company. But the abrasive personality of Jack Warner, the egoism of the actors and the bondage of the contract provoked many disputes between stars and studio. Errol Flynn, especially while shooting a film, would argue with Warner about money. Bogart mainly fought for better roles. In contrast to the reckless and self-destructive Flynn—who started at Warners at the same time as Bogart, peaked early and went down fast—Bogart took many long years to reach the top. He was not, like Flynn, a handsome, romantic figure with stunning though limited talent, but a serious actor with great range and skill. After slowly reaching stardom over a period of eight years, he retained his position until the end of his career.

Bogart's two main problems, apart from his personal dislike of Jack, were that Warners (sticking to the incremental raises specified in the contract) refused to increase his salary after the success of *The Petrified Forest* and forced him to act in many inferior films. Bogart had a pugnacious personality and fought for his rights. Hal Wallis, who had many difficult confrontations with Bogart, found him a formidable opponent. He criticized Bogart, who chose his own friends and led his own life, for not socializing with the other Warners actors (some of whom he despised): "Although people have written that offscreen Bogart was a soft and gentle man, I never found him so. . . . He drove a hard bargain, and every time he made a picture, he wanted an increase in salary. The moment the day's work was over, he drove home, and seldom mingled with the other players."[5] Like most corporations, Warners preferred obedient team players, but needed extraordinary stars to vitalize the mediocre scripts and arouse interest in their movies. But the unfair aspects of the studio system and constant jockeying for status angered many of the stars. They felt cheated of their due, refused to remain loyal to the company and constantly looked around for a better deal.

‹ III ›

THE STUDIO looked like a prison, with uniformed guards checking credentials at the front gate and high walls surrounding the vast space. The sound stage, sealed with huge steel doors against the outside world, was enclosed within the studio lot. It was not air-conditioned and could get very hot during the Los Angeles summer. Though top actors were well paid, working conditions were arduous and the apparently glamorous life had many degrading aspects. In the course of making movies Bogart was slapped, punched, knocked, bruised, crushed and bloodied; blown, dusted, muddied, shaken, submerged and drenched; bitten, choked, cut, thrown, singed and burned. Glaring lights and reflectors, supported by miles of thick serpentine wires, blazed in his eyes, and the heavy camera and crane-like sound booms loomed close to his face. He had to stay fresh while repeating the same scene over and over again until the slower actors finally learned how to do it and the director was satisfied with the take. He suffered early calls, sticky make-up, boring waits and exceptionally long hours. Bogart's eating habits were compulsively regular. He would bring a simple lunchbox with two tomato and cheese sandwiches, a hard-boiled egg and a bottle of beer, and eat in his dressing room. He would then lie down and sleep soundly for half an hour. As soon as he became a star, he put a 6 P.M. quitting-time clause in his contract.

Movie-making was and still is a collaborative enterprise. Fifty times a year, as soon as Jack Warner approved the project, a small army of artists and technicians—most of whom were on contract with the studio—were mobilized into production. The accounting department drew up a detailed budget, the screenwriters wrote and rewrote the script, the legal section checked it for libel and copyright, the censorship office for moral infractions.

The producer—the executive in charge of the budget and all personnel—was appointed, the director chosen, the roles cast, and there was great rivalry within the organization for the choicest projects. The art director built, painted and put up the exterior façades and three-sided roofless interiors, the set decorator furnished them, the costume designer created the wardrobes. Make-up artists and hair stylists glamorized and villainized, rejuvenated, aged or historicized the actors, who studied their parts, learned their lines and began to rehearse. The cameraman set up, lit and framed each shot, which took more time than the actual filming. Stunts and special effects—from hurricanes, earthquakes and fires to plane crashes and Indian arrows in the necks of cavalrymen—were conceived and executed. Music was composed and conducted, sound and sound effects recorded.

While the movie was being made the unit manager, who tried to keep the picture on schedule and on budget, sent a progress report to Jack Warner. He carefully noted the number of completed scenes, set-ups and takes, the total amount of footage shot and minutes of finished film each day. As soon as the film was developed in the lab and brought to the projection room, Warner, Hal Wallis and the director would see the daily rushes in order to decide which takes were best and judge the quality of each picture in production. A rough cut was made day by day, and after the movie was shot the film editor cut and spliced the footage into a ninety-minute dramatic sequence. During the filming hundreds of technicians, from electricians to firemen, were at work. Shooting on location —where permission, food and lodging had to be arranged, and equipment and crew transported to a distant site—was much more complicated. When the picture was finished, the publicity, advertising, sales and distribution departments took over.

Warners, like most studios, made "A" and "B" pictures. The former were more ambitious and more expensive to make, and became the main feature on the double bill that lured Depression audiences into the theaters. They were supervised by Hal Wallis and made in fifty to sixty days. The latter, more run-of-the-mill and made with smaller budgets, were overseen by Bryan Foy and shot in less than twenty-eight days. Both kinds of movies were released soon after completion. Warners' actors generally worked at a more frantic pace and received lower salaries than at more prestigious studios like MGM. The worst movies had the shortest schedules and forced the actors to complete them as quickly as possible. They would quickly rehearse a scene, try a few takes and then race on to the next one. The producers and directors, who had little time for detailed planning and careful thought, considered film-making a craft rather than an art.

The studio had two main problems in its frantic search for usable scripts. One was the sheer need for new material. Backed by the research department, the studio paid careful attention to the realistic details of make-up, costumes and settings; readers and writers, who worked in hive-like offices on the lot, raided history and literature for plots and characters. But in their haste to turn out saleable pictures, the studio tended to ignore the most blatant absurdities: ludicrous conventions, far-fetched coincidences, cardboard characters, crude plots, contrived conclusions, and lack of logic, structure and meaning. To emphasize the simplistic black and white morality, villains were always dark and fat, ate greedily and smoked cigars, while heroes were always young, slim and handsome. Intellectuals wore glasses and carried pipes. Whenever the screenwriters could not convey their meaning through dramatic action, the story came to a halt and someone made a long, cliché-ridden speech. Bogart and his fellow actors were hired to make this shoddy material convincing.

Another reason for predictable scripts was the film industry's self-regulating Production Code. Before the Code came into effect on July 15, 1934, movies had often violated the censorship laws of individual states. Censorship boards, with varying degrees of zeal, had proscribed a whole range of subject matter, including "profanity, nudity, drug trafficking, sex perversion, white slavery, miscegenation, sex hygiene and venereal diseases, scenes of actual childbirth, children's sex-organs, ridicule of the clergy and offenses against a nation, race or creed."[6] Local boards, prompted by the public's demand for moral standards, made radical cuts in films before they were shown.

The studios decided to set up a code of their own that would forestall such interference. Each script had to be approved before it could go into production; each film had to be viewed and passed by the censorship office before it could be released. The Code strictly controlled the cinematic portrayal of religion and patriotism as well as of vulgarity, obscenity, sensual dances, scenes in bedrooms, sex and crime. It banned the portrayal of repellent subjects—the sale of women, surgical operations, cruelty to children and animals—as well as scenes of brutality, branding, torture and hanging. By robbing films of a great deal of dramatic material, the Code encouraged fake and boring scripts. But its effect was not wholly negative. By insisting that criminal, violent and sexual acts could not be shown, the Code also forced writers and directors to express their themes and achieve their effects in subtle and indirect ways.

The casting of inexperienced actresses and the conventional roles of women in most Hollywood films did little to improve the quality of Bogart's movies. Predictable scripts, with bad and good guys, were similarly peopled with stereotyped madonnas and whores, with virtuous housewives or gangster sluts. These women either served breakfast in a frilly apron for Joel McCrea or draped themselves over a nattily-dressed George Raft. Bogart's on-screen wives—from Black Legion (1937) to The Harder They Fall (1956)—are always flat and wooden; they express conventional sentiments and stand for decent values. He had to appear in numerous movies with many now-forgotten performers, some of them products of couch-casting. As saccharine as Maud Humphrey's drawings, they stood in place, recited their lines and dragged the whole picture down to their level. The films became infinitely more animated when Bogart appeared with superior actresses, usually in shadier roles. Bette Davis, Ida Lupino, Mary Astor and Claire Trevor knew what they were doing and did it very well.

⟨ IV ⟩

NEARLY FIVE HUNDRED gangster murders took place in Chicago in one year in the 1920s. By 1935 movie versions of the John Dillingers and Al Capones of the Prohibition era had become enormously successful. Warners specialized in movies about mobsters in big cities, emphasizing both the social background of crime in *Dead End* (1937) and the regenerative effect of the family on criminals in *Crime School* (1938). Two of the dominant Hollywood genres, the western and the gangster film, dealt with the idealized rural past and the grim urban present (an escape from city to country was always a quest for innocence). In the western, the cowboy fights the gang and wins; in the crime film, the gang fights the law and loses. Robert Warshow pointed out that the excitement of crime movies is based on violent behavior and fatal punishment. The criminal in films is always doomed; the interest lies in how he meets his fate: "The gangster is a man of the city, with the city's language and knowledge, with its queer dishonest skills and its terrible daring, carrying his life in his hands. . . . Since we do not see the rational and routine aspects of the gangster's behavior, the practice of brutality—the quality of unmixed criminality—becomes the totality of his career." During the Depression, millions of people who felt they had been economically betrayed identified with those who had rejected and exploited the system. It was particularly important, therefore, that the transgressors be punished.

Hollywood's interest in gangsters was intensified in 1935 when two Chicago racketeers, George Browne, the new president of the International Alliance of Theatrical Stage Employees, and William Bioff, the Hollywood representative, seized control of the skilled workers' union. Over the next six years they extorted millions of dollars from studio executives by threatening to call strikes and then agreeing to limit their demands.

Though Bogart had usually acted in romantic roles on stage and in his early movies, he had also played convicts and criminals. By the late 1930s

59

he was deep into crime. Warners had wanted one of their established stars to play Duke Mantee, but Leslie Howard promised Bogart that he would have the role in the film and kept his word. When Bogart warned Howard, on holiday in Scotland, that Edward G. Robinson might get the coveted part, Howard refused to commit himself to the picture without Bogart and replied by telegram: "REST ASSURED IF YOU DON'T APPEAR IN PETRIFIED FOREST I WONT."

Duke Mantee was partly modeled on the notorious criminal John Dillinger, who had been in the newspapers almost every day in the early 1930s. Paroled after a sentence for robbery, he terrorized the Midwest, killed sixteen people and stole $300,000 before being shot by FBI agents in 1934 as he emerged from a gangster movie in Chicago. Each of the leading screen criminals at Warners imitated a famous mobster. Just as Bogart based the character of Duke Mantee on the WASP John Dillinger, so Robinson imitated the Italian Al Capone in *Little Caesar* and Cagney mimicked the mannerisms of the Irish train robber Dean O'Bannion in *Public Enemy.* In real life, George Raft maintained close connections with the mob. But Raft was stiff and wooden, Robinson an old softie and Cagney an animated midget. Only Bogart, the brooding, laconic psychopath of low-grade scenarios, conveyed real menace. In the 1940s, when Bogart kept his tough character while playing a private dick, Robinson became a monk in *Brother Orchid,* Cagney a song and dance man in *Yankee Doodle Dandy.*

The gangsters played by Robinson and Cagney had gesticulated, screamed and ranted. Bogart, who learned a great deal from Leslie Howard's calm and natural style of acting, was the first to convey a greater threat by speaking quietly. When Bogart appears, halfway through *The Petrified Forest,* he seems like a melancholy maniac at the extreme edge of exhaustion. Wearing a black vest and trousers, and a coarse gray flannel shirt, he has a slow, shuffling, penitential walk, as if still bound by chains. He has bristling hair and holds his curled fingers stiffly out in front of him like a robot about to strangle a victim.

The picture starred Leslie Howard and Bette Davis, who had been sensational in Maugham's *Of Human Bondage* (1934). Bogart got fifth billing, after the now-forgotten actors who played the rich Mrs. Chisholm and the athletic Boze. Like Bogart, Davis came from an upper-class family and had been trained in the theater. Though she also had a volatile temperament, the young and idealistic actress was repelled by his behavior and professional attitude. In contrast to Leslie Howard, who liked and respected Bogart, she hated his aggressive needling and found him "crude, overbearing and sullen . . . bad-mannered, ill-tempered, heavy drinking and downright boring." She remembered him as a "gruff and impatient" man who talked only of "making enough money in Hollywood to buy a yacht and sail off into the blue for good. . . . She was shocked by his lack of interest in picture-making and cynical attitude toward the studio." Though they appeared together in six films — including *Marked Woman* and *Dark Victory* — she never got to know him well.

The Petrified Forest opens with a realistic shot of the Arizona desert as the shabby yet elegant Leslie Howard trudges along a dusty path. Most of the film takes place in the cheap roadside restaurant. More like a stage play than a movie, it has long speeches and fake backdrops. The static pace and constricted setting, however, allow time for the characters to develop and for the actors to perfect their parts. In contrast to her usual roles as a neurotic harridan, Bette Davis, with a girlish manner and sensual figure, is charming and appealing. She wears a bow in her hair, white blouse, pinafore and bobby socks, and dreamily reads the love poetry of François Villon. Gabrielle's public declaration of her love and Squier's mournful desert *Liebestod* are naive yet poignant.

Squier's ponderous lines express the theme of disillusionment in the film. He describes his meaningless past life to the fascinated Gabrielle and quotes T. S. Eliot's "The Hollow Men," a pessimistic poem filled with desert imagery. He asserts that "nature's taking the world away from the intellectuals and giving it back to the apes," shares the condemned criminal's facial expression and grudgingly calls Duke Mantee "the last great apostle of rugged individualism in the Petrified Forest of outmoded ideas." Both are doomed figures, rebelling against and fleeing from a hostile world. When Squier describes himself as a "suitable candidate for extermination," Mantee looks astonished but quickly recovers himself and offhandedly says: "Lemme know when you wanna be killed."

Gabrielle's toothless, cantankerous Grampa, nicely played by Charley Grapewin, balances Squier's morbidity with a lively enthusiasm for the man on the run. Once shot at by Billy the Kid in the violent frontier days, Grampa distinguishes Dillinger-Mantee from the Italian mob and exclaims: "Gangsters is foreigners. He's an American. A real desperado." When the fugitive's arrival is dramatically announced by one of his henchmen: "This is Duke Man-tee, the world famous killer, and he's hungry," Grampa declares: "Sure is good to have a killer 'round here again." Gabrielle's father, by contrast, struts about in an ill-fitting soldier's uniform. His square moustache, pouchy face and round figure look amazingly like General Franco's (in the year the Spanish Civil War broke out) and link the militiamen to the dictator.

Bogart provides a sinister but sympathetic complement to the attractive, articulate Leslie Howard, and tersely summarizes Mantee's life and fate in the best line of the film: "I've spent most of my time since I grew up in jail, and it looks like I'll spend the rest of my life dead." He barks out commands with a curled upper lip, but tolerates Boze's insults and shows concern for Grampa's feelings when Squier coldly states the old man ought to die. The police blindly fire away, despite the presence of many innocent people inside the restaurant. But Mantee, faithful to his unspoken code, doesn't actually hurt anyone; he doesn't use hostages to prevent the shootout or to defend himself from the hail of bullets.

Following instructions, Mantee shoots Squier (who has named Gabrielle as his beneficiary) and fatalistically tells him: "Be seeing you soon." Squier dies melodramatically, and Gabrielle delivers an operatic speech while holding his corpse. In the play, Mantee escapes after the killing, but the inexorable movie Production Code insists he must be caught by the police. Ten years after the picture was released, Bogart saw it as the major turning point in his career: "I believe that if I had not been given the movie role of Duke Mantee, in *The Petrified Forest,* I'd be out of the films altogether."

Bogart's villainous, even melodramatic parts in *Three on a Match* and *Midnight,* and in the Broadway productions of *The Mask and the Face* and *The Petrified Forest* enabled him to develop his talents as an actor, perfect his film technique, and give a mature and masterful performance in the movie version of the play. Since he had been triumphant on stage, and the confined and concentrated film retained many characteristics of the play, the director Archie Mayo encouraged him to repeat his interpretation of Duke Mantee and "do the part with stage technique."[7]

Bogart-Mantee makes a dramatic appearance thirty minutes into the film, preceded by his fearsome reputation as a killer. He reacts quickly during crises, and immediately establishes his authority by giving sharp orders to the gang as they hijack the rich couple's car and enter the café. But he moves and talks very slowly, seems infinitely weary, shifts his eyes about and rolls his head as he walks. He shows his crude background by picking his teeth, spitting on the floor and smoking a cheap cigar. Bored by all the pretentious talk, his own staccato snarls are brief and monosyllabic, and he splits up the longer words into meb-be, bur-ried, moo-sick and Mex-ee-co. Barely in control and about to go berserk, he forces a sinister smile and shouts: "The foist time anyone makes a wrong move, I'm gonna kill the lot of ya."

The sad and vulnerable Bogart expresses Mantee's inner torment—a strange mixture of remorse and fear, swaggering self-assurance and brooding doubts—as he contemplates his own extinction. He closes his fingers into a clenched fist when trying to decide whether to stand or run from the police who have pursued him across the desert. The camera looks down on Bogart as if sitting in judgment. His dark, lined, shadowy visage provides a stark contrast to the brightly-lit, youthful and romantic faces of Bette Davis and Leslie Howard, just as his brusque commands contrast with Howard's eloquent diction. He plays brilliantly against the gloomy but still vivid Howard, who insisted on having Bogart to enhance his own performance in the film. In *The Petrified Forest* Bogart's voice, face, body and character all come together to create an unforgettable impression. His startling performance signaled the birth of a major star and kept him in infinite variants of this gangster role till 1942—and beyond.

It was ironic that Bogart's career at Warners began with this fine "A" movie, for he was not offered another good script for many years. Before becoming a star, he had to serve a prolonged apprenticeship in a series of "B" pictures. From 1936 to 1939 he kept up a killing pace and appeared in twenty-five films, an average of one every two months for four years. He sometimes went from one movie to the next without a break or sufficient time to prepare. Occasionally he worked in two different pictures on the same day, shooting one while doing retakes of another. Emphasizing the fact that movies were efficiently and economically shot from set to set, rather than in chronological sequence, Bogart explained: "Movie acting is strictly piecework. One day you do a scene walking out a door; two months later you do the scene of coming out the other side. You finish a love scene on one set, go next door—and you're shooting it out with the cops." The lack of connection with the emotions of the previous scene, the long waits and spurts of action, made it difficult for a serious actor, trained in the theater, to develop his character and give a good performance.

Bogart was one of the first male stars who was not handsome in the conventional way. But his expressive, craggy face had great interest and character. His raspy, nasal voice, metallic, adder-like hiss, and snarling mannerisms—his wince, his leer, his diabolical grimace—were riveting and widely imitated. The Bogart character, confronting his victim with an etiquette of violence, moved from illusory friendliness and courteous contempt through menacing chuckles and malicious threats to dangerous explosions and the promise of certain doom. Mocking his own screen image, Bogart described his memorable mannerisms: "I'd twisted the lower lip, spoken through the teeth, worn my hat over my eyes, pulled the coat collar up, put the right hand in the gun pocket, sneaked around corners, and climbed over roofs, until I was all out of sinister parts." He was, however, the consummate professional, planned his scenes beforehand and came to work with his part prepared. He was always punctual, always knew his lines and was willing to rehearse until the other actors had mastered their roles. In appearance and behavior, said the producer Jerry Wald, "he violated every rule of the movie business. But he was a good actor. He could project. He had tremendous force."[8]

The key to Bogart's effectiveness as both villain and lover was his unusual restraint, his ability to suggest inner turmoil with minimal expression. Bette Davis observed: "what women liked about Bogey, I think, was that when he did love scenes, he held back—like many men do—and they understood that." Bogart, who was usually convincing no matter what part he played, explained that it was more important to understand the role than to make dramatic gestures. He encouraged actors to learn by watching ordinary people react to violent situations: "If a guy points a gun at you, the audience knows you are afraid. You don't have to make faces. You just have to believe that you are the person you're playing and what is happening is happening to you. . . . If I had to do a scene in which my wife was run over, I'd just try to imagine how I'd feel if I saw my wife run over. If you watch newsreels, for instance, you see that human beings do not react like actors [during] massacres in Europe. People are not running around gesticulating. Some are not doing anything at all." Tawdry scripts and excessive emotions tried Bogart's patience. When Warners' dialogue director, Irving Rapper, urged him to deliver his lines "very dramatically and choking up," Bogart replied: "Irving, I can't cry. I'm not an actor."[9]

Bogart considered James Cagney the most impressive personality on screen and Spencer Tracy—also a natural minimalist—the best actor. He conceded that he himself was not a great performer, but felt he had something that was even more important than acting ability: when he came on screen he immediately captured everyone's attention. Nunnally Johnson acutely defined his strengths: "Bogart thinks his way through a part with a very keen intelligence, the emotions are there, the audience reads it from his eyes and subtle changes in his face and body, and finds itself living the part." The English critic James Agate also praised Bogart's restrained projection of an evil yet attractive character: "Bogart is always the same but he always delights me. He has charm and he doesn't waste energy by pretending to act. He has a sinister-rueful countenance which acts for him. He has an exciting personality and lets it do the work. His expression never changes, whether he is looking on his mistress, the dead body of a man he has murdered, or a blackbeetle." Bogart's "sameness," his enduring screen personality, enabled the audience to recognize and appreciate his essential qualities in a variety of roles.

Even in his toughest gangster roles, Bogart was sympathetic. Always the enemy of emotion, he nonchalantly accepted his inevitable doom while conveying an idiosyncratic mixture of high tension and sexy charm. "He would die with a shrug," wrote Kenneth Tynan, "no complaint, no apologies, no hard feelings. Indeed, he rarely displayed strong feelings of any kind." In the 1940s, when he finally graduated from gangster roles and became a private detective, a war hero and a disillusioned lover, whose lined and haggard face suggested that he had been through some terrible experiences, Bogart attracted millions of admirers. Sophisticated, self-mocking, stoical and self-reliant, but also lonely, romantic and vulnerable, he played men who were cynical about the corruption of the world but faithful to their personal code of honor. Arthur Schlesinger, Jr., perceived his essential qualities when he wrote that he "became a mythic figure, with his harrowed face, sharp, expressionless eyes, twisted mouth, weary walk; a figure mingling cynicism and duty as the moral man in an immoral society."[10]

‹ V ›

BETWEEN *The Petrified Forest* and his next major films—*High Sierra* and *The Maltese Falcon* (both 1941)—Bogart's numerous movies ranged from the marginally interesting to the absolutely dreadful. They gave him plenty of opportunity to develop his gangster mannerisms. *Bullets or Ballots* (1936) was the first of five movies made with Edward G. Robinson. A humane, cultured man, who spoke eight languages and built up the greatest art collection in Hollywood, Robinson was born in Bucharest, Romania, in 1893 and came from a humble Jewish background. Short and pudgy, with a puffy face and a huge frog's mouth, he was a charismatic actor. His performance in *Little Caesar* and his famous dying line— "Mother of Mercy, is this the end of Rico Bandello?"—had made him the prototypical movie mobster. In *Bullets or Ballots,* however, Robinson switched roles and played the good cop.

Warners loved to exploit the interest in contemporary crime and modeled Johnny Blake (Robinson) on the undercover policeman Johnny Broderick, and Al Kruger (Barton MacLane) on Dutch Schultz, a New York bootlegger and racketeer who had been killed in a gangland feud in 1935. Emphasizing (like Hemingway) the gangsters' interest in films, *Bullets or Ballots* opens with Bogart (Bugs Fenner) and his mobster friend watching a documentary about crime. Bogart pulls his lip and picks his teeth in the theater, speaks very slowly and pronounces "sure," with two syllables, as "shoo-were." A mad murderer, he first finishes off a vice crusader, then Al Kruger and finally Johnny Blake.

Warners frequently recycled its stories, and relied on shots of newspaper headlines to show the occurrence of events and the passage of time. The movie has the same undercover plot, in which a good guy infiltrates a mob or enemy organization, that would be used again in *The Amazing Dr. Clitterhouse* (1938) and *Across the Pacific* (1942). Blake smokes a pipe when he is a decent cop, but when he joins the mob (apparently dismissed by the police) he switches to a villainous cigar. Bugs suspects his rival, fears a double-cross and exclaims that the trouble has "all happened since Blake got in." But the gang boss, ignoring the obvious, does not realize Blake is treacherous. The movie reveals the hierarchy of criminals, from the corrupt bankers and political bosses down to the petty crooks and meanest hoods. The climax comes when Blake supplants Bugs in the gang (always a dangerous maneuver) and Bugs kills the boss so he can take over the numbers racket. In their fatal exchange of shots, prefiguring many others, Robinson, wounded by Bogart, finally kills him. After he makes the arrests and breaks the rackets, Robinson dies nobly in the arms of his police chief.

Four of Bogart's seven films in 1937 — *Black Legion, Marked Woman, Dead End* and *Stand-In* — were more interesting than the series of weak movies he had been forced to make in 1936 and marked an advance in his career. The topical, controversial *Black Legion,* made in August and September 1936, was named after a real racist organization that had terrorized Detroit auto workers with murders, hangings and bombings during the labor wars earlier that year. The Ku Klux Klan (which had inspired the Black Legion and was specifically mentioned in the movie) sued Warners for the "infringement of a design." They claimed to have patented the symbols that appeared on the robed and hooded figures in the film. Warners' lawyer argued that "it is not an infringement merely to take pictures of costumes or other articles, on which are affixed a patented design, and exhibit the films."[11] On April 1, 1938 an Atlanta court dismissed the case and made the Klan pay costs.

Robert Lord, who wrote the original story and produced *Black Legion,* later became Bogart's business partner. In the movie Bogart plays Frank Taylor, a happily married machinist with a house, car and radio, who is eager for promotion and envious of a more educated fellow worker. His hated rival Joe Dombrowski goes to night school (which in factory films inevitably leads to disaster) and gets the foreman's job that Taylor hoped to have. After listening to Black Legion propaganda on the radio, Taylor attends a secret meeting, takes a bloodthirsty induction oath and buys a gun. Frustrated at work, he joins the outfit to gain power and wreak vengeance.

When his best friend discovers the secret group, Taylor shoots him as he tries to escape. Caught by the police and accused of murder, Taylor repents and exposes the Black Legion for exploiting its own members and running "around in nightshirts gangin' up on innocent people." Bogart is quite good as a fearful little man, caught up and destroyed by a power he cannot control. The film's exposé of the Black Legion is a welcome contrast to the glorification of the Klan in D. W. Griffith's *The Birth of a Nation* (1915).

An editorial in the *New York Herald-Tribune* commended the crusading film for providing "not only excellent dramatic entertainment, if you are tough-minded enough to enjoy stark tragedy, but a sermon on American ideals worth all the emotional agony of the action." The critics also praised Warners' serious portrayal of a social problem in the age of Fascism. Graham Greene—who, with James Agee and Otis Ferguson, is one of the few contemporary film critics still worth reading—wrote that "*Black Legion,* an intelligent and exciting, if rather earnest film, is intended to expose the secret society of that name and the financial racket behind it. . . . It is an intelligent film because the director and script-writer know where the real horror lies: the real horror is not in the black robes and skull emblems, but in the knowledge that these hide the weak and commonplace faces you have met over the counter and minding the next machine."

Marked Woman was based on the career of Charles "Lucky" Luciano, a Sicilian-born Mafioso who ran prostitution, narcotics and extortion rackets in the Twenties and Thirties. In the spring of 1936 prostitutes testified against him in a New York trial that was widely reported, and he was sent to prison by the Assistant U.S. Attorney Thomas Dewey. (Released in 1946, Luciano settled briefly in Havana and inspired the criminal boss in *Key Largo*.) Bette Davis, in the title role, is marked both by the life she leads and the face that is scarred by the gangsters. After she's beaten up by the mob, she laments: "I got things wrong with me that all the doctors in the world can't fix." In the film the six women, euphemistically called nightclub "hostesses," have to soften up the customers "so they can be taken." As the director Lloyd Bacon told the actresses: "It's up to you girls to show what your profession is in your performances. The script is all innuendo because of the censorship code."[12]

Mayo Methot, who was having an affair with Bogart and would marry him in 1938, plays one of the "hostesses." The new boss, looking her over, says "Kind of old, ain't you?" and wants to fire her. Solidly built, with a hard, crass appearance, she pathetically asks her friends: "I don't really look old, do I?" Mayo looks more whorish than the jaded-looking sorority girls in the club, but the attractive and cheeky Bette Davis saves her job. Methot earned $2,500 for five weeks work on this film; Bogart (a co-star, but under contract) got only $3,184.

Instead of playing his usual part as head of the vice ring, Bogart is the idealistic and ambitious District Attorney, fighting the boss. He wears a three-piece suit, with a rep-striped tie and a handkerchief in his pocket, and is awfully *nice*. Deprived of his sinister mannerisms and the ambiguous attraction of evil, stuck with stilted dialogue and a predictable courtroom speech, he is much less effective as a respectable upholder of law and order. In the first trial Davis, intimidated by her evil boss (extremely well played by the smoothie Eduardo Ciannelli), saves him with false testimony. But when he kills her younger sister (the intolerably simpering Jane Bryan), Davis sheds her flashy clothes, dresses in black and tells the truth in court. Ciannelli is convicted by Bogart, who breaks up the vice ring and sends him up the river.

At the end of the movie Bogart asks Davis: "Where will you go?" and she answers: "Places." He asks: "But what will you do?" She says: "I'll get along. I always have." Though there is a flicker of interest between the lawyer and the prostitute, they realize that they belong to different worlds and can have no future together. At the end, the women walk through the misty streets as Bogart, congratulated by the press, is mentioned as the next D.A. While expressing sympathy for outcast and exploited women, the picture suggests that jailing their boss will solve their problems. In reality, they are damaged goods and can find no other work in the Depression.

Edward G. Robinson dominates *Kid Galahad* (Bogart's first film with director Michael Curtiz) as the tawdry but dynamic fight manager, Nick Donati. In the best scene Bogart humiliates a bellhop, who later becomes the boxer Kid Galahad, by slowly taking out a knife and telling him, "You think you're cute? Your pants are too long to be that cute." After cutting off his trouser leg and revealing his sock and garter, he ironically remarks: "Now you look real cute." Jealous of Bette Davis' love for the gentlemanly boxer, Robinson arranges for him to be mauled in the ring. Conniving with the gangster Bogart (wearing a double-breasted suit and gray homburg, and called Turkey Morgan), he bets against his own man. The suspicious Bogart, warning him not to renege on the deal, snarls: "I've been achin' to fill you full of slugs." During the crucial match between Kid Galahad and the heavyweight champion, Robinson, moved by the pleas of his sister and mistress, double-crosses Bogart and allows his fighter to win. They meet in the locker room and, as in *Bullets or Ballots,* kill each other in a fatal crossfire.

Bogart's character loves to taunt and provoke (as he liked to do in real life). Whenever he appears, there's confrontation, crisis and danger. Yet he communicates not only by words but also by physical gestures and facial expressions. Dapper, confident and cool, he suggests sleazy corruption by remaining cold, stony and impassive. In contrast to Robinson's animated conversation, he fingers his buttonhole, keeps his mouth taut and speaks slowly. He lifts his chin to look down on his pudgy enemy, raises his eyebrows when his fighter starts to lose and when betrayed pulls back his upper lip like a snarling animal. He loves pushing people around and is grimly determined to take revenge. Shot by Robinson, he holds up his arm with wrist bent, slowly crumples up and keels over.

Depression pictures are filled with fancy-dress dances and nightclub scenes to cheer up the unemployed with a bit of spurious glamour. But the boxing scenes are more realistic and convincing. As Kid Galahad (played by Wayne Morris) waits for his first fight, a battered, unconscious boxer, on the way down, is carried into the locker room. Otis Ferguson called *Kid Galahad* "the best prize-ring film I've seen — both for the explosive pace of its fight scenes and for the edge to its realism." In the potpourri fashion of Hollywood, the three Italians in the picture — Robinson, his mother and his sister (whom the Kid marries at the end) — were played by a Jew, a Mexican and a WASP.

Like *The Petrified Forest,* Sidney Kingsley's *Dead End* had been a successful Broadway play, and had run for 687 performances. After Samuel Goldwyn bought the film rights, George Raft refused to act the part of the gangster Baby Face Martin (named after the notorious criminal Baby Face Nelson) unless he could warn the delinquent Dead End Kids that crime did not pay. Bogart had no such qualms and was pleased to get the role. He had established a convincing screen presence as a gangster and was now in demand by other studios. Goldwyn paid Warners $2,000 a week for his services; Warners kept the difference between the contract salary and the loan-out fee, and made a substantial profit of $1,300 a week for seven weeks.

Lillian Hellman wrote the screenplay, William Wyler directed and Bogart, who got third billing after Sylvia Sidney and Joel McCrea, dominated the film. During the rehearsals Sylvia Sidney went to Elizabeth Arden's for a massage, slipped on the floor and split her forehead on the edge of a glass table. She suffered a concussion, was hospitalized and needed stitches; she remained under a doctor's care and held up the picture for two months. When she finally returned to work, she had trouble remembering her lines and "blamed it on her injury. Wyler didn't believe her. The more takes he made her do, the more tearful she became." When she recovered, she resented his cruelty, became bitter and found the whole experience "very distasteful."

Dead End refers to the street on the East River in New York where rich apartments stand next to crime-infested tenements as well as to the grim fate of the people who grow up there. Wyler hoped to shoot the movie on location, but Goldwyn wanted it filmed in the studio so he could retain control. Wyler explained how he used the camera to make the stage-like set seem more vivid: "We made—we faked, if you like—the opening ups, the cinematic thing. . . . We gave an illusion of movement by going from one room to another, and upstairs and downstairs, and so on, and you got an illusion." The slum, at Goldwyn's insistence, was unnaturally clean, but the cinematography by Gregg Toland (who later shot *Citizen Kane*) made it seem realistic. Wyler recalled that "we had flat, hard lights. We used open sun-arcs from behind the camera. We didn't try to make anybody look pretty."[13] The six Dead End Kids, who embody the atmosphere of the slum, had originally appeared in and taken their name from the play. Ugly, ragged and boisterous, the Kids talk tough and push each other around. But they do nothing worse than taunt the doorman of a fancy apartment house, beat up a wealthy boy and steal his watch. They now seem pretty harmless—more like pranksters than gangsters.

In *Dead End* Bogart gives his best performance since *The Petrified Forest*. Visiting the place where he grew up, he sees his childhood girlfriend and his old mother, and shows off the sharp clothes and jewelry that signify success. Tense and menacing, he runs through his arsenal of expressions. He pulls his ear, draws his lips together when angry and responds to Sylvia Sidney's hostility by ironically stating: "Lady, yer scarin' me." He wins the Kids' admiration by teaching them how to fight dirty and use a knife in their gang wars.

The rest of his visit is a disaster. He wants to marry his old girlfriend, played by Claire Trevor, and go straight. But he discovers that she has become a whore (the syphilis in the play is dropped from the film) and, repelled by her degradation, cannot even bring himself to kiss her. Their bitter exchange of dialogue, in which he's "moral" and she's realistic, epitomizes the tragedy of the Depression:

> MARTIN: Why didn't you get a job?
> FRANCEY: They don't grow on trees.

MARTIN: Why didn't you starve first?
FRANCEY: Why didn't you?

In this sharp exchange, Bogart exploits the contrast between the flashy and naive aspects of Martin's character, and arouses the sympathy of the audience by giving the nasty gangster more depth. He also makes clear that in Francey's degradation Martin sees evidence of his own decline.

Marjorie Main, who played Ma Martin both on stage and in the film, shatters his sentimental expectations about their long-awaited reunion. In the stage version—echoing Job 3:3, "Let the day perish wherein I was born, and the night in which it was said, There is a man child conceived"—she screams: "Baby-face! Baby-face! I remember. . . . *She begins to sob, clutching her stomach.* In here . . . in here! Kickin'! That's where yuh come from. God! I ought to be cut open here fer givin' yuh life . . . murderer!!!" The mother-son confrontation in the film—though toned down—is still the most powerful scene. Mrs. Martin slaps her son and then condemns him by exclaiming: "You're a killer, murderer, butcher, for sure. . . . Just leave us alone! You never brought nothin' but trouble!" Baby Face, much weaker than he seems, still needs maternal love. Devastated by her ferocious rejection, he loses his cocky swagger, crumples up and shrinks off into the shadows.

The main plot concerns the love between the respectable shopgirl Drina (Sylvia Sidney), who wants to rescue her brother and leave the slums, and the unemployed architect Dave Connell (Joel McCrea), who is also attracted to a rich girl and dreams of rebuilding the street. Baby Face cynically tells them: "I'm glad I ain't like you saps. Starvin' and freezin'. For what? Peanuts. I got mine. I took it. The fat of the land I'm livin' off of." In the play Baby Face is shot by government agents at the end of the second act. But he lasts until the very end of the movie, when Dave traps him on a fire escape and kills him with his own gun. After seeing her dead son, Ma Martin regrets her harshness, breaks down and weeps. Dave chooses Drina instead of the rich girl and uses the reward money to rehabilitate her delinquent brother.

In May 1932, during one of the worst years of the Depression, the Association of Motion Picture Producers explained their social policy by telling Jack Warner that "it would be unwise to lay any stress on the conflict between the rich and the poor whereby it is intimated that the rich can get away with anything."[14] There is a great deal of bitter Left-wing talk in *Dead End* about strikes, unemployment and poverty, about poor housing and reform schools as sources of crime. But Hollywood was committed to upholding the status quo. In this film, as in most others, the social protest is ineffectual and there is no radical social change. The rich keep their wealth and the poor keep their place. Despite the upbeat ending, Dave cannot get a job, Drina remains oppressed at work and everyone is still trapped by life in the slums.

Bogart once remarked: "I used to be the guy behind the guy behind the gun." But his evil character, far more interesting than the conventional roles of Sidney and McCrea, enabled him to steal the film. Graham Greene saw that Bogart had become a sophisticated actor, turning this stereotyped villain into a complex character, expressing ambivalent feelings about crime and sharp disappointments in love. He wrote that Baby Face "was brought up in the same dead end [as the Kids] and like a friendly Old Boy he gives them tips—how to catch another gang unawares, how to fling a knife. . . . In two memorable scenes sentimentality turns savage on him. His mother slaps his face ('Just stay away and leave us alone and die'), his girl is diseased on the streets. This is the finest performance Bogart has ever given—the ruthless sentimentalist who had melodramatized himself from the start."[15]

Stand-In is the greatest *unknown* Bogart film—clever, campy, witty— a rare treat for those lucky enough to see it. Shot in six weeks in July and August 1937, it provides an insider's view of the comic side of movie-making. It satirizes, in a high-spirited fashion, New York executives and Hollywood producers, financial skullduggery and exploitation of employees, arrogant studio heads and autocratic directors, Tarzan pictures and morals clauses, previews and script changes, waste and incompetence, alcoholic decline and sexual corruption. A dominant theme, as Bogart says, is that "in Hollywood, when you turn the other cheek, they kick it."

Leslie Howard is superb as the uptight English financial wizard and efficiency expert. Sent from New York to Hollywood to check the economic viability of Colossal Pictures, he must decide whether to save or abandon the studio. He becomes involved with Joan Blondell, the humble stand-in for the star of a jungle film, *Sex and Satan,* which will finally make or break Colossal. Startled by the lavish overspending at the studio, he sympathizes with the workers. To learn more about the business, he moves out of his luxurious hotel and into a modest theatrical boarding house filled with hopeless failures, and watches an ambitious but untalented child do a revolting imitation of Shirley Temple.

In a congenial role Bogart plays Douglas Quintain, a hard-drinking producer, romantically involved with the petulant star and trying, without much success, to save Colossal. After a long series of heavy parts, he seems delighted to return to the raffish, high-spirited comedy he had perfected on Broadway, and moves effortlessly from slapstick to satire. When he first meets Howard he slyly alludes to his juvenile leads by examining the warp of his tennis racket. He carries his own Scotch terrier in most of his scenes and, with aristocratic disdain, tells the temperamental, high-booted director (a fanatic who resembles von Stroheim and von Sternberg, and is ruining the studio by extravagantly demanding real instead of paper edelweiss): "I was making love to your fiancée long before they turned over that wet stone and you crawled out." Excluded from a posh nightclub for being rowdy (as Bogart often was), he pickets the place in evening dress and a top hat, carrying a sandwich board that protests, "This café is unfair to Quintain," and with a miniature version of the sign around his Scottie's neck. After Leslie Howard authorizes him to edit the disastrous movie, Bogart saves the film and the studio by cutting the star's scenes and replacing her with a more popular and talented gorilla. Like Nathanael West's *The Day of the Locust* (1939) and Scott Fitzgerald's *The Last Tycoon* (1941), which appeared a few years later, *Stand-In* satirizes the glamorous yet rotten atmosphere of Hollywood—dominated by the unscrupulous power of the executives, the meretricious star-system, and the crude toadyism that destroys artistic integrity and moral standards.

‹ VI ›

AT THE BEGINNING OF 1936, the conflict between Bogart's Hollywood film work and Mary Philips' career on the New York stage put a severe strain on his personal life and soon wrecked his second marriage. Despite Bogart's belief that marriage was more important than her career, Mary went East to appear with Richard Barthelmess in the dramatic adaptation of James M. Cain's novel *The Postman Always Rings Twice*. One critic wrote that Philips playing Cora was "as wrong as Florence Nightingale would have been as Cleopatra." But the failure of the play did not weaken her determination to remain in New York. While they were apart, Philips had an affair with the older English actor Roland Young, who had the title role in (the appropriately named) *Topper*, and Bogart became involved with the actress Mayo Methot, who would become his third wife.

The Bogarts formally separated on January 25, 1937 and were divorced on June 21. During the proceedings, which established the grounds for divorce, Bogart made the familiar assertion that married life was "too monotonous and did not give him the freedom he craved." Philips insisted that he had publicly criticized her, embarrassed her and said he no longer loved her. He had stayed out till all hours of the night without explaining his absence and had left home on January 25.[16] She later married Kenneth MacKenna, who had appeared on stage with Bogart and attended their wedding.

By 1936 Bogart was earning a substantial salary. Unused to handling large amounts of money, he followed the example of other stars and hired a business manager. Morgan Maree, whose family had originally come from France, was born in Columbus, Georgia (the hometown of Nunnally Johnson) in 1900. He had made a fortune in the Florida land boom of the 1920s and lost most of it when his bank was destroyed by a hurricane. In 1932 he moved west to Los Angeles and, during difficult times, started up as an investment counselor and financial adviser.

Maree was six feet tall and weighed two hundred pounds. Dore Schary described him as "sun bronzed, handsome as a Marlboro cigarette cowboy, lover of hunting and owner of horses and dogs." According to Jess Morgan, who succeeded him as Bogart's manager, he had a resonant voice, a friendly yet imposing manner and sound judgment. He built the biggest and most successful business management firm in the city, had twenty-five employees in his office on Wilshire Boulevard and attracted many prestigious clients: the executives Samuel Goldwyn and David Selznick, the directors John Huston and William Wyler, the actors Robert Taylor, Walter Pidgeon, Dick Powell, June Allyson and Ava Gardner. Maree received their pay checks directly from the studios or agents, handled their insurance, accounting and taxes, and advised them about how to invest funds and build up their estate.

The stars rarely used real money. Like royalty, they charged everything and had all their bills paid for them. Maree's formula, according to his obituary in the *Los Angeles Times,* "was to pay clients' bills, give them an allowance and invest the surplus in areas that would assure income after their film careers ended. . . . Maree steered entertainers' money into oil wells, shopping centers, marinas, government office buildings and even a television production firm."[17] In December 1954, for example, Bogart, along with Irene Selznick, Barbara Stanwyck, Cary Grant and the director Richard Brooks invested in the Bradco oil and gas project in Houston. Bogart paid Maree 5 percent of his salaried income and prospered under his guidance.

Managing his money was especially important to Bogart, who wanted to wrest some control of his life from the studio. When Warners gave him a part he felt would hurt his career, he refused it and went on suspension. Jack Warner called this "suspense" and Bogart said he had as many suspensions as the Brooklyn Bridge. Since he did not receive a salary and could not work on another film until, after months of negotiation, the agent, studio and star finally agreed on a suitable property, Bogart had to live below his income and put money aside so he could afford the luxury of refusing inferior roles.

He often advised young actors to be cautious. He said that if you get a big part, "grab it—but hold off on the big house and the big cars or you'll be up to your ass in studio brass the rest of your life." Keeping expenses down allowed him to go on suspension until he could get better ones. "The only reason to have money," he told *Time* magazine, "is to tell any s.o.b. in the world to go to hell."[18] Bogart shared the professional insecurity of most actors, who, it was said, were only as good as their last picture. His carefulness with money was influenced by fears that he might, like his father, suddenly lose it all.

Most actors were far less shrewd about money and easily intimidated by the powerful studio. Bette Davis, referring to Bogart, Cagney and herself, asserted: "There weren't many fighters in Hollywood; and we were punished for our unwillingness to compromise. An actor in genuine distress had no other recourse but to refuse to work." The feisty, independent Bogart said that when dealing with Jack Warner he had to be as tough off-screen as he was in pictures: "If you want to be an actor, be honest with yourself; don't let them push you around. When you believe in something, you fight for it even though you may suffer for it. We actors are better judges than any studio as to what is good for us."

Bogart's aggressive cynicism, his bluntness, his refusal to flatter people and tolerate phoniness, his open disdain for the studio's imperious commands, made him unpopular with the powers in Hollywood. Cagney remarked, "Not many people liked him, and he knew it." Though many colleagues did not warm to him as a person, they respected his integrity and his talent; his friends enjoyed his frankness and wit. He did not need the approval of others to know he did a good job, and took more pleasure from fan letters sent by prisoners who admired the authenticity of his acting than from the lavish but meaningless praise of Hollywood.

It was characteristic of Bogart to refuse to play the studio's game. He ironically called the leading gossip columnists—Hedda Hopper, Louella Parsons, Sheilah Graham—the Ladies' Aid Society. Whoever they were aiding, it wasn't actors. To fill their syndicated columns and their radio slots they used networks of tipsters, from hairdressers to hotel clerks, to discover the details of actors' private lives. Obligated to the studios for access to the sets, they frequently published "gossip" supplied by publicity agents to market a star or mitigate a scandal, and were paid off with expensive gifts and deferential treatment. Though they occasionally befriended a star (and always had their favorites) their threats of public exposure reinforced the studios' power over the stars. Female columnists generally resented Bogart's outspoken criticism of the world they tried to glamorize, and the Women's Press Club once named him the Least Cooperative Actor in Hollywood.

Bogart loved to throw people off the scent by making up bogus releases. When a *Time* reporter asked for the names of friends he could interview for a cover story, Bogart sent him to Robert Benchley, Mark Hellinger and the actor Charles Butterworth—all of whom were dead. In various interviews and in *Current Biography* (1942), he said that his favorite color was brown, his favorite flowers hibiscus and gladioli. His solemnly recorded recreations were playing the bull fiddle and cultivating angleworms, painting flowers on teacups and carving exquisite chessmen out of ivory. Asked to contribute to an anthology called *What Actors Eat* he sent in a most unlikely recipe—coconut custard flavored with orange extract: "The only time I do any cooking is when it is necessary for me to get my own ham and eggs in the morning, but I do have a favorite recipe. It is for a dessert which is not too heavy and is a very pleasant finish for most any dinner: Cocoanut Spanish Cream."

Many journalists, desperate to escape the anodyne and often absurd publicity releases, were drawn to Bogart's caustic, irreverent and highly quotable outbursts. He was especially popular with male reporters. Joe Hyams, Ezra Goodman and Jonathan Ruddy followed his career and later wrote books about him. Though he disliked the mystique of stardom and the demand that actors cater to public taste, he set up his own interviews, attracted a receptive audience and had ample opportunity to express his flashing wit. By frankly voicing his gripes, offering his opinions and acknowledging his faults, he projected an abrasive personality and was his own best press agent.

Louise Brooks wrote that "since publicity is the lifeblood of stardom, without which a star will die, it is obvious that he must keep it flowing through his private life, which feeds the envy and curiosity that bring many people into theatres." She thought Bogart was especially adept at the necessary evil of publicity, which created a private Bogey that complemented and enhanced his character on screen: "From the moment he settled at Warner Brothers, in 1935, [much of] his time . . . would be spent with journalists and columnists, who would invent for him the private character of Bogey. . . . Bogart allowed himself to be presented to the world by journalists as a coarse and drunken bully, and as a puppet Iago who fomented evil without a motive. He was neither."[19]

Though naturally contentious, Bogart was not really tough. But he had to be aggressive to protect his interests at Warners. Weary of self-revelation and the incessant scrutiny of the press, he resisted the unwritten agreement to deliver his private life to the public by devising a number of elusive stratagems. He imitated his screen persona in order to defend himself and protect his privacy. His gangster roles inevitably affected his behavior in private confrontations and remarks to the press. The public supposed he was a hard guy, though by temperament he was modest, even austere, and he cultivated a tough veneer that complemented the highly effective screen image of "Bogart." Warner's publicity department encouraged and helped create the rough side of his character to match his screen image and help the public believe in it. At the same time, in films like *Marked Woman* and *Stand-In,* they built up his respectable image to promote the belief that their films were wholesome and healthy. A somewhat divided personality, he was at once a puritan and hedonist, a gentleman and boor. He could be both fine-mannered and foul-tongued, charming and belligerent, consummately professional and wildly out of control.

◊ 4 ◊

Strife with Mayo

1937–1942

‹ I ›

BOGART MET Mayo Methot in Hollywood at the beginning of his long association with Warner Bros. During this time he worked extremely hard, played one gangster role after another, learned the techniques of screen acting and suffered intense frustration at the studio. Like his previous wives, Mayo was a professional stage actress, but had very little in common with Helen Menken and Mary Philips. She shared Bogart's tastes and interests, and they were close companions. But their relationship, happy at first, was marred by sexual and professional jealousy, and by public quarrels that made them known as the "Battling Bogarts." Their personal relations were turbulent even before their marriage and, as with Helen Menken, he gave friends the impression that he was reluctant to commit himself to her. Nevertheless, on August 20, 1938, more than a year after his divorce from Mary Philips, Bogart married Mayo at the Bel Air house of his friend Mary Baker.

Mayo was born at the turn of the century in Portland, Oregon. Her father, John Methot, was the captain of a ship that sailed to the Orient; her mother, Beryl, a police reporter. Called "The Portland Rosebud," Mayo began her career as a child actress, played in summer stock and made her Broadway debut in 1922. She achieved fame the following year as George M. Cohan's leading lady in *The Song and Dance Man* and then played a Louisiana belle in another musical hit, *Great Day* (1929). These roles led to an offer from Hollywood, where she made twenty-five films between 1931 and 1940. Her first husband was the film producer John LeMond; her second, a man called Percy Morgan, whom she was divorcing when she met Bogart in 1936. She was Bogart's third wife and he was her third husband.

Pat Bogart said: "Mayo was very small and a spitfire, just like my

78

mother." A short, bosomy blonde, with a round face and sharp features, she looked—like Mae West—rather sexy and vulgar. Dorris Johnson knew Methot in the Thirties and found her an overpowering woman who came on strong and was absolute in her assertions. When alcohol loosened her tongue she became even more talkative, quarrelsome and aggressive. In newspaper photographs she seems badly dressed, endearingly rumpled and caught by the camera in a bad moment. Propped at a bar with Bogart, she clutches her drink and shows her underwear.

When Bogart married Helen Menken, she was a well-established actress who could help him in the theater; when he met Mayo her career had already reached its peak. Her musical talent and brassy projection had been successful on Broadway, but her hard features made her look less attractive on screen and typecast her as a nasty, greedy, raddled woman. In *Mr. Deeds Goes to Town* (1936), starring Gary Cooper, she's persuasive as the avaricious Mrs. Semple and is as brazen and angry as in real life. In *Marked Woman* (1938), with Bogart, she is touching and convincing as a worn-out whore. Methot frequently maintained that she had given up her movie career to "concentrate" on Bogart's, but she envied his growing success and felt miserable when no parts came her way.

Bogart claimed: "I was besotted, I always married them." But he admired Mayo's unpredictability and combativeness, and seemed to enter their marriage without illusions. "I like a jealous wife," he boasted. "I can be a jealous husband, too. Mayo's a grand girl. She knows how to handle me. . . . When I go to a party and the party spirit gets at me I'm apt to flirt with any amusing girl I see. . . . We get on so well together [because] we don't have illusions about each other. . . . I love a good fight. So does Mayo. We have some first-rate battles. . . . One of the important things to master in marriage is the technique of a quarrel."[1]

In contrast to his other wives, Methot, like Bogart, loved to drink and argue, and was as tough in life as Bogart was in movies. Just as the timid James Joyce would get into drunken brawls with strangers and then tell his huge companion "Deal with him, Hemingway! Deal with him!" so Bogart would escape similar situations by crawling under a table and then reassuring his friends: "Everything's OK. Mayo's handling it." Mayo had a tough punch, and when she floored a heckler in a bar, Bogart proudly held her arm aloft and told the ringside fans: "She's marvelous. I wouldn't go anywhere without her." Mocking himself as well as his rival gangsters at the studio, he also remarked that "Sluggy's crazy about me because she knows I'm braver than George Raft and Edward G. Robinson."[2] Bogart was drawn to Mayo by her most unfeminine characteristics. The part of him that opposed conventional behavior valued Mayo's reckless extremism. He enjoyed the very spectacle they both presented to the world, their utter indifference to what other people thought.

Peggy Slater, one of Bogart's California sailing friends, recalled an embarrassing incident that showed how he used Mayo to shock people: "Enjoying a party aboard a large boat at Newport harbor, I heard him hail from the dock below. 'Peggy, can I join the party?' he had asked. The owner was willing and Bogart came aboard with a frowzy-looking young woman. Introduced to the group, he draped a possessive hand around her and flatly stated, 'And this is the woman I sleep with'"—without mentioning that Mayo was his wife. Slater recalled that "his language was notorious, his domestic quarrels loud and public."

Mayo came from a maritime tradition and shared his passion for boats. After their marriage, he bought a thirty-six-foot motor cruiser, which he kept south of Los Angeles at Newport Beach. He called it the *Sluggy*, and they spent most weekends at sea. Just as Mayo helped Bogart flout social conventions, so the boat also became part of his public image. Speaking to a reporter, Bogart used the boat to emphasize his laziness: "I love the water almost as much as I dislike work. I don't believe I was born to be bad—on the screen or off. I was born to be indolent. That may be the reason I'm an actor. Most certainly it is one of the reasons I bought a boat, a boat that has a motor in it to do most of the work."[3]

Life with Mayo helped him discard the last vestige of his parents' old-fashioned gentility. For the first three years of their marriage they lived at 8787 Shoreham Drive, just around the corner from Horn Avenue, where he had resided with Mary Philips. In January 1942 he moved back to his old, steep street and bought a modest house at 1210 Horn Avenue. He christened the place—after his wife, his boat and his Scottie dog— Sluggy Hollow. James Thurber's cartoon "Jolly Times" hung on the wall and immortalized one of their notable fights. Next to the drawing was a framed bill for $400, the cost of breakage on a destructive night at the Algonquin Hotel in New York.

The house had an arched doorway, a fireplace and an upstairs porch, and was decorated with chintz curtains and a litter of silver boxes. On the piano stood Maud's rather somber crayon portrait of Bogart, his head turned slightly and shaded on one side, signed and dated: "Maud H. Bogart, 1938." A journalist described the seedy neighborhood, which appealed to Bogart's unpretentious character and funky taste: "The Bogarts live in a 15-year-old Hollywood-Spanish house in a part of town that Better Addresses have long since by-passed. In the same block is the Café Gala, a weird-looking night club and a supercolossal drive-in restaurant and down the hill I noticed the varied attractions of Princess Zoraida, Clairvoyant, and the Utter-McKinley Mortuary." "I was born with [class]," Bogart said. "I've had it all my life—and I can also do without it." This modest house and eccentric wife suited him best.

Mayo shared his tastes and humor, and could be lively, defiant, curious, interesting and original. As Verita Peterson observed, Mayo was "everything Bogie loved: intelligent, vivacious, independent, witty, charming, and, above all, a character." Even her destructive influence—the way she encouraged his drinking and accentuated his truculent nature—had a positive effect on his acting, if not on his life. Louise Brooks has convincingly observed that "except for Leslie Howard, no one contributed so much to Humphrey's success as his third wife, Mayo Methot . . . who set fire to him" and freed a sleeping giant. "Those passions—envy, hatred, and violence, which were essential to the Bogey character, which had been simmering beneath his failure for so many years—she brought to a boil, blowing the lid off all his inhibitions for ever."[4]

< **II** >

DURING HIS EARLY YEARS with Mayo Bogart led a pleasant and fairly normal existence. Much of his social life revolved around his friendships with a lively group of writers. In New York his drinking companions were James Thurber and Mark Hellinger, a journalist and columnist who later moved to Hollywood and became a screenwriter. He liked Robert Sherwood (author of *The Petrified Forest*) and Louis Bromfield (who wrote the story that was made into Bogart's film *It All Came True*). He saw a great deal of the screenwriters Nunnally Johnson, Eric Hatch, John Huston and Richard Brooks.[5]

Time reported that Bogart read "voluminously." In two photographs of him at home in the 1940s, the titles of several books are legible and give some indication of his taste: Assen Jordaneff's *Through the Overcast: The Art of Instrument Flying* (1938), which provided background for his aeronautical films; *The Middle Aged Man on the Flying Trapeze* (1940), a satire by James Thurber; *Great Sea Stories,* a nautical anthology that he read on the boat; *American Harvest: Twenty Years of Creative Writing in the United States* (1943), which provided ideas for future films; Bill Mauldin's popular *Up Front* (1945), with drawings and text about army life in World War II; and *Nothing to Fear: Selected Addresses of Franklin Delano Roosevelt, 1932–1945* (1946), published soon after the death of the president. He had to read scripts, devoured newspapers, liked current best-sellers and was addicted to murder mysteries. While reading and talking to literary friends he kept his eye open for good parts. In 1940 he read Henry Bellamann's novel *Kings Row* and told Ann Sheridan that she ought to play the female lead in the film. She took his advice and made the movie in 1941.

Three of his closest friends made shrewd comments about Bogart's intellectual interests. Mike Romanoff defined his restless, unfocused intelligence: "He has an insatiable hunger to know things but is without the energy to acquire learning." His last and most important agent, Sam Jaffe, suggested that Bogart was well educated, picked up a lot from talking to his writer friends, and grasped the essence of current topics and ideas without actually having to read: "He was intelligent. He respected writers. He always surrounded himself with writers. I don't recall that he read a lot, but he found interesting conversation with writers. . . . I can never picture him reading a book, but he gave the impression he did." And the writer-director-actor John Huston recalled his love of stimulating and often volatile conversation: "Bogart used to sit at the writers' table in the Green Room of the studio restaurant and argue. That was my first observation of him. He revelled in argument, debate, discussion, and the exchange of ideas. He enjoyed being provocative. Bogey liked writers, scriveners, newspapermen. He said he had an affinity for them, and would often challenge a writer-pal with 'Fine. Make with the words!'"[6]

Bogart disliked writing, usually kept in touch with friends by phone and sent very few letters, but his leg-pulling notes to Eric Hatch give some idea of his amusing epistolary style.[7] Hatch's life ran parallel to Bogart's and they had a natural affinity. He was born in New York City three years after Bogart, came from a wealthy family and was educated at St. Paul's. He did not go to college but served in World War I, worked in business, got divorced and remarried, and wrote witty stories and screenplays (including the script for *My Man Godfrey*). Hatch was an experienced yachtsman and—an essential quality for friendship with Bogart—a convivial drinker.

In November 1940 Hatch and his wife, who were staying at Bogart's house on Shoreham Road, went to see a sneak preview of a movie called *Road Show*, which had been adapted from Hatch's early novel. He later explained that "Bogie was drinking pretty heavily at the time (as were lots of us) and apparently he got to brooding—and drinking—while we were out. When we came home the enclosed note was waiting on my dresser."

In this playful letter, in large, looped handwriting, Bogart adopted the role of a drunken, gushing, ignorant female fan. He refers to Roosevelt,

Dr. Belmont DeForest Bogart, c. 1900:
Handsome, sturdily built and nearly six feet
tall, he was a natural athlete, a keen sailor
and a superb wing shot.

Maud Bogart with baby Humphrey, 1900:
The stately, fastidious woman — with caustic
wit and imperious manner — was known as
"Lady Maud."

Maud's sketch of baby Humphrey, 1900: "There was a period in American history when you couldn't pick up a goddamned magazine without seeing my kisser in it."

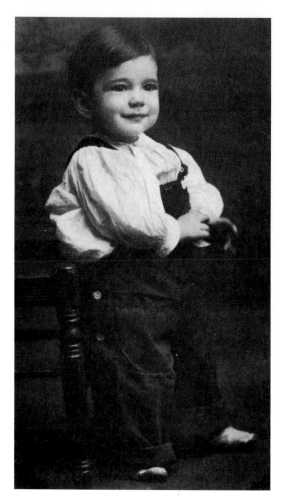

Humphrey, 1901: He was a robust, chubby-cheeked two-year-old, with neatly combed hair, a billowing shirt and side-buttoned overalls with rolled-up cuffs.

Humphrey, 1907: "Kay had a boil on her arm and I opened it. She nearly bled to death."

Bogart at Andover, 1917: Dr. Bogart wrote: "The boy has given up his mind to sports and a continuous correspondence with his girl friends."

Bogart in naval uniform, 1918: "At eighteen war was great stuff. Paris! French girls! Hot damn!"

Stuart Rose, 1918: Bogart's brother-in-law had served in the Cavalry in World War I, and was a keen fox-hunter and steeple-chaser.

William A. Brady, 1928: The big, hard-drinking, cigar-smoking man had a wide florid face and shock of fair hair.

Cradle Snatchers, with Mary Boland (center), 1925: Bogart played a cynical college boy, paid by a middle-aged wife to attend a "three-day petting party" on Long Island.

Helen Menken, 1923: She was mad about clothes, had a "perfect mania for shoes and was as high-strung as a thoroughbred horse."

Mary Philips, 1936: Mary, like Helen, had a fierce temper and once bit a cop's finger when he tried to arrest her for being drunk.

I Loved You Wednesday, with Rose Hobart, 1932: "He seemed to accept the fact that he was doomed to play poor parts in bad plays."

The Petrified Forest, with Bette Davis and Leslie Howard, 1936: "I've spent most of my time since I grew up in jail, and it looks like I'll spend the rest of my life dead."

Jack Warner and his studio, 1940s: Jack built up and ran a multi-million-dollar business, and was not nearly as stupid, philistine and mercenary as he seemed to be.

Marked Woman, 1937, with Bette Davis and Mayo Methot: Davis and Methot play nightclub "hostesses"; Bogart's the crusading D.A. who breaks up the prostitution racket.

Angels with Dirty Faces, with James Cagney, 1938: Cagney tells Bogart, before filling him full of lead: "I know you're a smart lawyer. Very smart. But don't get smart with me."

Dead End, with Marjorie Main, 1937: Main tells Bogart: "You're a killer, murderer, butcher, for sure. You never brought nothin' but trouble!"

Bogart and Mayo, drunk and kicking, early 1940s: "I wouldn't give you two cents for a dame without a temper."

King of the Underworld, 1939: "Don't tell 'em dat a dame tripped me up."

Horn Avenue house, with Bogart and Mayo, 1942: "a 15-year-old Hollywood-Spanish house in a part of town that Better Addresses have long since by-passed."

Virginia City, 1940: Dressed in villainous black, he plays a half-breed outlaw with a dubious Mexican accent.

The Return of Doctor X, 1939: "I was this doctor, brought back to life, and the only thing that nourished this poor bastard was blood."

High Sierra, with Ida Lupino, 1941: Lupino said: "Each of us thought the other was being nasty, and we were both offended."

The Maltese Falcon, with Peter Lorre and John Huston, 1941: Lorre recalled that the film "was one of my happiest memories because for a few years we had a sort of stock company, an ensemble there at Warner Bros."

The Big Shot, with Irene Manning, 1942: Confronted with a life sentence, Bogart hopelessly asks: "Why feed a dead man even if he's still walkin' around?"

Verita Peterson, 1943: She was his toupee-minder, bartender, boat-mate, traveling companion, confidante, adviser and mistress.

who had just been elected to his third term, and to Hitler, who had recently conquered most of Europe and been satirized in Chaplin's *The Great Dictator* (1940). He deliberately confuses his words, writing "magnitude" instead of "magnum," and pretends that he cannot spell "psychic." But he shows some knowledge of nineteenth-century poetry by signing the letter "Barbara Fritchie." In this once-famous poem by Whittier, the ancient heroine bravely raises the Union flag as the Confederate Stonewall Jackson enters Frederick, Maryland. His postscript quotes from another old favorite, Longfellow's "Paul Revere's Ride":

> Dear Eric,
>
> Of course I feel like an old fool, calling you "Eric," but this is the really first fan letter I've ever written—except once to that "awful man in the White House."
>
> I've written a lot of your readings—oh, dear, things go stumbling over my own tongue—my husband says I'm such a fool—I just can't seem to get anything straight he says—of course, Eric, that's what I tell him. "Tee Hee!"
>
> Well, anyway, Eric. I saw your picture tonight and I can't tell you. I just can't tell you! My husband says I shouldn't, but you know him. Quote (The Son-of-a-bitch) Unquote!
>
> If they ever repeal the Prohibition act and we can drink once again like Dad's cruel gentlemen I will personally buy you a magnitude of champagne and we will drink it out of my goddamn slipper!
>
> My Husband Quote (The Son-of-a-bitch) Unquote says I'm drunk. I am—sh!!
>
> I liked your picture better than "Birth of a Nation" which I saw last night and I think that Theodore Roosevelt is just lovely, don't you—him and his big stick!
>
> What I can't understand is why all the people in your picture talked so goddamn much—last night in the [silent film] Birth-of-a-Nation nobody said a word and I liked it better.
>
> Now I have to say goodbye because my Husband Quote (The Son-of-a-bitch) Unquote—says so.
>
> Dear Eric, could you spare a dime for the [unemployed] boys at Valley Forge who need shoes—they liked your picture too.
>
> I'm P yic [Psychic] (I can't spell it) and I just looked into my crystal ball and I see all hell breaking loose on account of

a funny man with a mustache who looks like Charlie Chaplin
and I see your picture previewed once again like it was new.

Now I lay me down to sleep.

Barbara Fritchie.

P.S. One if by land—two if by Sea—lucky me!

Barbara.

His second letter to Hatch, written from Shoreham Road in the
summer of 1941, recalls the zany style of Groucho Marx. The daughters
of Hatch and his friend Carl Timpson were to be presented to society at
a Long Island cotillion that September. Bogart, who had attended many
of these affairs, pleaded poverty and sent his regrets. He parodies an
appropriately genteel response to this invitation, and mocks both etiquette
books and the social pretensions of a coming out party:

Dear Mr. and Mrs. Hatch,

We, Mr. and Mrs. Bogart, are so distressed, and please tell
Mr. and Mrs. Timpson, because we really feel it's going to cost
too much.

For instance, just a glance at our estimated expenses should
convince you that this matter is out of the question.

Railroad fare $600

Side trip to Grand Canyon (no sales resistance) $150

4 Indian blankets $20 (no sales resistance)

Hotel food in N.Y. (couple of hundred)

Liquor on trip and in Twenty-One (God knows!)

Breakage (couple of hundred)

So as you can see this trip is really out of the question—
please explain to the Timpsons.

Incidentally how well do you know the Timpsons—are
you sure they aren't using you to further their own ends. I
simply want to ask you one question—why should Miss Timpson come out before Miss Hatch—after all H comes before
T in the alphabet, if we're going to be fair and democratic about
all this.

Oh, and one more question—What are they coming out
of—because I gather this is a mild "coming out party." And
dear Mr. and Mrs. Hatch we haven't been to a tea dance since
the Plaza Grill—cinnamon toast and martinis—never!!

And finally I've looked all through Emily Post, Tiffany and

an old book on behavior and convention and I can't figure out that Hewlett [Long Island] on the bottom to the left under R.S.V.P.

Is this Hewlett a place or the forgotten man who started the whole thing.

Anyway Mr. and Mrs. Bogart refuse with pleasure your kind invitation on account of how it's too far away—and anyway how do Mr. and Mrs. Timpson know our company would be pleasant.

You see, the whole thing's silly.

> Love
> Mayo and Bogie[8]

‹ III ›

BOGART ACCURATELY defined himself as a "Democrat in politics, Episcopalian by upbringing, dissenter by disposition." He regarded Hollywood as a world of fake images and social pretense, rebelled against its insincerity and sycophancy, and took pride in exposing phonies and maintaining a grip on reality. Vincent Sherman, who wrote or directed four of Bogart's films, emphasized that "Bogie was always a skeptic. His favorite phrase was 'Let's cut the crap.' I think that if he was asked about the big cult of worship that has developed around him, I think he would be pleased. But I also think he would say, 'Cut the crap, fellows.'" Unlike most members of his profession, Bogart, an essentially modest man, was surprisingly free of the narcissism and vanity that impels actors to exhibit themselves in public. He did not take himself or anyone else too seriously. Richard Brooks perceived that "he could never equate the money he was making with what he was doing. He was constantly mocking himself. And that's a good thing."[9]

One observer, describing the social atmosphere in Hollywood, wrote that "warm words of endearment and great cordiality set the tone. But underneath is hostility amounting frequently to hatred, and even more important, a lack of respect for each other's work." Bogart despised this hypocritical world, and in reaction deliberately set out to say whatever he felt, whenever he felt like saying it. He attributed this outspokenness to his father, who had always encouraged him to be unrestrained and independent: "I'm full of opinions and don't hesitate to let fly with them. . . .

I never learned to bridle myself in conversation. I never had to. My father was a successful physician. One of his chief concerns was that his kids should not get ingrained complexes. . . . We grew up in a good neighborhood in New York and associated with a lot of other young free agents with unhampered views. As a result the junior Bogarts developed a talent for individuality because there wasn't any penalty attached to it."

Bogart justified his frankness in an interview of 1937. He claimed that all he wanted was to dissociate himself from the phonies and be free of the inventions of the publicity department:

> Why can't you be yourself, do your job, be your role at the studio and yourself at home, and not have to belong to the glitter-and-glamor group? Actors are always publicized as having a beautiful courtesy. I haven't. I'm the most impolite person in the world. It's thoughtlessness. If I start to be polite you can hear it for forty miles. . . . It's an effort for me to do things people believe should "be done." . . . I'm a human being with a pattern of my own and the right to work out my pattern in my own way. . . . I really can't understand why actors can't have human frailties like other people; why they can't make the same mistakes, guess wrong now and then; why they must be presented to the world as of a uniform and unassailable virtue. . . .
>
> I take my work seriously, but none of this art for art's sake. Any art or any job of work that's any good at all sells. If it's worth selling, it's worth buying. I have no sentimentality about such matters.[10]

His cri de coeur was deliberately naive. As an experienced actor he knew that make-believe was part of the glamour, that in mass entertainment an actor's personal life influenced the public's perception of his art. He never quite gave up his wish to have a truly private life, and devised ways to evade the attempts of the studio and the press to control his life. Taking a no-nonsense approach, he emphasized that acting was a job that one tried to do well.

Bogart remarked that cautious film stars did not invite him to private parties at their houses because they were afraid he might provoke Mayer, Goldwyn, Zanuck or other great powers. (He made up for it by insulting his own boss, Jack Warner, in public.) He defended his behavior by insisting that executives and actors were not uniformly virtuous and smart: "All over Hollywood they are continually advising me, 'Oh, you mustn't say that. That'll get you into a lot of trouble.' . . . This local idea that anyone making a thousand dollars a week is sacred and beyond the realm of criticism never strikes me as a particularly sound reasoning."

Bogart knew the consequences of his bluntness. But when informed that he was the best-hated guy in Hollywood, the news hit him "like a swift kick in the ego." He retaliated by asserting that he hated Hollywood even more than it hated him. In 1940, before he became a star and was still in a vulnerable position, he described Hollywood society as gangsters, fakes and vulgar *nouveaux riches,* as "the clique of ex-bootleggers and phony baronesses that get all dressed up in chinchillas and tailcoats to see the world premiere of a movie that played Fall River, Mass., three weeks ago." Bogart once advised Robert Mitchum—another tough, rebellious actor, who had been arrested for smoking marijuana—about how to survive in that jungle: "'Whatever it is, be against it.' I told him, 'I've got a lot of scars already from being an againster.' He said, 'You've got a lot of scars, but you're still alive.'" The others, Bogart felt, were all dead.

Truman Capote suggested Bogart's values and work ethic by listing the categories of people Bogart scorned as bums: "Bums were guys who cheated on their wives, cheated on their taxes, and all whiners, gossipists, most politicians, most writers, women who Drank, women who were scornful of men who Drank; but the bum true-blue was any fellow who shirked his job, was not, in meticulous style, a 'pro' in his work."[11] Truly Protestant in his attitude to work, despite his professions of indolence, Bogart measured his worth by his professional expertise. Not even Jack Warner could take that away.

‹ IV ›

BOGART'S SMOKING and drinking were notorious, and alcohol often revved him up from frankness to cruel needling. He had cigarettes before breakfast and consumed more than two fatal packs of Chesterfields a day. His films were suffused with smoke (cigarettes conveniently occupied his nicotined-stained fingers), and if he were alive today he could revive the tobacco industry singlehanded.

One of his most famous cracks was "I don't trust any bastard who doesn't drink." When Jess Morgan, a young man from his business manager's office, brought some papers for Bogart to sign at ten in the morning, he said: "Listen, kid, have a drink. If everyone started the day with two scotches, it would be a better world." Bogart had catholic taste. He would begin with martinis or Rob Roys (Scotch, vermouth and bitters) before dinner, have beer (not wine) with his meal and Drambuie afterwards. He would continue to drink throughout the evening, but was never quite as drunk as he pretended to be. According to Nunnally Johnson, he carefully calibrated his alcohol in order to maintain a pleasant sensation without actually becoming intoxicated: "He never gets drunk. Just . . . pumps in some Scotch, and stays a nice even glow all day, automatically redosing as necessary. . . . He is likely to nurse two Scotches with a moderate dash of soda all evening." Richard Brooks agreed that Bogart didn't need much Scotch in his drink to make him tight and emphasized that he never drank when working in a film. Nicholas Ray, who directed two of Bogart's movies, said they shared a taste for alcohol, but that "Bogie was more elegant than I, especially with booze."[12]

Bogart's favorite New York bars, apart from "21," were Bleeck's Artists and Writers on West 40th Street and Tim Costello's (also a favorite of James Thurber, John O'Hara and Dylan Thomas) on Third Avenue. In Hollywood he drank at the Cock and Bull pub, at the Château Marmont, and at the restaurants of Dave Chasen and Mike Romanoff. Drink changed his appearance as well as his behavior. His remark "I have character in my face. It's taken an awful lot of late nights and drinking to put it there" was substantiated by Richard Avedon's revealing photographs of his lined and ravaged countenance. Bogart also rather elegantly said, "I'm formal till I get stiff. Then when I'm stiff I'm not stiff any more."[13] He belonged to the Prohibition era, when drinking had a special mystique. It stood for every relaxation of morality and convention, every forbidden pleasure. Alcohol loosened and sharpened his tongue, and inspired lively talk about chess, boats, gossip, inside information, the current news and politics. Scotch lubricated his male friendships, and he never formed close bonds with men who did not drink.

Bogart was basically a polite, charming and often endearing person, yet he was reluctant to show any feeling but hostility. His desire to provoke and disturb often turned into an irrational urge to misbehave, an urge that his marriage to Mayo encouraged. When angry he moved from deflation of pomposity to insulting and often merciless provocation of any target within range. "You never have a discussion with Humphrey," one friend said. "It's always an argument." Even good pals like David Niven found this habit rather tiresome. Like his parents before him, Bogart needled in order to relieve the monotony of ordinary conversation, to make contact, however negative, with others, to test and shock people and force them to reveal their personal weaknesses. Sometimes, with an elderly adversary, he was relatively gentle. Sylvia Thompson, the daughter of a friend, recalled Bogart's meeting with her grandmother, a rather sharp-tongued old lady. After one of her characteristic remarks, "he turned to her with his famous slow toothy smile and said, 'Why, we should call you Alice Vinegar!' But he was always darling to me, my Uncle Bogart." On other occasions he would amuse himself by tormenting the innocent. At a dinner party, in her husband's absence, he once reduced a young wife to tears. When a fellow guest asked him to stop, Bogart aggressively demanded: "Why should she be left alone?"[14]

Most of the time, however, Bogart was merely trying out his wit, challenging his adversary and willing to risk hostility to get a response. Several of his half-serious remarks have become classics in the history of cruel insults. When the actors Paul Douglas and Jan Sterling told Bogart they were going to get married, he growled: "Don't come to me with your fucking troubles." Noel Coward met Bogart through David Niven. Referring to Bogart's annual birthday party, he ironically wrote that "Bogey, justly celebrated for his Dix-Huitième manners, said to [the fastidious, mother-fixated Clifton Webb] at a party, apropos their own projected Christmas Eve Rout, 'Bring your fucking mother and she can wipe up her own sick!' Clifton was not pleased."[15]

Bogart disliked producers, who knew very little about writing, directing or acting, but gave orders to those who did. He asked his burly neighbor Sid Luft, the husband of Judy Garland: "They tell me you're a producer. What makes you think you have the taste to be a producer?" The producer Armand Deutsch, who (Bogart felt) had bought his way into pictures by acquiring MGM stock, was the victim of his most protracted needling. Bogart's agent Sam Jaffe recalled that Bogart walked up to Deutsch at a party and said: "'You're a dreary, dull man.' . . . He had a certain idiocy about attacking people when he was drinking. I guess that gave him courage or nerve." Deutsch, pushed beyond endurance after many insulting remarks, turned white with rage and screamed: "You've tormented me for years. I'm gonna kill you." But Bogart, who had achieved the desired effect, merely laughed, settled himself comfortably on a sofa and said: "Nobody can fight a man sitting down."

Though he sometimes got punched, Bogart took the greatest pleasure in needling the victim to the point of explosion and then using every trick he had to escape punishment. Deutsch himself recorded a number of unpleasant incidents. On their first encounter Bogart merely said: "Listen, kid, don't confuse inheriting money with having talent." At their second meeting, Bogart hit his target and then, as Deutsch rushed toward him, hastily grabbed a pair of glasses from the man next to him, put them on and said: "It's not right to hit an older man." The third time around, Bogart defused Deutsch's rage by coolly remarking: "You should never strike a smaller man. It's a cowardly thing to do."

Though Bogart bullied people who were physically or psychologically weak, he would always back down if challenged, refused to step outside and frankly confessed he was a physical coward. He enjoyed getting dangerously close to an uproar and relied on his status to get him out of it. He might hit a man first and get the waiter to break up the fight before his victim could hit back. At the house of the director Edward Dmytryk, Bogart needled a man who angrily called him out. When Bogart asked, "Can you fight?" and the man said, "Pretty well," he replied: "Then let's forget the whole thing."[16] In this fashion Bogart livened up parties that he felt were devoted to mutual admiration and meaningless chat.

‹ V ›

THIS CAT-LIKE GAME of attack and retreat gave Bogart the illusion of always winning the argument, and if all else failed he could use his tough screen reputation to face down his adversary. This technique did not work so well with Mayo, who played the game to the gruesome end. Bogart clearly enjoyed fighting with Mayo, whose flash point was instantaneous, and their disputes were primarily for display. Though they had tender moments in private, many friends had never heard them exchange a civil word in public. Sam Jaffe remembered how "he used to tease her! It was a cat and mouse game. It was awful. He enjoyed that. He knew she was pugnacious and threatening, and he would bring it on." As Bogart said in *High Sierra:* "I wouldn't give you two cents for a dame without a temper."

In their struggle for dominance, any divergence of opinion could start a row and politics was a favorite source of contention. Bogart was a New Deal liberal, Methot a confirmed Republican who poured scorn on Roosevelt. She adored General Douglas MacArthur and got livid when Bogart made cracks about his vanity and egomania. The actress Gloria Stuart recalled how the strong-willed Mayo would constantly put him down, disdainfully saying, "So *you* think so-and-so," and calling him "a 4-F coward and a phony." He would give her a push and the fight would escalate to scratches, bites and kicks. But Bogart liked the excitement. "Speak your piece," he said, "tell what's on your mind, let the little woman know what you're really thinking—and then duck, but fast!" She would hit him with an ashtray, lamp or bottle, and friends were warned not to visit Horn Avenue for fear they would be cut by flying glass.

One evening, when drinking with Peter Lorre, Bogart forgot that he was supposed to meet Mayo for dinner. She suddenly appeared, "took off her jewelry, rings, wrist watch, bracelets, whatever, got mad and threw them at Bogie." Bogart carefully retrieved the valuables and wrapped them in his handkerchief.[17] He encouraged Mayo to play the virago and confirm his satiric view of domestic life. On their fifth wedding anniversary in August 1943, he sent Sluggy a hand-carved rolling pin.

In time the Battling Bogarts became a less comic and more disturbing couple. At Slapsie Maxie Rosenbloom's nightclub, when they were dining with Arthur and Gloria Sheekman, Bogart rose to Mayo's bait and warned her: "You say that once more and I'll get you." Inevitably, she took up the challenge and he pushed her backwards over a table. Realizing perhaps that he had gone too far, he turned to Arthur and said: "Wouldn't you also have done that?" To which Sheekman mildly replied: "Not necessarily." Another friend, leaving an elegant restaurant on Sunset Strip, discovered Methot sitting on Bogart's back and mechanically banging his head on the sidewalk. On another occasion, when a friend came to his rescue, Bogart triumphantly announced: "I've got her down now." Methot was lying on the deck of the boat, with blood all over her, but happy, he said, "as she always was after she had forced me to lose my temper and hit her back." Neighbors across the street on Horn Avenue, alerted by screaming, saw them fighting on the roof. He had a noose around her neck and, trying to strangle her, was shouting: "Sluggy, you miserable shrew, I'm going to hang you!"[18] His favorite song, appropriately enough, was "Mean to Me."

These fights were part of their powerful sexual bond. Mayo responded passionately to his provocations, found their violence quite thrilling and continued the display by telling a reporter: "I married a man who conducts himself like a man. A man who doesn't only offer me security, but a certain excitement." Their fierce foreplay, an elaborate mating dance, released Bogart's normally repressed and sealed emotions. She always smothered him with kisses after an especially bitter fight, and during the tender reconciliation their lovemaking was always more passionate. In this respect, they resembled D. H. and Frieda Lawrence, whose violent battles repelled and astounded their friends. Katherine Mansfield wrote: "I don't know which disgusts one worse—when they are loving and playing with each other, or when they are roaring at each other and he is pulling out Frieda's hair and saying 'I'll cut your bloody throat, you bitch.'" Howard Hawks, who directed Bogart's first two films with Lauren Bacall, "once asked Bogie if he could get an erection without first having battled with Mayo."

Eventually Mayo's hard drinking took its toll, and she became, like her mother, an alcoholic. At night she often passed out in a stupor before they got to bed, injured herself and even broke her bones by falling down. Alcohol also affected her appearance and hurt her career. She lost her beauty and her figure collapsed; her face became puffy, her skin scaly, her looks blowsy. Like the hero of Hemingway's *To Have and Have Not* (1937), Bogart "hated the way she had coarsened and grown heavy, was repelled by her bleached hair, her too big breasts, her lack of sympathy with his work." As Bogart's enormous success in *The Maltese Falcon* and *Casablanca* coincided with her physical and professional decline, she became jealous of his fame and of the beautiful actresses (Mary Astor, Ingrid Bergman and Lauren Bacall) to whom he made love in his increasingly romantic films. She was stung by Bogart's claim that Ingrid Bergman was "the only lady in Hollywood." Bitterly unhappy, she called him "that cheap little ham actor."[19] Alcoholism and mental illness propelled her into vengeful outbursts.

Their colorful domestic fireworks now revealed their profound unhappiness. On one occasion Methot set the house on fire and threatened him with a gun. Sometimes things really got out of control. The worst episode occurred after he came home from the Finlandia Baths. Bogart and Lorre would "come down there, after a hangover, and steam out. Then they'd go right across the street to a place called the Villanova, a bar, and start all over again." But Mayo, believing it was a high-class whorehouse, stabbed him in the back with a kitchen knife. As he passed out and fell into a pool of blood, she panicked and screamed: "I didn't do anything, I didn't do anything." After he came to, Bogart called Mary Baker, who rushed over and got her doctor to treat the wound. Mindful of the morals clause in his contract and keen to keep the incident out of the press, she did not notify the police. When Methot couldn't wound Bogart, she injured herself, intimidated and bound him to her. On several occasions she slashed her wrists and tried to commit suicide.

As their sexual display turned deadly, the Mayo he loved became a source of emotional anguish. Bogart, overwhelmed by guilt, got close to breakdown over the failure of his marriage. He and Mayo became locked into their endless quarrels, which derived from her resentment, lack of purpose and mental instability. Bogart's restless and contradictory nature also contributed to their problems. Like many intelligent people, he was easily bored. The long waits on the set, the company of egoistic and intellectually limited actors, and life in the stultifying milieu of Hollywood all tried his patience. "I don't like placid things," he remarked, in a calmer time. "I get bored if there isn't a little action going on. There should be a little more color in this town." His verbal sparring with Jack Warner turned into physical combats with Methot. Releasing his professional frustrations, he got pleasure out of quarreling with his boss and his wife. After he left both Mayo and Warner Bros., he said: "I kinda miss the arguments. . . . It's like when you've fought your wife and gotten a divorce. You kind of miss the fighting!"[20]

‹ VI ›

In 1942, as his marriage to Mayo deteriorated beyond repair, Bogart began his twelve-year love affair with his make-up artist, Verita Peterson. Though he was usually attached to only one woman at a time, he had affairs with Philips, Methot and Bacall when married to someone else. Bogart did not normally have close women friends, but Verita—who became his toupee-minder, bartender, boat-mate, traveling companion, sympathizer, protector and adviser—was the exception. He called her "Pete," confided in her and treated her like one of the boys. She was as lively and as sexy as Mayo, but younger, more amusing, attractive, responsive and devoted. When his domestic life became unbearable, he took refuge with Verita, and often turned up drunk, exhausted and disheveled on her doorstep.

Bogart first met Verita through the actress Ann Sheridan during the filming of *Casablanca* in the summer of 1942. When Verita arrived on the Warners set with the producer Henry Blanke, Bogart bluntly asked: "Where'd a creep like you find such a good-looking broad?" A western girl, like Mayo, Verita was orphaned when young and had been brought up by relatives in Arizona. After the death of her grandfather, a wealthy surgeon, she inherited a considerable fortune. She went to Hollywood, acted in a few films and got a job in the make-up department of Warners.

She admired Bogart's lack of vanity. As she applied his make-up, he would grumble: "If you work on my mug any longer, you'll have me looking like the leading lady." Though he had to look his best on screen and on publicity tours, Bogart either reduced make-up to an absolute minimum or did not use it at all. He called the cosmetic department "Boys' Town" because it could rejuvenate the faces of the older actors, and openly told reporters about the shoe lifts, which he mockingly called "wedgies," that were used to increase his height. He had hairy arms, chest and legs, but was getting bald. He made fun of his own hairpiece, in contrast to other actors—Charles Boyer, Fred Astaire, Bing Crosby, Gene Kelly and Frank Sinatra—who solemnly disguised their baldness. According to Verita, Bogart joked that his toupee was "Jack Warner's diabolical plot to make him look like a fag." He wittily suggested she "bring his hairline down to his eyebrows to give him the Neanderthal look of a movie mogul," and once exclaimed: "I'm not going to prance around the studio with a fucking *beaver* on my head!"

Always on the lookout for ways to torment the studio, Bogart even used his hairpiece to pick a fight. In March 1946, he came in for two days to have a cast made of his head for a toupee and told Perc Westmore, the head of the make-up department: "I have the Company over a barrel." He had agreed to come in for one day but not for two, and said that "a couple of months from now we can cause trouble and claim a breach of contract." Bogart deliberately fed this line to Westmore, knowing quite well that he would tell the management. Steve Trilling, Jack Warner's executive assistant, took this threat seriously. He reported the incident to the studio's lawyer Roy Obringer and asked him how to deal with the troublesome actor. Bogart was delighted to have stirred up the studio brass.

When Verita's husband unexpectedly came back to their house at 722 Roselli Street in Burbank and discovered them naked in the shower, her marriage was over. She and Bogart often talked about getting married when their divorces came through, but he met the unattached Bacall before Verita was free. Verita praised his kindness, gentleness and warmth, and wrote that "he was very loving, very kind and considerate, and very tender. . . . He was a very unselfish lover, and he knew how to make a woman feel like a woman." In a recent interview, she said the secrecy and danger of their affair made it more exciting for both of them. Though he could have lost his job if the studio found out, they were willing to take the risk. In those more puritanical days, when men and women did not live together, it was either marriage or secrecy. Nathaniel Benchley, who knew Bogart quite well, claimed that "although he had four wives there were never any girls on the sidelines," which shows how well they kept their liaison hidden.[21]

✦ 5 ✦

Professional Gangster

1938-1940

< I >

IN 1938, the year he married Mayo Methot, Bogart made six movies for Warner Bros. Four of them were abominable; two had some interest; but none was as good as *Dead End* or *Stand-In*. The studio was keen to satisfy the public's demand for gangster movies. It put Bogart under contract because he was good in these roles, but did not see his potential or try to develop his career. So he slogged mechanically along, playing stereotyped criminal characters. The work was hard, his parts unrewarding, his status low. Despite efforts to get better roles, his career remained as stagnant as it had been on Broadway before the success of *The Petrified Forest*.

Type-casting served Warners' purpose, but consigned actors to an assembly-line job in return for a regular paycheck. The system took an emotional toll on Bogart. As his long run of inferior pictures extended into 1939 and 1940, he became intensely dissatisfied, made caustic comments about other actors and had a number of sharp but futile quarrels with Jack Warner. Despite, and partly because of, his protests he remained, both in salary and status, far below the leading Warners stars—Robinson, Cagney, Raft, Flynn and Bette Davis. His frustrations at work put additional strain on his rocky marriage.

The title of *Swing Your Lady* (1938), a bit of Ozark idiocy which Bogart called his worst movie, puns on the athletic and musical elements in the story. Bogart as a boy had wrestled at Andover. He now plays a wrestling manager, with flat cap and watch chain, trying to promote a powerful lady blacksmith called Sadie. This pointless exercise limped along with numbers like "Mountain Swingeroo" and even flopped with rural audiences. As *Variety*'s famous headline put it: "STIX NIX HIX PIX."

In *Crime School* (1938), another formulaic film, the Dead End Kids (as one collective name) got higher billing than Bogart. The screenwriter Vincent Sherman explained how such movies were manufactured. Warners "had an A department run by Hal Wallis and a B department run by Bryan Foy. Wallis would make about twenty pictures a year and Foy about thirty-five. When a picture got to be, say, seven or eight years old, Foy would turn around and take that A picture and make it into a B picture." *Crime School* was made by doing "half of *The Mayor of Hell* [1933], which was an old Cagney film, and half of a picture called *San Quentin* [1937]." Though the formula seemed hackneyed, it worked quite well. The picture cost only $186,000 and grossed over $2 million.

Jack Warner told Sherman to try Bogart out in a good-guy part to "see if you can get him to do something besides Duke Mantee," and the actor was pleased to play a character who didn't have to die at the end of the film. When the director Lewis Seiler asked the actors for ideas about their scenes Bogart, good at improvisation, ad-libbed. Sherman thought he was a serious actor who did his best with poor material.

Crime School opens as six rough boys fracture the skull of a pawnbroker who refuses to pay what he owes them. They are caught, appear at the trial with their broken-down parents and are sentenced to reform school. The conditions are predictably horrible: the warden is sadistic, the doctor is drunk, the guards are ex-convicts and the boys are whipped. Bogart, a social worker who has observed the trial, has (like Baby Face Martin in *Dead End*) the same slum origins as the boys. He inspects the school, fires the warden and takes charge himself. He rescues an injured kid when the boiler explodes and covers for the boys when they try to escape. At the end of the picture he brings out the inherent goodness of his wards and arranges their parole. He also courts the gang-leader's goody-goody sister and gets her into the marriage bed.

The Amazing Dr. Clitterhouse (1938), inevitably referred to on the set as *Dr. Clitoris*, had a strong cast (including the boxer Maxie Rosenbloom as one of the heavies) and an intriguing screenplay by John Huston. A chemical retort bubbles over behind the titles, though Dr. Clitterhouse (Edward G. Robinson) does no mad-scientist lab work. Writing a book on criminal behavior, he joins a gang of jewel thieves to find out more about how they operate. Claire Trevor is the hard-nosed fence who falls for Robinson. Bogart plays the head of the gang, Rocks Valentine, whose nickname pays tribute to his previous heists. He habitually polishes his diamond ring, has brilliantined hair and wears—like the gangsters in Hemingway's "The Killers"—a derby hat. When Rocks discovers the doctor's true identity and threatens to kill him, he gives Rocks a poisoned drink and coolly studies his reactions as he dies. Caught and tried for murder, Clitterhouse pleads insanity, but under cross-examination changes his plea and insists that he is sane. The jury believes that anyone who claims to be sane while pleading insanity must, in fact, be crazy—and promptly acquits him. The Warners research department found the correct legal formula for the jury verdict, "Not guilty on grounds of insanity," and gave the apparently absurd ending a touch of realism.

Huston's script has some witty touches and unusual scenes. The name on the gang's office door is "Hudson River String Quartet," an allusion to the location of Sing Sing prison as well as to the violin cases they use to carry machine guns. During an exciting fur robbery Bogart locks Robinson (later freed by Rosenbloom) in a claustrophobic refrigerated vault. There is a meaningful contrast between the dress, speech and behavior of Bogart and Robinson. A review in the *Louisville Courier-Journal,* recalling that Robinson had shot the evil Bogart in both *Bullets or Ballots* and *Kid Galahad,* opened with the headline: "Robinson Ends Bogart's Life For Third Time—Poison Does the Work in *Dr. Clitterhouse.*"[1]

Just as Thomas Dewey's crusade against "Lucky" Luciano's prostitution ring had inspired *Marked Woman,* so his suppression of the trucking rackets, which made headline stories in the mid-1930s, inspired *Racket Busters* the following year. Bogart, the intimidating racketeer who controls the drivers and attempts to take over the New York produce market, is responsible for a great deal of nastiness: beating up potential witnesses, tampering with brakes to cause a crash, blowing up the trucks of his enemies, shooting a strike-breaking speechmaker and pushing Pop, a sympathetic old man, in front of a train.

Racket Busters exhibits all the faults of a Warners "B" film. The dialogue is flat and familiar, dull speeches replace dramatic action, romantic scenes are excruciating and good simple-mindedly conquers evil. Fearful men always answer when criminals knock on the door and are immediately beaten up. Disputes are settled by a predictable punch on the jaw, which rarely harms the victim. George Brent, a law-abiding union man, finally knocks down Bogart, who is arrested by the police and sent up the Hudson for twenty years. The audience is left with the comfortable illusion that the racketeers have been driven out of New York.

Angels with Dirty Faces, Bogart's last film in 1938, was made in two months between June and August. The budget was $602,000, of which Bogart earned $8,800 and Cagney, with a salary of $85,667, nearly ten times more. The deadbeat Dead End Kids appear with Bogart for the third and last time. Pat O'Brien—the Doris Day of crime films—guided by the "technical adviser" Father J. J. Devlin, plays a smug and sanctimonious priest. This movie repeats, in the timeworn Warners fashion, the plot of *Public Enemy*. In the earlier picture two brothers grow up in a rough Irish neighborhood. The good one keeps his nose clean, fights in the war and faithfully returns to his old job on the trolley. The baddie, played by Cagney, becomes a ruthless gangster. In *Angels with Dirty Faces* two tough childhood friends, Cagney and O'Brien, take different paths after they rob a boxcar. Cagney, caught and sent to reform school, goes on to a life of crime; O'Brien escapes, makes it through the seminary and enters the priesthood. As in *Dead End,* the boyhood friends meet in their old neighborhood when the bad one returns to show off his wealth and corrupt the local kids who have read about his exploits in the newspapers.

During his latest term in prison Cagney has taken the rap for a crooked lawyer, played by Bogart, who kept a huge sum of his money and promised to return it when he's released. Enjoying the good life as a nightclub owner and gambler, Bogart decides to kill Cagney and keep the cash. There is a fine scene when Cagney, pursued by the mob, stuffs a rival gangster into a phone booth where he is shot by his own men. Cagney finally confronts Bogart with wisecracks, threats and violence. He warns Bogart, who flutters the fingers of his trembling hands as if he were scratching the air—"I know you're a smart lawyer. Very smart. But don't get smart with me"—before filling him full of lead.

The film, directed by Michael Curtiz, moves with fast-paced panache as Cagney runs through his repertoire of tough-guy mannerisms: shoulder hunching, neck twisting, jaw jutting and finger snapping. When the cops, tipped off by the gangsters, come to arrest him, Cagney is casually reading *Police Detective* magazine. Chased up to the roof of the nightclub (gangsters always go aloft before meeting their doom), he's captured with the friendly assistance of the priest. O'Brien convinces him that he must pretend to be yellow when he goes to the chair so that he won't be a bad example to the slum kids.[2] "They've got to despise your memory," Pat tells Cagney, who agrees to follow his advice and "straighten himself out with God." As the dead hand of the Production Code exerts its influence, the exciting film turns into sentimental tripe: *The Bells of St. Mary's* meets Al Capone. In *Angels with Dirty Faces,* as in many other movies, Bogart, stereotyped as a callous and evil character, must be eliminated to assure the viewers that crime does not pay.

In the middle of 1938, before his marriage to Mayo, Bogart tried to find a way out of his impasse at Warners by getting a new and more effective agent. He replaced Leland Hayward, who had succeeded Myron Selznick, by Sam Jaffe. A New Yorker, close to Bogart's age, Jaffe became an agent after several years in a studio. He began as a messenger at Paramount, where his brother-in-law B. P. Schulberg was general manager, became a production manager in 1922 and joined the Schulberg-Feldman Agency in 1934. That year, with the literary agent Mary Baker (who had worked for Hayward), he founded his own agency. His clients included, in addition to Bogart, the actors Joan Bennett, Lee J. Cobb, Jennifer Jones, Fredric March and Zero Mostel (all of whom appeared, with Jaffe's help, in Bogart's films), and the directors John Cromwell, Fritz Lang and Stanley Kubrick.

Mary Baker, petite, pretty and smartly dressed, put Bogart in touch with Jaffe, who arranged a lunch with him. Jaffe said: "Look, I need you and you need me. You need somebody to look after your interests. Leland Hayward doesn't do it." Jaffe thought Bogart's career had suffered because "he didn't have anybody going to the front office and pleading his case." Jaffe frequently went to the front office but had a hard time with Jack Warner. He regarded agents as the enemy and loathed anyone who tried to come between the studio and the actors. "Warner resented very much any time we acted on behalf of a client," Jaffe bitterly recalled. "I had a lot of trouble with him. He barred me [from entering the studio] many times, and he was very vicious about it. . . . He didn't have any respect for the director or the writer or the actor, no feelings about their choices." When Warner told him, "'I'm not going to talk to Jaffe,' Bogart said, 'Well, that's fine. Then I won't talk to *you.*'" Bogart, Jaffe said, "was very smart that way."

Jaffe deflected some of Warner's hostility, the traditional role of an agent, and dealt with complaints from both sides. He remained a vital ally in Bogart's attempts to break out of stereotyped roles, but sometimes brought dubious scripts that made him exclaim: "You're not going to sell me on that goddamned lousy picture." Jaffe was a candid, cultivated, knowledgeable man who owned a valuable art collection and could talk about a wide range of subjects. He understood Bogart's temperament and was proud of his talent. Bogart thought Jaffe too formal and proper, and would openly needle him by asking: "why don't you loosen up, you stiff son of a bitch?" But they had great rapport and affection, and became firm friends. Bogart admired his integrity and later told Bacall: "I trust Sam more than anyone else in the world."

⟨ II ⟩

OF THE SEVEN FILMS Bogart made in 1939, four were pointless but peppery exercises, and three—*Dark Victory, The Roaring Twenties, The Return of Doctor X*—tried for something beyond the conventional, the trite and the mediocre. *King of the Underworld* was a remake of *Dr. Socrates* (1935), in which Paul Muni played a small-town doctor who is forced to treat a wounded criminal and becomes implicated in the crimes of his gang. In the remake a young doctor tries to extricate himself from gambling debts by treating wounded members of Bogart's gang. When he is killed in a raid, the police accuse his innocent wife (also a doctor and leadenly played by Kay Francis) of being their accomplice.[3] Forced to exonerate herself or lose her medical license, she persuades the desperate crew to allow her to put drops in their eyes. Temporarily blinded, they are captured by the police. Though the movie effectively contrasts the good doctor and the evil mobster, her mode of escape is highly implausible.

Bogart lounges about reading a biography of Napoleon and quotes the Emperor to justify his own criminal exploits and ruthless megalomania. He has also taken hostage an English author and hitchhiker (a weak imitation of the Leslie Howard character in *The Petrified Forest*), whom he orders to write his biography. Just before Bogart's death provides a dramatic conclusion to the book, he informs his Boswell, "I guess you'll have to finish it without me," and delivers the classically macho line: "Don't tell 'em dat a dame tripped me up."

Between their two crime films, *Angels with Dirty Faces* and *The Roaring Twenties*, Bogart and Cagney also made a western, *The Oklahoma Kid*. Both city boys look ill at ease in the Tulsa land rush in 1893, though Bogart's youthful riding in Central Park helped him handle a horse. The evil Bogart, dressed in black, with greasy curly hair, is devious, sulky and snarling. The jaunty Cagney, in cowboy boots and fringed buckskin jacket, wears an enormous western hat that makes him look like a giant mushroom. In the picture Bogart jumps the gun on the land grab and takes control of the drinking, gambling and vice on the new frontier. Resisting attempts to run him out of town, he persuades the crowd to hang the crusading mayor. At the height of Bogart's villainy, Cagney, the mayor's outlaw son, exacts vengeance by tracking down each one of his father's murderers. Finally he kills Bogart and wins the vapid Rosemary Lane. Cagney, an untouchable superman during all the shooting, takes daring risks but is never hurt.

Cagney, who grew up in a rough part of New York, mocked the posh "Park Avenue" Bogart and said, "when it came to fighting, he was about as tough as Shirley Temple." As the well-paid star of the film, he also sympathized with Bogart's frustration and bitterness:

> *The Oklahoma Kid* was something of a fiasco. Bogart and me on what you might call new territory, stalking around the set like a couple of city slickers dolled up in Western rigout. . . . Bogie played a heavy in it, doing his usual expert job. By this time in his career he'd become entirely disillusioned with the picture business. Endlessly the studio required him to show up without his even knowing what the script was, what his dialogue was, what the picture was about. On top of this he would be doing two or three pictures at a time. That's how much they appreciated him. He came into the makeup depart-ment one morning and I said, "What is it today, Bogie?" "Oh, I don't know," he said. "I was told to go over to Stage 12." There he was fulfilling his contract, doing as required, however much against his will.

In February 1939, shortly before he and Mayo went to Oklahoma City for the opening, Bogart was interviewed by the *New York Times*. Instead of puffing the picture, as actors usually did, he angered the studio by ex-pressing scorn for its mechanical product. "I speak the same lines," he said, "and do the same things as I do in any other Warner picture. The only difference is that I snarl at the Injuns from under a ten-gallon hat."[4]

Dark Victory (1939) was an important picture for Bette Davis and George Brent, who had an affair during the filming, but Bogart had only a minor role. Borrowing the setting from Scott Fitzgerald, it takes place in a Gatsby-like mansion on Long Island. Like Fitzgerald's *Tender is the Night,* it concerns a doctor's unsuccessful attempt to save the woman he loves. But in the movie her illness is physical rather than mental and leads to an early, romantic death.

Hollywood maintained its vitality by buying or stealing both material and expertise. In order to ensure the psychological accuracy of the story, the producer Hal Wallis came up with the idea of asking Sigmund Freud, with whom Davis had graciously agreed to work, to come to Hollywood and act as technical adviser. Freud—eighty-two years old and with fatal cancer of the jaw—had lived under the absolute monarchy of the Em-peror Franz Josef and had just escaped from the totalitarian regime of Adolf Hitler. But he was unwilling to submit to the dictatorship of Jack

Warner. On August 1, 1938, a month before filming began, an American psychiatrist, predicting that Freud would refuse, jumped into the breach and offered "to bring with me a number of normal and abnormal people (of various degrees) to California, should this be desirable." Wallis, who felt there were more than enough abnormal people in Hollywood, turned down the offer.

In *Dark Victory* Davis' youthful vitality and acting skill turned the mawkish material into a moving portrait of a spoiled and doomed young woman. Davis made her stage debut at the age of twenty in 1928 and her first film three years later. She was then married to the musician Harmon Nelson. Since appearing in *The Petrified Forest* with Bogart, she had won Oscars for *Dangerous* in 1935 and for *Jezebel* in 1938. George Brent plays the doctor who treats the heiress' incurable brain tumor and falls in love with his plucky patient, who tells her friend: "Confidentially, honey, this is more than a hangover."

Their off-screen love affair intensified their performance, but disrupted the filming when they saw the absurdity of their romantic dialogue. On November 7 the unit manager told the studio production manager that the stars had cracked up: "the peculiar wording of the dialogue was suggestive, which got Miss Davis and Mr. Brent laughing so they had to go into 10 takes on the scene." The following month Davis, overcome this time by the pathos of her role, once again went out of control: "Miss Davis was taken hysterical in this scene and they had difficulties in getting it. She cried very heavily and it was very difficult and very trying for everybody to get the scene."[5]

Despite her extraordinary ability and success, Davis was still being assigned to mediocre movies. Like Bogart, she had bitter fights with Jack Warner and was frequently suspended. In the past Bogart's rude behavior had angered and alienated the tough but vulnerable actress. By the time they made *Dark Victory,* their last picture together, they had formed a kind of edgy truce: "We finally had a sort of grudging admiration for each other, Bogart and me," said Davis. "We'd both come up the hard way, and in those days we were married to people that we didn't have much in common with. . . . I thought his performance in this [film] was just perfect. We had some very difficult scenes to play together. I thanked God for the help his performance gave me in playing mine."

Struggling with an Irish accent, Bogart plays "a barnyard Romeo," a pipe-smoking, impertinent horse-trainer, Michael O'Leary. The script once again borrows the characters and plot from modern literature. O'Leary has, through his intimate contact with racing thoroughbreds, the same sullen, animalistic sexual energy as Lewis, the Welsh groom, in D. H. Lawrence's *St. Mawr* (1925): "'He's a common little fellow,' [the heroine] thought to herself. 'But he knows a woman and a horse, at sight.'" Like Lawrence's earthy Celtic heroes, O'Leary tries to transcend the barriers of class through a sexual connection with his aristocratic employer.

In their main scene together Judith Traherne (Davis)—knowing she is doomed, eager for pleasure and aware of Michael's love for her—visits him in the stables. Michael wears jodhpurs, puttees and high boots; Judith is dressed in an evening gown and fur coat. Her sick horse has been saved by the vet, but she knows she herself cannot recover. Responding to Michael's offer to warm herself, she enters his dark room, which glows from the heat of the stove. As they talk about the prospects of her favorite horse, he exclaims: "You know, you and I are kind of alike. . . . You've got the spirit in you the same as I have in me. It's the fighting that counts. You've got to have action in your life just like I've got to have action in mine"—and urges her to seize the sensual moment. O'Leary's speech was influenced by the scene in Conrad's much darker *Victory* (1915) in which Ricardo, trying to seduce Lena, says: "You and I are made to understand each other. Born alike, bred alike, I guess. You are not tame. Same here! You have been chucked out into this rotten world of 'yporcrits. Same here!"

When Michael lights her cigarette, Judith asks if he's afraid to burn —and afraid to die. Inspired by her question, he claims that he's more of a man than her doctor and passionately declares his love: "The nights I've laid awake thinking of you. . . . The things I've wanted to say to you ever since the first time I saw you." He kisses her and she seems to submit, but suddenly breaks away. He says she's rejected him because he's a stable hand; she tells him that she has only a few months to live. Shocked by her confession, he refuses to believe her. She then says that when death comes "it's got to be met finely—beautifully" and collapses onto the straw as the scene dissolves.[6]

Unable to respond to her servant's redemptive vitality, the heiress rejects earthy passion, marries her doctor and enjoys a brief idyll in Vermont before the onset of blindness and death. His more idealistic love enables her to achieve victory over the dark. Just as Methot had helped Bogart become less inhibited and more extrovert in his personal relations with his wife and women in general, so Davis' intensely emotional, highly skilled acting stimulated him for the first time to express sexual feeling in a realistic way. Though ill at ease in curls and a fake Irish accent, Bogart (like Hemingway) never missed the chance to profit from the best teachers and learned as much from Bette Davis as he had from Leslie Howard. His emotions would flow more freely with Mary Astor in *The Maltese Falcon,* with Ingrid Bergman in *Casablanca,* and with Lauren Bacall in *To Have and Have Not* and *The Big Sleep.*

Bogart and Cagney's last film together, *The Roaring Twenties,* "was a troubled production from the start. Three writers were required to turn Mark Hellinger's sprawling original story into a concise and workable screenplay; [Raoul] Walsh stepped in late as a director when producer Hal Wallis dropped Anatole Litvak; and there were several last-minute casting changes as well." It opens with newsreels and with scenes of Bogart and Cagney in the trenches of World War I. Bogart, nasty and aggressive, enjoys killing Germans and becomes a bootlegger after the war. The decent Cagney, who can't get a job, also joins a gang and drifts into crime. Bogart reappears later on as a boat captain (one of his most congenial roles) who delivers contraband whiskey and is robbed by Cagney. They decide to become partners (a fatal pact), Bogart bringing the booze in by sea, Cagney looking after the distribution. The greedy Bogart once again tries to betray Cagney, who discovers the plot and shoots a rival gangster in a spaghetti-house killing. He then returns to kill Bogart, whose body trembles and fingers twitch as in *Angels with Dirty Faces.* Cagney, in a famous death scene, tries to shoot his way through Bogart's gunmen. Seeking sanctuary, he's killed as he stumbles up the steps of a church. A lady friend bitterly pronounces his epitaph: "He used to be a big shot."

The romantic scenes with the simpering songbird Priscilla Lane, who is loved by Cagney but marries a good lawyer, nearly wreck a promising movie. Bogart supplies the wisecracking lines and corrosive comments that undermine the sentimental strain and inject some gritty reality into the picture. Indifferent to the high mortality rate of his colleagues, he continues to play cards when he hears that Cagney's buddy has been murdered. When let down by Cagney, he ironically complains: "My feelings is gettin' hoit." The low-life novelist James Farrell noted the weaknesses of the movie: "There was a little bit of falseness in the picture . . . the boy scout lawyer. . . . Certain of the values brought out were—well, the old stuff. The home life of the young lawyer, the motto that crime does not pay." But he admired Cagney's acting and wanted to write a screenplay for him.

The Return of Doctor X (1939)—an allusion to a Warners horror film of 1932—is, like *Stand-In,* campy and quite funny. The sharp-eyed Jack Warner, concerned as always with efficient production, thought it was just another "B" movie. When the director Vincent Sherman tried to film with care, Warner thought he was being too arty and ordered him to speed things up. "The first day of Sherman as a director," Warner told the producer Bryan Foy, "he took a 45-second take ten times. If he does this again he won't be on the picture any longer. I will not stand for over three takes and they will have to be good enough."

In this grisly film Bogart, a hollow-cheeked, languid vampire with a fiendish grin, has been executed, buried and brought back from the dead. He plays a mad scientist, puttering around with coils of wire and cylinders of glass that bubble over with vile liquids. (Warners' publicity department boasted that the picture had used $17,000 worth of hospital equipment and lab apparatus.) Made up in a white mime-mask, with dark lips to emphasize his ghastly pallor, Bogart wears a glittering pince-nez and speaks in a sepulchral voice. Electrocution has left him with a white-streaked, two-tone crew cut, which makes him look like a skunk. Instead of the Scottie in *Stand-In,* he carries a white rabbit in his paralyzed hand, and strokes the portable blood bank to get some animal warmth and sustain his second life.

In the ghoulish graveyard scene the keeper, who never gets lonely in his job, says the corpses "are all my friends." Wayne Morris, passing Bogart in the cemetery, asks: "Doesn't he look just like the man who was electrocuted a few months ago?" When he opens the empty grave and confirms his theory, the keeper exclaims: "I've been robbed!" Rosemary Lane escapes Bogart's clutches just in time to keep the blood circulating in her *own* veins. Recalling his unusual part, originally intended for Bela Lugosi, Bogart said: "I was this doctor, brought back to life, and the only thing that nourished this poor bastard was blood. If it had been Jack Warner's blood maybe I wouldn't have minded as much."[7]

Invisible Stripes was based on the memoirs of Warden Lewis E. Lawes of Sing Sing, which Warners bought for $12,500. George Raft, Jane Bryan and William Holden (who had just become a star in *Golden Boy,* 1939) got top billing. Bogart, who had a much smaller role, appeared under the title with Flora Robson. Raft earned $50,000, Bogart $10,000 and Holden $2,500. The filming did not go smoothly. Jane Bryan, marooned on Catalina Island during a storm on a Sunday, could not get back the following day. The director, Lloyd Bacon, also had problems with Raft, who had close connections with "Bugsy" Siegel and was sensitive about his public image. Bacon told Warner that "Raft was upsetting Humphrey Bogart, William Holden and the other actors by changing his lines so that he would appear less hard-bitten." Instead of removing the troublesome actor from the set, Warner thought of "killing Raft off early by having a prison guard knock him down a flight of steps." Threatened with premature death, Raft obediently fell into line.

The title refers to the way prison marks a convict for life. It suggests the difficulty of rehabilitation and expresses sympathy for prisoners who try to reform. But the trite melodrama is a compendium of all the clichés in Warners' crime films of the 1930s. There is the long-timer in prison who says: "I'll still be here when you come back"; the con who tries to go straight after his release and the one who goes straight into crime; the good younger man who is corrupted by the gang; a final shootout, after a series of robberies, in which Raft and Bogart are killed; and a reunion of Holden with his girl.

The movie has neither a mob tart nor a redemptive girl for Bogart. Once more he plays the cynical crook and jailbird who gets good guys like Holden into trouble. Disillusioned and fatalistic as always, he says, just before the final crossfire: "I ain't got no chance. But I ain't got no love for the hot seat." His characteristic last words (always important in crime movies) are: "This is it, I guess, and it's okay with me. You can't live forever." Though the plot demands that the vicious crook must die, his offhanded insouciance wins the sympathy of the audience. By 1939 Bogart, thoroughly fed up with these unrewarding roles, could act them blindfolded. But he still had to run through a few more before he could break out of Warners prison.

While playing these gangster parts, Bogart formed a close friendship with the real-life con-man and restaurateur "Prince Mike Romanoff." The pint-sized, jug-eared Romanoff, five feet five inches tall, always wore dapper clothes. He had an Oxford accent, leathery complexion, thin moustache, bulbous nose and incongruous crew cut. Charming and witty, an amusing charlatan and consummate actor (who played bit parts in a number of films), he insulted his customers and ate at a table with his pet dogs. A total fraud himself, he was an infallible authority on phonies and had them all thrown out of his classy joint. Bogart saw him as a living satire on the social pretensions of Hollywood, as "the practitioner of the biggest, longest-lasting, and most successful rib [he'd] ever seen."

Born Harry Gerguson in 1890 in Vilna, Lithuania (then part of the Russian Empire), he came to New York at the age of six and grew up in Brooklyn orphanages. He surfaced in Paris in 1919, where he borrowed his title and name from the Russian Imperial family, and returned to America in 1922. The following year, claiming his academic records had been destroyed in the Russian Revolution, he enrolled briefly at Harvard. In 1927 he moved to Hollywood, which tolerated and even encouraged his pose. The U.S. government spent ten years trying to deport Romanoff, who had done time in prison, as an undesirable alien. In 1938, backed with money from Bogart and others, he opened his expensive and fashionable restaurant on Rodeo Drive in Beverly Hills. Twenty years later, having eluded and outwitted the authorities, he became an American citizen.

When he was not actually filming Bogart loved to lunch at Romanoff's, where he drank, misbehaved and greeted his friend with "Good morning, your royal phoniness." He had the first booth on the left as one entered the restaurant and Spencer Tracy had the next one. They conversed in a friendly fashion, but stayed in their separate booths and maintained their own little fiefdoms. Bogart sometimes ate alone, sometimes had guests. Everyone who knew him stopped to say hello on the way in and he always had a flow of visitors. He loved ham and eggs and often ordered it at both breakfast and lunch. Fond of plain cooking, he was a meat-and-potatoes man who liked hamburgers, roast beef, lamb chops and T-bone steaks.

He came early, before noon, and had a drink with Romanoff at the rear of the premises. He lunched until two, then played an intense game of chess with Romanoff, savoring the silence and the concentrated thought. When they could not get together they would play by phone or mail. Bogart once astonished Romanoff by a series of brilliant telephoned moves — secretly dictated by his master, Herman Steiner. Bogart liked to turn up in a polo shirt and sports jacket, unshaven and without a tie. One day Romanoff joked that he was bringing down the tone of the place and would have to put on a tie or take his business to the Brown Derby. The next day Bogart appeared with a minute, barely discernible metal bow tie slyly pinned to his collar.

In May 1952 Nunnally Johnson reported that Romanoff had renovated his restaurant and moved down Rodeo Drive to the south side of Wilshire Boulevard: "Romanoff's has opened again and it's a beautiful place, except that there are three steps down from the bar into the dining room and it's only a question of time before Bogey and I and many of our friends of like tastes are going to enter la salle [à] manger on our kissers. Something's got to be done about that. I think Mike's pretty worried over the size of the proposition now. The waiters all wear black jackets now, with gold buttons and food spots — very smart effect." Bogart, who found Romanoff a kindred spirit, said: "I like Mike very, very much. He is a very entertaining, interesting and kind man, a civilized citizen. I can meet my friends here. It's kind of like a club."[8]

‹ III ›

In 1940, during his final phase of purgatory at Warner Bros., Bogart made a series of dud films. *Virginia City,* his third and mercifully last western, was shot—partly on location in the Painted Desert of northern Arizona—between late October 1939 and early January 1940. Errol Flynn and Miriam Hopkins earned $50,000, Randolph Scott received $35,000 and Bogart got killed for only $10,000. As usual Jack Warner and Hal Wallis put pressure on Michael Curtiz—though he was one of their most efficient and economical directors—to stop rewriting and reshooting the scenes. His efforts, they felt, increased the cost without improving the film.

The short-tempered, hard-driving Hungarian director (out of his element, like Bogart, in a western) also had difficulties with the leading lady. On December 16 the unit manager, trying to play the peacemaker, wrote to headquarters that "it becomes tougher every day to handle Hopkins and Mike Curtiz together, for each show their utter contempt and disregard for the other." The star's inability to ride a horse also inspired a tactful memo to the home office: "Miss Hopkins informed Mr. Shourds [the assistant director] that she is unable to ride a horse today and we are therefore cancelling the Process shot of her and Flynn on horses. This is the time of the month when she may be indisposed for one or two days."

Virginia City proves that no play or film in which Bogart wore a moustache was any good. Dressed once again in villainous black, he plays a half-breed outlaw with a Mexican accent that was no better than his Irish brogue in *Dark Victory.* The plot concerns an attempt to ship gold from a mining town in Nevada to support the tottering Confederacy during the Civil War. Scott arranges the shipment, Flynn stops it, Bogart tries to steal it. The best scene focuses on the stunt man, who leaps from one coach horse to another, falls between them, drops to the ground, catches the axle and pulls himself up. As with *The Oklahoma Kid,* the publicity department arranged a lavish premiere, this time in Nevada, which "attracted the governors of six sovereign states of the Union; and thousands of un-Western visitors from all over the land [who] turned Virginia City into an inferno of cowboy suits, ten-gallon hats, and joy unconfined."[9] Bogart must have wondered what the hell he was doing there.

They Drive By Night, shot in five weeks in April and May 1940, was Bogart's second and last movie with George Raft. Raft began as a professional ballroom dancer, achieved fame as the gangster in *Scarface* (1932) and moved from Paramount to Warners in 1939. His career went into a steep decline as Bogart's ascended and his last film, ironically enough, was *The Man With Bogart's Face* (1980). But in *They Drive By Night* Bogart, who earned $11,200, has fourth billing and Raft, the top star, wins Ann Sheridan.

In the days before Italy became America's wartime enemy, Bogart and Raft play good Italian brothers, Joe and Paul Fabrini. Exploited by their boss, they dream of having their own trucks. Bogart not only loses his arm in a crash, but also has a boring wife who wants to have a baby. Raft, hired as the manager of a trucking company, is pursued by the boss's passionate, deranged and sexually predatory wife, played by Ida Lupino. Spurned by Raft, Lupino accuses him of asphyxiating her buffoonish husband. But — in a spectacular scene that made her a star and got her a handsome new contract at Warners — she cracks up on the witness stand and confesses her guilt. This wobbling picture starts off as a social protest documentary, becomes an obvious murder mystery and lapses into a capitalistic success story as Raft starts his own trucking firm.

Raoul Walsh, the one-eyed director known for his action films, recorded (as Davis and Cagney had done) Bogart's extreme disgust with the wretched movies he had made during the last four years. Underpaid and unappreciated, "Bogey the Beefer" bitched about the difficult conditions and long hours: "They get you up before daybreak and work your ass off all day until sundown. In the theater I went to work at eight in the evening and was through by eleven; had all the rest of the night and the next day to play and catch up with my drinking. Working in pictures is for the birds." Adopting a hedonistic pose, he seemed to complain about the hard work, but he really resented the pointless parts he was forced to play.

Bogart took some of his anger and bitterness out on his fellow actors. Raft had more clout than Bogart in the studio, and refused to work with him because of Bogart's cutting comments about his performance. In 1941, scheduled to appear with Raft in Mark Hellinger's *Manpower,* Bogart was bumped from the film and replaced by Edward G. Robinson. This setback to his career (though partly self-induced) inspired Bogart's long telegram of March 6, 1941 to Hal Wallis. Assuming the posture of an aggrieved and powerless employee, Bogart portrayed himself as a solid company man who needed protection:

> I am sending you this wire because I am extremely upset and
> wanted you to know the true facts, and you can take my word
> for it that any statements to the contrary are untrue. . . . I have
> never had anything but the very finest feeling of friendship for

George. I understand he has refused to make the picture if I
am in it. . . . I tried to get George to tell me this morning what
he was angry about and what I was supposed to have said but
he wouldn't tell me. I feel very much hurt by this because it's
the second time I've been kept out of a good picture and a
good part because of an actor's refusing to work with me. . . .
I could see no way to protect myself against these insinuations
and accusations and I think it's up to the company to protect
me inasmuch as we are all concerned in the business of making
good motion pictures.

In response, Warners not only kept him out of a good film, but also
tried to force him into a poor one. "For many, many years on the Warner
Bros. lot," wrote Vincent Sherman, "he was considered nothing more than
a heavy who would never be able to play anything else but that." But
Bogart did not want to make any more bad pictures. On March 17,
recalling his dreadful westerns, he turned down *Bad Men of Missouri*
(which Warners made in 1941 with Dennis Morgan) and bitterly told
Steve Trilling: "Are you kidding? This is certainly rubbing it in. Since
Lupino and Raft are casting pictures, maybe I can." Warners retaliated
the next day by suspending him. "Bogart attempted to come back April
2nd," their lawyer told Jack Warner, "but we continued his suspension
until the time it will take Dennis Morgan to finish the picture."[10]

Bogart's situation at Warners, though scarcely enviable, was not quite
as bad as he claimed. In a frequently quoted but exaggerated statement
he maintained that "in my first 34 films I was shot in 12, electrocuted or
hanged in eight, and was a jailbird in nine." David Niven seemed to
confirm this by repeating that "in the next four years [1937–40] he was
forced to pump out no less than twenty-nine gangster films, in each of
which he played a carbon copy of Duke Mantee." Though Bogart's poor
films tend to blur into one another, he actually appeared in thirty-six
pictures between *Three on a Match* (1932) and *The Big Shot* (1942).
Though he had a high mortality rate, he was in fact arrested or killed in
only twenty-two (not twenty-nine) of these movies. There was but one
execution, and he was actually reformed and released in two of them.
Despite Niven's assertion, he played positive roles in twelve other pictures.[11]

Resentful of being typecast as an ill-fated gangster, Bogart said: "I
played more scenes writhing around on the floor than I did standing up.
My principal problem was finding new ways to say 'Aaagh' and different
ways of spitting blood. . . . I made so many pictures like [*Racket Busters*]

I used to get the titles mixed up. People would ask me what I was working on, and I'd have to think about what it was called." It *seemed* that Bogart always played the criminal because that's what he did best, most frequently and most memorably. The trouble was not in the kind of parts he was given, but in the inferior quality of most of his 1930s movies. He first achieved fame as a gangster in *The Petrified Forest*, would reach the second stage of his climb to stardom as a criminal in *High Sierra* and play a similar role at the very end of his career in *The Desperate Hours*.

Bogart was not physically tough and never actually won a fight with anybody. He once remarked: "I could use a foot more in height and 50 more pounds and fifteen years off my age and then God help all you bastards." It amused him, however, to play a hard, sardonic guy, off screen as well as on, and he struggled to live up to his film persona in real life. Belligerent drunks would come up to him in bars and try to impress their girls by challenging him to a fight, and Bogart often found himself in a sticky situation. Richard Brooks described a typical confrontation:

> "What are you, a tough guy?" Ratchek grasped Taggart's arm. Taggart tried to pull loose, realizing he was about to get into trouble.
> "You got the wrong fella. I'm no tough guy."
> "Sure you are. You're the tough *Mr.* Taggart, the brave *Mr.* Taggart, the famous *Mr.* Taggart."
> "You've been seeing too many movies, friend."
> "Some tough guy. Go ahead, do something tough."[12]

Sometimes, when *he* was drunk, his desire to play the part and live up to expectations led to reckless bravado. One night at a party he met a man who chewed glass in a circus. Taking up the challenge and the bet, he smashed a glass, chewed the pieces and tried to swallow. But he could not quite get the rough bits down. As he coughed them up, blood gushed out of his torn mouth and lips. "The trouble with Bogart," said the restaurateur Dave Chasen, "is that he thinks he's Bogart." But, conscious of his gentlemanly background as well as his tough-guy image, he sued *Rave* magazine for writing that he behaved like "a prize oaf and boor."

Despite the poor quality of his pictures, Bogart appeared with the most popular Warners actors: Robinson, Cagney, Raft and Flynn, and with some of their best leading ladies: Blondell, Sheridan, Davis and Lupino. He acted in western, adventure, horror, detective, spy, war, murder, boxing and comic films. He would have been very good in musicals like *Guys and Dolls* and fascinating as Shakespeare's *Richard III*. The problem was that his few good pictures were invariably followed by many bad ones. If a movie succeeded, Warners would repeat the formula and churn out "great batches of musical, newspaper, gangster, historical and war films . . . until each vogue was done to exhaustion." Bogart justly complained of his repetitive roles and said that "half my career has been spent in a horizontal position—having been beaten up, shot, stabbed or all three at once." He also used the press and fan magazines to voice his complaints. In the *New York Times* he mocked the absurd plots and rigid conventions that made bad guys poor marksmen who could never kill the heroes: "I always have a gun in my hand and I'm always shooting, but I never hit anybody. Sometimes they let me wing a small fry, but my bullets never get the big shot."[13]

Though the physically unappealing Edward G. Robinson had a mob girl to keep him happy in all five pictures he made with Bogart (*Bullets or Ballots, Kid Galahad, The Amazing Dr. Clitterhouse, Brother Orchid* and *Key Largo*), Bogart, who was much more attractive, acerbically remarked: "I always wound up dead and never got the girl. A gangster is never allowed to have any sex life." He managed to get the girl in very early films and was married in two of them, but his amorous record in the 1930s was not good. He is rejected by Bette Davis in *Dark Victory* and drinks the heroine's blood in *The Return of Doctor X.* He is killed by his girl in *Midnight* and is shot by the police before he can escape with Ida Lupino in *High Sierra.* In *The Maltese Falcon* he falls in love with Mary Astor, but must send her to jail for murder.

Bogart made a lot of money for Warners but was grossly underpaid until he signed his new and lucrative contract with them in 1947. Though he fought for more pay in the early 1940s, he was willing to work for less money if he found an appealing part. "I'm sick to death of being a one-dimensional character," he said in 1942. "I'm just a guy in a tight suit and a snap-brim hat. I have no function except to carry the plot and get killed in the end to prove that virtue is triumphant. . . . I would like to play . . . a role that you could get the feel of and actually do something with." The pattern of refusing the poor parts and losing the good ones, partly as punishment by Warner Bros., continued into the next decade. In 1940, after Warners had refused to lend him to Hal Roach and United Artists to make a Steinbeck film, Bogart wrote in *Screen Book:* "When producers steer me out of a sweet picture, as they did when I had an offer to do *Of Mice and Men,* I'm not too shy to stand up and beef about it." The following year, trying to secure the lead in a film based on Irwin Shaw's 1939 play about gangsters who move in and terrorize an innocent Brooklyn family (the same role he would later act in *The Desperate Hours*), he wrote Jack Warner: "It seems to me that I am the logical person on the lot to play *Gentle People.* I would be greatly disappointed if I didn't get it. I would like very much to talk to you about it."[14] But John Garfield got the lead in *Gentle People,* renamed *Out of the Fog* (1941), and Bogart continued to waste his talent in trashy pictures.

During his exhausting marital struggle with Methot and his professional wrangles with Jack Warner, Bogart also had serious problems with what Mayo called his "crazy family." In 1935, after his father's death and sister's divorce, Maud and Pat followed him out to Hollywood and took an apartment near Shoreham Road. Pat, who had several nervous break-downs, wandered around Sunset Boulevard in her nightgown and was picked up by the police. Bogart knew how to handle her, and was kind, patient and gentle with both his sister and his mother.

Maud later moved to the Château Marmont hotel, near Horn Avenue on Sunset Boulevard. Those acquainted with the aging grande dame, who seemed to speak with a New England accent, found her charming, gracious and pleasant. She was also "sickly sweet" and voiced platitudes like "we must all be kind to each other." Now extremely proud of her son's success, she remarked: "What an adorable boy he was—sweet and darling. I don't know why he has to play all those dreadful parts." One of his friends, strolling with her in Bogart's garden during a party for James Thurber, discovered that Maud had a mad streak. When she saw a butterfly, Maud grabbed the guest by the throat and screamed: "I can't stand flying things! I'm afraid of things that fly!"[15] On November 22, 1940, after slipping into a coma, Maud died of cancer at the age of seventy-five. She was buried, as her son would be, in Forest Lawn cemetery.

◆ 6 ◆

John Huston and
The Maltese Falcon
1941-1942

⟨ I ⟩

JOHN HUSTON had written the script for *The Amazing Dr. Clitterhouse*, but did not actually meet Bogart until the filming of Huston's *High Sierra*. He soon became Bogart's closest friend, and would direct five of his best films: *The Maltese Falcon, Across the Pacific, The Treasure of the Sierra Madre, The African Queen* and *Beat the Devil*. Huston, an incorrigible risk-taker, was born in Nevada, Missouri, a town his grandfather was supposed to have won in a poker game. The son of the famous stage and film actor Walter Huston (who would appear in two films with Bogart), John had a weak heart and had been an invalid in childhood. But he was also a man of wide interests, restless energy and fierce appetites. He had been a teenage boxing champion, had served in the Mexican cavalry, become an actor and playwright on Broadway, and studied painting in Paris. He was a fisherman, big game hunter and art collector, a superb actor, writer and director, and would make first-rate documentaries under fire during World War II. A persuasive, charismatic charmer, he impressed studio executives and won the affection of actors by giving them a free hand. Tall and rugged, courtly and eloquent, gambler and raconteur, he had a passion for horses, married five times and had many mistresses.

The Warners producer Henry Blanke thought Huston's second wife, Lesley Black, whom he had married in 1937, was a dominant influence on his artistic development. In his youth, Blanke said, John was "just a drunken boy; hopelessly immature. You'd see him at every party, wearing bangs, with a monkey on his shoulder. Charming. Very talented but without an ounce of discipline in his makeup." Lesley "set standards and incentives which brought his abilities into focus."

Huston had always wanted to direct a movie from horseback, and his wild, freewheeling films had more *hauteur* than *auteur*. His great theme was the tremendous struggle to achieve the impossible and the loss of the goal at the moment of triumph. Arthur Miller, who worked with Huston on *The Misfits* (1961), found him a macho figure with a sunken chest, expert with horses, full of life and adventurous stories, sensitive as well as brutal. He was a good writer, appreciated literary value and put more emphasis on the composition of scenes than on acting. Miller admired Huston and ranked him high as a director. Truman Capote, who wrote *Beat the Devil* with Huston, emphasized the ruthless side of his personality: the "riverboat gambler's suavity overlaid with roughneck buffooning, the hearty mirthless laughter that rises toward but never reaches his warmly crinkled and ungentle eyes, eyes as bored as sunbathing lizards."[1]

Huston, like the writer Eric Hatch, had deep temperamental affinities with Bogart. Just as Bogart recalled Maud's grudging praise after his naval service and harsh criticism of his acting on Broadway, so Huston confessed: "Nothing I ever did pleased my mother." Both men were rebellious and iconoclastic, with a cruel, sometimes sadistic streak. Consummate professionals in their work, both were restless and easily bored. A few years younger than Bogart, Huston called everyone "kid." Like Bogart, he was a good listener as well as a witty and stimulating conversationalist. They liked to stir things up and amused each other with a teasing rivalry. When a secretary praised Bogart's sex appeal, he told Huston: "I yield to no man in the animal magnetism field." The actress Evelyn Keyes, Huston's third wife, recalled that both men indulged in childish pranks and acted like a couple of schoolboys. They often got drunk together, and once played football with a precious Ming vase.

Bogart, who admired Huston's creativity and his exciting, quixotic character, observed: "Risk, action, and making the best use of what's around is what makes him tick. When he isn't actually on the set, he sees his surroundings as a forest of windmills, bottles, women, racehorses, elephants and oxen, noblemen and bums." He also said that John was "one of the few sons of a famous father who equalled if not surpassed his old man's successes" and praised him as "the only real genius in Hollywood, a real poet." But Bogart, who liked to see a job completed, was also aware of Huston's limitations and his reluctance, once he had realized his artistic vision, to finish his films: "He's murder to work with during the last three weeks of shooting. Always restless, wanting to quit for some new idea."[2]

Thus far, William Brady and Leslie Howard had been Bogart's greatest benefactors. After he met Huston, his career was inadvertently advanced at Warner Bros. by George Raft. Bogart's rival, though not very bright, was too cocky to seek good advice and too concerned about his public image. A notoriously poor judge of scripts, despite many years in the business, Raft turned down a number of important roles that eventually went to Bogart. Raft's refusals, in fact, built Bogart's career and allowed him to break through to stardom in 1941. Sam Jaffe called Raft "an illiterate, uneducated, ordinary man." In a letter of August 1941 to Warners' Steve Trilling, Jaffe argued that the studio ought to develop Bogart's career and enable him to use his talent instead of assigning him to a random series of parts that other actors didn't want: "A story," Jaffe insisted, "should be prepared for which they have Bogart in mind and no other actor because it seems that for the past year he's practically pinch-hitted for Raft and been kicked around from pillar to post."

Raft, a natural heavy who was sensitive about his underworld connections and always wanted to play the good guy, first turned down *Dead End* —Bogart's best part in the late 1930s—because he did not like the vicious character of Baby Face Martin. He refused the inconsequential gangster-in-a-boarding-house picture *It All Came True* (1940) and the gangster-on-the-run film *High Sierra* (1941) because he disliked criminal roles. Paul Muni refused *High Sierra* because it had first been offered to Raft, and the choice part was also rejected by Cagney, Robinson and John Garfield. After Warners had run through its entire roster of tough guys, Bogart—keen to work with Huston, the producer Mark Hellinger and the director Raoul Walsh—got the role by default.

When an interviewer asked W. R. Burnett, co-author of the screenplay, if Bogart got the part because "Raft didn't want to die at the end of another picture," Burnett said: "That's bullshit. Bogie talked Raft out of it and got the part himself." Bogie could not have talked Raft and all the other actors out of a role they really wanted. But, as with *The Petrified Forest,* he eagerly went after the lead in *High Sierra.* In May 1940, three months before shooting began, he showed better judgment than Raft by writing Hal Wallis: "You told me once to let you know when I found a part I wanted. A few weeks ago I left a note for you concerning *High Sierra.* I never received an answer so I'm bringing it up again as I understand there is some doubt about Muni doing it."

Raft continued his passive patronage, despite the success of *High Sierra,* by rejecting more promising parts. He turned down *The Maltese Falcon* (1941), Huston's debut as a director, because he did not want to appear in a movie made by an inexperienced young man. Though Huston was one of the few directors who could have teased a decent performance out of him, Raft considered himself too good for what he thought was a cheap "B" picture. Expressing disdain for his rival, he also told Jack Warner: "I was afraid the studio would put me into parts that Humphrey Bogart should play and you told me that I would never have to play a Humphrey Bogart part."[3] Raft groped blindly into the early 1940s, making commonplace pictures like *Manpower* (1941), *Broadway* (1942) and *Background to Danger* (1943). Bogart had the brains and talent to take the parts that Raft turned down and transform them into something greater than anyone had ever imagined.

< **II** >

HUSTON ADMIRED Burnett's novel *High Sierra* and wrote the screenplay with him. In March 1940, while working on the script, he told Wallis that he wanted the film to remain faithful to the book and transcend the mediocre gangster melodrama: "It would be very easy for this to be made into the conventional gangster picture, which is exactly what it should not be. With the exception of *Little Caesar,* all of Burnett has suffered sadly in screen translation." The writer John Wexley agreed in a memo to Wallis that if the story were "emasculated," it would be just another gangster movie, with "Sierras instead of skyscrapers" in the background. Huston wanted to emphasize "the strange sense of inevitability that comes with our deepening understanding of his characters and the forces that motivate them."

Burnett and Huston, despite their different modes of operation, were also kindred spirits. "I never had so much fun in my life, John and I working together," Burnett recalled. "We got along fine. But we didn't work well together, because I work fast on the typewriter and he dictates. He likes to sit down and completely talk out a scene, which would take a day and wear me out." He was also extremely pleased, despite twenty-seven pages of objections from the Production Code censors, that they had managed to evade some moral restrictions: "we had a girl living with two guys and we got away with it — in 1940!" Asked if he took credit for creating the part that made Bogart a star, Burnett replied that Bogart's potential had been there since *The Petrified Forest:* "Bogart needed a *break.* He had the makings of a star, and Warners didn't know what to do with him. And he wound up in B pictures. . . . Bogart was ready for the part and the part suited him. . . . For once I got something on the screen pretty much as I saw it."[4]

High Sierra was made in August and September 1940. The final scenes were shot on location at Big Bear Lake, east of Los Angeles, in the San Bernardino mountains. The film cost $455,000, of which Lupino got $12,000 and Bogart $11,200. When night shots were required, he worked from 9 to 11:30 A.M. and then for almost twelve more hours, from 2 in the afternoon until 1:30 the next morning.

The director Raoul Walsh had made three earlier Bogart films, including *The Roaring Twenties.* Now in his fifties, he had been a seaman and ranch-hand, played John Wilkes Booth in Griffith's *The Birth of a Nation* and directed scores of silent films. He had lost an eye when a jackrabbit crashed through his windshield in Arizona, and wore a black patch. A master of action pictures, he understood the forces of nature and was skilled at filming cowboys, criminals and war heroes in a natural landscape. He had recorded Bogart's complaints while making *They Drive By Night,* and also "remembered the actor grousing continually about the long hours moviemaking required in contrast with the stage. And about the early morning calls. And about the bad food on location. And, of course, about the [mediocre] roles." When, on location, Walsh withheld Bogart's lunch as a joke, the actor exclaimed: "That bastard Jack Warner, eating in his private dining room, sinking his puss into a filet mignon with asparagus and trimmings and such and I'm up here starving to death. What a lousy business."

The fifteen-year-old Joan Leslie, who played Velma, took her screen test for *High Sierra* with Walsh and Bogart. To protect her, Walsh forbade all rough talk on the set. While making the film she spoke to Bogart about the scenes, the set and the studio. He would reassure her by putting his hand on hers and kindly saying: "that was a good take." Leslie once heard someone warn, "Look out, Mayo's on the lot," which made Bogart tense, nervous and upset.[5]

The sharp-tongued Bogart had several run-ins with Ida Lupino, who played the sympathetic and loyal Marie, a very different role from the snarling vixen in *They Drive By Night.* He disliked aggressive women, especially those who earned more money and had more power than he did, and they got off to an edgy start. Lupino recalled: "I have a way of kidding with a straight face; so has Bogey. Neither of us recognized the trait in the other. Each of us thought the other was being nasty, and we were both offended." Bogart was so openly critical of her performance that Lupino (like George Raft) made Jack Warner promise that she would never have to work with him again. In her self-enhancing recollection of their films together, she didn't mention that she had blackballed Bogart and fondly said: "We became great, great friends. He was quite a guy."

When the picture was finished, Jack Warner, referring to Lupino's fine crack-up scene in her previous film, wrote Wallis: "Don't you think we ought to reverse the billing on *High Sierra,* and instead of billing Bogart first, bill Lupino first? Lupino has had a great deal of publicity on the strength of *They Drive By Night,* whereas Bogart has been playing the leads in a lot of 'B' pictures, and this fact might mitigate [i.e., militate] against the success of *High Sierra.* The billing has just gone through with Bogart's name first, and I think we should reverse it." The billing was in fact reversed, which enraged Bogart and made him even more hostile to both Lupino and Warner.

Bogart's role gave him more scope than *The Petrified Forest. High Sierra* was more realistic and avoided the high-minded palaver of the earlier film. During the latter part of the picture, he is alone rather than part of a gang. Instead of arriving at the roadside café after committing his crimes, he pulls off two robberies in the course of the film. He is a more sympathetic figure, involved with two women instead of waiting for one who never appears. He lives in a city, at a mountain lake and in the high sierras instead of being confined to a stage-set desert café.

Bogart's Roy Earle once again "incorporated elements of [John Dillinger's] life and legend—his folk-hero status, his supposed sex appeal, his skill as a master bank robber, his unwarranted reputation as a 'mad-dog' killer." Dillinger was not a member of a mob but a kind of western bandit, fighting, like the heroic outlaws of the American frontier, against the corrupt economic system. Earle's crimes are committed in towns and cities. He smiles when paroled from a life sentence, and immediately goes to a park to breathe fresh air and to "make sure that the grass is still green and the trees are still growin'." While driving west, he revisits his boyhood farm in Indiana. He always gets into trouble when he leaves rural settings, and finally seeks refuge in the mountains.

Bogart's character in *High Sierra* is made emotionally complex and credible (despite trite aspects of the plot) by his feeling for nature, his unlucky attachment to his dog Pard, his friendships with men and his hopeless love for two women. Unlike the earlier, one-dimensional gangsters, Earle is a criminal with integrity. Though he comes from a poor background and bitterly unhappy family, he's "never let nobody down." He helps unfortunate outcasts, is loyal to his friends and has a code of honor. Huston eloquently described how Bogart realized his role: "Bogie was a medium-sized man, not particularly impressive offscreen, but something happened when he was playing the right part. Those lights and shadows composed themselves into another, nobler personality: heroic, as in *High Sierra.*"[6]

"Mad Dog" Earle's fate has tragic dimensions. Once sprung from prison, he cannot leave the life of crime and must commit another robbery to pay back the dying boss who fixed his pardon. When he cases the posh resort hotel before the jewel robbery, with his close-cropped convict's haircut, he takes off his jacket and tie and makes a feeble attempt to fit in to the informal atmosphere by carrying a tennis racquet (an allusion to Bogart's youthful roles on stage).

Instead of being drawn to the sexy "dance-hall girl" Marie, who has been rescued and taken up to the mountains by his gang, and who falls in love with him, he is drawn to the vapid Velma, who he hopes will reform him and enable him to lead a normal life. Attached to and momentarily in harmony with nature, Earle gets close to Velma as they gaze at the stars, which he learned about in prison and which suggest the vast distance between his aspirations and his fate. In an unusually tender, even lyrical moment, Earle tries to close this gulf and express his love for Velma. Holding her hand, he says that at night sometimes when you look at the stars you "can feel the motion of the earth. Just like a little ball turning through the night, with us hanging on to it."

In an unusual reversal of conventional roles, the "good" girl is treacherous, the "bad" girl loyal. Earle pays for the operation on Velma's clubfoot, inadvertently transforming her from a crippled outcast into a bourgeois bitch. After her recovery, she adopts pretentious middle-class values and jilts her benefactor for a more attractive but superficial suitor. When Earle tries to leave Marie so he can carry out his dangerous job alone, she alludes to the angelic girl in *Uncle Tom's Cabin* and bitterly asks: "Are you trying to ditch me on account of that Little Eva from the corn belt?"

While waiting to be paid for the stolen jewels, he gives all his cash to Lupino and sends her out of danger. But he runs out of gas and has to commit a second robbery. A single fugitive, pursued by a huge police operation, he heads for the mountains—the rural equivalent of the tenement roof in *Dead End*. After a high-octane car chase he encounters a road block, abandons his car and, followed by swarms of motorcycles, takes to the hills on foot. He can never come down again and will never be free till he's dead. Exposed by his all-too-faithful dog, he calls out to his girl, who has followed him into the high sierras. As a radio announcer narrates the fatal events, he's trapped and killed by a marksman with a high-powered telescopic rifle. His ironic epitaph is spoken by the reporter Healey: "Big shot Earle! Well . . . look at him lying there. He ain't much now, is he."[7]

Bogart's performance in *High Sierra*, his last important gangster film, shows his progress from the psychopaths in *The Petrified Forest* and *Dead*

End to a more sympathetic kind of criminal. Bogart's Earle begins as a hardened killer. But he regrets the past, is capable of affection and aspires to a better life. He immediately shows his teeth and his toughness by slapping the face of Jake Kranmer, a treacherous ex-cop who's recently joined the gang. At a gas station he puts his thumbs in his belt and ironically tells Velma's grandpa that he's going "up in the mountains . . . for my health." Self-assured and commanding, he's a man of few words but, unlike Duke Mantee, speaks rapidly and with a half-closed mouth.

When he first meets Lupino at the mountain hideout, he offers her a cigarette — a gesture that expresses rapport — and smokes throughout the movie. After she warns him that Mendoza, their accomplice in the jewel robbery, is unreliable, he stares hard and silently at him and then tells a menacing story. He first wants to get rid of Lupino, who provokes fights in his gang, but establishes intimacy by allowing her to watch him shave and serve his breakfast. With great reluctance, he starts out on a caper with a woman and a dog.

During the jewel robbery Bogart breaks the glass of a cabinet, steals a cigar and pours water from the tray of a trembling waiter before killing a guard who stumbles into the lobby. He's wounded in the gut during an exchange of gunfire with Kranmer, quarrels with Velma's boyfriend and warns the fence: "If I don't get my end I'll come gunnin' for you." When he moves from his gang to solitude, he paces around with his hands in his pockets. He establishes his humanity in the park near the prison, his toughness with Kranmer and his gang, his vulnerability with Velma and compassion with Marie. In *High Sierra* he's more thoughtful and decent, less intense and morbid than in *The Petrified Forest,* and shows, through movement and gesture, that Earle is both killer and trapped human being.

The American reviews of the movie were excellent and Bogart received high praise. *Variety,* noting the complexity of his character, said: "He's properly silent and hard with an underlying tenderness that's incongruous with his ability to kill." The *Kansas City Star* agreed that "the picture brings Humphrey Bogart and Ida Lupino to long deferred and long deserved stardom. . . . Mr. Bogart gives one of the great performances of this dramatic season." Howard Barnes, writing in the *New York Herald-Tribune,* noted that Bogart "is at once savage and sentimental, fatalistic and filled with half-formulated aspirations. . . . A fine actor, he deserves enormous credit for the success of *High Sierra.*" Otis Ferguson, in the *New Republic,* also felt Bogart had done justice to the role and come into his own as an actor. His "conception and rock-bound maintenance of the hard-handed, graying, and bitter ex-con is not only one of the finest projections of character in any story of men in action, but the whole vertebrate structure of this one. . . . Bogart makes it true, for there is not one minute in this picture when the intensity of his presence is not felt."

The one significant dissent came from George Orwell, reviewing films for *Time and Tide,* who was repelled by the characteristic violence of American movies. For Orwell, *High Sierra* represented the extremes of sadism, bully worship and gunplay, repugnantly combined with sentimentality and perverse morality: "Humphrey Bogart is the Big Shot who smashes people in the face with the butt of his pistol and watches fellow gangsters burn to death with the casual comment, 'They were only small town guys,' but is kind to dogs and is supposed to be deeply touching when he is smitten with a 'pure' affection for a crippled girl, who knows nothing of his past. In the end he is killed, but we are evidently expected to sympathise with him and even to admire him."[8]

Orwell ignored the moral complexity that distinguished *High Sierra* from the simplistic morality of Bogart's crime films of the Thirties. The film also aroused the wrath of community groups who felt the movie could have a dangerous influence. In March 1941, two months after the film was released, the Milwaukee Better Films Council objected that "a hardened criminal, who is tender and kind to a lame girl, affectionate to a dog, and understanding and protective in his relations to his moll, is just too fascinating a character to put before our boys from fourteen to twenty."

Like most movie stars in the 1940s, Bogart earned a great deal of extra money from advertising endorsements, including imitation-Bogart cartoon characters, and from appearances on radio and television. In 1941, for example, his film salary was $63,000 but his total income from all other sources came to $105,000. After he had appeared in two notable pictures as a private detective, he posed for a shirt ad, wearing "super-strength Bogart collars." He also endorsed Raleigh cigarettes. After examining the "scientific evidence," he claimed that Raleighs had less nicotine and tar, and were "safer to smoke" than other leading brands.

Warners permitted contract players to keep most of the money they earned from radio and television appearances if they donated part of their fee to Jack Warner's charities. This of course cost Warner nothing and made the studio look good. The actors resented these donations, especially since they were providing the studio with free publicity. In May 1939 Sam Jaffe, trying to diminish the studio's cut, wrote Jack Warner: "It was our understanding that when he gave up half [his fee] on the last three broadcasts that would be all he would be required to donate. Bogart has been very cooperative with personal appearances, on which he has done a great deal of work."

In two fatuous performances on Edgar Bergen's radio program, Bogart played a tough cowboy and a hard guy urging civilians to buy war bonds. He also appeared on Louella Parsons' show, on the Philip Morris Playhouse (pushing even safer cigarettes), on the Theatre Guild of the Air and in dramatized redactions of four films — *Bullets or Ballots* and, later on, *To Have and Have Not, The Treasure of the Sierra Madre* and *The African Queen* — on the Lux Radio Theater. In an all-star musical film, *Thank Your Lucky Stars* (1943), the unshaven Bogart, in a cameo role, parodied his gangster persona and was thrown out of a theater by S. Z. "Cuddles" Sakall, who had played the endearing waiter Carl in *Casablanca*.

Nathaniel Benchley described Bogart's highly successful personal appearance in a Broadway movie theater late in 1940: "His act started in a darkened house while one after another of his death scenes was flashed on the screen. The house lights came up and there he was, lying flat on his face on the stage. He rose, smiled, and said, 'It's a hell of a way to make a living,' then dusted off his hands and went into a brief routine. It was the first time most people had seen the cheerful side of him, and the effect was startling. Hordes of people, the majority of them women, mobbed his dressing-room door."[9] Such evidence of Bogart's sex appeal helped convince Jack Warner that Bogart could also be a romantic hero.

‹ III ›

IN *The Maltese Falcon* (1941), Huston created a new style as well as a new role for Bogart. His first great film has brilliant pace, characters, dialogue and plot. *High Sierra* and *The Maltese Falcon* stress the lonely individual rather than, as in earlier, more conventional films, the gang and the police. The former focuses on a single doomed criminal, the latter on a single private detective. In a perfect fusion of serious drama and sophisticated wit, Bogart gave a performance that was crucial for both his career and the history of *film noir* detective movies.

The novel by Dashiell Hammett was first published in the pulp magazine *Black Mask* in 1929 and became a best-seller the following year. Warners bought the movie rights for $8,500 in 1930 and got its money's worth by making three versions during the next decade. In the pre–Production Code first version, which had the same title as the novel, Spade forces Brigid to undress in front of him (but off-camera) in order to see if she has stolen a thousand-dollar bill. The second version, called *Satan Met a Lady* (1936), was a semi-comic melodrama that deviates from

Hammett and portrays the detective as roguish, flamboyant and showy. Dissatisfied with the exotic resonance of the original title, Jack Warner wanted the third version, written and directed by John Huston, to be called *The Gent from Frisco.*

The key to Huston's success with *The Maltese Falcon,* as with *High Sierra,* was his extraordinary fidelity to the original. The dialogue, style, action and ambience were taken straight out of Hammett's novel, which, as Edmund Wilson said of Steinbeck's *Grapes of Wrath,* poured "on to the screen as easily as if it had been written in the studios." Huston said that he "'took two copies of the book, tore each page and just pasted it together on script pages and edited it a little.'. . . [He then] gave the novel to the secretary and told her to recopy the text, but to break it down routinely into script format with the usual scene numbers and shot descriptions." Huston also described his unusual method, which provided a salutary contrast to the typically pointless revisions by an army of authors: "*The Maltese Falcon* was done in a very short time, because it was based on a very fine book and there was very little for me to invent. It was a matter of sticking to the ideas of the book, of making a film out of a book. . . . I tried to transpose Dashiell Hammett's highly individual prose style into camera terms—i.e., sharp photography, geographically exact camera movements, striking, if not shocking, setups."[10]

In June 1941, just before shooting began, George Raft, whose prose was as bad as his acting, told Jack Warner: "As you know, I strongly feel that *The Maltese Falcon,* which you want me to do, is not an important picture and, in this connection, I must remind you again, before I signed the new contract with you, you promised me that you would not require me to perform in anything but important pictures." Raft was convinced that the third version of the movie would be as bad as the previous ones. Bogart was as eager to play Sam Spade as Raft was to avoid it.

Meticulously planned by Huston, the picture was shot in thirty-four days (including a full day's rehearsal for the long scene in Gutman's apartment, when the characters gather to get the falcon) in June and July 1941. It cost only $327,000—$54 under budget. To create the statue of the fabulous bird, the art department made a sketch, the plaster shop cast a mold and turned out six hollow reproductions, and the paint shop sprayed them with black enamel—at a cost of $114 each. After the shooting of the blaze aboard *La Paloma,* the studio kept two firemen in the boat in case the sparks flared up at night.

The Maltese Falcon, like *Casablanca,* combines perfect casting and collaborative acting. Huston and the leading players were all good friends and morale on the set was extremely high. Sydney Greenstreet, who weighed as much as 360 pounds, played Kasper Gutman, described by Hammett as "flabbily fat with bulbous pink cheeks and lips and chins and neck, with a great soft egg of a belly that was all his torso, and pendant cones for arms and legs." Born in England and twenty years older than Bogart, the massive Greenstreet had been a tea planter in Ceylon and had acted on stage in London and in America since 1902. Somewhat nervous during the shooting of his first film, he asked Miss Astor, "Mary dear, hold my hand, tell me I won't make an ass of meself!"[11] He played an urbane, sybaritic, attractive villain, and was particularly good in scenes with Peter Lorre.

Lorre, born in Hungary in 1904 (a year later than the birthdate on Joel Cairo's Greek passport, which Sam Spade inspects in the movie), had a distinguished career in the German theater. After a painful gallbladder operation in the late 1920s, he became (like Bogart's father) a morphine addict — a problem that plagued him for the rest of his life. Lorre, who could launch into alarming spasms of fury and fear, had achieved fame as the psychotic child murderer in Fritz Lang's German film classic *M* (1931). He had come to America in 1934 and still had a strong central European accent. He said "gen-oo-ine" and "d" instead of "th," and the studio urged him to enunciate more clearly so that he could be understood. Yet his strange accent and high nasal voice provide a wonderful contrast to Greenstreet's plummy tones. Huston considered him "one of the finest and most subtle actors I have ever worked with. Beneath that air of innocence he used to such effect, one sensed a Faustian worldliness." Lorre became a close friend of Bogart and made four more films with him, including *Casablanca* and *Beat the Devil*. He later attributed the success of *The Maltese Falcon* to the unusual quality of the acting: "*The Maltese Falcon* was one of my happiest memories, a very nostalgic one, because for a few years we had a sort of stock company, an ensemble there at Warner Bros. . . . In each one of those people . . . there is one quality in common, that is quite a hard quality to come by, it's something you can't teach, and that is to switch an audience from laughter to seriousness."

Mary Astor, the leading lady, had been a child star, acted while still a teenager in films with John Barrymore and Douglas Fairbanks, and appeared with Walter Huston in *Dodsworth* (1936). A stormy love affair with Barrymore, the death of her first husband (the brother of Howard Hawks) in a plane crash, three divorces, the scurrilous publication in 1936 of her personal diary, describing in detail her secret affair with the playwright George S. Kaufman, as well as her alcoholism and suicide attempts, had filled the Hollywood gossip columns and nearly ruined her career. But these lurid events made her perfect for the role of the elegant and sophisticated deceiver, Brigid O'Shaughnessy. While making *The Maltese Falcon,* Astor also had an affair with John Huston.

The producers, Hal Wallis and Henry Blanke, thought Astor was originally too coy and ladylike when lying to Bogart in their opening scene. The beginning of the film, when she first enters his office, had to be reshot to make the story clearer. Huston made her run around the set a few times before appearing on camera in order to give her a characteristically nervous, breathless appearance. She felt that shooting most of the film in chronological sequence improved her performance.

Though Bogart was fond of Astor, he could not resist needling her. During one of their kissing scenes (when he was not at his best) he irritably said: "Try not to knock my teeth out next time." But when the actors made fun of her intellectual pretensions and she broke into tears, he comforted her by saying: "You're okay, baby, take it easy. So you're not very smart, but you know it and what the hell's wrong with that!" Mary Astor, like Bette Davis, later paid tribute to his skill as an actor: "His personality dominated the character he was playing—but the character gained by it. His technical skill was quite brilliant. His precision timing was no accident. He kept other actors on their toes because he *listened* to them, he watched, he *looked* at them. He never had that vague stare of a person who waits for you to finish talking."[12] Everyone had a good time making the film. Every night after shooting was completed, Astor, Huston, Bogart, Lorre and Ward Bond (who played a detective) would drive over to the Lakeside Country Club, have some drinks, eat the buffet dinner and talk convivially till midnight.

Warners' pictures of the Thirties and Forties were characterized by frenetic pacing. Scripts were cut down to the minimum, actors spoke their lines rapidly, editors cut the frames and producers trimmed the footage. On June 12, during the second week of shooting, Wallis (as usual) told Blanke to speed things up: "my criticism is principally with Bogart, who has adopted a leisurely suave form of delivery. I don't think we can stand this all through a picture, as it is going to have a tendency to drag down the scenes and slow them [down] too much. Bogart must have his usual brisk, staccato manner and delivery." Huston agreed and the following day said that he had begun with deliberate slowness, but was now increasing the pace: "I am shrinking all the pauses and speeding up all the action. You understand so far I have done all the slow scenes of the picture. After Brigid's apartment scene, the story really begins to move. By the time we reach the Cairo-Brigid-Fat Man scene, it will be turning like a pinwheel. . . . This picture should gather momentum as it goes along. . . . I am doing as you say . . . making Bogart quick and staccato and taking the deliberateness out of the action."

Meta Carpenter, William Faulkner's mistress and the script girl on *The Maltese Falcon,* gave a detailed account of Huston's technical innovations, his complex patterns of light and shadow, and his extraordinary camera set-up during Bogart's second encounter with Greenstreet, who drugs him with a drink:

> We rehearsed two days for the twenty-two uninterrupted moves that Huston and cinematographer Arthur Edeson devised. The camera followed Greenstreet and Bogart from one room into another, then down a long hallway, and finally into a living room; there the camera moved up and down in what is referred to as a boom-up and boom-down shot, then panned from left to right and back to Bogart's drunken face; the next pan shot was to Greenstreet's massive stomach from Bogart's point of view; Greenstreet slowly rose from his chair and moved to the fireplace to stand facing Bogart as our camera followed him. The choreography of it was exacting and exciting. One miss and we had to begin all over again. But there was the understanding that we were attempting something purely cinematic, never tried before, and everyone — stars, camera operators, and cablemen — worked industriously to bring it off. . . . A hushed silence fell over the company as Huston called for a take. After a nerve-wracking seven minutes or so, in which actors and camera crew were incredibly coordinated, Huston shouted "Cut!" and "PRINT IT!" A shout went up and crew members heartily applauded.[13]

‹ IV ›

THE BLACK, enameled, foot-high falcon appears behind the titles, which are followed by a quaint printed prologue. Extracted from Whitworth Porter's *History of the Knights of Malta* (1858), it gives a brief history of the jeweled statue: "In 1539 the Knights Templars of Malta paid tribute to Charles V of Spain, by sending him a Golden Falcon encrusted from beak to claw with rarest jewels — but pirates seized the galley carrying this priceless token and the fate of the Maltese Falcon remains a mystery to this day — ." The falcon is not mentioned again until a quarter of the way through the film when Joel Cairo (Lorre) asks Sam Spade (Bogart) to help him to get it. Later on, Kasper Gutman (Greenstreet), in a perfect bit of solemn nonsense, gives Spade a more elaborate description.

The film opens in San Francisco as Brigid O'Shaughnessy, calling herself Miss Wonderly, comes to Spade's austere office. Spade appears in every scene, except the murder of his partner, Miles Archer. He reels through a series of increasingly dangerous confrontations with O'Shaughnessy, Cairo, Wilmer Cook (played by Elisha Cook, Jr.), Gutman and the police in what could be called six characters in search of a falcon. The audience meets the other figures only when Spade does, sees only what the private eye sees and knows only what he knows.

Bogart's previous gangster characters, like Duke Mantee and Roy Earle, were criminals hunted down by the police. In *The Maltese Falcon* he plays an isolated individual, hounded by the police, who opposes a gang of elegant and sophisticated criminals. The character of Sam Spade, the private detective who is more intelligent, imaginative and effective, more honorable and principled than the stolid, flatfooted police, originates in the stories of Edgar Poe and Conan Doyle. The part suited Bogart, who brings to it a credible, hard-boiled seriousness that is a perfect foil to the other characters. His cold, appraising glance contrasts with Astor's fluttering eyelids, Lorre's childish alarm and Greenstreet's genial villainy. Next to Elisha Cook's perverse nastiness, Bogart seems all the more capable and courageous.

Bogart's Spade—a shrewd, dapper figure—rolls his own cigarettes, lives in a modest one-room apartment and does not carry a gun, though he twice disarms both Cairo and Wilmer. He must at once help his client, find out who murdered his partner and maintain his idealistic code. Rebellious and misogynistic, he risks his life for $25 a day. In their hostile love scenes, as Brigid tells him, "You're absolutely the wildest, most unpredictable person I've ever known," he tugs at his ear and pulls his lips back into a grimace. Looking at her with sceptical disdain, he ironically says, "You're good. You're very good" and then calls her a liar. After their first ambiguous kiss, he pushes her face back with his fingers. Though he looks up expectantly as Brigid prepares to overpay him, he is contemptuous of the materialism that dominates the other characters and drives them to destruction. He has had an affair with Archer's wife, despises his partner and removes his name from the office window immediately after his death. But when he discovers that Brigid, whom he loves, has killed Miles Archer, he feels compelled to turn her over to the police.

Spade's defiant encounters with Cairo and Gutman are the high points of the film. Cairo is preceded into Spade's office by the penetrating odor of gardenias. The Levantine homosexual has brilliantined curly hair, wears a wing collar and outsized bow tie, carries white gloves and a white-topped cane, whose rounded tip he suggestively puts next to his mouth. Huston was forced to cut one scene in which Cairo seductively slips his arm around Wilmer's shoulder and is hit by the outraged young man. Foppish, affected and exquisitely polite, Cairo usually speaks with elaborately formal diction. "Our private conversations," he informs Spade, "have not been such that I'm anxious to continue them." The two characters are contrasted in a terse exchange when Cairo complains, "This is the second time that you laid hands on me!" and Spade replies: "When you're slapped you'll take it and like it." Cairo also shifts from pathetic whining ("Look what you did to my shirt!") to a comically vituperative outburst when Gutman chips off pieces of the falcon and discovers it is a fake: "You imbecile! You bloated idiot! You stupid fat-head, you!"

Spade's conflict with Wilmer, who tails and loses him, provides a structural link between Cairo and Gutman, and reinforces the homosexual theme. Spade constantly taunts the tough but childish-looking "gunsel"—underworld slang for a young homosexual used by an older man—just as Bogart needled people in real life. Though it's dangerous to provoke him, Spade can't resist doing it. "Keep on ridin' me," Wilmer warns him. "They're gonna be pickin' iron out o' your liver!" To which Spade dismissively replies: "The cheaper the crook, the gaudier the patter." When Gutman says of Wilmer: "If you lose a son it's possible to get another. There's only one Maltese falcon" and agrees to hand him over to the police, the camera prolongs the crucial moment by moving slowly across the faces of the other four protagonists. In *The Maltese Falcon* Elisha Cook, Jr. played the kind of character he would always be required to play: what he resentfully called a series of "pimps, informers, cocksuckers."[14]

When Jacoby of *La Paloma* (an uncredited part, played by Walter Huston) is shot by Wilmer, staggers into Spade's office and dies, Spade gains possession of the falcon from the captain of a ship whose name means "the dove." With the help of his only ally, his secretary Effie ("You're a good man, sister!"), he appears for a final showdown with the fat man. In their first interview, as the camera shoots from below to emphasize Gutman's massive bulk, the giggling, baby-faced malefactor recognizes Spade as a kindred spirit who also likes to talk and drink. But they cannot agree on how to do business. Pretending to be angry with Gutman, Spade blusters and storms out of the apartment. In the hallway he pauses, amused at his own bad acting, and grins at his successful deception. Bogart's comic turn gives the stark film a sly tongue-in-cheek quality.

Gutman pretends to be more amenable during their second meeting, but gives Spade knock-out drops (Wilmer kicks him when he's passed out) so he can seize the falcon without having to pay him. In their third and final encounter, Gutman, echoing Brigid's description of Spade's character and using the same eloquent diction as Cairo, tells him: "By gad, sir, you are a character. That you are! There's never any telling what you'll say or do next, except that it's bound to be something astonishing." Gutman, who has spent seventeen years searching for the precious statue, is not easily discouraged when he wants something. Realizing that the falcon is more of a curse than a treasure, he remains monomaniacally obsessed by the quest. He intends to devote his life to finding it and leaves Bogart with a courtly compliment: "frankly, sir, I'd like to have you along, you're a man of nice judgment and many resources."

Spade must next deal with Brigid. He tells her that he knows she killed Archer (no one else could have taken him by surprise with a gun) and, choking her with his hand on her throat, says: "I hope they don't hang you, precious, by that sweet neck. . . . If you're a good girl, you'll be out in twenty years. I'll be waiting for you. If they hang you, I'll always remember you." As the pathological liar appeals to him for protection against the police, he exclaims: "I don't care who loves who! I won't play the sap for you! I won't walk in Thursby's, and I don't know how many others' footsteps! You killed Miles and you're going over for it." To explain his callous attitude, Spade states his Hemingwayesque code of honor, which transcends his personal feelings and expresses the theme of the film: "When a man's partner's killed, he's supposed to do something about it. It doesn't make any difference what you thought of him. He was your partner, and you're supposed to do something about it." He confesses "maybe you love me and maybe I love you," but is willing to sacrifice personal feelings to achieve justice. As the police arrive to arrest her, Spade brushes past Brigid as if she doesn't exist.

The source of the last line of the film has inspired a good deal of discussion by professors, film critics, biographers and Huston himself. When Detective Polhaus asks what the statue is, Spade replies: "The stuff that dreams are made of." Lawrence Grobel, for example, preparing the reader for a real revelation, states: "for forty-eight years the line has been attributed to Huston." He then quotes Huston's assertion that this phrase "was Bogie's idea. It's been quoted a number of times, but this is the first opportunity I've had to tell where the credit for it lies. Before we shot the scene Bogie said to me, 'John, don't you think it would be a good idea, this line? Be a good ending?' And it certainly was."[15]

Bogart may have supplied the line, but Shakespeare wrote it. Toward the end of *The Tempest* (1611), the magician Prospero breaks off the masque he has presented to the lovers, Ferdinand and Miranda, and declares it has all been an illusion: "Our revels now are ended. These our actors, / As I foretold you, were all spirits and / Are melted into air, into thin air." Human lives, he says, are just as frail as make-believe: "We are such stuff / As dreams are made on, and our little life / Is rounded with a sleep" (4.1.148–158). The line is indeed a wonderfully appropriate conclusion. Spade's reference to the famous Shakespearean epilogue rounds out the film, parallels the formal prologue at the beginning, and emphasizes the illusory yet fascinating quest for a falcon that had melted into thin air. Many of the lives have certainly been rounded with a sleep: Archer (killed by Brigid), Thursby and Jacoby (killed by Wilmer) are dead. Brigid, Gutman, Cairo and Wilmer have been arrested. Spade remains alone in a deceptive, hostile world. And the real falcon, somewhere between Istanbul and Hong Kong, has once again disappeared.

The critics were ecstatic about the picture. *Films and Filming* praised Huston's "exact manipulation of actors, cameramen, set designers and others, to capture such a rich, near flawlessly correct mood throughout the length of the film. . . . It is finally a study of people affected by the weakness of greed, realized with a force and a psychological aptness that gives it moral purpose. . . . More than just a private-eye picture, this is a compelling study in human frailty." Bogart agreed that "it was practically a masterpiece. I don't have many things I'm proud of . . . but that's one." It was nominated by the Academy for best screenplay, best picture and best supporting actor (Sydney Greenstreet). Released nine months after *High Sierra,* the film catapulted Bogart to fame and soon became a classic as well as a cult favorite. In September 1941, after the 101st Cavalry had advertised in the *New York Times* for a falcon mascot, Bogart—advertising the film, emphasizing the theme of illusion, and substituting the fake for the real—sent them "the falcon which appeared with me in *The Maltese Falcon.* I think this will more than fill the qualifications stated in the advertisement."[16]

◆ 7 ◆

War Movies and
Casablanca

1943

⟨ I ⟩

IN 1941 Bogart showed that his wit, skill and timing could help transform the remake of a conventional mystery into a stylish *film noir* classic, *The Maltese Falcon*. But instead of being treated like a star, he was put back into the Warners assembly line. During the next few years he made several war movies, a genre which in the early 1940s killed the gangster film. From 1942 to 1945 the Hollywood studios joined the war effort by churning out more than five hundred features that dealt with war material. Patriotic and propagandistic pictures matched Warners' dramatic style, and they made more military and political movies than any other studio. Bogart followed this trend. He had joined Flotilla 21 of the Coast Guard Auxiliary and patrolled once a week off the shore near Balboa. In 1942 he made his last gangster movie, an anti-Nazi melodrama and an anti-Japanese espionage film. As parliamentary democracy was crushed by dictators in Occupied Europe, Bogart moved from criminal roles to private eyes to war heroes.

The Big Shot was Bogart's farewell to "B" crime films. Jack Warner, emphasizing as always speed, efficiency and economy, adopted the gangsters' lingo when he told the director, Lewis Seiler: "I do not want this picture to get cold from any more delays. . . . If Bogart starts to stall out, just tell him it doesn't go." Irene Manning, an operetta singer who lent some class to the part of the gun moll, found Bogart a reserved and distant man but patient teacher. He would arrive on the set and say: "All right, you guys, what are we going to do today? . . . Good, then let's get it done." "He was basically all business," Manning said, and "not really my kind of guy. He used a lot of four-letter words, which shocked me. Still, he was

132

always prepared and professional and he did give me some good advice." When Seiler, to establish his authority and put the cheeky young lady in her place, upset her by asking if she was going to *sing* her lines, Bogart encouraged her by saying: "Never mind the camera, never mind the lights. Just get to the set, and say the lines."[1]

In *The Big Shot,* an inferior version of *High Sierra* and a compendium of gangster motifs, Bogart (having once played Duke Mantee) now plays Duke Berne. Forced into crime by poverty and recruited by a crooked lawyer, he had taken part in a foiled attempt to rob an armored car and been sent back to prison. Confronted with a life sentence, he echoes *The Petrified Forest* and hopelessly asks: "Why feed a dead man even if he's still walkin' around?" His girl smuggles in a rope and he escapes after shooting out the stage lights during a convicts' show. She waits outside the walls with a car and eagerly kisses him as he drives to his high sierra retreat. But, concentrating on the getaway, he pushes her aside and drily remarks that he "can't do two things at once."

Despite his evil little "heh-heh" laugh, Bogart decides to give himself up in order to save the decent kid who took the rap during the escape. As he drives down the mountain road, pursued by the police (why run away if he wants to surrender?), his girl is shot dead and one of the cops falls spectacularly off his motorcycle. In the final shootout, Bogart and the crooked lawyer fatally wound each other (as Bogart and Robinson had often done in earlier films) and Bogart dies in the hospital, smoking his last cigarette. His ironic dying words recycle Cagney's epitaph in *The Roaring Twenties* and his own in *High Sierra:* "Knew all the angles. Big shot." Though the plot is ridiculous, *The Big Shot* is better than most of his gangster movies of the 1930s. Bogart is now a reluctant criminal, haunted by his past, goaded by his gang, tormented by his conscience. The mountain idyll is poignant, the car chase and final shootout quite exciting. This picture, unlike most of the others before it, makes us care about the fate of the doomed criminal.

When George Raft turned down *All Through the Night,* Bogart once again inherited the leading role. Playing a natty Broadway gambler with a bossy Irish ma, he uses his criminal skills against the Nazi fifth column, foils their attempt to blow up a ship in New York harbor and changes from gangster to war hero. The director Vincent Sherman described the origins of the movie: "I stole most of it from the Hitchcock films I'd seen. The auction [a respectable front for the Nazis] was a typical Hitchcock scene. I think I got the idea from *The Thirty-Nine Steps,* where [Robert] Donat accidentally walks into a political meeting, but I twisted it around." The picture begins with comic scenes and puns ("We'll catch them with their panzers down") by Phil Silvers and Jackie Gleason, who later became famous on television. Sherman, taking an off-the-cuff approach, told the comedians: "'Look, fellas, I don't have time to write anything for you. Write some gags, do a few ad-libs, bring them in and I'll work some into the script.' Being comics, they came back with pages of stuff. I used what I could." But the low humor jars with the crime, action and violence in the rest of the film.

In this complicated story, the Nazis—played by Conrad Veidt and Peter Lorre, who have dachshunds and speak German to each other—blackmail a nightclub singer whose father is in a concentration camp. Bogart infiltrates a Nazi meeting, makes an ironic speech to the German sympathizers and knows how to deal with Lorre: "We got a special little gadget in Sing Sing that will melt him away." In the end, forced to pilot a speedboat filled with explosives, Bogart throws Veidt over the side, saves the American ship and gets the girl, Kaaren Verne. (Later in life, she married Peter Lorre.) The tone of *All Through the Night,* which joked about the Nazi threat, seemed crudely inappropriate when it was released in January 1942, a month after America entered the war.

Vincent Sherman recalled that while making this film Bogart once turned up for work in terrible shape. He had been locked out by Mayo, slept on their front lawn and "froze his ass." On another occasion, drunk and hysterical, Mayo suddenly appeared on the set. She called Sherman into a dressing-room, wept bitterly and said: "'He doesn't love me any more.' I went out to Bogie and said, 'Why don't you just go into the dressing-room and talk with Mayo?' He said no. He was very angry and said that she had no business in coming to the set." Embarrassed and irritated, Bogart resented Mayo's demand that he find work for her at the studio: "Oh, fuck her. I'm tired of actresses. I'm sick of hearing all day long, 'Why don't you get me a part?'"

When the film was completed, Bogart phoned Sherman and said: "'Vince, I just want to let you know that I wanted to apologize for causing you so much trouble on the picture.' I said, 'Bogie, you didn't cause any trouble.' He said, 'Well, I was having trouble with my wife. We are going to get divorced. I just want you to know, kid, that any time we had a disagreement or an argument, I didn't mean it. I was going through hell.'"[2]

Across the Pacific, Bogart's best war movie, takes place in November and December 1941 along the *Atlantic* from Canada to Panama. The title refers to an attack on Hawaii in the original story and has nothing to do with the actual film. Mary Astor explained: "The first version wasn't bad. It was all about thwarting a Japanese plot to attack Pearl Harbor. By the time we had commenced work on it late in December of 1941, Pearl Harbor *had* been attacked [the screenwriters foresaw the threat before the U.S. Navy], and the story was changed to thwarting a Japanese plot to blow up the Panama Canal. Bogart said, 'Let's hurry and get this thing over with before the Canal goes too.'"

In this film, originally directed by John Huston, Bogart has another witty and sophisticated relationship with the duplicitous Mary Astor and the evil Sydney Greenstreet. It also features the slimiest Japanese villains who had ever appeared on the screen. Astor recalled: "The government started shipping out our Nisei cast. A little indignation and some wire-pulling held them at least until the picture was finished." But her memory was unreliable. All the Oriental roles were played by Chinese actors, made to look as ugly and sinister as possible and to reflect the current hatred of the Japanese enemy.

The plot recalls *Bullets or Ballots,* in which Edward G. Robinson, apparently kicked out of the police force, infiltrates and destroys a gang of criminals. In *Across the Pacific* Bogart, apparently dismissed from the army, sails with Astor and Greenstreet on an eerie Japanese ship whose blinds cast shadows into the striped pattern of the enemy flag. She is going to her father's plantation, which (Bogart discovers) is being used as a secret base by the Japanese. Quoting Byron's "Hebrew Melodies," he says that she "walks in beauty."

The large and luscious Greenstreet, an admirer of Japanese culture and sympathizer with the enemy, tries to get strategic information from Bogart and enlist him in his plot. Called "the fat man," as in *The Maltese Falcon,* he again tells Bogart: "You're always furnishing surprises." Greenstreet wears a homburg, Bogart a fedora. Greenstreet claims that "Japanese make great servants," Bogart observes that "they all look alike." Greenstreet boasts: "My gun is bigger than your gun," Bogart retorts: "I told you—mine is bigger than yours." At the end, Greenstreet, about to be arrested, tries but fails to commit hara-kiri.

Huston, who completed most of the film from February to April 1942, before he was suddenly called in to military service, also contributed to the myths surrounding *Across the Pacific.* In his autobiography, *An Open Book,* he hyperbolically wrote: "I proceeded to make things as difficult as possible for my successor. I had Bogie tied to a chair, and installed about three times as many Japanese soldiers as were needed to keep him prisoner. There were guards at every window brandishing machine guns. I made it so that there was no way in God's green world that Bogart could logically escape. I shot the scene, then called Jack Warner and said, 'Jack, I'm on my way. I'm in the Army. Bogie will know how to get out.'"

The scene in which Bogart was hopelessly trapped may have been planned or fantasized by Huston, but it was never shot by Vincent Sherman, who took over, for the last ten days, on April 23. Jack Warner, fed up with all the delays, told Sherman to "get in there and finish the goddamn thing." Sherman arrived on the set to find actors still walking around with the script and learning new lines. The Japanese airplane and Bogart's machine gun were already in place for the final scene. But the melodramatic conclusion of the movie was much less interesting than the beginning, in which suspense had been built up, and Huston (always weak on endings) didn't know what to do with it. The army would have let him finish the picture and continued the war without him for a few more days, but he wanted to escape from the picture and from his current affair with Olivia de Havilland.

Alone at the end of the film, and trapped by the menacing villains, Bogart enacts a James Bond fantasy, triumphs against overwhelming odds and proves (as he tells the enemy): "You may start the war, but we'll finish it." After one of the Japanese soldiers goes beserk, Bogart overpowers his guard, captures a machine gun and shoots down a Japanese plane as it takes off to bomb the Canal. When someone questioned the logic of the scene, Sherman exclaimed: "Listen, if you ask me, we were lucky to get the bastard out of there at all."[3]

Playing an officer entrusted to carry out espionage and willing to risk his life for his country, Bogart stands stiffly and draws in his breath when he's sentenced by the army court and quickly changes from military uniform to his trademark trenchcoat. He tests the hard bed in his ship's cabin, shifts his eyes suspiciously back and forth as Greenstreet speaks to his servant in Japanese, and wriggles his fingers after a hard handshake with the chief engineer. He also carries on a playful, even roguish flirtation with Mary Astor. He blinks with pleasure after first kissing her, runs his fingers along her neck after their second kiss and smiles at her discomfort when she's seasick.

His scenes with Greenstreet reveal the more serious side of his character. They drink congenially, but he stumbles out of the lounge to be seasick himself when Greenstreet gets him drunk. His face drops when Greenstreet inquires about his trouble in the army, he pushes the bribe money around on the table with his index finger, as if reluctant to take it, and stares at Greenstreet's extended hand before shaking it. Bogart moves effortlessly from apparent disgrace through light comedy to wartime heroics. Combining toughness with moral commitment, he preserves an ironic distance from the propagandistic aspects of the picture.

< **II** >

Casablanca (1943), based on an unsuccessful play, *Everybody Comes to Rick's,* began as an imitation of *Algiers,* made in 1939 with Charles Boyer and Hedy Lamarr. The title was nearly changed when the studio feared it would remind the audience of a popular Mexican beer, Carta Blanca. The excellent screenplay—tightly-structured, literate, allusive, poignant and memorable—was written by the identical twins Julius and Philip Epstein and by Howard Koch. (Koch was known for his frightening radio dramatization of H. G. Wells' *The War of the Worlds,* which had convinced a huge audience that America was being invaded by Martians.) The budget was about $950,000, including $20,000 for the rights to the play, $47,000 for the three screenwriters, $73,400 for the director, Michael Curtiz, $53,000 for the producer, Hal Wallis. The shooting of *Casablanca* began without a completed script on May 25, 1942, lasted nearly ten weeks and came in eleven days behind schedule. In the Parisian flashback Curtiz casually drew attention to the novel use of a rear projection screen. The shot of Bogart and Bergman "in a convertible with typical Parisian scenery in the background is obviously process work. But, strangely enough, the background of the scene *dissolves* into another scene of Paris while the car and its two occupants remain in focus."

The leading actors and supporting cast were, as in *The Maltese Falcon,* absolutely superb. Of the first nine top-billed actors, only Bogart was American. Ingrid Bergman was Swedish, Paul Henreid was Austrian, Conrad Veidt was German, Peter Lorre and S. Z. Sakall (as well as Curtiz) were Hungarian, Claude Rains and Sydney Greenstreet were English, Madeleine LeBeau was French. Some of the refugees in *Casablanca* were actually played by refugee actors. Marcel Dalio (the croupier) had appeared in Jean Renoir's *Grande Illusion* (1937) and had (like Bogart in the film) escaped from France after the German invasion. While making *Casablanca* he learned that his parents had died in a concentration camp. Dalio, who was married to LeBeau, later wrote: "Bogart was a very generous man. He clearly saw that I was troubled and couldn't master English. He helped me and taught me to pronounce it. Noticing that he feverishly rubbed his thumb against his index finger before playing a scene, I forgot my stage fright."

The other American actors included Joy Page (Annina), who was Jack Warner's stepdaughter; Dooley Wilson (Sam), a black actor who could *not* play the piano but sang Herman Hupfield's nostalgic song, originally written for a 1931 stage revue, "As Time Goes By"; and Dan Seymour (Abdul the doorman). At more than three hundred pounds each, Seymour and Sydney Greenstreet together weighed nearly a third of a ton. Bogart earned $36,667, Bergman, Henreid and Veidt $25,000 each, Rains $22,000, Greenstreet $7,500 and Lorre (killed early on) $2,333.

Curtiz, once a circus strongman, had directed Bogart in three mediocre films: *Kid Galahad, Angels with Dirty Faces* and *Virginia City*. His English was bad, his temper even worse, and he often berated and bullied his actors. Though the finished script is excellent, *Casablanca's* three writers added to the tense atmosphere on the set by barely keeping ahead of the shooting. On July 19, with nearly two months of filming finished and the cast still straining to master their parts, Bogart and Curtiz had a fierce quarrel. The unit manager, Al Alleborn, reported to Jack Warner: "During the day the company had several delays caused by arguments with Curtiz the director, and Bogart the actor. I had to go out and get Wallis and bring him over to the set to straighten out the situation. At one time they sat around for a long time and argued, finally deciding on how to do the scene." Everything would come to a halt when the cast had to learn new dialogue for a scene that had been hastily rewritten the night before.

Lorre, Bogart's close friend, had a similarly sardonic sense of humor and tried to break the tension with elaborate practical jokes. Knowing that John Barrymore had spent his final alcoholic days in the house of the Warners actor Errol Flynn, he contrived a bizarre plot. Paul Henreid recalled: "I was making *Casablanca* with Peter Lorre the day of Barrymore's death, and he took Humphrey Bogart, and me, and two other friends aside. 'I have a fantastic idea,' Lorre said, his bulging eyes glistening. 'For very little, maybe two or three hundred dollars, I can get Barrymore's body away from the mortuary.' 'What the hell for?' I asked. 'Yeah,' Bogart seconded. 'Why would you want his body?' 'Now get this. We take the body into Flynn's house—I know he's shooting and gets home late, and we arrange it in that chair in the living room he always used to sit in, then we hide and watch Flynn's face. Is that or isn't it fantastic?'" The trick was successful and gave Flynn (himself a heavy drinker) a real scare.

Jack Warner and Hal Wallis wanted a new face for the female lead. They managed to convince David Selznick, who had Ingrid Bergman under contract, that *Casablanca* would advance her career, increase her box-office appeal and make her more valuable to his organization. Born in Stockholm in 1915 and classically trained at the Royal Dramatic Theater, she had come to America in 1939 and made her debut that year with Leslie Howard in *Intermezzo*. Fluent in English, with an attractive accent, she did not have the fake veneer of most Hollywood stars. Tall and elegant, her natural looks made her a perfect romantic heroine.

Intimidated at the prospect of appearing with Bogart, who had a reputation for being abrasive, Bergman said she "saw *The Maltese Falcon* over and over again so I could get used to him so that when I met him I wouldn't be so frightened." Unaware of his miserable marriage to Mayo Methot and of her intense jealousy of his leading ladies, Bergman recalled: "He was very much by himself and I think he was very worried about it. He used to go into his little trailer on the set and close the door [and play chess with his friends]. . . . He wasn't sitting around on the set and making jokes and was not in a very happy mood." Though their love scenes are among the most magnetic on film, Bergman revealed that they had little to do with personal feelings: "I kissed him, but I never really knew him."[4] Bergman's innocent sensuality provided a fine contrast to Bogart's bitter disillusionment, just as her self-sacrificial love (so unlike the egoistical duplicity of Mary Astor in *The Maltese Falcon*) brought out his idealism and tenderness.

The costume designers suggested the foreign setting in a rather blatant and unrealistic way. Though the average temperature in Casablanca in December is only 56° (I've been there in the winter), the civilians wear white tropical clothing. The names of the characters in *Casablanca* are also oddly assorted. Some seem chosen for brand recognition: Louis Renault (Rains) and Signor Ferrari (Greenstreet) are named for foreign cars. Some are simply inconsistent. Ferrari, presumably Italian, wears a Moslem fez. Victor Laszlo (Henreid), a Czech fighting for the Allies, has a typically Hungarian name, although that country was an Axis power. Since Sweden was neutral in World War II, Ilsa Lund (Bergman), though named after a town in Sweden, is Norwegian. One Warners writer told Wallis: "this guy Rick is two parts Hemingway, one part Scott Fitzgerald," and Rick Blaine (Bogart) is named after Amory Blaine, the romantic hero of Fitzgerald's first novel, *This Side of Paradise* (1920). Almost everyone calls him Rick, but three of the characters suggest their more intimate friendship by addressing him in a different way. Sam (Dooley Wilson) calls his boss "Mr. Richard," Ilsa calls him "Richard" and Renault calls him "Ricky."

Bogart knew a great deal about screenplays and contributed significantly to the conception of his role. He improved the script by thinking up the famous line "Here's looking at you, kid," and changing "Of all the cafés in all the cities in all the world, she walks into my café" to the more colloquial and elegant "Of all the gin-joints in all the towns in all the world, she walks into mine!" According to Julius Epstein, Bogart "felt that in the early drafts Rick's character was heavy with self-pity and that he was too cold, too suspicious, and too hostile."[5] So the Epsteins softened his character by giving him a committed Left-wing past. He had joined the nobler but losing side of the two anti-Fascist wars that led to World War II, running guns to the Ethiopians who were battling the Italian invaders in 1935 and fighting (like Hemingway's hero in *For Whom the Bell Tolls*) with the Loyalists in Spain in 1936. After two bitter political defeats, Rick has set up his business in Casablanca and is determined to "stick his neck out for nobody." But Renault perceives that under his shell he's "at heart a sentimentalist." By the end of the film he is shown to be loyal to friends and employees, able to take swift and violent action, politically committed to the French Resistance and capable of romantic renunciation.

Bogart had played a young lover on stage, but *Casablanca* was his first romantic lead with a major star. The playwright Mel Baker (his agent's husband) gave him some good advice about how to act with Bergman: "You stand still, and always make her come to you. Mike [Curtiz] probably won't notice it, and if she complains you can tell her it's tacit in the script. You've got something she wants [both his love and the letters of transit], so she has to come to you." Bogart's distance gave him a certain mystery and made the audience wonder what he was thinking. The passionate restraint in the two love scenes — in the Paris flashback and in his room in Casablanca — intensifies the powerful conflict between personal desires and political commitment, and enhances the theme of sacrifice for a higher cause.

Bogart rather modestly observed: "I didn't do anything I've never done before. . . . But when the camera moves in on that Bergman's face, and she's saying she loves you, it would make anybody look romantic." Paul Henreid (as Victor Laszlo, who flies off with Ilsa but knows she loves Rick) was unhappy with many aspects of his role. He was an Old World gentleman, disliked Bogart's rough manners and was highly critical of the way he played Rick: "Before *Casablanca* he was nobody. He was the fellow [of whom] Robinson or Cagney would say, 'Get him.' Bogart was a mediocre actor. He was sorry for himself in *Casablanca*. Unfortunately, Michael Curtiz was not a director of actors; he was a director of effects. He was first rate at that, but he could not tell Bogart he should not play like a crybaby. It was embarrassing, I thought, when I looked at the rushes." Bergman disagreed with Henreid and admired Bogart's ability as an actor: "What an enormous talent he had with that rough, tough way, yet he brings out so much love." Pauline Kael has convincingly defined his achievement as both lover and hero: "In the role of the cynic redeemed by love, Bogart became the great adventurer-lover of the screen during the war years. There isn't an actor in American films today with anything like his assurance, his magnetism, or his style. In *Casablanca,* he established the figure of the rebellious hero—the lone wolf who hates and defies officialdom."[6]

< **III** >

Casablanca opens and closes with a plane taking refugees to neutral Lisbon. The contrast between Vichy-controlled North Africa, where a German courier has been murdered and important documents stolen, and freedom in America, is emphasized by the recurrent phrase: "Round up all suspicious characters. . . . Round up twice the usual number of suspects." Rick Blaine, first seen wearing a white dinner jacket and playing chess alone in his Café Américain, reacts to all the major characters who come to his nightclub and gambling casino. He despises but agrees to help the ingratiating Ugarte (Lorre)—who has killed the courier and stolen the letters of transit—by hiding the valuable papers in the piano. But the sniveling, whimpering Ugarte is soon arrested and killed. Rick gets rid of his French mistress Yvonne (LeBeau), and refuses to sell his café to the oleaginous Ferrari, the owner of the Blue Parrot (a sly allusion to the Maltese Falcon). His ironic exchanges with Captain Renault (who ought to know that Casablanca is on the coast, not in the desert) reveal his witty, mysterious character, and suggest that he's much more than an entrepreneur:

> RENAULT: And what in heaven's name brought you to Casablanca?
> RICK: My health. I came to Casablanca for the waters.
> RENAULT: Waters? What waters? We're in the desert.
> RICK: I was misinformed.

Renault, who wears his kepi at a sympathetically jaunty angle, suggests his covert opposition to the Nazis by quoting W. E. Henley's defiant and stoic poem "Invictus" (1875): "I am the master of my fate. I am the captain of my . . . [soul]."

These brief but telling encounters also anticipate the themes that recur in scenes with Rick and Ilsa Lund later in the film. Ugarte asks Rick: "What right do I have to think?" Ilsa asks: "You'll have to think for both of us, for all of us"—and his final decision determines her fate and Laszlo's. Rick rejects Yvonne's invitation by stating: "I never make plans that far ahead"; Ilsa later evades his marriage proposal by saying: "That's too far ahead to plan." Renault, referring to Rick's fighting in Ethiopa and Spain, remarks: "The winning side would have paid you much better."[7] This foreshadows Rick's refusal of money for the precious letters of transit and his resolution, when he gives them to Ilsa and Laszlo, to be on the losing side in the battle to possess her.

Meanwhile, the Nazi Major Strasser (Conrad Veidt) has also arrived in Casablanca and been greeted at the airport by the German Consul (in full military uniform), Herr Heinze. Just as Bette Davis' militaristic father in *The Petrified Forest* resembled Francisco Franco, so Heinze—with square moustache, thick rimless spectacles and jowly face—looks remarkably like Heinrich Himmler. Veidt (by contrast), who had played the somnambulist Cesare in the classic Expressionist film *The Cabinet of Dr. Caligari* (1919), masks his evil with refinement and culture. He also comes to Rick's, orders (like all the decadent, high-booted, monocled Hollywood Nazis) champagne and caviar, and is subjected to Rick's wisecracks:

> STRASSER: What's your nationality?
> RICK: I'm a drunkard.

Parrying Strasser's questions, Rick advises him not to invade certain (Jewish) parts of New York—an allusion to Warners' previous anti-Nazi film *All Through the Night* (1942). Later on, Strasser orders Renault to close the café because everybody's having "much too good a time"—a sly but unmistakable dig at the autocratic Jack Warner, who once told the director Howard Hawks: "Word has reached me that you are having fun on the set. This must stop."

After the fast-paced plot has been set in motion and the principal characters introduced, the heroic Underground leader Victor Laszlo, who has escaped from a German concentration camp, appears at Rick's café with his charming wife, Ilsa Lund. Unaware of Ugarte's fate, they hope to get the stolen letters of transit and must exchange icy pleasantries when Major Strasser comes to their table. Ilsa recognizes Sam from the old days in Paris and asks him to play the love song she associates with Rick: "Play it, Sam. Play 'As Time Goes By.'" Rick, astonished by Laszlo's unexpected appearance with Ilsa, is overwhelmed by anguished memories. He acts with restraint when she is present, but becomes drunk and embittered with Sam as soon as she leaves.

Casablanca, effective as propagandistic entertainment, skillfully blends the romantic story of Rick and Ilsa with the war that threatens to destroy them. In the last sentence of *Homage to Catalonia* (1938), a memoir of the Spanish Civil War, George Orwell wrote that we are "all sleeping the deep, deep sleep of England, from which I sometimes fear that we shall never wake till we are jerked out of it by the roar of bombs." In the film, Rick expresses Orwell's cogent warning against isolationism and pacificism. Just before the crucial flashback to his Parisian idyll with Ilsa, he mentions that "it's December 1941 in Casablanca," just before the Japanese attack on Pearl Harbor, and announces that America must be prepared for war: "I bet they're asleep in New York. I'll bet they're asleep all over America."[8]

Their love song leads to a dissolve and to a flashback of Rick and Ilsa in Paris a year and a half earlier, in June 1940. He moves from the shadows of his café into the spring sunshine, wears a daisy in his buttonhole, and lives in an elegant and romantic atmosphere. Their love seems all the more moving when threatened by the German occupation of Paris (shown in actual wartime newsreels) and by Rick's need to flee from his enemies. He expresses his happiness in one of his rare laughs, and Ilsa, while urging him to leave the city, subtly conveys the feeling that she will not be able to go with him. After their last kiss, he knocks over a glass, just as he does after the flashback ends and the story returns to the present in Casablanca. Ilsa suddenly reappears, but the angry Rick doesn't let her explain why she left him, with his guts kicked out, in the rain at the Paris railroad station. Instead, he mocks her deceitful promise: "Richard, dear, I'll go with you anyplace. We'll get on a train together and never stop." These poignant and powerful words both echo and contravene an eloquent passage in the Book of Ruth, 1:16: "whither thou goest, I will go; and where thou lodgest, I will lodge; thy people shall be my people, and thy God my God."

Writing in the French Resistance newspaper *Combat,* Albert Camus appealed to patriotic feelings and expressed the idealistic beliefs that had sustained the Allies since the beginning of the war: "[We] know that a thousand rifles aimed at a man will not stop him from believing in the justice of his cause, and that when he is dead, there will be other men to say 'no' until force itself is worn out." During the second confrontation between Victor Laszlo and Major Strasser in Captain Renault's office, Laszlo, in a passionate speech, uses the same image to express another dominant political theme of the film—the solidarity of those willing to sacrifice their lives for the Allied cause: "And what if you track down these men and kill them? What if you murdered all of us? From every corner of Europe, hundreds, thousands, would rise to take our places. Even Nazis can't kill that fast."

In a moment that foreshadows Rick and Ilsa's second love scene, the young married refugee, Annina, who has offered herself to Renault in exchange for exit visas, asks Rick to approve her immoral but sacrificial act: "If someone loved you very much, so that your happiness was the only thing that she wanted in the whole world, but she did a bad thing to make certain of it, could you forgive her?" Rick, with offhanded cynicism, remarks: "Nobody ever loved me that much." He then tells his croupier to let her husband win enough money to buy the visas.

While Laszlo is trying unsuccessfully to buy the elusive letters of transit from Rick, the German officers gather round the piano in the café and sing "Die Wacht am Rhein" (The Watch on the Rhine). This nationalistic poem, written in 1840 when France was threatening to annex part of the Rhineland, had been popular in Germany ever since the Franco-Prussian War of 1870. Laszlo emerges from Rick's office and, echoing Ilsa's and Rick's "Play it," commands the orchestra to "Play the Marseillaise! Play it!" As Rick nods significantly to confirm the order, everyone else in the café stands up to sing the French national anthem, drown out the Germans and suggest the promise of victory in the war. Ilsa weeps and Yvonne, rejecting her German escort, cries "Vive la France!" Though it doesn't really matter whose song is louder, the emotionally charged scene works perfectly on both the literal and symbolic levels.

In Rick's café and just before leaving for an Underground meeting, Laszlo tells Ilsa, "I love you very much, my dear." She mutters, "Yes. Yes, I know," but does not say that she also loves him. While he's away, she goes to Rick's room to see if *she* can somehow get the letters of transit. Once jilted by Ilsa, Rick is now in control of her destiny and her husband's, and can even influence the course of the Resistance movement in Europe. Echoing Annina's plea to Renault, Ilsa says: "You can ask any price you want, but you must give me those letters." Shifting her argument, she next refers (as Laszlo had done) to the greater cause Victor is fighting for. She also tries to arouse Rick's feelings by mentioning their past love, then calls him a coward and a weakling, and finally threatens him with a silver pistol. After none of these attempts has worked, she finally declares her love for Rick (as she had failed to do with Victor): "If you knew how much I loved you, how much I still love you! . . . I'll never have the strength to leave you again. . . . I wish I didn't love you so much."[9] She now reveals that she discovered, just before they were to leave Paris together, that Victor was still alive and desperately in need of her. Learning the truth and knowing that Ilsa still loves him, Rick moves from disengagement to commitment and decides — as she had done in Paris — to renounce personal feelings for a nobler ideal.

The scenes glide swiftly into each other, and when they all meet in the great shadowy climax at the airport the complex elements of *Casablanca* come inevitably together. Victor thinks he is leaving with Ilsa, Ilsa believes she is staying with Rick. But what now seems like a perfect conclusion was not written until *after* most of *Casablanca* had been made. New lines were being fed to the actors until the very end. Jack Warner, as always, was frantic about having to pay the extra costs if the unfinished script delayed the shooting and Bergman's contract expired before they were finished. Julius Epstein, who came to dislike the film, gave an amusing account, in a privately printed pamphlet, of how it was completed: "For each additional day Selznick would be paid a huge sum, a prospect that caused the four pairs of eyes of the Brothers Warner to glaze over. So speed in the writing of the screenplay was essential." But the writers found it difficult to come up with an ending and rumor had it that Jack Warner "was also consulting psychiatrists, psychics and even Rabbi Magnin" of the Wilshire Boulevard Temple. Epstein also recalled that Bogart grumbled a bit at the constant uncertainty and that in "the last days of *Casablanca* there was a definite look of concern on his face, but most likely it was caused by the fears that there might not be enough wind that weekend to fill the *Santana*'s sails."

In fact, the writers knew from the start that Ilsa belonged to and with Laszlo, and that Rick could not leave Casablanca with her unless Victor was dead. The explanation of why Ilsa had failed to appear at the Paris railroad station had to be delayed until late in the plot. Since the heroic Victor had to remain alive to lead the Resistance, the film had to maintain the love interest and suspense until he could escape with his wife. Rick's prewar idealism (revealed in Ethiopia and Spain), which he had lost when Ilsa left him in Paris, is ignited when she reappears in Casablanca and declares her love. His political beliefs, while transcending his personal feelings, are also based on his enduring love for Ilsa.

The final parting at the airport in Casablanca (during which midgets were hired to stand in the swirling fog to make the plane look larger) is an effective reprise of the farewell scene at the railroad station in Paris. The steam of the train foreshadows the fog on the runway. "Swifty" Lazar, the Hollywood agent, once told Bogart: "Without an Aquascutum you couldn't even get arrested." But he appears in his raincoat (with belt always tied, not buckled) at the Paris station and again, to link the two scenes and emphasize the recurrent loss of Ilsa, at the Casablanca airport. Wallis (in one of his less inspired moments) told Curtiz that Bogart should *not* wear a hat at the airport.[10] But the similarity of their broad-brimmed, turned-down hats suggest the powerful bond between Rick and Ilsa as they part for the last time.

Rick convinces Ilsa to leave with Laszlo by telling her: "Inside of us we both know you belong with Victor. You're part of his work, the thing that keeps him going." He then echoes her previous speech by saying: "Where I'm going you can't follow. What I've got to do, you can't be any part of." Though his renunciation is certainly idealistic, Rick retains some of his bitter cynicism. After rekindling Ilsa's love ("We'll always have Paris. . . . We got it back last night"), he is now able to give her up. He rejects Ilsa, not only for ideological reasons, but also to repay her previous rejection.

Bergman—unaware throughout the film of how it would actually end—was uncertain about how to act in her scenes with Bogart and with Henreid. But her very doubts about the role enabled her to suggest her ambiguous feelings for both men. She later recalled: "It's obvious from the start that she loved Bogart very much, in the true sense of love—she respected and admired her husband and went with him because there was a cause and he needed her and so she went with him from a sense of duty. But her love as a woman was certainly for Humphrey Bogart. . . . I'm sure that's how I played it." Bogart remarked, with characteristic irony: "Miss Bergman is the kind of lady that no man would give up willingly, even to the tune of a lot of high[-sounding] philosophy. But that was the story and I had to let her slide right out of my arms."[11] The farewell scene, a fine example of Hemingway's "grace under pressure," combines poetic beauty and quiet realism.

Having put Victor and Ilsa safely on the plane, the wrought-up Rick still has to deal with Major Strasser, who arrives at the airport and tries to stop the flight. Since everyone wanted to see Strasser killed by Rick, his death was inevitable. But, as Wallis explained to Curtiz, they could not use Rick's corny line, " 'All right, Major, you're asking for it,' because of censorship reasons. . . . This would make Strasser's shot one of self-defense." Instead, Strasser pulls out his pistol and shoots first. Following the convention that bad guys are always poor marksmen, he misses and is killed by Rick. Renault, knowing Rick has shot Strasser, saves him by exclaiming, "Major Strasser's been shot," pausing for a moment to reveal his sympathetic attitude and then repeating the ironic command: "Round up the usual suspects." This wittily suggests a whole group of professional villains, hanging around the bazaar of Casablanca and patiently waiting to be rounded up every time a new crime is committed.

In the final scene Renault, like Rick, moves from cynicism to commitment. He has lost his bet with Rick about Laszlo's escape from Casablanca and will use the ten thousand francs to pay for their passage to the Free French garrison in French Equatorial Africa. As Renault replaces Ilsa in Rick's life, the last line of the film was changed from "Louis, I might have known you'd mix your patriotism with a little larceny" to the more virile and idealistic: "Louis, I think this is the beginning of a beautiful friendship."[12]

Julius Epstein felt *Casablanca* was overrated and resented its elevation to a cult film. Though he and his brother gave it wit and saved it from sentimentality, he came to hate the work with which he was always associated and frequently attacked it. He maintained "there wasn't one moment of reality in *Casablanca*" and condemned it as "slick shit":

> *Casablanca* is one of my least favorite pictures. I'm tired of talking about it after thirty years. I can explain its success only by the Bogie cult that has sprung up after his death. I can recognize that the picture is entertaining and that people love it. But it's a completely phoney romance, a completely phoney picture. For instance, nobody knew what was going on in Casablanca at the time. Nobody had ever been to Casablanca. The whole thing was shot in the back lot. There was never a German who appeared in Casablanca for the duration of the entire war, and we had Germans marching around with medals and epaulets. Furthermore, there were never any such things as letters of transit around which the entire plot revolved. . . . The movie is completely phoney!

But Epstein's statement is not entirely accurate. The film was tremendously successful long before Bogart's death, and the research department at Warner Bros. had worked hard to create a realistic representation of the city. Some Germans *were* in the strategic port before the Allied invasion (the French commander arrested the German Armistice Commission when he heard the Americans had landed), and vital visas and exit papers were certainly bought and sold.

Epstein did not, however, mention the most serious logical flaws in *Casablanca*. Victor Laszlo, an Underground leader, is prominently *above* ground. Though followed by the Germans, he walks from his hotel to a supposedly secret meeting. He wants to reach Lisbon and go on to America. But once he has raised funds to support the Resistance, he would have to resume his clandestine work in Europe. Ilsa—following him on his dangerous missions and repeating, as she does in the film: "Victor, please don't go to the Underground meeting tonight"—would be more of a liability than an asset. Rick's speech to Ilsa at the end—"Where I'm going you can't follow. What I've got to do, you can't be any part of" —applies to Laszlo as well as to himself.

Worst of all, Laszlo has escaped from a concentration camp and has been pursued all over Europe by the Nazis. As Renault says of Ugarte: "If you are thinking of warning him, don't put yourself out. He cannot possibly escape." The screenwriters tried to deal with this difficult point by having Laszlo tell Strasser: "You won't dare to interfere with me here. This is still Unoccupied France. Any violation of neutrality would reflect on Captain Renault."[13] But Renault's administration, like the Vichy regime, has been portrayed as hopelessly weak and corrupt. Though technically part of Unoccupied France, the Vichy government, under the primacy of Admiral Jean Darlan, actively collaborated with Hitler and was controlled by the Nazis. In fact, the easiest way to prevent Laszlo's escape would be to shoot him. As one of the most wanted Resistance leaders in Europe, as a man who tried to obtain stolen documents and had attended an illegal Underground meeting, he would have been quickly assassinated or executed by the Germans.

Henreid, an anti-Nazi émigré, realized all this and did not want to play Laszlo: "He felt the role of an Underground leader who appeared in a white tropical suit and hat in a famous nightclub, and talked openly with Nazis, was ridiculous." Confronted with this fundamental criticism, Curtiz brushed it aside by saying: "Don't worry what's logical. I make it go so fast no one notices." But it was Bogart's performance rather than Curtiz' pace that made the film convincing.

Rick Blaine, Bogart's most memorable character, inspires the respect and loyalty of his engaging employees—the croupier, Sasha, Karl and Sam —two of whom escort his girls, Yvonne and Ilsa, home from the café. Ugarte, Renault, Laszlo, even Strasser, also express admiration for Rick until he becomes, in our eyes, worthy of Ilsa's love. Bogart makes Rick both attractive and convincing by showing his change from a sullen, introspective egotist to an emotionally engaged and politically active patriot.

Bogart tenses up and tightens his mouth to indicate wounded anger at the first mention of Laszlo's name, and looks up for a moment when Strasser questions him. He angrily rushes toward Sam when he hears the old love song and stares hard, when he first sees Ilsa, as if trying to recapture whatever they had lost. Drinking and brooding about the past, he constantly handles two of the most familiar objects in his actual life: cigarettes and drinks. Alcohol (in films as in reality) breaks down his reserve and allows his true feelings to emerge. Filled with anguished memories, he bangs the table with his fist, clasps his head in torment and slurs his words.

In the flashback at the Paris railroad station he reads Ilsa's farewell letter with shocked incredulity, goes limp and is pushed on to the train by Sam. He smiles bitterly when she reappears in the café. Angry and disillusioned after he drives her away, he bends his neck and mumbles to himself, rests his head on the table (and shows the ring he had inherited from his father). He can also be patient and protective with Annina. He shows, through the movement of his eyes, that he's thinking about Ilsa when Annina tells him of her intended sexual sacrifice; and awkwardly disengages from her grateful kiss after he's let her husband win at roulette.

He's stone-faced when Laszlo requests the letters of transit. When Ilsa begs for them, he fends her off with hostile remarks that hide his true feelings. The shadowy lighting suggests their ambiguous situation. When he sees the tearful anguish of her love, he melts and embraces her; then, in a businesslike manner, extracts the reason for her devastating rejection in Paris. He seems to smile pleasurably when Laszlo is arrested for buying the letters of transit, reassures Ilsa about their own escape and sternly pulls a gun on Renault. He commands Ilsa at the airport, but shows he still loves her by saying: "We'll always have Paris." In his greatest and most difficult scene, he persuades us, as he persuades her, that renunciation is the only right, honorable and inevitable thing to do, and then walks in step with Renault as they march off to fight in Brazzaville. Bogart is an intensely reflective actor. His characters do a good deal of thinking and seem eternally preoccupied with some inner voice or memory.

The Office of War Information, responsible for routine propaganda, was unhappy about Renault's sympathy with the Vichy regime ("I have no conviction, if that's what you mean. I blow with the wind, and the prevailing wind happens to be from Vichy") as well as with Rick's prolonged reluctance to abandon his dubious neutrality. Troubled by *Casablanca*'s political message, the New York office "withheld it for shipment to North Africa 'on the advice of several Frenchmen with our organization who feel that it is bound to create resentment.'" Richard Raskin has pointed out that *Casablanca* did *not* reflect contemporary American policy. The film was "pro-[de Gaulle's] Free French and anti-Vichy" at a time when the United States was exactly the opposite, "pro-Vichy and anti-Free

French," and when de Gaulle's followers "had been totally excluded from the Operation Torch" landings in North Africa.[14]

Despite its ludicrous, corny and sentimental elements (in Paris Ilsa asks Rick: "Was that cannon fire, or is it my heart pounding?"), *Casablanca* transcends its absurdities. The various writers, in various drafts, emphasized different elements of the story: action, melodrama, politics and romance. Its exotic setting, brilliant cast, fast pace, witty dialogue, meaningful allusions, poignant love scenes, political idealism and timely military context ensured its tremendous success. Umberto Eco, noting its weaknesses, perceptively called it "a hodgepodge of sensational scenes strung together implausibly; its characters are psychologically incredible, its actors act in a manneristic way. Nevertheless, it is a great example of cinematic discourse." He accounted for its triumph by explaining that it combines many disparate story elements and motifs: newsreels and war propaganda, patriotism and exoticism, the test and the enemy, sacrifice and unhappy love, escape and salvation, the visa as Magic Key, the plane as Magic Horse. Eco concluded that "*Casablanca* has succeeded in becoming a cult movie because it is not *one* movie. It is 'the movies.'"

The reception of *Casablanca* was also helped by two extraordinary military and political events. It opened in New York on November 26, 1942, only eighteen days after the Allied armies had landed in Oran, in Algiers and (led by General George Patton) in Casablanca and after newspaper headlines had pushed Casablanca into the public consciousness. The film was also shown at the White House on December 31, 1942. Robert Sherwood recalled that during the evening "there were very few of those present who had any idea as to the significance of the selection."[15] A few days later, Roosevelt left Washington to meet Churchill at Casablanca. The film was released throughout the country on January 23, 1943 during the vitally important Casablanca Conference, when the two wartime leaders planned the invasion of Sicily, the bombing of German territory, the demand for unconditional surrender and the transfer of British forces to the Far East after victory in Europe.

Bogart was nominated by the Academy for best actor (though Paul Lukas won it for his more patriotic role in *Watch on the Rhine*), and *Casablanca* won Awards for best film, best screenplay and best director. When accepting his Oscar, Curtiz pleased the crowd by saying: "So many times I have a speech ready, but no dice. Always a bridesmaid, never a mother. Now I win, I have no speech." When Hal Wallis, the producer of the film, started down the aisle to receive the Oscar for best picture, he was humiliated and outraged by Jack Warner. His boss suddenly leaped to his feet, ran to the stage ahead of him and with a look of great satisfaction grabbed the Award. The film earned a spectacular $3.5 million dollars in 1943. It has been shown more frequently than any other movie on television, and was called by the British Film Institute "the best film ever made."

Like *The Petrified Forest* in 1936, and *High Sierra* and *The Maltese Falcon* in 1941, *Casablanca* (1943) marked a new phase of Bogart's film career. After *The Big Shot* (1942), his last criminal role, he began to play more positive parts—a private detective, a war hero and a romantic idealist—though most of his roles in the 1940s remained stereotypes. The studio always viewed actors as commodities. The better the actor, the more he could be relied upon to breathe life into hackneyed plots and clichéd dialogue. Even as Warners acknowledged Bogart's skill, the studio executives saw him as their own creation. As early as July 1940, just before he made *High Sierra,* Charles Einfeld, Warners' director of advertising and publicity, recognized Bogart's potential and planned to change the image they had created: "Bogart has been typed through publicity as a gangster character. We want to undo this. . . . Sell Bogart romantically. Sell him as a great actor . . . predicting great success for him as a star."

Casablanca finally made Bogart a major romantic star—and once he had achieved that status, he retained it for the rest of his life. In 1941 he ranked fourth—after Cagney, Davis and Flynn—on Warners' roster. His new contract, signed that year, paid him an annual salary of $195,000, while Flynn got $213,000 and Cagney, at $368,000, earned nearly twice as much. In 1946, after the tremendous success of his two films with Lauren Bacall, Bogart's salary shot up to $432,000. The following year his $467,360 salary made him the highest paid actor in the world.[16] Bogart's years of greatest popularity came between 1943 and 1949, when (the only Warners star to make the list) he was named to the exhibitors' top-ten poll for seven years in a row.

In 1945, when Warners tried to prevent the Marx Brothers from making *A Night in Casablanca* (1946), Groucho came up with a brilliant retort:

> I had no idea that the city of Casablanca belonged exclusively to Warner Brothers. . . . It seems that in 1471, Ferdinand Balboa Warner, your great-great grandfather, while looking for a shortcut to the city of Burbank, had stumbled on the shores of Africa and, raising his alpenstock (which he later turned in for a hundred shares of the common), named it Casablanca. . . .
>
> You claim you own Casablanca and that no one else can

use that name without your permission. What about "Warner Brothers"? Do you own that, too? You probably have the right to use the name Warner, but what about Brothers? Professionally, we were brothers long before you were.

〈 IV 〉

BOGART COULD NOT sustain the heights of *Casablanca*. During 1942–43 he was assigned to three mediocre war propaganda pictures and a conventional murder mystery. He finally got into combat with *Action in the North Atlantic,* which reminded him of his convoy duty in World War I and was a kind of wet-run for *The Caine Mutiny.* Ruth Gordon, who had acted in a Broadway show with Bogart in 1928 and played Raymond Massey's wife in this film, noted that Bogart had now reached the top of his profession: "In 1942 Humphrey Bogart was king. No more diffidence, no more insecurity, his dressing room was like the throne room, things went the way *he* said." But all this, she noted, did not change his character: "When he was important, he didn't try to ingratiate any more than when he'd got hired for *Saturday's Children* on our road tour."

Action in the North Atlantic (1943), a somber movie that lacks the high-spirited wit of *Across the Pacific,* began shooting in September 1942 —a month after Bogart completed *Casablanca*—and finished in mid-December. Raymond Massey, who played the captain of the merchant ship, described the elaborate special effects of the most impressive scene, which put the movie forty-three days behind schedule: "The burning tanker was really terrifying, to actors as well as audiences. The effect was achieved by dozens of gas jets controlled at a set of valves which looked like an organ console. This was operated by the so-called 'smokebum' who could play his valves with such skill that the actors seemed to walk through the flames."

The action picture opens realistically as a German submarine torpedoes and sinks Bogart's ship, and then ruthlessly rams the survivors' lifeboat. After eleven days at sea, they are rescued, brought ashore and assigned to a cargo ship in a convoy bound for northwest Russia. Bogart's ship, detached from the convoy, is attacked by planes and again set ablaze by U-boat torpedoes, fired by Germans wearing leather and barking out orders in their guttural tongue. When the captain is wounded, First-Mate Bogart takes command and rams the submarine to get even for the lifeboat. Then, in a "miracle of American seamanship," he brings the ship through rough seas and safely into Murmansk, where he's greeted by a jubilant crowd of fur-trimmed Russkies. Echoing Laszlo's speech in *Casablanca,* Bogart concludes: "A lot more people are going to die before this is over. And it's up to the ones that come through to make sure that they didn't die for nothing."

The movie expresses all the traditional patriotic and propagandistic wartime themes: "the role of the Allies, the importance of the merchant marine, the responsibility of civilians at home . . . the need for everyone to do his part, the toughness of the enemy, and the certainty of eventual victory"[17] as well as the commitment to international solidarity and to the wartime alliance with the Soviet Union.

Having clobbered the Krauts in the North Atlantic, Bogart next trounces Rommel's gang in the Libyan desert. Since Warners wanted Cary Grant, then under contract to Columbia, to star in *Arsenic and Old Lace,* Harry Cohn, the head of Columbia, demanded Bogart for *Sahara* (1943) —his first film outside Warners since Goldwyn's *Dead End* in 1937. The credits suggest the tortuous evolution of the weak script: "Screenplay by John Howard Lawson and Zoltan Korda. Adaptation by James O'Hanlon. From an original story by Philip MacDonald, based on an incident in the Soviet film *The Thirteen.*" No wonder Bogart, trying to squirm out of the heroic though unrewarding role of a tank sergeant, telegraphed Jack Warner: "I can't make myself read lines or play scenes if I think they are phony." Though his built-in shit detector was working well, the studio forced him to take the part.

Sahara, like *Action in the North Atlantic,* contains an ethnic mix that would now satisfy the most stringent advocates of diversity: an American tank crew, five stranded British tommies, an Australian, a South African, a Free Frenchman, a blond-beast German prisoner, a repentant Italian prisoner (of whom Bogart unkindly remarks: "I'm not taking on a load of spaghetti") and a heroic black Sudanese corporal who speaks English like an Oxford graduate. Since the soldiers are stranded in the distant desert, there are no women in the film and no sentimental reunions of soldiers on leave. Bogart—stoic and cool—portrays the kind of heroic soldier who would win the war. The tank that wins the battle and rescues the men stranded in the desert symbolizes America's ability to defeat the Nazis and save the Allies.

Shot in the Mojave Desert, near the Mexican border, using hundreds of army recruits in the battle scenes, *Sahara* takes place in June 1942, after the fall of Tobruk. In a tremendous effort to rejoin their command, the tank crew, cut off by the advancing Germans, slogs through sandstorms and explores empty water-holes (the script cleverly alludes to

Numbers 20:11 when one of the soldiers says, "You'll have to hit a rock to get water, like Moses"). After the usual patriotic palaver about the need for sacrifice in war, Bogart and his last surviving companions make their final stand at a dry well and persuade five hundred thirst-crazed Germans (screaming "*Wasser, Wasser!*") to surrender. At the end, an enemy missile hits the well and provides an abundance of water for all the men. As Bogart reads the roll of the noble dead, he learns that the British have stopped the Germans at the First Battle of Alamein. James Agee, his taste for war films not yet sated, unaccountably called *Sahara* "the best [war melodrama] since *Bataan.*" Though its heroics now seem rather absurd, contemporary audiences found it poignant and inspiring. It earned $2,300,000 in the first three weeks and was Columbia's biggest money-maker in 1943. During the shooting of the film a ten-year-old boy, sceptical about Bogart's role as a war hero, supposedly refused his autograph and said: "I wanna be sure you stay straight."[18]

Conflict, made between mid-June and late August 1943, was not released until June 1945 when Warners stopped concentrating on war films. In this odd conjunction of life and film, Bogart kills his nagging wife (Rose Hobart) so he can marry her attractive younger sister (Alexis Smith). The plot seems to reflect his domestic discord with Mayo Methot and affair with the young Lauren Bacall. But in the movie his dead wife makes him even more miserable than when she was alive. As "funny things happen inside people's heads," Sydney Greenstreet, playing a cunning psychologist, exposes the guilty Bogart by undermining his ability to reason.

The story, though far-fetched, is psychologically interesting. After breaking his leg in a car crash and secretly recovering within a few weeks, Bogart, pretending he cannot walk, follows his wife up a lonely mountain road and murders her. When Bogart says that his wife left their house with a rose, Greenstreet, who gave her the rose when she stopped to see him on the way to the mountains, knows he is guilty. He contrives to trap him by planting an elaborate, hallucinatory sequence of clues: her stolen ring, her perfume, her safe key, her wedding ring, her phone calls, her handkerchief, her letter, her theme song, her locket and her signature. All these clues make Bogart doubt his sanity and convince him—though "she's supposed to be dead"—that she's still alive. To quell his doubts, he returns to the scene of the crime where the police, led by Greenstreet, arrest him. Bogart is unconvincing as Alexis Smith's lover. But he is good at conveying the kind of acute tension and psychological disintegration he would later portray in far greater films: *In a Lonely Place, The Treasure of the Sierra Madre* and *The Caine Mutiny.*

An upper-class smoothie, Bogart's bored and irritated by his nagging wife, and twists his mouth regretfully as Alexis gives him an affectionate peck on the cheek. He sits next to his wife at a dinner party and forces a laugh when she criticizes him publicly, but gazes lovingly at Alexis and watches her in the rear mirror as they all drive home. He stares malevolently at his wife as he plans her murder, is cold and deliberate as he pushes her car over a cliff and looks satisfied when he knows she's dead. He also has to dissemble. He affects concern when he hears that his wife hasn't arrived at the mountain lodge. He lies convincingly to the police and remains debonair with Alexis while brooding about his crime. Nervous and incredulous when a pickpocket brings in his dead wife's ring, he becomes increasingly confused and tormented, and shows signs of his crack-up by slowly drawing his fingers across his face, smiling reflectively, rubbing and biting his lower lip.

In this film the clues are left not by the criminal, but by the police. Everything is staged and all the accomplices have to play their parts perfectly. As Bogart remarks: "Nothing has been taken [from his house] but something has been added." When he tries to bully Alexis into confessing her love for him, the tilt of his limping body makes him seem sinister. His face falls when he realizes that his wife may still be alive, and he foreshadows his fate by grasping the bars of the pawnbroker's cage. Shrinking under Greenstreet's intense scrutiny, he begins to drop his guard and nearly gives himself away. When arrested, his mouth hangs open. The great irony is that he kills for Alexis and then discovers that she doesn't love him. Bogart (as we shall see) didn't want to appear in this film, but he transcended the rather absurd plot and made it all seem quite convincing. Throughout the movie he acts out the inner conflicts between marriage and mistress, tolerance and murder, escape and punishment, conscience and passion.

On September 22, 1943, while making his next film, *Passage to Marseilles* (1944), Bogart's disgust with his rotten pictures and domestic chaos began to interfere with his work. The unit manager reported that Bogart was "suffering from a very bad hangover and being very unruly and hard to manage." The French actress Michele Morgan, who played his wife, agreed with Irene Manning and Ingrid Bergman that he was withdrawn and rather difficult to reach: "Bogart was a strange man, I thought. He was nice to me, but not over-nice. I was very young and shy, and he was at the height of his career. . . . My strongest impression of him was . . . a man who was always on his guard."

Based on a Nordhoff-Hall adventure novel and directed by Michael Curtiz, the film was photographed by the talented James Wong Howe.

The cameraman said the set-ups and lighting would reflect the blunt wartime characters: "There isn't going to be any of that [glamour] stuff in *Passage to Marseilles*. . . . It will be straightforward, nothing tricky. The camera will just happen to be there, a natural spectator."[19] The movie, starring Rains, Greenstreet and Lorre, tries unsuccessfully to recapture some of the magic of *Casablanca*. It also has a French character called Renault, flashbacks of Bogart's idyllic prewar days with Michele Morgan and dialogue that recalls Rick's witty exchange with Strasser. When asked about his nationality in the later film, Bogart, echoing the earlier "drunkard," replies: "Eskimo."

The picture unfolds in a series of complex flashbacks. It begins in 1940 with Bogart, a French pilot, flying from an English air base against Germany. When a visiting journalist remarks, "I've never seen a stranger face or a stronger," Rains, a French liaison officer, narrates Bogart's story. For his opposition to the Munich Pact, in which the Allies had abandoned Czechoslovakia to Hitler, Bogart, a crusading French reporter, has been framed by his political enemies and sent to Devil's Island. He escapes with Lorre and four others and, after several days as a castaway, is picked up by a French freighter, bound for Vichy-controlled Marseilles with a cargo of strategically valuable nickel.

Greenstreet, pro-Japanese in *Across the Pacific,* is now a pro-Vichy French officer, while Rains, who joined the Free French at the end of *Casablanca,* helps steer the ship away from the Nazi port. When a traitor signals their position to the enemy, German planes attack the ship, Lorre is killed and—in the most interesting scene—Bogart cruelly machine-guns the downed pilots. When they finally reach England, instead of Marseilles, he becomes a Free French pilot. Shot down by the enemy, he reaches the base while fatally wounded. The movie ends, like so many others, with a long speech in which propaganda replaces plot. Though the domestic version included Bogart's vengeful murder of the enemy pilots, this unpalatable footage had to be cut before the federal government allowed Warners to send the movie abroad.

< V >

From December 1943 to February 1944 Bogart and Mayo helped the war effort by entertaining troops near the front. They performed from Algiers to Casablanca in North Africa and from Sicily to Naples in Italy, worked seven days a week and gave a hundred and fifty shows in three months. Wartime conditions were extremely difficult but the Bogarts, who sometimes had a wildly enthusiastic audience of eleven thousand men, soldiered on. Mayo, an old trouper, wrote: "We slept in blankets on floors, we bounced in jeeps for endless hours over incredibly rough roads, we trudged through mud, and we still did our stuff." They sometimes had to create a makeshift stage by backing up two army trucks and putting planks between them.

Bogart, who wore a military uniform and army boots, also recalled that their work was arduous: "We wanted to stay in Italy as long as possible because there seemed to be such a terrific need for entertainment there. Usually we were playing to boys who had just left active combat for three or four days' rest, and we would spend the entire leave period with one division. We always played at least two shows a day, not counting the time spent visiting hospitals."[20] The tour made Bogart realize how much affection and appreciation he had inspired in his audience, and how closely they identified him with his movie roles. After one show a Chicago gangster, now a soldier in uniform, approached him and discreetly asked for news of the mob.

Their show, similar to his personal appearance on Broadway in 1940, began with clips from a dozen movies in which Bogart was shot and tumbled to his death. He then came on stage live, pretending to be gravely wounded, and fell down a flight of steps. Picking himself up, he told some jokes and actually sang a few songs. After "getting tough" with the master of ceremonies, Don Cummings, he delivered one of Duke Mantee's speeches from *The Petrified Forest*. Mayo appeared next with the accordionist Ralph Hark, sang "More Than You Know" in her still vibrant voice and then responded to requests for other songs. Finally, Bogart gave a brief but moving speech that concluded: "There's nothing I can say, no words to tell you what the folks at home think about you, what a good job you're all doing. All I can say is, good luck and God bless you."

Though Bogart and Methot were bound together by their adventures and hardships, they continued to fight with each other. Their private war opened a second front in North Africa and they were thrown out of two continents. Bogart's friend John Huston, who was making war documentaries in Italy, visited them in Naples and drank through the night to celebrate their reunion. Bogart, alluding to the supposed impasse at the end of *Across the Pacific*, exclaimed: "John, you sonofabitch! Leaving me tied to a chair!" Huston also recalled that the news of Bogart's arrival received more attention among the troops than the Russian counteroffensive on the Eastern front. According to Huston, Bogart, who had access to bountiful supplies of liquor, fought with the military as well as with Mayo. "He threw a party in his room for a large group of enlisted men, and it got out of hand. A general across the hall came to the room and objected to the noise, and Bogie answered appropriately with something like 'Go fuck yourself!' Bogie was shortly shipped out of Italy."[21]

The Bogarts reached New York on February 15, 1944. They quarreled violently and Bogart, who enjoyed a certain element of sexual intrigue, spent a few nostalgic days visiting Helen Menken. Later that year film clips of the Bogarts' trip, together with combat shots narrated by Bogart, were made by the Red Cross into an effective propaganda short, *Report from the Front*.

Bogart had a fortunate war. The Allied landings and Roosevelt's Conference helped the success of *Casablanca*. He was good at playing military heroes, and they liberated him from gangster stereotypes. The increasing attendance at movie theaters during the war, when people were desperate for diversion, earned huge profits for the studio and prompted Warners to offer him a new and more generous contract in 1947.

Bogart attributed his long-lasting popularity to his professional training on stage. He was also talented, self-confident and willing to work very hard. He had been helped at a crucial moment by Leslie Howard, and was chosen for several excellent parts after George Raft and other actors had turned them down. He capitalized on physical defects, like his hissing lisp and intriguing scar, and carefully exploited his public image. He was shrewd about choosing literate scripts, was eager to work with innovative directors like John Huston and Howard Hawks, and would click magnificently in his first two films with Lauren Bacall. He had the intelligence to see the meaning of the whole film and move effectively within it. His comic gifts and ironic awareness—invaluable in patriotic action movies and essential to balance the villains and caricatures in *Casablanca*—led directly to his triumphs in *The Big Sleep* and *The African Queen*.

♦ 8 ♦

Warner, Bacall and Howard Hawks

1944-1946

⟨ I ⟩

BOGART'S PRICKLY RELATIONS with the autocratic Jack Warner deteriorated during a series of personal clashes in the mid-1940s. After the triumphs of *The Maltese Falcon* and *Casablanca,* Bogart became more confident about choosing his parts and angrily protested when Warner, following the strict terms of the contract, tried to force him to accept inferior roles. The studio's desire to make money with cheap productions and repetitions of successful formulas inevitably clashed with the actor's desire for interesting roles that would display his talent.[1]

Rebellious actors like Peter Lorre and Ann Sheridan have described the belligerent atmosphere of the studio as well as their own conflicts with Jack Warner. On one occasion Lorre could not resist provoking his boss's rage: "Warner asked what I thought of a picture I had made with Humphrey Bogart. I told him I didn't go to see it. Mr. Warner was furious. I said that I only get paid for making pictures. If he wanted me to see them, he'd have to pay me extra." Sheridan said actors had to protest in order to avoid being ground down by the system. She also "had to fight for everything at Warners. From the casting director up to Jack Warner. Of course, at Warners everybody seemed to have to fight. Cagney and Davis. That's the only way it was done. A knock-down, drag-out fight. You didn't always win, but it let them know you were alive."

Just after he completed *Sahara* in May 1943, Bogart began a prolonged dispute with Jack Warner. He had been assigned to *Conflict,* whose plot seemed to reflect his tumultuous personal life. When he refused to report for work and remained incommunicado on the *Sluggy,* he was suspended. Three days later he came ashore to speak to Warner. Their acrimonious phone conversation, transcribed by a studio secretary, illuminates Bogart's relations with Warner, the power of the studio executives and the subservient position of actors.

Knowing he had to work or remain suspended, Bogart attempted to bargain from a weak position. Appealing in vain to artistic values and human sympathy, he was humiliated by his boss. Warner, who held all the legal and contractual cards, tried to be polite but kept turning the screws. Both men hated each other, but wanted to keep the dispute impersonal in order to maintain their working relationship. Bogart kept repeating his refusal while Warner, getting the better of the argument, kept coming up with new reasons why Bogart should agree to do the picture. At first, as Warner appealed to his team spirit, Bogart placated him by recognizing his power, by mentioning their "friendship" and by insisting that he could not betray his professional standards:

> B: I don't want to get into any personal fight with you.
> W: This is nothing personal. I'm running a big business and try to call the shots for the good of all concerned, as it is a herculean task to get everyone paid each Wednesday.
> B: This is personal between you and me, Jack. I am more serious than I have ever been in my life and I just do not want to do this picture [*Conflict*]. If you want to get tough with me you can, and I know how tough you can get, but if you do get tough, and do the things you say you will, I will feel that I have lost a friend. I ask you as a favor to me to take me out of this picture, for I feel very strongly about it. . . .
> W: We have everything all set, people engaged to work in the picture, so come on and come to work tomorrow.
> B: I'm sorry, Jack; I just can't do it. My stomach will not let me. I'm an honest man and I have to be honest with myself in this matter.

Warner, calling him Humphrey (not Bogey), tried to coerce the actor by flattery and moral exhortations. Emphasizing his paternal interest in Bogart's welfare and need to enforce the terms of their contract, he urged him to be more loyal and more flexible. Bogart insisted that he loved Warners as much as Warner did, but had to consider his own career and reject the inferior story:

> W: All I know is, if you are the artist you think you are, and I know you are, you should do this picture. . . .

B: I just can't do it no matter what you do to me; I just can't
do it. . . .

W: Believe me, Humphrey, I bought it for you exclusively. . . .

B: I know something about this business and do not think it
is good. This thing has upset me more than anything else
in this town. I think Warner Bros. is the best studio in the
business, and always want to work at Warners. . . . [But] I
also have my career at stake.

W: Well, I cannot let everybody do what they want and I have
to go by the contract. . . . You must remember, Humphrey,
that it is not Jack Warner that is asking you to do this
picture. You are doing this for the company. . . . I say you
are making a serious error in not making this picture. Besides, once in a while you must give and take, and so far
you haven't done this. I think you are just stubborn.

Bogart was particularly upset by Warner's assumption that actors were
too stupid to judge scripts. He told Warner that both Wallis and Curtiz
had advised him not to do the film, and tried to get him to admit the script
was rotten. Warner refused to be drawn on the subject of artistic merit,
which did not concern him. He asserted that it would be a successful
product and resorted to threats:

W: In this business you can't always take the apples off the
tree, you have to take some of them that are on the ground.

B: Then you admit that this is a rotten apple. . . .

W: You may think it is not good for you, but I think it will be
great, and want you to rely on my judgment. . . . I have
heard the same talk from twenty people who talk just like
you are doing, and I know one of them is now trying to get
a job as just an extra.

Warner's calculated insult to an actor who had recently completed *Casablanca* and had contributed so much to the studio's success was tasteless
and absurd. Bogart's reluctant acceptance of the remark reveals the psychological price the stars had to pay at Warner Bros.

Bogart then reminded him of all he had done for the studio and Warner
(who said he never made threats) threatened to suspend him and to
withdraw him from the forthcoming *Passage to Marseilles*. Becoming more
and more personal but fearful of escalating the fight, Bogart exaggerated
his devotion. But he resisted coercion and claimed that Warner treated
him worse than his other stars:

B: I work for Warner Bros. and am willing to die for Warner Bros. When you asked me to appear at the Hollywood Bowl on Easter Sunday at 4 a.m., and dance in a musical comedy, I did so. I will do anything, but I cannot do this picture. . . .

W: Don't make the mistake that some people have made.

B: What are you doing? Threatening me? . . .

W: We will have to suspend you and we will not put you in *Passage to Marseilles*.

B: I know what you can do to me, and am thoroughly aware of this.

W: Please understand that I am not threatening you. I don't threaten anyone.

B: I am glad that you are not making this a personal thing. . . . You would never have offered this script to Flynn, Bette Davis or anyone else, but you think I am a sucker, and because I signed that contract you are forcing me to do this.

Bogart, apparently weakening, deserted the high ground of artistic merit and begged for pity. He tried to flatter Warner by claiming that he loved the studio (which he loathed) and said he would rather do the film version of Patrick Hamilton's *Hangover Square*. (It had an appealing title and was made by Twentieth Century–Fox in 1944 with George Sanders and Linda Darnell.) Warner, also employing strategic lies, retorted that Bogart *had* to act in *Conflict* and was the only man who could do justice to the magnificent part:

B: All I am doing is talking to you as a man. . . . Why be so tough with me? . . .

W: I told [your agent] we are not going to keep this other picture and are going to hold *Conflict* until you come back to work on it. . . .

B: Did you ever read a book called *Hangover Square*. That is what this picture should be. . . . Jack, I like the way the studio is run, and I have always liked it, but I do not think I am the right guy to play it.

W: I am positive you can do it. When I read the script I thought you were the only man in town who could play it.

Finally, Bogart returned to his previous arguments: that he knew as much about movies as anyone else at Warners, that Jack ought to respect his judgment and that the studio would be better off destroying the script than making the film. Eager to conclude the business, Warner urged

Bogart not to make a great mistake. He could finish the picture in only a few weeks and then happily return to the high seas:

> B: I don't think Trilling or anyone knows what the hell they
> are talking about. I know I can direct or produce a picture
> better than most of the people you have on the Lot. . . .
> W: All I ask you to do is to come in Monday, and five or six
> weeks will go by, then you can go back to your boat. . . .
> B: Why don't you burn this script and forget about it. . . . I am
> sorry, Jack, but I can't do it.[2]

Bogart held out during the month of May. But the outcome of the uneven skirmish was clear from the start, and he finally had to submit. He gave up in early June, came off suspension and joined the cast of *Conflict* in the summer of 1943. Though by no means "great," even in Jack Warner's sense of the word, the film was better than many others Bogart had made.

Having lost the dispute about *Conflict,* Bogart was determined to win the next round. A year later, on May 26, 1944, he sent Warner an angry, resentful telegram explaining his refusal to do formulaic war propaganda, like *God is My Co-Pilot,* about the Flying Tigers in China. More self-confident and aggressive after falling in love with Bacall and after completing *To Have and Have Not,* Bogart asserted that he had read the script and Jack had not. He relied on his own good judgment and rejected the studio's spurious appeal to patriotism. He resented Warner's patronizing attitude, was unhappy about his current contract, and wanted to get the same treatment as other stars. He also claimed poor health and — defending himself psychologically as well as professionally — insisted that he, not Warner, was responsible for his own achievements:

> When picture in question was offered by Wallis I turned it
> down as did Mike Curtiz because I did not think it would make
> a good picture and did not think the part suited me. We have
> made this picture many times. I have read carefully the script
> as it is now and my opinion has not changed. The part is no
> good and is not for me and I consider myself as well equipped
> to judge scripts and parts as anyone else. I question Jack
> whether you have had time to read the completed script. . . .
> I do not think our business relationship has anything to do with
> patriotism and I resent your putting it on that basis. You con-
> tinually refer to the seven year contract as if it were a favor to
> me. At the time it was signed it was good. Now it is no good.
> I would be very happy to tear it up and start again. I have not

been ill advised. . . . I alone have read the script and have
made my decision which I am fully capable of doing. I am tired
of the studio's attitude that I am a half-witted child. Don't like
to be threatened and should like the same consideration as
shown to Davis and Flynn. You are not thinking of me when
you put me in this picture. You are using the box office value
I fortunately have at the moment to bolster a picture even to
the extent of forcing me into a mediocre part for which I am
not suited. You have assigned a director who has never been
associated with first class productions and in whom I have no
confidence. My part in *Passage to Marseilles* was a very bad one
which could have been played by anyone, as can this. I trusted
the studio to protect me in that case, which they did not. In
closing, I have waited one solid year for a chance to get a few
uninterrupted weeks to gain back my health and prevent a
breakdown and one and a half weeks after the start of it the
wires and the threats and the same old story start again. You
speak of my success as if you alone were responsible for it. I
feel that I had something to do with that success.

Bogart did *not* make *God is My Co-Pilot* (1945), which was directed
by Robert Florey and starred Dennis Morgan, who took Bogart's rejected
roles as Bogart had taken Raft's. Bogart was on suspension during the
emotionally turbulent summer of 1944, and began his next film with
Bacall, *The Big Sleep,* on October 10. But he continued to refuse inferior
pictures. In 1946 he turned down *Cheyenne* (1947), a western made with
Dennis Morgan, and *Stallion Road,* a horse-racing movie starring Ronald
Reagan and Zachary Scott. In 1947, when Mark Hellinger was making
Brute Force, Bogart appeared on the set, painted "Jack Warner Peniten-
tiary" on the prison wall and posed for a picture in front of it.

‹ II ›

IN LATE FEBRUARY 1944, just after returning from his unhappy USO
tour with Mayo, Bogart met and fell in love with his fourth wife, Lauren
Bacall, while they were shooting her first film, *To Have and Have Not.*
Born Betty Perske in 1924 (twenty-five years after Bogart), she came from
a poor Jewish family and grew up in the Bronx. Her father sold medical
supplies and her mother, who worked as a secretary, supported the family

after their divorce in 1930. Betty was raised by her German-Romanian grandmother, whose family names were Weinstein-Bacal. After graduating from Julia Richman High School in Manhattan and studying for a year at the American Academy of Dramatic Arts, she worked as an usher in the Shubert Theaters, had a walk-on part in a Broadway show and a speaking role in a play by Mary Astor's lover George S. Kaufman.

Bacall also worked as a model. Her big break came when the editor Diana Vreeland put her on the March 1943 cover of *Harper's Bazaar* and she was noticed by a former model, Slim Hawks. Her husband Howard, a leading independent director, placed Bacall under his personal seven-year contract and brought her out to Hollywood. She would start at $100 a week and reach $1,200 a week in the final year. This enabled her to rent an apartment, buy a car and bring out her mother to live with her in Los Angeles. Hawks named her by dropping the "ce" from Laurence and adding an "l" to Bacal, and molded her as his dream girl. He supervised all the details of her make-up and wardrobe, and arranged her photographs and publicity. She realized that Hawks regarded her as his property. But as a hardworking and ambitious nineteen-year-old, she was good at following direction and eager to be a protégée. In February 1945 she pulled off a real coup by appearing in a famous leggy photograph, lounging on top of an upright piano and gazing down as Vice-President Harry Truman played a tune.

Both Bogart and Bacall sought a marriage partner who could fulfill their childhood needs: he chose a dominant woman, like his strong-willed mother; she had grown up without a father and wanted an older man. Bogart helped Bacall's career in films as Helen Menken had helped his on stage. (In 1944, when Bacall asked Hedda Hopper: "I'm not getting anywhere with my career. What do I do?" Hopper advised her to "marry a star.") Their first meeting was brief, casual and undramatic. Bogart, slighter than she had pictured him from his image on screen, was unusually friendly and said: "I just saw your test. We'll have a lot of fun together." As Louise Brooks shrewdly observed: "He could only love a woman he had known for a long time or . . . one who was flung at him in the intimacy of a play or film. . . . [Bacall became] his perfect screen partner, as seductive as Eve, as cool as the serpent."[3]

Bacall represented a new kind of cover-girl beauty. Thin, flat-chested and angular, she had the perfect figure for the tailored suits and dresses of the 1940s, with their bold stripes and wide shoulder pads. Five feet six inches tall, she weighed 120 pounds, had tawny blond hair and blue-green eyes. Bogart, not a "bosom man" (Maud, Menken and Philips were all rather thin), was instantly attracted to her and said: "you've got the map of Middle Europe slung across those high cheekbones and wide green eyes." He found her earthy, witty, amusing; liked her outspoken honesty, admired "her youth, her animal-like behavior and don't-give-a-damn attitude." Quoting Kipling (in the last five words), he also noted that "she wasn't jealous of other actresses because they happened to be more talented or beautiful than she. And, brother, that's a rare trait in the female of the species."[4]

Their romance began, three weeks into the shooting, when Bogart—who never fooled around with women at work—came to her dressing room to say goodnight. Suddenly (lovers take note) he leaned over, put his hand under her chin and impulsively but shyly kissed her on the lips. He then asked her to write her phone number on the back of an old matchbook. She was both attracted to and intimidated by the upper-class WASP and leading actor at Warner Bros., and was afraid he might think less of her because she was Jewish. But religion was not important to Bogart, who had many close Jewish friends: Leslie Howard, Sam Jaffe, Mike Romanoff, Mark Hellinger, Peter Lorre, Richard Brooks and Swifty Lazar.

Bacall was astonished to discover that the famous film star was lonely and miserable, and drank to escape the frustration at work and unbearable tension at home. Despite the differences in age, background, experience—he had been married three times, she was still a virgin—they soon fell deeply in love. They had emotional and physical rapport, and made a dynamic pair. She respected him as an actor and wanted to learn from him. Flattered by her interest, he became her mentor and tried to protect her. Excited by her new romance, she wrote to her mother that they shared the same sense of humor and had great fun together: "Bogie has been a dream man. We have the most wonderful times together. I'm insane about him. We kid around—he's always gagging—trying to break me up and is very, very fond of me."

Untainted by the corruption of Hollywood, she seemed to offer him a new life, while he obviously had much to give her. By marrying him the ambitious actress would solidify her early success and assure her fame, wealth and status. Since Bogart was still married and Methot (whom he referred to as "Madam") was fiercely jealous, their courtship had to be kept secret and they had very little time together. They sometimes invited Marcel Dalio to join them for coffee or dinner and help them maintain a respectable front. They would also drive to quiet residential areas, talk, hold hands and kiss in the car, and keep in touch with passionate, frustrated letters. Bogart's, written in the summer of 1944 after the filming ended, are just as good as the love letters of major authors like Graham Greene and Hemingway. Bogart's first letter, in fact, is uncannily like

Hemingway's description in *A Moveable Feast* (1964) of leaving his first wife for another woman:

> When I saw my wife again standing by the tracks as the train came in by the piled logs at the station, I wished I had died before I ever loved anyone but her.

Bogart wrote Bacall with similar bittersweet melancholy:

> I wish with all my heart that things were different—someday soon they will be. And now I know what was meant by "To say goodbye is to die a little"—because when I walked away from you that last time and saw you standing there so darling I did die a little in my heart.

Sometimes at night Bacall would drive down the coast to Balboa and meet him at the Coast Guard station during his break from his weekly volunteer duty. Once again they would sit in the car like two kids, talk, hold hands, kiss, and exchange letters they later read and reread. Bogart expressed his love and his desire to protect her from harm. She aroused his long-suppressed yet powerful romantic feelings, and he begged her to be patient while he gathered strength to disengage himself from the volatile and violent Methot:

> Baby, I do love you so dearly and I never, never want to hurt you or bring any unhappiness to you—I want you to have the loveliest life any mortal ever had. It's been so long, darling, since I've cared so deeply for anyone that I just don't know what to do or say. I can only say that I've searched my heart thoroughly these past two weeks and I know that I deeply adore you and I know that I've got to have you. We must just wait because at present nothing can be done that would not bring disaster to you. . . .
>
> Baby, I never believed that I could love anyone again, for so many things have happened in my life to me that I was afraid to love—I didn't want to love because it hurts so when you do.

A week later he described the life they would have together when she had transformed him and he had recovered the old friends who had drifted away during his flying-glass battles with Methot. Imitating the characters they had played in *To Have and Have Not*, Marie Browning and Harry Morgan, they called each other Slim and Steve. (Bogart, called Steve in Richard Brooks' *The Producer*, called their son Steve.) The romantic association of this film and the triumphant outcome of that story—when the hero and heroine "rescue" each other and make their escape—heightened the intensity of their love affair. As Hawks later observed: "Bogey fell in love with the character she played, so she had to keep playing it for the rest of her life." Bogart wrote to her:

> All the nice things I do each day would be so much sweeter and so much gayer if you were with me. I find myself saying a hundred times a day, "If Slim could only see that" or "I wish Slim could hear this." I want to make a new life with you—I want all the friends I've lost to meet you and know you and love you as I do—and live again with you, for the past years have been terribly tough, damn near drove me crazy. You'll soon be here, Baby, and when you come you'll bring everything that's important to me in this world with you.

On June 14—after her mother had tactfully stayed away and they had had a few hours together in Bacall's apartment—Bogart thanked her for her patience and repeated the phrase "fun together" he had used at their first meeting. He also emphasized their age difference (she made him feel old rather than rejuvenated), mentioned his personal and professional burdens, and voiced his fear that they might have only a few years together:

> Darling, sometimes I get so unhappy because I feel that I'm not being fair to you—that it is not fair to wait so long a time —and then somehow I feel that it's alright because I'm not hurting you, not harming and never shall.
>
> I'd rather die than be the cause of any hurt or harm coming to you, Baby, because I love you so much.
>
> It seems so strange that after forty-four years of knocking around I should meet you, know you and fall in love with you when I thought that that could never again happen to me. And it's tragic that everything couldn't be all clean and just right for us instead of the way it is because we'd have such fun together. Out of my love for you I want nothing but happiness to come and no hurt ever.
>
> Slim, darling, I wish I were your age again—perhaps a few years older—and no ties of any kind—no responsibilities— it would be so lovely, for there would be so many long years ahead instead of the few possible ones.

In July Bogart called her at four in the morning and made her mother furious. He was drunk and had no car; he had quarreled with Mayo, left his boat at Newport Beach and was walking to town in the rain. Bacall ran off to meet him, found him at sunrise and drove him to a friend's trailer. There, for the first time (Bacall wrote) they had complete privacy: "We could do or say anything we pleased—it was our nest—it was the most natural thing in the world." They seem to have slept together that day. On July 12 he thanked her for rescuing him and for revitalizing his existence:

> Sunday was so beautiful, so sweet, my dearest, and you were wonderful to come to the rescue of poor befuddled me—I was just about ready to give up and die under an oil well when I saw your blessed face—never was so glad to see anyone, and I must have been a beautiful sight. And then that lovely day with you darling—and the moments that were ours alone to cherish always in our hearts.[5]

The contrast between Bacall and Methot was extreme. Betty—tall and thin rather than short and chunky—had a lean figure and a cascade of long smooth hair, and dressed elegantly in the latest fashions. She was virginal, not blowsy, temperate, not alcoholic, a rising, not a fading star. Most importantly, she was self-effacing, devoted and adoring. Unlike his other wives, she wanted to have children. Though ambitious, she was willing to give up her career for him. Although impatient and upset by Bogart's insistence on slowly severing his ties to Mayo, she wisely retreated, kept her dignity and did not press him to leave his wife before he was ready to do so. Confident of their love, she was prepared to wait and ride out the storm.

Bogart misleadingly maintained: "I should like to make it positively clear that Betty had nothing to do with my divorce." Though his seven-year marriage was doomed, it had lasted until Bacall provided the impetus for its dissolution. On one occasion Methot appeared unexpectedly and Bacall, terrified of a confrontation, had to hide in the toilet of the boat. Another time Mayo—no great laundress herself—grabbed the phone from the drunken Bogart and screamed: "Listen, you Jewish bitch—who's going to wash his socks? Are *you*? Are *you* going to take care of him?" The next day Bogart, ashamed that he had subjected Bacall to such vilification, reached an all-time low and was too drunk to work.

Bacall later described the deterioration of his marriage to Methot: "He felt he had to marry Mayo—he was a marrying man, she expected it, it was the gentlemanly thing to do, so he did it. And it got worse and worse. . . . He said he had to drink—it was the only way he could live with her. She was jealous—always accused him of having affairs with his leading ladies—always knocked him as an actor, making sarcastic references about the 'big star.' She'd sung 'More Than You Know' in a Vincent Youmans musical, had been successful and was a good actress—but drink took over and the minute there was a third person present, she'd start on Bogie."[6]

‹ III ›

IN THE MIDST of this emotional turbulence, and partly inspired by it, Bogart made two of his greatest and most literate films, *To Have and Have Not* (1945) and *The Big Sleep* (1946), with Bacall and Howard Hawks. Like Huston, Hawks was a man of action, a virile director who brought out the best in the screenplay and in Bogart. But unlike Huston, a meticulous planner, Hawks emphasized spontaneity and improvisation. He rehearsed very little, kept changing the script and handed new scenes to the actors as the film was shot. Raymond Chandler, who wrote the novel *The Big Sleep* and liked the film version, noted that "Hawks shoots [off] the cuff more or less, he tells me, merely using a rough script to try out his scenes and then rewriting them on the set."

Born in Goshen, Indiana, in 1896, the son of a wealthy paper manufacturer, Hawks went to Exeter and graduated from Cornell in 1917 with a degree in mechanical engineering. He was a lieutenant in the Army Air Corps in France in World War I, and after the war built airplanes and the racing car that won the Indianapolis 500 in 1936. Physically impressive (like Huston), Hawks was "six-feet-three, broad shouldered, slim-hipped, soft-spoken, confident in manner, conservative in dress, and utterly distinguished overall." The screenwriter Niven Busch found him formidably distant and frigid: "He gave me his reptilian glare. The man had ice-cold blue eyes and the coldest of manners. He was like that with everyone— women, men, whatever. He was remote; he came from outer space. He wore beautiful clothes. He spoke slowly in a deep voice. He looked at you with these frozen eyes."

Hawks' tall, blond and beautiful wife, Nancy (known as Slim), a former socialite, was born in California in 1918 and later married another powerful Hollywood figure, Leland Hayward. Hawks adored his wife, but was undemonstrative, and Bacall felt they didn't have much fun or sex. While

Slim helped transform the young actress into her own image, Hawks tried to dominate and control Bacall's life, and expected her to follow his orders. Though Bogart gave her a great deal of help on the set, Hawks claimed that the actor was distracting her and interfering with her work. Slim and Hawks both tried to discourage her involvement with Bogart. "When the picture's over," they told her, "he'll forget all about it—that's the last you'll ever see of him." Hawks resented Bogart's growing influence on his latest creation and threatened to get rid of her, to destroy her career (if Bogart didn't) by sending her to Monogram, which made the worst movies in Hollywood. Bogart reassured her by dismissing the threat and explaining Hawks' motives: "No, Baby, he won't send you to Monogram—don't you worry, you're too valuable to him. He just can't stand to see your attention diverted from him, that's all—he's jealous."[7]

Hawks claimed that while fishing with Hemingway (who had a passion for Slim), he had boasted: "'I can make a picture out of your worst story.' 'What's my worst story?' asked Hemingway. 'That god damned piece of junk called *To Have and Have Not.*' 'You can't make anything out of that,' said Hemingway and Hawks said, 'Yes I can'"—and did. Howard Hughes had originally bought the rights of the novel from Hemingway for $10,000 and sold them to Hawks for $97,000. Hawks then resold the rights to Warners for $108,500 plus 20 percent of the gross receipts up to $3 million.

The only characters and scenes in the film that have any connection to the novel concern the fishing episodes on Harry Morgan's boat, his relations with his dishonest client, Johnson, and his friendship with his drunken mate, Eddy, who (Hemingway wrote) "walked with his joints all slung wrong." In the novel Morgan loses his clients, fishing equipment, contraband liquor, charter boat, right arm, shipmates and, finally, his life. The theme is: "No matter how, a man alone ain't got no bloody fucking chance."

In the film, this negative idea is reversed and Morgan, though acting alone, helps the French Resistance and defeats his Vichy enemies. Hemingway's novel was set in Cuba. But the locale was changed when the Office of Inter-American Affairs complained that the political theme of the picture might hurt America's relations with the Batista regime in Cuba. Instead of smuggling twelve Chinese to Cuba, as in the novel, Morgan, in the film, smuggles a Resistance leader and his wife to Martinique.

The script was written by the veteran Jules Furthman, who earned $3,000 a week, and the "amateur" William Faulkner, who got $300 a week. According to Hawks, Faulkner enjoyed changing the novel just because it was Hemingway's. Hawks told Jack Warner that he would show the finished screenplay to Hemingway, who promised to "write on it for nothing."[8] But Hemingway never saw or worked on the script. In 1955, after Hemingway had won the Nobel Prize, he condemned Faulkner for alcoholism and for selling out to Hollywood by writing an inferior version of his novel.

After the opening scenes, *Casablanca* becomes the dominant influence on *To Have and Have Not*. Hawks' film also has a tough American expatriate who helps the Free French and fights the Nazis in Vichy-controlled territory, a Resistance leader and his wife (de Bursac and Helène) and an excellent cast of minor characters. Marcel Dalio and Dan Seymour, who had appeared in *Casablanca,* now graduate to more important roles: from nightclub croupier to hotel owner (called Frenchy in a town where most of the people are French) and from loyal doorman to villainous police captain (Renard, the fox, instead of Renault).

Both pictures have a sentimental and sympathetic piano player (Hoagy Carmichael instead of Dooley Wilson) whose songs are not, as in most films, a trite distraction but an integral part of the story. Marie suggests she's had a rough time with her lovers when she "sings" (in a voice dubbed by Andy Williams) that she feels blue 'cause her plan for a man has fallen through. Cricket (Carmichael) describes her plight, stranded between Brazil and America and forced to live by her wits, when he sings that he needs someone to love him and carry him back to San Francisco.

Bogart, who was fond of the sweetly naive Carmichael, had found him one morning examining the wrinkles in his eyes: "When I asked what the trouble was, he said he had been out pretty late the night before last, but that last night he had gotten to bed early and he was afraid the wrinkles around his eyes would not match up with the previous day's shooting." When Hoagy invented the business of playing the piano with a match in his mouth, Bogart gave him "a large box consisting of several dozen plain kitchen matches but painted different colors, which we presented to him, and told him these were mood matches which he could use while portraying various moods."[9]

In both *Casablanca* and *To Have and Have Not* the authorities question Rick Blaine and Harry Morgan about their nationality; the Vichy police chief closes the nightclub and hotel; the police ask Marie, as they had asked Rick, why she came to the territory (she cheekily answers: "To buy a new hat"); pockets are picked and wallets stolen; the Free French hold secret Underground meetings; the Resistance leader wonders whether he should leave by himself or take his wife; and de Bursac (who hides from his enemies instead of chatting with them in public) makes the same stirring speech as Victor Laszlo: "There is always someone else. That is the mistake the Germans always make with people they try to destroy. There will always be someone else."

Most importantly, both Blaine and Morgan have been jilted and embittered by a woman, but are brought from isolation ("I don't care who runs France or Martinique") to political engagement by a woman's love. Harry forces Renard to fill out the exit papers, and when asked by the Resistance fighters why he finally agrees to help the de Bursacs, laconically explains: "Maybe because I like you and maybe because I don't like them." At the end of *Casablanca,* Rick leaves with Renault to fight the Nazis in Brazzaville. At the end of this film Morgan leaves with Slim and Eddy to pick up a Resistance leader on Devil's Island. Though the themes are similar, *To Have and Have Not* has a more upbeat ending than *Casablanca.* Marie, unlike Ilsa, is free to go with Morgan to a new, adventurous and dedicated life.

To Have and Have Not was shot in ten weeks between February and May 1944. Hawks fancied himself as a tough guy in a Bogart role. Imitating Cagney's line in *Angels with Dirty Faces* ("But don't get smart with me"), he was pleased, in a late interview, to portray his leading actor as fearful, docile and obedient: "I had trouble the first day with Bogart. I think I grabbed him by the lapels and pushed his head up against the wall, and said, 'Look, Bogie. . . . I tell you how to get tough, but don't get tough with me.' He said, 'I won't.' Everything was fine from that time on. He had a couple of drinks at lunch, and that's what caused it." In a more realistic account, Hawks confirmed Nunnally Johnson's view of Bogart's acting ability while completely suppressing his violent opposition to Bogart's affair with Bacall: "He was . . . really underrated as an actor. My kind of actor, you know. And the little queer things he did because he had a nerve cut in his upper lip—so his upper lip wouldn't smile—only his lower lip would smile. We seemed to understand one another and work very well together. Without his help I couldn't have done what I did with Bacall. The average leading man would have got sick and tired of the rehearsal and the fussing around. Not very many actors would sit around and wait while a girl steals a scene. But he fell in love with the girl and the girl with him, and that made it easy."

Warners took a great risk by starring an almost untrained and inexperienced actress. But under the tutelage of Bogart and Hawks, Bacall made a sensational debut in *To Have and Have Not.* Hawks taught her how to make her high-pitched voice huskier and sexier. Bogart not only let her steal scenes, but told her how to do it. He gave her confidence and a sense of herself. She explained that "when Bogie was in the scene and saw that I was just standing there, rather blank, he'd change his line or he'd say

'What?' That shook me up. I'd say, 'Why did you do that?' He'd say, 'Because you weren't listening.'" He also made her think more seriously about her role by asking: "'Where are you coming from?' 'My bedroom,' I said. 'Weren't you doing something before the doorbell rang? You just don't walk to the door because the director says 'Action.'"[10]

Bacall also described how Hawks improved the script, enhanced her role and brought out the best in her: "Each morning when we got to the set, he, Bogie, and I and whoever else might be in the scene, and the script girl, would sit in a circle in canvas chairs with our names on them and read the scene. Almost unfailingly Howard would bring in additional dialogue for the scenes of sex and innuendo between Bogie and me. After we'd gone over the words several times . . . we'd go through the scene on the set to see how it felt. Howard said, 'Move around—see where it feels most comfortable.' Only after all that had been worked out did he call Sid Hickox and talk about camera set-ups."

In the film Bacall wears thick 1940s-style shoulder pads, as if she were trying out for a women's football team, and slinks around in satin like a languid panther. Hawks wanted to make the innocent, virginal Bacall utterly unlike Ingrid Bergman's idealized, devoted Ilsa. Bergman romantically tells Bogart: "I'll go with you anyplace"; Bacall—witty, brazen, impertinent and acidly affectionate—says: "You could do anything to me. I wouldn't care." Hawks, who liked to pretend that Bogart resented Bacall's character, when he was actually doing everything he could to help her, wrote that he told Bogart: "watch yourself because you're supposed to be the most insolent man on the screen and I'm going to make a girl a little more insolent than you. . . . In every scene in the picture she's going to walk out and leave you. You're going to be left standing with egg on your face. He said that isn't fair, and I said I know but I'm the director and I can do that."

Bacall wrote that Hawks conceived her character as "a young woman who'd knocked around a lot in her life, a woman of the world, a woman with humor, with insolence, who in traveling alone had developed a certain veneer as protection against the men who preyed on her." Her tough background is shown when she takes a slap from a Vichy policeman without turning a hair. "You hardly blinked an eye," Morgan tells her. "That takes a lot of practice. Yeah, I know a lot about you, Slim."[11] Later on, Morgan slaps Eddy (Walter Brennan) for hiding on the boat without permission and Marie lightly slaps Morgan's face after they kiss. The slap motif unites the three characters, who have all been humiliated and who leave the oppressive island together at the end of the film.

Bacall noted that "worldliness in sex, total independence, the ability to handle any situation, had no more relation to me then than it has now." But her character, which avoided the usual clichés, was absolutely convincing. In Furthman's original scene, Hawks sardonically recalled, someone stole Marie's purse: "Jules says, 'How do you like it?' And I said, 'Jules, that's just a great scene. If there's anything that gives me a rash, it's a poor little girl whose purse has been stolen.' 'You sonofabitch,' he says, and the next day, in the scene, *she* steals the purse'" from the fisherman Johnson and flashes a sly smile when Morgan makes her return it.

In contrast to conventional films, where the lovers hate each other at first sight and marry ninety minutes later, Morgan and Marie are instantly attracted to each other and reveal an urgent and palpable desire. As they exchange wisecracks, he tries to keep her at a distance so he can carry out his dangerous work for the Resistance. Her first line is, "Have you got a match?" and lighting and holding cigarettes, one of his trademarks as an actor, becomes a kind of mating dance until chain smoking finally chains them to each other. As Bogart hooks his fingers in his belt and thoughtfully pulls his ear, they also carry a bottle of whiskey back and forth between their hotel rooms. He warns both Marie and Helène de Bursac to "Quit that baby talk," but Marie has the best lines and always gets the better of him. During their sharp but affectionate verbal fencing, they keep cutting each other off but he allows her to have the last word. When he calls her by her nickname and orders her to hand over Johnson's stolen wallet, she says: "nobody calls me Slim. I'm too skinny to take it kindly." When she slides into his lap and he asks what she's doing, she kisses him and answers, "Well, somebody has to make the first move." When Helène faints as Morgan removes the bullet from her husband's wound and he tenderly carries her out of the room, Marie cracks: "What are you trying to do, guess her weight?" As they leave the hotel at the end of the film, she wiggles her bottom to a sexy little rumba rhythm that parodies Eddy's jerky alcoholic gait.

In her now immortal scene, Marie kisses the still passive Morgan and boldly tells him: "It's even better when you help." Annoyed by his lack of response, she then adds: "You don't have to say anything and you don't have to do anything. Not a thing. Oh, maybe, just whistle. You know how to whistle, don't you, Steve? You just put your lips together and blow." Hawks originally wrote these lines for Bacall's screen test, and they went over so well that he decided to use them in the picture: "Faulkner was the one who found a place to put it. He said, 'If we put these people in a hotel corridor where nobody else is around, then I think we can make that scene work.'"[12] Bogart's Christmas present to Bacall was a gold whistle with the inscription: "If you want anything, just whistle."

This scene is a good example of how writers and directors circumvented the Production Code in the 1940s by creating a subtle tension between repression and expression. The film became a raid on inarticulate feelings as the sexual theme was conveyed through the language of reticence and evasion. As the director Peter Bogdanovich wrote: "You never doubted for a moment what Bogart and Bacall were talking about in *To Have and Have Not* — I mean, it was clear they wanted to sleep together, and we didn't need it discussed; in fact it was much sexier left unspoken."

In this film Bogart exhibits his repertory of gestures and facial expressions. He moves his hands irritably while waiting for the dock official to produce his daily exit papers. He occupies himself with practical tasks on the boat. He rubs his hands with excitement as his client hooks the huge marlin. He smiles with recognition when Frenchy asks for his help and rolls up the blinds as if to clarify the murky political situation. When he shoots the Vichy cop, he brings out the old gangster grimace. Walter Brennan plays Bogart's faithful sidekick as he had done with Gary Cooper and John Wayne. Bogart smiles indulgently at Brennan's feeble jokes and is horrified when he hears the police are interrogating him.

When Bacall first asks for a light, Bogart quickly sizes her up and throws the matches instead of striking one for her. He smiles and shifts pleasurably in his seat when hearing her sing. He pushes her into his room to retrieve his client's stolen wallet and, having established rapport, now lights her cigarette. He pushes her to the safety of the floor as gunfire breaks out and gasps when she's slapped by the police. He shudders when she angrily slams the door and (to signal intimacy) smells her perfume when entering her room. He registers surprise when she first kisses him, blinks and whistles to himself when she leaves. He's surprised but pleased to discover that she hadn't left (as planned) on the afternoon plane and, while contemplating their future, reflectively scratches his chin with his thumbnail. Though he is usually aloof, unresponsive and cool, his face is mobile and expressive in this movie. He reveals in turn disdain for his client, comradeship for Frenchy, solicitude for Brennan and passion for Bacall.

According to Bette Davis, Bacall released Bogart's emotions in films as Mayo had done in real life: "Up until Betty Bacall, I think Bogart was really embarrassed doing love scenes, and that came over as a certain reticence. With her he let go, and it was great. She matched his insolence." Since Bogart and Bacall really did want to sleep with each other, their sexual dynamism and passionate excitement came through on the screen. Bogart had complained that he always had trouble getting women in films and that movie gangsters have no sex life. In *High Sierra* he had a girl, but was killed. In *The Maltese Falcon* and *Casablanca* he had a girl, but was forced to renounce her. Not until *To Have and Have Not* did he get to keep his girl and escape (albeit to Devil's Island) with her. James Agee, in an enthusiastic review, called Bogart "Nietzsche in dungarees" and described the film as "a leisurely series of mating duels between Humphrey Bogart at his most proficient and the very entertaining, nervy, adolescent new blonde, Lauren Bacall."[13]

⟨ IV ⟩

In December 1944, while making *The Big Sleep*, Bogart was still torn between loyalty to Methot and passionate love for Bacall. Drunk and depressed, plagued by anxiety about the quarter-century difference in their ages, he said that he was old enough to be her father, that their marriage would never last, that she would leave him for a younger man. Though full of doubts himself, he also tried to reassure Bacall about his love and their future. By this time both Methot and Hawks had found out about his affair. They were giving him absolute hell at home and at work, and he drank more than ever. On December 4 he tried to break from Methot, left Horn Avenue and moved into the Beverly Wilshire Hotel.

The atmosphere on the set of *The Big Sleep* was tense; the joyous mood of *To Have and Have Not* had vanished. Bacall was frequently in tears, and Bogart's emotional chaos provoked a series of frantic memos at Warner Bros. As early as November 24 the unit manager, Eric Stacey, reported that the delinquent had "overslept this morning and will delay the company somewhat getting their first shot." Toward the end of December he went out of control, was unable to work and—for the first time in his career—repeatedly held up the film. On the 22nd, with the script being rewritten by Hawks as they went along, "the Company lost quite a lot of time during the day due to conferences regarding the story and discussions with Mr. Bogart, Hawks and Lauren Bacall." Two days earlier T. C. Wright, the studio production manager, had told Warners' lawyer Roy Obringer that it had been "necessary for Mr. Hawks to speak with Mr. Bogart for a half an hour to straighten him out relative to the 'Bacall' situation, which is affecting their performances in the picture. . . . I understand there have been several instances when Hawks had had to take him to one side and talk with him at great length because he was dissatisfied with his performance, which was no doubt caused by his domestic troubles."

Frightened and alone, Methot appealed to Bogart to return. In an effort to save their marriage, she agreed to enter a hospital for alcoholics. Bogart was still strongly attached to Methot, whose temperament resembled his in so many ways, and felt partly responsible for her heavy drinking. Behaving in a gentlemanly fashion, he promised to stay with her till she was well and reluctantly went home to Horn Avenue for Christmas.

But Christmas with Mayo, who knew all his weak points and where to put the knife in, was a nightmare. The following day, as Hawks waited for Bogart to arrive on the set, Methot called to say that he had been out on a binge all night and had turned up drunk at their house that morning. While scores of actors, staff and technicians stood idly by and Jack Warner fumed, Sam Jaffe, Stacey and the assistant director rushed to Horn Avenue to sober up the star. Methot told them that Bogart, in bad shape, was trying to sleep off his hangover. When he finally appeared, Stacey reported, "the atmosphere became extremely strained and I felt that my presence there would serve no useful purpose since Bogart himself kept asking, 'Are we holding a wake?' I really do not feel that Bogart's condition can be straightened out overnight since he has been drinking for approximately three weeks and it is not only the liquor, but also the mental turmoil regarding his domestic life that is entering into this situation." Despite the efforts of Warners' emissaries, Bogart could not and did not report for work that day and Hawks could not shoot anything without him.

Warners' troubles were not yet over. Bogart came back for a day or two, then lapsed into alcoholic oblivion. On December 29 Stacey told Wright, yet again, that the "company did not work due to Mr. Bogart's absence. Mr. Hawks had time to sit down with his writers and completely rewrite the end of the story." Hawks, who couldn't control Bogart, then tried to protect his investment by putting the screws on the more malleable Bacall. He claimed that Bogart still loved Mayo and would never leave her, demanded obedience and once again warned her that she was risking her career by having an affair with a married man: "Look, I'm not going to go on with this. I can't have anyone under contract who won't listen to me. Bogart likes his life—he likes the drinking and he likes his wife—you're throwing away a whole career because of something that's just not going to happen. You're a damn fool—I'll just sell your contract—I can't be bothered anymore. If I'd known anything like this could happen, I'd never have signed you. So you'd better make up your mind—this is your last chance." When threats didn't work, he tried to distract her by inviting Clark Gable to dinner. But she was not impressed by the handsome hunk. In January 1945 it was obvious that Methot's treatment for alcoholism had failed and that their marriage was finished. After Bogart finally decided to leave her, she agreed on a divorce settlement of $300,000 and went to Reno. No wonder, with all these problems, that *The Big Sleep*, which finished on January 28, 1945, was five weeks behind its six-week schedule and $50,000 over its budget.

In February 1945 Bogart and Bacall publicized *To Have and Have Not* in New York, where they had to behave discreetly in public. Though Methot had agreed to a divorce, she was still drinking heavily and was quite unreliable, and their legal arrangements were by no means certain. Bogart met Bacall's uncles (who were about his age) and she completed the tour of his past life by meeting Helen Menken and Mary Philips. Most of the publicity focused on the rising young star. Resenting the intrusion on their personal affairs, Bogart complained: "Fucking Warner Brothers are running your life!"[14]

‹ V ›

Just as *To Have and Have Not* echoes *Casablanca*, so *The Big Sleep*, in which Bogart again plays a private detective, recalls *The Maltese Falcon*. Bacall also links *To Have and Have Not* to *The Big Sleep* by again wearing a stylish checked suit and black beret, singing in a nightclub and hiding with another woman in the hero's room. Bogart also fingers his belt and pulls his ear as if it might come loose. Both Hawks films have a witty but sympathetic crossfire of insults and wisecracks.

The title of the film, as Raymond Chandler explains in the book, refers to death: "You were dead, you were sleeping the big sleep." The names of the characters are also vivid and suggestive: Marlowe is taken from the narrator of Conrad's *Heart of Darkness* and *Lord Jim*; Mars, the violent god of war, is a shortened form of Marlowe; Geiger is jumpy and unpredictable; Canino, feral and savage; General Sternwood, austere and monolithic.

The Big Sleep starts with a big heat as Marlowe visits General Sternwood in his hothouse. Marlowe is first drenched in sweat, then in rain. Sternwood says of his orchids, which have the same qualities as his daughters: "Their perfume has the rotten sweetness of corruption." The general is troubled by the disappearance of his youthful surrogate son, Shawn Regan, who was also a military man. Though he does not ask Marlowe to find that mysterious figure, his daughter Vivian (Bacall) tells Marlowe: "You're a lot like Shawn Regan. . . . Your face is like Shawn's too —clean and thin, with hard bones under it." When Marlowe returns to the hothouse toward the end of the film, the general also tells him: "You have a lot that Shawn had. Strength—and a steady eye." Eddie Mars asks Marlowe if he is looking for Regan. Harry Jones offers to sell information that will help him locate Regan. Vivian tries to discourage him from finding Regan. Regan is the key to the mystery that surrounds all the other characters. In searching for Regan, his alter ego, Marlowe is also searching for his own identity.

Hawks explained that in *The Big Sleep* (as in *The Maltese Falcon*) "the audience knows . . . everything that Bogart knows. He's in on every scene, and the scene ends when he goes off." Yet Hawks made Chandler's plot more complex and difficult to follow by eliminating many details and connections that would have made it much clearer. One critic called the film "confusing, chaotic, senseless, illogical, indecipherable, and unfathomable." Chandler had also complicated matters by leaving some loose ends in his story. He confessed that when "Hawks was making *The Big Sleep,* the movie, he and Bogart got into an argument as to whether one of the characters [Owen Taylor] was murdered or committed suicide. They sent me a wire asking me, and dammit, I didn't know either."[15]

The plot becomes clear (during the second viewing) if one keeps close track of who commits each of the spiraling series of murders. Arthur Geiger, the owner of a pornographic bookstore, is killed by the chauffeur, Owen Taylor, for blackmailing his lover Carmen Sternwood. Taylor is killed by Joe Brody, the boyfriend of Geiger's assistant Agnes, to get the valuable nude photographs of Carmen. Brody is killed by Geiger's male lover Carol Lundgren in order to get the same photos. Harry Jones (Elisha Cook, Jr.), Agnes' loyal new boyfriend, is killed by Eddie Mars' gunman Canino to prevent him from telling Marlowe about Shawn Regan. Canino is killed (in self-defense) by Marlowe for killing Harry Jones. Regan (Marlowe discovers toward the end of the film) had been killed by the jealous Carmen for rejecting her advances. Finally, as Marlowe forces Eddie Mars to leave Geiger's house, he is machine-gunned by his own men. Vivian, knowing Carmen had killed Shawn, had hired Mars to hide the evidence and conceal the crime. Mars had used this knowledge to blackmail her.

The Big Sleep has a fascinating cast of female characters. The sexually irresistible Marlowe flirts with Vivian, her sister Carmen (who sucks her thumb and has to be weaned), Geiger's assistant, Agnes, the prim girl across the street in the Acme Bookshop, even the cheeky lady cabdriver. The cabby says: "Anything you want, bud, I can give you," to which Marlowe salaciously replies: "Tail job?" In contrast to the hard-boiled, sophisticated Agnes—who is disgusted when he chuckles to himself, turns up his hat, puts on and looks over his glasses, and minces about like a stereotyped homosexual (a bit of comic business that Bogart invented) —the Acme girl (played by the twenty-year-old Dorothy Malone) satisfies Marlowe's male fantasies. Though young, virginal and spinsterish, she is also instantly responsive. After a bit of chat, she takes off her glasses, lets down her hair, closes the shop, gives him a drink and (we understand) has sex with him during a thunderstorm. Though Marlowe is potent with women, Vivian, Carmen and Agnes all have guns while he is unarmed.

Marlowe's cynical sparring contests with Vivian are one of the high points of the film. When the rich and arrogant Vivian mocks him, Marlowe allusively promises: "Next time I'll carry a tennis racket." Her ambiguous line, "I thought you worked in bed like Marcel Proust," not only alludes to the homosexual relations of Arthur Geiger and Carol Lundgren, but also anticipates her seductive overtures during which Marlowe suggests —in contrast to the asthmatic Proust—how *he* works in bed.

Chandler revealed that the beautiful and sexy Martha Vickers, who played "the nymphy sister, was so good she shattered Miss Bacall completely. So they cut the picture in such a way that all her best scenes were left out except one." Bacall's agent, Charles Feldman, wanted her to repeat the success of her first film by sexually dominating Bogart and told Jack Warner: "Give the girl at least three or four additional scenes with Bogart of the insolent and provocative nature that she had in *To Have and Have Not*. . . . In *To Have and Have Not* Bacall was more insolent than Bogart and this very insolence endeared her in both the public's and the critics' mind when the picture appeared. It was something startling and new." Warner agreed and, several weeks after the picture was completed, Hawks added their daring exchange of sexual innuendoes. Vivian tells Marlowe that she likes to see horses "work out a little first. See if they're front-runners or come from behind. Find out what their hole-card is—what makes them run. . . . I'd say you don't like to be rated. You like to get out front, open up a lead, take a little breather in the back stretch, and then come home free." He adds, "You've got a touch of class, but I don't know how far you can go." Rising to the challenge, she responds: "That depends on who's in the saddle."[16]

This bold repartee somehow managed to slip past the censors. The film was less explicit and, for that reason, more intriguing than the novel. The script played down Geiger's homosexuality and pornography, Carmen's drug addiction and nymphomania. In August 1948, however, the Censor's Office, refusing an export license to Ireland and Scandinavia, finally woke up and called it "a thoroughly immoral film in the widest sense of the word. Blackmail and murders are mere incidents in it. The entire atmosphere is sordid, and there are many suggestive situations and not a little double-meaning dialogue. Altogether an unsavory picture for which a certificate cannot be granted." Shocked by the violence and missing the moral dimension of the film, the producer John Houseman wrote of the hero and heroine of *The Big Sleep*: "It is these people — spiritless, zombies, utterly lacking in moral or tragic sense — that are really frightening, not their forays with blackjack and pistol."

Bogart's slight swagger suggests he can handle anything. He's not fazed by sexual advances or intimidated by wealth and social position, and easily disarms all the crooks. He's surprised but pleased when Carmen faints in his arms, and reflectively purses his lips when speaking to General Sternwood. He smiles benignly when Vivian insults him by saying "you're a mess" and gives a high-pitched, ironic "Ooohhh" when she becomes indignant about his rudeness. In the bookstore he quickly moves from pushy hostility with the first woman to gentle rapport with the second.

Every telling gesture suggests his commanding character. He impatiently twists his mouth and snaps his fingers when he finds the film's been taken from Geiger's camera, and dumps (rather than lowers) Carmen on the huge satin-covered bed. He grabs Vivian's wrists and cracks: "I don't slap so good," sits next to her on top of his desk to establish intimacy and greets her with a drawling "We-ell" when they meet in an obscure restaurant. His hands are particularly expressive. He lifts one up and drops it before punching a robber, rolls his fist in his palm when he finds Carmen in his flat, pushes the change around the breakfast counter while deciding what to do and rests his fingers on the table as he calls Mars for the final showdown. He continues to smoke while tied up, and allows Bacall to take the cigarette from his mouth so he can order her about — and then kiss her.

Despite their trouble during *The Big Sleep*, Hawks maintained good relations with Bogart and admired his acting skill: "He certainly could do anything that you asked him to do, and he also took criticism without a murmur. . . . Bogey was one of the best actors I've ever worked with." Raymond Chandler defined the various qualities that made Bogart's Marlowe absolutely convincing. Bogart, he wrote, is "so much better than any other tough-guy actor. . . . [He] can be tough without a gun. Also he has a sense of humor that contains that grating undertone of contempt. . . . Bogart is the genuine article." Leigh Brackett, who wrote the screenplay with Faulkner and Furthman, was tremendously impressed by Bogart's theatrical background, his rapid mastery of the script and patient professionalism with the rest of the cast: "Bogart was the greatest actor that ever happened. . . . It was a joy to watch him on the set because he was stage trained. On a Hawks film nobody gets their pages until five minutes before they're going to shoot. Bogart would put on his horn-rims, go off in a corner, look at it, then come back on the set and they'd run through it a couple of times, and he'd have it right down, every bit of timing, and he'd go through about fourteen takes waiting for other people to catch up to him."[17] In the film Bogart, though thinner and older than the fictional Philip Marlowe, gives the character more interest, compassion and depth than Raymond Chandler does in the novel. He conveys the inner strength and moral rectitude with outward cynicism and disrespect that perfectly embodies the *film noir* detective.

Chandler, influenced like Hammett by Hemingway's style and values, adapted the Hemingway hero to popular culture. In *A Farewell to Arms,* Hemingway's Frederic Henry, fighting a dirty war and troubled by the conflict between high-minded ideals and the reality of death, thinks: "Abstract words such as glory, honor, courage, or hallow were obscene beside the concrete names of villages, the numbers of roads, the names of rivers, the numbers of regiments and the dates." Marlowe, who fights his battles in an urban jungle of criminals and perverts, is paid to take chances against these predatory animals and to clean up the slime. In *The Big Sleep* the detective is even more disgusted than in *The Maltese Falcon* by the corrupt world in which he lives. "I try to do my job and keep my nose clean," he tells the now respectful and responsive Vivian. "I risk my whole future, the hatred of the cops and Eddie Mars' gang. I dodge bullets and eat saps. But I'm not supposed to feel anything about it either way, because anybody can buy my immortal soul with a few bucks—or maybe just a kiss." Though he takes punishment, suppresses his emotions and can be cheaply bought, he does have an obstinate integrity. In a key passage, he upholds his code of honor, like Frederic Henry, in a corrupt and confusing world: "Pride is a great thing, isn't it? And courage—and honor—and love. All the things you read about in the copybooks—only in the copybooks nothing ever gets tangled. The road always lies so straight, and clear, and the signs say to love and honor and be brave."[18]

◊ 9 ◊
Fourth Marriage
1945-1950

‹ I ›

WHEN BOGART MET BACALL early in 1944 he was forty-four, in the prime of his life and at the top of his profession. She was a young girl, groomed and trained by Hawks, and assiduously managed by her agent, Charles Feldman. She had signed a personal contract with him and he legally "owned" her. He paid her a weekly salary, as if staking a competitor or sponsoring an athlete, and eventually sold her contract to Warners at an enormous profit.

Bogart's marriage to Methot had been on the rocks for years, and he was intensely frustrated with both his wife and his studio. He had a long-term relationship with Verita, and had other liaisons during the frequent spells of unhappiness with his previous wives. But the love affair with Bacall was quite different. Her youth, freshness and adoration flattered and inspired him. She was someone he could teach and help to shape, and who could save him from the nightmare of drinking and despair.

The impulsive kiss in the dressing room of *To Have and Have Not,* after working with her for three weeks, was out of character for Bogart. This affair touched his deepest emotions and was Bacall's first serious romance. But it took an entire year to work out his true feelings, to choose what was best for all of them and to decide what he ought to do. After that agonizing Christmas of 1944 he was relieved to escape from Methot and delighted to be finally free to marry Bacall. He repressed his doubts about his three previous failures and their great differences in age and background, his fears that she would be attracted to younger men and that they would have only a brief time together. Bacall (whom he called Baby or Betty) dismissed his doubts with a witty one-liner: "I think eighty is the proper age for getting married because then you can be sure it will last."

Bogart announced their engagement on January 29, 1945, three days after they completed *The Big Sleep,* and was divorced in Reno on May 10. He married Bacall on May 21 (in the midst of his filming *The Two Mrs. Carrolls*) at Louis Bromfield's six-hundred-acre Malabar Farm, eighty miles southwest of Cleveland, Ohio. Bacall described the charming and good-humored Bromfield as "one of Bogie's oldest and best friends." The once popular and now forgotten author of *The Rains Came* was born in Ohio three years before Bogart, had served in World War I, and had been a journalist in New York and Europe. Bogart had known him in the New York theater world in the 1920s—the good old days which (as Edmund Wilson said) seemed much more fun than the war-torn 1940s. Bogart met him again in Hollywood in 1939 while making the dreadful movie *It All Came True,* based on Bromfield's whimsical story. Though Bromfield was politically conservative, and they were rarely able to meet, he and Bogart had an intuitive affinity.

Bacall and Bogart traveled all the way to Ohio to have a quiet country wedding, amid polished copper pans and antique furniture, farm and cooking smells, animals grazing and trees blowing in the wind. It would be an authentic, natural and purifying contrast to their tacky Hollywood houses, fake studio sets and swimming pools lit up by colored lights. The warm rural family, complete with white-haired granny and homespun judge, completed the perfect tableau. Bromfield was best man and Bacall's mother matron-of-honor. They took their mandatory Wasserman test for syphilis at a nearby hospital in Mansfield. Bacall wore medium heels, Bogart put on elevated shoes. As the wedding march began, the nervous Bacall had not yet appeared. Bogart asked, "Where is she?" and a friend romantically replied: "Hold it—she's in the can." After the simple ceremony she said: "Oh, goody." He felt more in love, more committed, "more married" than on his previous tries.

Jack Warner, who gave Bacall the Buick from *The Big Sleep* as a wedding present, wanted to generate publicity and cash in on the romance. He alerted the Hollywood press, who pursued the actors across the country and invaded the farm. When *Life* sent their best cameraman to board the wedding train, Bogart refused to cooperate. "Great," he said caustically, "maybe he'd like to photograph us fucking."[1] In the fan magazines, heated accounts of the romantic courtship and wedding, which took place soon after the release of *To Have and Have Not,* replaced the old stories of the Battling Bogarts and gave him a more appealing public image.

Bogart and Bacall spent their one-week honeymoon cruising the California coast on the *Sluggy,* and they first lived at the Garden of Allah. He had stayed there with Mary Philips in the fall of 1935, and a few years later, while still married to Mary, he had a secret affair with Mayo in that congenial setting. Now, as he carried the slender Bacall across the threshold of their small suite, he alluded to her famous wisecrack in *To Have and Have Not* ("What are you trying to do, guess her weight?") and joked: "You weigh a ton."

After a couple of months in the hotel, they moved into their first house, above Sunset Strip on Kings Road, which winds steeply into the Hollywood Hills. The genteel suburban neighborhood, less than a mile from his old house, was light-years away from the parlor of Princess Zoraida and the Utter-McKinley mortuary on Horn Avenue. The modern, completely furnished home was built on three levels and had a study, a patio and a fine view. But it had no land and was close to the other houses.

In 1946, inspired by Bromfield's farm and wanting to try "country life," they bought Hedy Lamarr's much larger house at 2707 Benedict Canyon Road. Remote and isolated, it was built on top of a steep drive that branched off the far end of the winding canyon. The white L-shaped ranch house, with shuttered front windows, a wide front lawn and a picket fence, had eight rooms on one floor. With six and a half acres of land, there was space for a swimming pool and coops for ducks and chickens. Bogart's den was decorated with hideous plaid wallpaper, "masculine furnishings" and photographs of Bacall.

From childhood Bogart was used to having servants around the house. Since Methot returned to Portland after their divorce, he kept their household staff. The wives came and went, but the servants stayed on. In addition to his agent, his business manager and his secretary, Kathy Sloan, he employed May Smith, the black cook, Fred Clarke, the very British Jamaican butler, and Aurelio Salazar, the handyman and gardener. May had a sense of humor and Bogart would kid her about the lunch she had prepared until she asked: "Is he eaten them sandwiches or thrown 'em out?" He also liked to tease the rather proper butler, who amused the Bogarts by calling them "milord" and "milady," and affectionately told him: "Where's your chauffeur's cap, you bastard? I bought it for you and you better put it on!" Aurelio, who had many children, would sometimes cut the grass like a drunkard, leaving many ragged patches. The servants were more eccentric than efficient, but Bogart loved their idiosyncratic characters.

Louis Bromfield had given them Harvey, a boxer puppy, as a wedding gift, and Bogart acquired two others, George and Baby. On October 7, 1948 the New York *Daily News* reported that Bogart played the hero in real life. He first killed a rattlesnake that had bitten one of his dogs on the nose. Then, after he returned from the vet and found a wildcat threatening his other dog, he shot the beast with a .22 rifle. Bacall loved the dogs and felt she needed them to protect the house; Bogart would get fed up with them and tell the butler: "Get rid of those damned dogs, and let me drink in peace."

Bogart liked good cars. He bought an MG and then an XK-120 Jaguar convertible for himself and a Mark VII for Bacall. When he tired of shifting the gears on his four-speed sports cars in the 1950s, he traded them in for a black Ford Thunderbird and a black Mercedes. A friend's daughter still retains a vivid image of the stylish Bogart, wearing a flat cap and driving an MG down their long straight Brentwood driveway, with two boxer dogs perfectly aligned in the front seat. Dorris Johnson recalled that on another occasion, after drinking at the Beverly Hills Hotel, Bogart drove up Benedict Canyon in his MG. A heavy storm had turned the road into a river of mud, and he had to abandon his car and trudge back to the hotel in filthy clothes.[2] After a few years the Bogarts tired of their isolated country life. Bacall was frightened of rattlesnakes, and began to search for a house in a more settled neighborhood.

‹ II ›

BOGART'S MARRIAGE to Bacall was a happy one, and she soon learned to cook and be a Hollywood housewife. But living together brought out the contrast in their habits and interests. Bogart had grown up with luxury and now did not want or need it. He was frugal with money, disliked material possessions and preferred to live in modest comfort with some of his mother's old furniture. But he did not try to restrain his wife's extravagance. Bacall came from a poor family and craved the material evidence of success — what Bogart ironically called "instant tradition." A great shopper and free spender, she would buy six pairs of the same shoes, wore couturier clothes, acquired increasingly grand houses, and filled them with expensive knickknacks, antiques, paintings and furniture. On their first trip to Paris she "bought everything in sight." When Bogart forked out for the requisite fur coat, she took off her shoes, trod on the pelts and rather vulgarly exclaimed: "I've always wanted to walk on mink."

He was a homebody and went to bed early, she liked to go out and stay up late. She confessed that she became more strong-willed after the wedding: "Bogey doesn't have the interests I have — going places, traveling, meeting new people. He's definitely content to live in his home or live on his boat. That's not for me. He says I was great and did everything he wanted until I got him in my clutches." Howard Hawks, who had introduced them and at first opposed the marriage, believed, on reflection, that it had expanded his interests and "changed Bogart for the better. She did a lot of good with him. . . . She was terribly eager for anything, to learn, to try things, and she interested him in them, so that his life was broadened and happier and wasn't full of the strife that he found in his early career."[3]

Bogart admired both sides of his wife's character: Lauren Bacall, the glamorous model groomed for success by Diana Vreeland, the ambitious actress carefully coached and launched by Howard Hawks; and Betty Bacall, the youthful and energetic, direct and practical, brassy and managing domestic partner, who took good care of him, put up with his drinking pals (though she did not drink much herself) and tolerated his long absences on the boat. After the emotional chaos with Methot, Bogart loved his pleasant home life with Bacall. "He can't live in any kind of unsettled atmosphere," she told a journalist. "He loves to stay home. . . . He doesn't do a thing, no, not a thing around the house." She understood, as Swifty Lazar noted, that "he had to be [or seem to be] the master of the house. . . . They had dinner when he wanted, and they had guests when he cared to see people." They dined in restaurants and in the houses of friends, went to nightclubs, parties and premieres. But they also valued privacy and led a surprisingly conventional bourgeois life. "Our idea of a perfect evening," Bacall said, "was dinner on trays in front of the television."[4]

With an elaborate staff of servants, which Bacall soon learned to manage, there was no need for Bogart to do anything around the house. He hated occasions when you were supposed to give presents and disliked New Year's Eve—the only night he refused to get drunk. She loved to plan dinners and give parties, and they were well equipped to entertain in style. Every year they gave two big bashes: on May 21, their wedding anniversary, and on Christmas Eve, the night before Bogart's birthday. But he really didn't like all the parties, and participated mainly to please her. His cruel needling expressed his rebellion against a social life that seemed as constricted as his work at the studio.

Though Bacall appeared to be a devoted and submissive wife, her tough character—which appealed to Bogart and was probably influenced by him—had a good deal in common with Methot's. After their marriage, she became the dominant partner and was much more aggressive with him. Friends described her as abrasive and outspoken, biting, demanding and intimidating. She quickly picked up sophisticated mannerisms, and once fascinated a young woman by asking for a martini and saying (as if in a film): "Just pass the vermouth over the glass." When she met the Shah of Iran at a glamorous New Year's Eve party in the 1950s, he graciously remarked that she danced very well and she replied: "You bet your ass, Shah!"

According to Warren Stevens, who appeared in two of Bogart's films, when she overstepped the mark Bogart would say, "*Miss* Bacall!" and she'd back down. But their son later said Bacall was a "controlling sort of woman . . . who usually gets what she wants." She dominated Bogart and he found it very difficult to oppose her wishes when she was (as she put it) "determined." She'd push for what she wanted and he'd eventually give in. She gradually persuaded him to change his way of life—to live in luxury, travel widely and have children.

Bogart went out of control when he drank too much, needed to be looked after and wanted a wife who would manage him. During their arguments, Bogart, who amused himself by playing the role of "Bogart," would adopt his screen role and shout "Listen to me!" Bacall gave him a lot of freedom to do as he wished, but was very good at restraining his smoking and drinking. When he drank too much and argued too much, she would jerk the reins and shout: "For God's sake, shut up!" He'd give a little embarrassed laugh—and do as she ordered.[5]

They sometimes quarreled about her closely-knit Jewish family. Bogart, who had never been close to his sisters and (now deceased) parents, was afraid of being overwhelmed by her mother and "goddamned relatives." He resented the endless obligations laid on by her family ("You *have* to see your cousin Marvin at West Point"), and exploded when they dropped in without asking permission. Mrs. Perske had opposed her daughter's marriage to a hard-drinking, thrice-divorced gentile who was old enough to be her father, but accepted her daughter's decision and attended their wedding. Richard Brooks, in his convincing fictional portrayal of their quarrels, emphasized Bacall's nagging, confrontational style and his hard-nosed role-playing:

> "You promised we'd go out and see my mother."
> "What do I want to see your mother for?" . . .
> "Do you have to be a bastard twenty-four hours a day?" . . .
> "It's the most consistent performance I give. . . . Your mother
>   bores me."
> "God, but you're selfish." . . .
> "Why don't you get out of here!" Taggart said to her in his
>   tight-lipped style, his movie style. "Go see your mother."

The marriage survived these minor disputes because Bacall was flexible about his behavior and Bogart—though set in his ways—generally submitted to her wishes. But (Bacall wrote) even Bogart, who liked to spoil her, had his limits and often behaved unexpectedly: "You had to stay awake married to him. Every time I thought I could relax and do *everything* I wanted, he'd buck. There was no way to predict his reactions, no matter how well I knew him. . . . He never expected to settle down. He liked keeping people off balance." One evening, on the way to a party at Danny Kaye's, he felt she was taking him for granted and exclaimed: " 'Damn it, I am not an escort. I'm not here just to take you to parties and take you home. Get it straight—I'm your husband.' That must have been a moment when I'd gone too far."

He wanted her to be with him most of the time, but didn't want to feel tied down by a ball and chain. "She can take a guy like me," he said, using a hanging metaphor derived from his experience with Mayo, "with my moods, give me my rope," and yet not make him feel as if she were wringing his neck.[6] Since she did not play chess, drink heavily or lunch at Romanoff's, and disliked the boat, Bogart could retain considerable independence and divert himself with male friends.

Just before his marriage he called Bacall a "tigress" and then, mixing his metaphor, told Mark Hellinger that he felt like a "mouse that's going to be torn apart by a rabbit." He also admitted that he had always been attracted to—and submitted to—dominant, predatory, Maud-like women: "Of my other wives . . . one [Methot] was a witch, all were demanding, all were back-seat drivers and all were a little masculine." Mary Astor, who had a great deal of experience with men, explained the successful dynamics of the Bogarts' marriage: "The remarkable Lauren Bacall knew who he was, let him be who he was. And in return, he was at last able to give something no other woman could grab from him: his total commitment."[7]

< III >

AFTER ALL HIS YEARS on stage and in films Bogart found acting rather a bore. He said, for public consumption, "it's more fun to go to Rome or Africa to make a picture than to stay [in a theater] on 44th Street." In fact, he disliked filming on location, which may have been exotic and adventurous, but was certainly more arduous. He preferred to maintain his more comfortable suburban routine in Hollywood, where he would stop work promptly at six, have a drink, drive home to Benedict Canyon for a simple dinner and go to sleep by ten o'clock to be ready for an early call the next day. When he was not working, he became a night owl and sat up drinking and talking till very late.

Bogart worked to make money, to practice his profession and fulfill his potential as an actor as well as to avoid dissipation and remain psychologically sound. He took a straightforward, no-nonsense approach to acting, and became restless and depressed when he was not in a film: "Working is therapy I guess—it keeps you on the wagon. [Hollywood] is a bad town to be out of work in. After a week or so of not working, you're so bored you don't know what the hell to do." But he did not like to talk about his work, once he had left the studio, unless something unusual had happened. Though he criticized his own lack of ambition in an article called "Things I Don't Like About Myself," he became one of the most successful and highly paid actors of his time. His attitude toward his career, like his manners, was influenced by his parents: pride in his work, disdain for his own achievements, fear (deep-rooted in a late-developing son of high achievers) that whatever he did well wasn't worth doing. When Bacall asked him how he got so many good parts, he told her: "Because I keep working."

Like his previous wives, Bacall felt a constant conflict between her marriage and her career as an actress. By the age of twenty-one she had achieved instant success in two important films and was happily married to a rich and famous star. In contrast to Bogart, who had taken twenty years to achieve fame and had endured three unhappy marriages before he met her, Bacall had peaked early, could not sustain a career at that level and had nowhere to go but down. Her first films—witty, wisecracking thrillers—had been carefully managed by Hawks to bring out her best qualities. But in conventional roles (even with Bogart in *Key Largo* and *Dark Passage*), she could not play her own screen character and gave disappointingly dull performances. Hawks defined her problem when he remarked: "I felt I had done as much as I could with Betty. I didn't feel I could keep on doing the stuff she did best and ought to do. She was not an actress. She was a personality."[8]

During the first five years of their marriage, Bacall made—in addition to her four films with Bogart—three mediocre movies with Warners. She refused many other roles and in 1950, soon after Bogart left to form his own independent company, bought out her Warners contract and signed with Fox. Though she made six more films by 1957, they were all poor and she seemed lost without the help of Hawks.

During a dinner in Hollywood with Walter Winchell and a Warners publicity man, the journalist casually asked Bacall if she'd like to appear in a New York play and she impulsively answered "Yes." Bogart, still bitterly sensitive about the conflicting careers that had destroyed his previous marriages, exclaimed: "You goddam actresses! If that's your plan, go ahead and go—forget about me. . . . If you want a career, don't get married. You can't have both." She remained in Hollywood, but did in fact have both.

Bogart was also troubled by the fear that Bacall might want to leave him for a younger and more attractive man. He warned her that love affairs often tempted actresses, but that a quick romance was not worth the damage it could do. In his decent, old-fashioned, gentlemanly way he told her that he would not try to hold her: "if she ever found someone she preferred she should tell him, and if he thought the man would be good for her he'd step aside and let her go." He then added that he would not tolerate deceit: "don't do it behind my back. Come to me and tell me. If you did anything dishonest, I'd never like you again."[9]

‹ IV ›

In 1946, the same year he reluctantly acquired the house in Benedict Canyon, Bogart (possibly as a trade-off) fulfilled his lifelong ambition to own a racing yacht and bought the *Santana* for $55,000. Named after the hot desert wind that blows onto the Pacific, the yawl was fifty-five feet long, weighed sixteen tons and had an eighty-five-horsepower engine. The cabin was made of Honduran mahogany, the decks of teak. Built in 1935 from an Olin-Stephens design by the Union Oil executive William Stewart, it had won several important races. It also had a distinguished Hollywood lineage and had been previously owned by one of Eva Gabor's husbands, by George Brent, by Ray Milland and by Dick Powell, from whom Bogart bought it. The change from a rough-and-ready power cruiser to an elegant yacht marked his transition from Methot to Bacall.

Bogart had courted Bacall on the *Sluggy,* their secret hideaway and trysting place. He tried to interest her in his passion for the sea and in the only possession he really cared about. He wanted her to escape with him on the *Santana* as he sailed to Catalina Island on most weekends during the year, share his isolation from the "gossip and leeches" of

Hollywood, and see his real self emerge as he took command and showed his skill as a yachtsman. As he watched his graceful boat heel in the wind and glide through the water, he felt clean, relaxed and healthy, isolated, independent and free.

The *Santana* was tended by Carl Petersen, a Swedish-born retired fireman, who lived on the boat, set the (illegal) lobster traps and kept the bar well stocked. Bogart called him "Dumb-Bum," "Squarehead" and several other affectionate nicknames. The boat was tied up first at Newport Beach and then closer in at San Pedro, about twenty-five miles south of Hollywood. Most members of the Yacht Club were wealthy conservatives who thought actors were freaks, but Bogart, an expert sailor, won their respect and got on well with them. Though he tended to be sloppy at home and let the servants pick up after him, on the *Santana* he helped Carl keep everything glistening and shipshape.

Bogart's experience at sea—in the navy, the coast guard and on his own yacht—made him self-assured on boats and gave his nautical scenes an authentic look. At the end of *All Through the Night* he prevented a Nazi motorboat filled with high explosives from destroying an American battleship. In *Across the Pacific* he sailed to Panama on a Japanese ship; as first mate in *Action in the North Atlantic*, he brought a merchant marine ship safely through a German attack and into Murmansk. In *Passage to Marseilles* he prevented a French freighter from falling into Nazi hands; in *To Have and Have Not*, as the skipper of a small cabin cruiser, he picked up an Underground leader in Martinique and rescued a Resistance hero from Devil's Island. His sailing roles are more significant in his later films. In *Key Largo*, forced to take five gangsters to Cuba on a boat named *Santana*, he kills them one by one and returns to the Keys to marry Bacall. As skipper of *The African Queen*, he steers his derelict steamer through perilous rapids and blows up a German gunboat. He even takes Audrey Hepburn sailing in *Sabrina*. As the paranoid Captain Queeg in *The Caine Mutiny*, he panics and loses control of the destroyer during a typhoon.

Always queasy on the boat, Bacall did not feel obliged to accompany him once she became pregnant and gladly abandoned her feigned interest in sailing. Clearly exasperated and repelled by the cramped quarters and by her duties in the small galley, by the heavy seas and heavy drinking, she exclaimed: "I spent three years on that so-and-so yacht of his. I had to have my first baby to escape. . . . I've had it with no shoes and a little stove."[10]

‹ V ›

BOGART AND BACALL —with their careers, house, boat, cars, servants, dogs and poultry—also began to think about having children. He had always led a rather unstable and precarious existence, with many wives, moves, houses, plays and films, and said: "My life was, I thought, too unsettled for children. I was either going on tour with a play, or going in and out of things on Broadway, or something like that. Show business, I felt, was a pretty tenuous field. You might be on top one day and broke the next." Bacall had bought the big house in Benedict Canyon partly for the children she planned to have and soon convinced him to give in to her wishes.

After three years of marriage, however, Bacall was still not pregnant. Bogart's sperm count was low and he submitted to a series of hormone injections to increase it. He was warned that a high testosterone level would cause hair loss—a serious problem for an actor who had to preserve his masculine image—but he kept up the treatments, began to go bald and had to wear a toupee. When Bacall finally announced that she was pregnant, she did not get a joyful response. All his fears about losing her exclusive companionship and of being an inadequate father surged up, and they had the worst quarrel of their marriage. In this emotional explosion (Bacall wrote) he said that "he hadn't married me to lose me to a child—no child was going to come between us. The next morning he wrote me a long letter apologizing for his behavior."[11]

Bogart continued to be ambivalent about the prospect of fatherhood. Emphasizing the deep division between the sexes, he celebrated the change in his status with a stag party, a bizarre mockery of the baby shower given to Bacall. In a raucous bit of horseplay Dr. John Huston forced mother Bogart onto the floor and delivered the baby with fireplace tongs. Both men acted out their fantasies and fears as Bogart, playing Bacall's part, mimicked her power to produce a new life and transform his old one.

The Bogarts' first child, Stephen Humphrey, was born in the Cedars of Lebanon Hospital on January 6, 1949. Steve was named for the Bogart character in *To Have and Have Not*. Their daughter, Leslie, named for the actor who had helped Bogart at a crucial time in his career, was born three and a half years later on August 23, 1952. Bacall was surprised and pleased when she overheard her husband on the intercom speaking to the new baby, on his first morning home, in an unusually tender and gentle voice: "Hello, son. You're a little fella, aren't you. I'm Father. Welcome home."

He was, as all fathers would be, panic-stricken when his three-year-old boy had to have surgery for a hernia. Though Bacall was Jewish and Bogart had no religious beliefs, she followed his family tradition and sent their boy to Sunday School at All Saints Episcopal Church.

Little Steve addressed him as "Father," but quickly picked up Bogart's irreverent attitude toward others. Like many children, he imitated obscene language without knowing what it meant, and would call distinguished visitors "Mr. Blubberhead" and "Mr. Dog-Do-in-the-Pants." Steve once asked their neighbor Art Linkletter, who was washing his car: "What the fuck are you doing?" Bogart—who asked: "What do you do with a kid? They don't drink"—tried to entertain his children by taking them to lunch at Romanoff's. Confused about what to say and do with a godson, Romanoff played "Bogart," bought him a drink and confined his religious instruction to "Listen, kid, there are twelve Commandments."[12]

Though deeply moved by the birth of his son, Bogart was not a warm and affectionate parent, and had very little to do with his small children. He felt he was too old to be a father, found the whole experience quite alien, and let Bacall and the servants take care of the kids. He thought bringing up a child was a mysterious business and confessed to a journalist: "I don't understand the children and I think they don't understand me and all I can say is 'Thank God for Betty.' I find my son looking at me as if I was some kind of monster from another planet." Sam Jaffe, confirming Bogart's remoteness, recalled that "one of his children walked up to him, and I saw a look in [Bogart's] eye, it was a very curious look, as if to say, 'Who is that?'" Most men in Bogart's position—with money, success and fame, a pretty young wife and healthy children—would consider themselves lucky and ready to live forever. But he felt gloomy and fatalistic about the future. He hoped to establish some rapport when the children got older, but also told Verita Peterson, "I'll never live to see the little bastards grown up."[13]

Bogart was the professional mentor, but Bacall the mover and shaker in their marriage. She enjoyed spending money and wearing expensive clothes, acquired the houses and furniture, initiated the party-giving and party-going, wanted to travel in Europe, made Bogart do things he'd never done and was "determined" to have children. She helped control his drinking and made him happy. Bogart's response to her managing was generally compliant, but he compensated by keeping her "off balance." He could be unpleasant and difficult, but he tolerated her flirtations and tendency to hero-worship. Deeply committed to Bacall, he never lost the romantic, protective feeling of their early courtship.

✧ 10 ✧

A Celebrity in Politics

1947–1951

⟨ I ⟩

A NEW DEAL LIBERAL and loyal supporter of Franklin Roosevelt, Bogart became actively involved in politics during the early years of his marriage to Bacall. His political activities began in 1940, between the Nazi-Soviet Pact and America's wartime alliance with Russia, and ended during the Korean War in 1952. Given his combative nature, his belief in free speech and his idealistic wife, Bogart's life was inevitably convulsed by the congressional committee that mounted an attack on the Hollywood film industry.

For three and a half years, during the war against the Nazis, the Soviet Union had been America's valuable ally. But after Germany was defeated in 1945, Russia extended its political and military influence by setting up Communist puppet-governments throughout Eastern Europe. As the Soviet Union raced, with the help of espionage, to develop its own atomic bomb, and the former allies became engaged in a volatile and dangerous Cold War, an Iron Curtain fell between East and West. In March 1947 the American president announced the Truman Doctrine, which promised economic and military aid to Greece, Turkey and other countries threatened by Communism. War broke out in China, and in 1949 the Communists defeated the Nationalists and took over that vast country.

Americans saw Communism as an alien and seditious movement that threatened to undermine the democratic form of government and destroy political freedom everywhere. The once sympathetic Russians were now transformed into a terrifying Red menace. In the atomic age conservative politicians, eager to reverse the economic and social programs set in motion by Roosevelt, generated and thrived in an atmosphere of fear. In 1945 Congress permanently established the House Un-American Activities Committee (HUAC), which had evolved from Congressman Martin

196

Dies' Special Committee of 1938–44, to investigate and root out Communist influence in the United States.

Communist Party cells had been set up in Hollywood in the late 1930s in response to the Spanish Civil War, the rise of Fascism in Europe and the visible suffering of hungry and homeless Americans during the Depression, when a quarter of the work force was unemployed. A small number of the more intellectual writers, directors and actors, who felt capitalism was bankrupt and America needed a new social system, belonged to the Party for brief periods. Many of them soon became disillusioned by its autocratic policies, by the Purge Trials in Soviet Russia and by the Nazi-Soviet Pact of 1939. Many Left-wing sympathizers, who were not Party members, attended political meetings to raise money and support progressive causes.

Membership in the Communist Party was and still is legal—though generally covert—and its influence was extremely limited. But the members of HUAC believed Communism was a national conspiracy, and claimed Hollywood was filled with subversives who used the propagandistic power of movies to indoctrinate a gullible public. At the HUAC hearings, a riveting public spectacle on radio and newsreels, leading writers and directors were accused of being Reds or Communist sympathizers. They appeared before the cameras, blinked in the bright lights and were shouted down by the chairman. After the hearings, present and former members of the Party—without evidence, trial or a chance to defend themselves—were condemned as pariahs and deprived of their jobs.

The public adored the fantasy figures of the screen, and the HUAC hearings became part of America's rapt obsession with celebrity. The real aim of the Committee was not to root out Communists, whom they knew all about through the covert inquiries of the FBI, but to denigrate celebrities. The attack on Hollywood captured the attention of the press, justified the Committee's existence and advanced many political careers. Richard Nixon, then a young congressman, first gained national attention through his zealous participation in the Communist witch hunts.

The actors, protected and controlled by the big studios, faced two opposed and oppressive forces: wealthy, conservative studio heads, hypersensitive to public opinion and desperately worried about their profits, and the Right-wing elements in Congress, determined to bait and humiliate anyone they perceived as Communist. The self-righteous condemnation of political opponents as "Un-American" suggested the politicians' isolationism, anti-Semitism and fear of all things foreign. Hollywood, run mainly by Jewish executives and filled with aliens who had fled from

European dictatorships, soon became victimized by a native ideology that seemed as autocratic as Communism.

Bogart was a victim of the first congressional investigation into Communist subversion in Hollywood. In the summer of 1940 Buron Fitts, running for reelection as Los Angeles district attorney, persuaded John L. Leech, a former Communist official, to testify before a grand jury about Communist influence on motion pictures. Fitts then leaked the testimony to the press and planned to help his campaign by taking charge of the hearings. Leech had joined the Party in 1931, served as a Party organizer for two years and become executive secretary of the Los Angeles branch. He was expelled in 1937. During those years he was also a paid police informer.

Leech's revelations were immediately picked up by the national press, and the publicity fueled the investigation. On August 15 a front-page headline in the *New York Times* announced: "Hollywood Stars Accused as Reds before Grand Jury. . . . Actors Deny Charges." Leech had named Bogart, Cagney, Fredric March, Melvyn Douglas, Franchot Tone and thirteen others as Communists. Martin Dies, a Texas Republican and chairman of the temporary House Un-American Activities Committee, carefully questioned Leech about his accusations. Dies asked: "Are you contending that Mr. Bogart was a member of the Communist Party?" and Leech replied: "Yes; I am. . . . I have sat in organized study groups, organized by the Communist Party, and have known Mr. Bogart to contribute money to that Communist Party." After making these false but damaging charges, Leech hastened to add: "I have nothing but the kindliest feeling toward [the accused] and I have no desire either to slander these people or in any way injure them."

Bogart was furious and outraged. He demanded an investigation and the right to be heard, and left the set of *High Sierra* to deny the accusations. On the stand he alluded to the name of the Committee and exclaimed: "I think it's completely un-American that a man [Leech] who has been, as far as I can read in the papers, called a liar, be allowed to testify before a grand jury without the people accused being permitted to have an opportunity to answer those charges." Questioned by Dies, Bogart emphasized his patriotism and denied all involvement with Communist organizations: "My family were born American; I've been born an American; I've always been a loyal citizen; I have great love for my country. Anytime I would be called upon I would serve my country. . . . I'd say [the charges] were 100 percent untrue; they couldn't be more ridiculous or absurd because I've never been a member of any party or contributed one cent."

When asked how the Communists were able to carry out their subversive activities, Bogart said: "I think Hollywood people are dupes in the most part." He himself had received many requests to contribute to Popular Front organizations, "but somehow God in Heaven guided me along the correct path" and he had always refused to give money. Asked to speculate about the informant's motives, Bogart correctly observed that Leech had mentioned well-known names in order to "sow the seed of mistrust around the country." When challenged, Leech was unable to substantiate his charges. Dies, after exposing the lies of his own witness, exonerated Bogart and told him that "this committee has absolutely no evidence in its possession that involves you in any un-American activity."[1] Bogart's first encounter with HUAC revealed his vulnerability and made a profound impression. It alerted him to the personal and political dangers of Communist witch hunts, which threatened the constitutional rights of all citizens, and made him sympathetic when colleagues had to face similar charges in 1947.

In the 1940s famous movie stars were told to keep their political opinions private. The studios did not want actors to offend their audience, hurt their standing at the box office and lose money for the company. Bogart, as usual, defied the current practice. He had resisted the studio's attempts to control his life, and now insisted on an actor's right to his own opinions. On election eve, November 6, 1944, in the midst of the war, he endorsed Franklin Roosevelt's campaign against Thomas Dewey. In a five-minute speech on CBS radio, organized by the Hollywood Democratic Committee, Bogart (along with several other stars) urged soldiers to use their right to vote and join the "millions and millions of people riding on the Roosevelt special." He told listeners that he personally was voting for Roosevelt because "I believe he is one of the world's greatest humanitarians; because he's leading our fight against the enemies of a free world." The broadcast swung an estimated one million votes, contributed to the Democratic landslide in California and helped Roosevelt win his fourth term as president.

During the next few months Bogart received a mountain of offensive and hostile mail that called him (for example) a "cheap sissy — portrayer of gangster parts, [who has] the asinine impudence to attempt to tell [his] superiors how to vote." In the February 10, 1945 issue of the *Saturday Evening Post* Bogart struck back at his critics, attacked Hollywood trade papers that urged actors to keep silent about public issues and defended his constitutional right to express his political beliefs: "I believe we must pay our freight in this democracy by working with all our intelligence . . . to keep it a living, vital force." Then, thirty-five years before Ronald Reagan entered the White House, Bogart shrewdly predicted: "Give us time, and we [actors] may produce a prime minister or a president."[2]

The Warners strike of 1945, coming after Bogart's appearance before HUAC in 1940 and endorsement of Roosevelt's New Deal policies in 1944, also influenced his political beliefs. We have seen how the Chicago gangsters Bioff and Browne took over the Hollywood unions in 1935. They were convicted of extortion in 1941 and sent to jail.[3] But their influence persisted. In October 1945 a violent labor union conflict erupted in Hollywood between the "militant, independent and left-wing trade coalition called the Conference of Studio Unions, [and Bioff and Browne's old] racket-dominated set-up known as the International Alliance of Theatrical Stage Employees."

On October 5 the Conference of Studio Workers, opposing the racketeers' union and demanding a guaranteed thirty-six-hour work week, went on strike at Warners and took part in full-scale riots. More than a thousand men formed a picket line outside the gates in Burbank and prevented the production staff from entering the studio. After the workers had beaten and stabbed people trying to cross their lines, studio guards threw tear gas bombs into the crowds, firemen turned their hoses on the mob and police reserves clubbed them off the streets. A *Los Angeles Times* editorial of October 12, 1945 claimed: "The Communists are trying to take over the studios to make use of films for their own propaganda." This explosive labor-union dispute—in which legitimate grievances, gangsterism and Communist agitation were inextricably mixed—infuriated Jack Warner. "His anger against the strikers spilled over into a determination to fight the Communists who . . . [seemed to be] behind the disorders, and he became the first major convert from the top of the industry's hierarchy to the anti-Communist front."[4] Jack Warner's rabid and ill-informed testimony before HUAC in 1947 encouraged the blacklisting of suspected Communists and the destruction of the screenwriters and directors known as the Hollywood Ten.

⟨ II ⟩

IN MARCH 1947, Richard Nixon, serving his freshman term (in a Republican-dominated Congress) as a representative from Southern California, wrote to Eric Johnston, the president of the Right-wing Motion Picture Association, which represented the Hollywood executives. Nixon, a prominent member of HUAC, referred to the Left-wing Screen Writers Guild and laid the groundwork for the persecution of the Hollywood Ten by asking: "Is the motion picture industry doing anything to stop the infiltration of Communist influence in Hollywood, or to root out any of those who are . . . sympathizers and use their positions in some subtle manner to affect the film?"

There had been some pro-Russian propaganda in wartime films like *Mission to Moscow* (based on a book by Ambassador Joseph Davies and made at Roosevelt's request) and Bogart's own *Action in the North Atlantic* (both 1943). But the conservative studio heads controlled the content of films and writers could hardly introduce political ideas without their approval. Nevertheless, HUAC, chaired by Nixon's colleague J. Parnell Thomas, a New Jersey Republican, saw political conspiracies everywhere and felt anything that opposed Right-wing thought was pro-Communist. They wanted to undo Roosevelt's social policies, to weaken trade unions and to outlaw the Communist Party. The Committee feared artists and intellectuals, thought films were a dangerous propaganda weapon and wished to eliminate all liberal content from motion pictures.

In September 1947 HUAC subpoenaed forty-three producers, directors, writers and actors, who were required to appear at the Committee's hearings in Washington the following month. Most people in Hollywood felt HUAC was a serious threat to the film industry, which had to be defended. Artists and intellectuals feared the oppressive social and intellectual climate; studio heads worried that political attacks would hurt business. John Huston, the screenwriter Philip Dunne and William Wyler (who had directed Bogart in *Dead End*) responded to the subpoenas by setting up the Committee for the First Amendment (CFA). Its name referred to the part of the Constitution which guaranteed that "Congress shall make no law . . . abridging the freedom of speech . . . or the right of the people peaceably to assemble." Dunne said that the idealistic CFA was established to fight four specific abuses: "the threat of a blacklist, the threat of censorship, official inquiry under threat of contempt of any citizen's legal political beliefs and affiliations, and the indiscriminate trial and conviction by headline of hundreds of persons deprived of any legal opportunity to defend themselves." Huston added that "we stated our opposition to Communism, but argued that mass hysteria was no way to fight it." The CFA eventually attracted five hundred members, from leading film stars to distinguished intellectuals like Albert Einstein and Thomas Mann.

Of the forty-three Hollywood people subpoenaed, nineteen were known as "unfriendly" witnesses. They refused to cooperate with the investigating committee, to state whether they were members of the Communist Party or to name other Party members or sympathizers. Eleven of the nineteen actually testified, including the German playwright Bertolt Brecht, who denied he was a Communist and immediately left the country. The remaining Americans became known as the Hollywood Ten. Despite Huston's statement of the CFA's opposition to Communism, these witnesses mistakenly assumed that its protest against HUAC meant personal solidarity with their political beliefs. As Ceplair and Englund point out in *The Inquisition in Hollywood*, "while liberals had loyally stepped forward, it was not to support suspected Communists, whom many regarded as 'agents of a foreign power,' but to defend civil liberties and oppose political reaction."[5]

The CFA sponsored two national radio broadcasts, took out several advertisements in the *Hollywood Reporter* and other trade newspapers, and chartered a plane to fly fifty prominent members to Washington to attend the hearings. Bogart, though not one of the three main organizers, was the most conspicuous, vehement and outspoken actor. As Edward G. Robinson said: "He stuck his neck out and didn't hesitate to be counted whereas a lot of actors played it safe." Just before flying East on Sunday October 26, 1947, Bogart released a statement to the press that dissociated himself from the Communists and made clear that he was defending the freedom of speech guaranteed by the Constitution:

> This has nothing to do with Communism. It's none of my business who's a Communist and who isn't. We have a well organized and excellent agency in Washington known as the FBI who does know these things. The reason I am flying to Washington is because I am an outraged and angry citizen who feels that my civil liberties are being taken away from me and that the Bill of Rights is being abused and who also feels that nobody in this country has any right to kick around the Constitution of the United States, not even the Un-American Activities Committee.

Bogart reinforced this statement with a "Hollywood Fights Back" speech that was broadcast on ABC radio on the day of the flight. He based his argument on an editorial in the *New York Herald-Tribune* which, like most serious newspapers, had questioned the danger of Communist subversion and attacked HUAC's unconstitutional procedures:

This is Humphrey Bogart. Is democracy so feeble it can be subverted merely by a look or a line, an inflection, a gesture? There was an editorial in the New York Herald-Tribune which says it perfectly, and I quote: "If moving pictures are undermining the American form of government and menacing it by their content, it might become the duty of Congress to ferret out the responsible persons. But clearly this is not the case. Not even the Committee's own witnesses are willing to make so fantastic a charge. And since no danger exists, the beliefs of men and women who write for the screen are, like the beliefs of any ordinary men and women, nobody's business but their own. As the Bill of Rights mentions. Neither Mr. Thomas nor the Congress in which he sits is empowered to dictate what Americans shall think."[6]

Bogart and Huston interrupted their preparations for *Key Largo* and joined the fifty actors (many others were making films and could not leave) on the CFA flight from Los Angeles to Washington. Press photos showed Evelyn Keyes, Richard Conte, Danny Kaye, Gene Kelly, Bacall, Bogart, Marsha Hunt, June Havoc, Paul Henreid and Geraldine Brooks standing on the steps leading to the plane. In addition to Huston and Dunne, Ira Gershwin, John Garfield, Jane Wyatt, the screenwriter Robert Ardrey, the producers Jules Buck and Joseph Sistrom, David Hopkins (the son of Roosevelt's adviser Harry Hopkins), the harmonica player Larry Adler and Sterling Hayden were also on the flight.

Huston and Dunne spoke to the press and placed Bogart and Bacall, the most charismatic couple, at the head of the group. The plane stopped along the way in Kansas City, St. Louis and Chicago, where throngs of people turned up—sometimes in the middle of the night—to greet them. Huston, Bogart, Bacall, Kelly and Kaye made short speeches to counter the negative publicity about Hollywood and arouse support for their cause. They explained why they were making the trip and why the charges of Communist subversion were absurd, denounced HUAC and reaffirmed the right to free speech. According to Marsha Hunt, the mood on the plane was both festive and serious. All the actors were well established, and did not need publicity or controversy. They had decided to fly into the eye of the storm to set the record straight. No one dreamed that they would become victims and that some careers would be destroyed when public sympathy turned against the Hollywood Ten and the CFA was smeared as a Communist front.

‹ III ›

As EARLY AS 1938 J. Parnell Thomas, the current chairman of HUAC, and Martin Dies, the chairman in 1940, had denounced the government-sponsored Federal Theater Project as a hotbed of Communism. They claimed the Communists were using the Theater to express their ideology in plays and to distribute their propaganda in books and works of art. But the October 1947 hearings, which (in Max Lerner's words) tried "to track down the footprints of Karl Marx in movieland" were the "most flamboyant and widely publicized" in HUAC's history.

The investigation of Communist infiltration in Hollywood began on October 20, a week before the CFA flight, in the crowded Caucus Room in the Old House Office Building. Nixon attended the opening session and then, because his California constituents were being named, disappeared from the subsequent sessions. The "friendly" witnesses, who deplored the Communist influence in Hollywood and named prominent Communist sympathizers, were called during the first week. They included the actors Ronald Reagan, George Murphy (elected U.S. Senator for California in 1964), Gary Cooper, Robert Montgomery, Robert Taylor and Adolphe Menjou as well as the studio executives Walt Disney, Louis Mayer and Jack Warner. Ceplair and Englund wrote that these actors "had cast themselves in the role of 'concerned patriotic citizens' defending a shrinking studio beachhead against an invading Bolshevik menace. . . . [They] related how they had vigilantly scrutinized prospective scripts for their 'Communistic' content, tried to warn their colleagues and superiors of 'subversive' activity, and generally tried to set a high standard of patriotic Americanism."[7]

The most significant testimony, from Bogart's point of view, was that of Jack Warner, who was called first. Eager to display his patriotic credentials, he launched into a long-winded, incoherent attack on Communism and told HUAC that "Communists injected 95% of their propaganda into films through the medium of writers." Though he admitted that he had never actually seen a Communist or "wouldn't know one if I saw one," he mentioned the names of twelve "Reds" (including five of the Hollywood Ten) he had somehow spotted and fired from his studio. Joining the hysteria about a secret conspiracy, Warner also exclaimed that "ideological termites have burrowed into many American industries, organizations, and societies. Wherever they may be, I say let us dig them out and get rid of them. My brothers and I will be happy to subscribe generously to a pest-removal fund."

Warner's willingness to betray his own screenwriters on admittedly flimsy evidence horrified the Hollywood Ten, the CFA and his colleagues at the studio, and intensified Bogart's hatred of his boss. Even Eric Johnston, president of the Motion Picture Association, told the writers that the producers were "embarrassed by the fact that Jack Warner . . . made a stupid ass of himself." Warner, later appalled by his own testimony, asked Huston: "That makes me a squealer, doesn't it?" Unwilling to let his boss off the hook, Huston mercilessly replied: "Yes, it does."[8] Nevertheless, Warner's testimony was extremely damaging. It emphasized the split between executives and actors, reinforced the suspicion that Communists were indeed making propaganda films and served to justify the witch hunt that threatened to destroy his own industry.

Bogart and the CFA resented not only the testimony of Warner and other "friendly" witnesses, but also HUAC's quite different treatment of the witnesses. The "friendly" witnesses confirmed the existence of Communist infiltration in Hollywood; the "unfriendly" ones were accused of subversion. The former did not know the names of Communist Party members; the latter refused to give them. The former were allowed to read speeches and testify at great length; the latter were cut off before they could speak and sometimes dragged from the room by armed guards.

All the Hollywood Ten—producers, directors and writers—had been Communists, though Edward Dmytryk and Adrian Scott had left the Party by 1947, and five of them had worked for Warners. Their contradictory aims while on the stand were to attack HUAC and keep their jobs, avoid naming names and stay out of jail. As soon as the hearings began, Chairman Thomas and HUAC were strongly criticized by newspaper editorials throughout the country for violating the First Amendment. And Eric Johnston announced that the Motion Picture Association would never blacklist writers who were accused of being Communists. With the support of the press, the backing of the CFA and the apparent guarantees of the producers, the Ten believed they could afford to take a defiant stance at the hearings.

The large, drafty stone hall, with its mass of bright lights and whirring cameras, its grim interrogators, screaming witnesses and gavel pounding right next to the microphone created a theatrical atmosphere. It had fierce dialogue, intense drama and a highly emotional audience. The CFA had agreed, Dunne wrote, on the basic premise that "any *official* inquiry into political beliefs and affiliations was unconstitutional." If any of them were called to the stand and asked the crucial question: "Are you now or have you ever been a member of the Communist Party?" they would reply: "I must respectfully decline to answer that question, on the grounds that the information is privileged under the First Amendment to the Constitution."

Dunne and Huston wanted the Ten to seize the moral high ground and adopt this dignified procedure. But the Ten hoped to give the appearance of cooperating without actually answering the questions. They decided not to be bullied by the Committee, but to insist on responding in their own way and unleashing a diatribe against HUAC. The first of the Ten to be sworn in was John Howard Lawson, the leading Communist in Hollywood. When he asked if he could read a statement, a privilege that had been granted to all the "friendly" witnesses, the short, bald, cigar-smoking Thomas refused permission and began the bullying interrogation. He had a copy of the statement in front of him, and had no intention of allowing Lawson to discredit the Committee with a violent denunciation. Lawson fenced with them for half an hour, refused to say whether he was a Communist (an admission that would have been followed by a demand to name the members of his cell) and managed to shout a few furious protests over the pounding gavel: "The Committee is on trial here before the American public. . . . The question of Communism is in no way related to this inquiry, which is an attempt to get control of the screen and to invade the basic rights of American citizens." Another hostile witness, Dalton Trumbo, shouted: "This is the beginning of the American concentration camp."[9] Though all of the Ten were professional writers and directors, with extensive experience in plays and films, they completely miscalculated the effect of their performance.

After belligerently challenging the Committee and acting as rudely and vulgarly as the chairman, Lawson was cited for contempt and roughly removed from the stand by the police. Bogart and the other actors were appalled and outraged by Thomas' arbitrary treatment of the witness, but they were also disgusted by Lawson's undignified behavior and disdain for the congressional hearing. His arrogant refusal to answer the questions alienated the public and smeared the stars with his own Communist views. The other nine witnesses, like sheep rushing over a cliff, followed Lawson's example and made an equally disastrous impression. Dunne felt that the transparent ploy "of pretending to answer the questions while actually evading them and indulging in combative political speeches . . . inevitably—and perhaps deservedly—backfired." He also said that "this blustering and shouting—getting in the gutter with the committee, and it was a gutter committee"—obscured the real issue and missed the chance to defend an important principle. Victor Navasky agreed that Lawson's aggression had upset the audience "who thought they had come to cheer on a group of civil libertarians and instead found themselves listening to what sounded suspiciously like Party rhetoric." Only Ring Lardner, Jr., who said "I could answer [the question], but if I did, I would hate myself in the morning," replied in a dignified manner.[10]

In his definitive book on HUAC Robert Carr concluded: "the Hollywood hearings revealed the committee at its worst. . . . No other major investigation of the committee ever ended so anti-climactically or produced so little tangible evidence in support of a thesis which the committee set out to prove." Thomas—who had been criticized by the press but felt he had achieved his political aims—indefinitely adjourned the hearings after only ten of the nineteen "unfriendly" witnesses had been called. The CFA, feeling victorious, had a celebratory party at "21," one of Bogart's favorite hangouts in New York.

Yet the discreditable performances of Lawson and his colleagues had suddenly turned editorials against the Hollywood Ten and their supporters. Since the Hollywood Ten had obscured the constitutional issue in a cloud of Leftist jargon, the CFA now seemed to be defending Communism rather than democracy. The actress Evelyn Keyes, then married to Huston, said: "We faced a hostile, sophisticated, worldly press who made us look like stupid children interfering with grownup problems." David Selznick, Mayer and even Warner had originally contributed to the CFA. Louella Parsons had publicly supported them. President Truman had invited them to lunch. But, as Paul Henreid recalled: "We woke up the next morning to find that the press, which had praised us so fully, had done a complete about-face. We were no longer knights in shining armor. We were 'dupes and fellow-travellers,' 'pinkos,' who were trying to undermine the country." The strategy of the Ten had played directly into the hands of HUAC, whose propaganda victory would have far-reaching effects.

The studio heads met at the Waldorf-Astoria Hotel on November 24 and reversed their previous stance. They announced that they would not employ Communists, and would fire the Hollywood Ten; they would not rehire any of them until they had cleared themselves of contempt and declared under oath that they were not members of the Party. Bogart explained that "the industry—Warner and the rest of them—felt that the government heat was on. They had to have scapegoats. That's why they set up the blacklist of stars, writers, producers and all the rest. They had to show the government they were willing to cooperate." The CFA was listed by HUAC as a "Communist front" and its members, now tainted and threatened by the prospect of unemployment, felt betrayed by the men they had come to Washington to help.

The CFA quickly began to dissolve and within a few weeks there was almost no one left in the fight. As Navasky explained: "Liberal Hollywood, which had been with the Ten on arrival in the East, abandoned them as they left—partly out of shock at the confrontation with the Committee, partly in reaction to the indictment for contempt of Congress, and partly out of fear, after the Waldorf meeting, that they themselves would be tainted. The Committee for the First Amendment, which had announced a major propaganda campaign on behalf of the Ten, folded almost as fast as it had formed."[11] Bogart and other prominent figures came under public and private pressure from journalists, gossip columnists, studio executives, financial backers, managers, agents, family and friends. To save their careers, they had to withdraw their opposition to HUAC and obtain a clearance from the FBI—as if acting were equivalent to working for the State Department or doing atomic research.

‹ IV ›

MIKE ROMANOFF said that Bogart "really got himself into serious trouble by going to Washington." He had appeared in the pro-Russian *Action in the North Atlantic* (which Lawson had written), had played a starring role in the CFA and had been one of the most outspoken members of what was now considered to be a Communist front organization. The CFA, their ranks shattered, returned home separately. Huston said that Bogart, met by (unnamed) friends in Chicago who urged him to withdraw from the CFA, later publicly admitted he had been "ill advised" (by Huston and Dunne) to go to Washington. Henreid angrily claimed that Bogart made his public retraction as soon as he reached Chicago: "'I didn't know the people I was with were fellow travelers,' he told the reporters, acknowledging in his statement the validity of the false accusations against us. . . . I felt Bogart's statement was a form of betrayal, and it was also the end of our friendship—and the end of many of Bogart's other friendships. The rest of us stood firm."

But Henreid was always hostile to Bogart and his assertion is suspect for several reasons. Bogart's broadcast of November 2, *after* he returned to Hollywood from Washington, described his horrified reaction to the hearings and harshly condemned HUAC. (A photograph in Nathaniel Benchley's book shows him standing up, tense and furious, during the hearings.) And Bogart knew that the CFA were *not* fellow travelers, but defenders of the Constitution. Finally, the rest of the actors did not stand firm. Work in the movies was always precarious, subject to the whims of the studio heads and casting directors, the vagaries of popular taste and availability of suitable scripts. When threatened by the United States government, the CFA splintered and scattered, trying to take cover and salvage their own careers.

In his broadcast of November 2 Bogart alluded to *It Can't Happen Here* (1935), Sinclair Lewis' novel about the threat of a Fascist takeover in America. Through a forceful repetition of "We saw," he conveyed his angry response to the disgraceful fiasco, and concluded with a biting last sentence:

> This is Humphrey Bogart. We sat in the committee room and heard it happen. We saw it and we said to ourselves, "It *can* happen here!" We saw American citizens denied the right to speak by elected representatives of the people. We saw police take citizens from the stand like criminals, after they had been refused the right to defend themselves. We saw the gavel of a committee chairman cutting off the words of free Americans. The sound of that gavel, Mr. Thomas, rings across America! Because every time your gavel struck, it hit the first amendment to the Constitution of the United States!

Despite Bogart's passionate appeal, Right-wing newsmen like Ed Sullivan, the Broadway gossip columnist for McCormick's New York *Daily News,* and George Sokolsky, a columnist for Hearst's New York *Daily Mirror,* seized the initiative in the media. They became the moral arbiters of American politics and gave Bogart well-intentioned advice that he could not afford to reject. Bogart said Sullivan had warned him: "the public is beginning to think you're a Red! Get that through your skull, Bogie." On November 24, a month after the hearings, the FBI's file on Bogart noted that Sullivan, while trying to defend Bogart, had asked them for secret information about him: "Sullivan stated he would like to know anything that we could tell him about Bogart, because he certainly is not going to let Bogart sell him a bill of goods, although he was frank to confess that he did not believe there was anything sinister about Bogart but that he had probably just been misled."[12]

Hedda Hopper and Louella Parsons also jumped into the controversy (which continued to capture the headlines) and tried to threaten and patronize him. Horrified by his politics, Hopper called him one of "the four most dangerous men in America." Parsons, in an influential broadcast of November 9 (a week after Bogart's second "Hollywood Fights Back" talk) played the schoolmarm and seemed unaware that her conclusion was illogical and absurd: Bogart "was ill-advised when he went to Washington to protest the procedure of the Thomas Committee. . . . Because [actors'] names make news they must be doubly careful that their motives are clearly understood. Bogie went to Washington with good intentions but every day I receive hundreds of letters from people who insist he is a Communist because there were some [other] people questioned at the hearing who were under suspicion."

Bogart's friends were also alarmed. In January 1947, ten months before the Washington hearings, he had signed a lucrative contract with Warners. Both his business manager and agent feared that this profitable arrangement would be ruined by his political activities. Morgan Maree and Sam Jaffe, who made a great deal of money from Bogart, urged him to leave the CFA. Maree told him: "You'd better step out or you won't be able to get jobs." Later on, Jaffe rather hypocritically criticized Bogart for following their advice: "He got frightened. He withdrew. . . . He *talked* big, but he didn't take any risks. He wanted to play it safe." Both urged him to "step out," precisely because he *had* taken great risks.

Bogart's new contract with Warners allowed him to make pictures outside the studio. When the hearings began in October 1947, he was planning to form an independent film company with his old friend Mark Hellinger, who also told him that their project was threatened. The screenwriter Malvin Wald remembered: "I was in Hellinger's office when he told me that the backers of their new venture, in Chicago, didn't want Bogart involved with a Left-wing group. They said he was free to take any political stance, but they were also free to withdraw their funding. Hellinger called Bogie in Washington and relayed this message. Bogart chose prudence over valor and returned immediately to Hollywood."[13]

The key figure in Bogart's public recantation was the journalist George Sokolsky. According to John Cogley's *Report on Blacklisting,* Sokolsky played an important role "in making judgments as to who of the Hollywood penitents were worthy of immediate absolution and who should be referred to the 'experts' on the West Coast for further consideration." Sokolsky, in one of his columns, challenged Bogart to name the people who had persuaded him to defend the Communists. Bogart, giving in to the pressure put on him by all his associates, followed what turned out to be good advice. As Ian Hamilton wrote: "The Committee for the First Amendment had gone to Washington in support of what had seemed a glorious cause, the cause of free expression, and had found themselves lined up with a group of writers who had come across as shifty, ill-mannered, fanatical, and—well, frankly, un-American."[14]

Casablanca, with Claude Rains, Paul Henreid and Ingrid Bergman, 1943: At the airport Bogart tells her: "Where I'm going you can't follow. What I've got to do, you can't be any part of."

Slim and Howard Hawks, 1940s: "The man had ice-cold blue eyes and the coldest of
manners."

To Have and Have Not, with Lauren Bacall and Marcel Dalio, 1945: "Watch yourself," Hawks told Bogart, "because you're supposed to be the most insolent man on the screen and I'm going to make a girl a little more insolent than you."

Bogart and Bacall, with her gold whistle, late 1940s: "You know how to whistle, don't you, Steve? You just put your lips together and blow."

The *Santana*, 1940s: Bogart thought: "The sea is the last free place on earth."

The Big Sleep, with Bacall, John Ridgely and Howard Hawks, 1946: "You've got a touch of class," Bogart tells her, "but I don't know how far you can go," to which she replies, "That depends on who's in the saddle."

Dark Passage, with Bacall, 1947: When the mummy-like wrappings come off after plastic surgery, Bogart (not surprisingly) looks exactly like Bogart.

Bogart signing the Warners contract, with Morgan Maree, Sam Jaffe, Bacall and Mary
Baker, December 1946: The fifteen-year contract guaranteed him $3 million.

Committee for the First Amendment, flying to Washington: Geraldine Brooks, Paul Henreid, June Havoc, Bogart, Marsha Hunt, Bacall, Gene Kelly, Danny Kaye, Richard Conte and Evelyn Keyes, October 1947.

The Treasure of the Sierra Madre, with John Huston and Walter Huston, 1948: Walter says: "I know what gold does to men's souls. . . . You lose your sense of values and your character changes entirely."

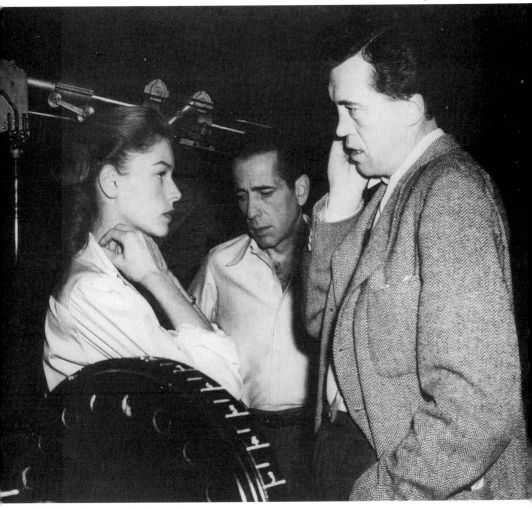

Key Largo, with Bacall and John Huston, 1948: "We're fighting to cleanse the world of ancient evils, ancient ills."

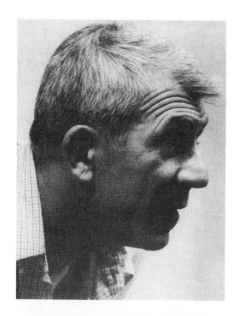

Richard Brooks, 1950s: Bogart would work his friend into a rage and then exclaim: "Look at him now. His eyes are getting big and red!"

Bogart drinking with Bacall and Mike Romanoff, late 1940s: Bogart saw him as "the practitioner of the biggest, longest-lasting, and most successful rib he'd ever seen."

Bogart with his panda, September 1949: "I can take my panda any place I want to. And if I wanna buy it a drink, that's my business."

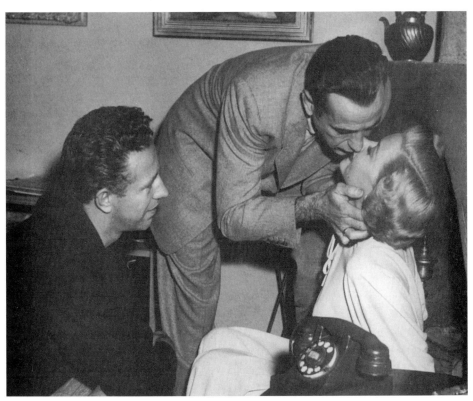

In a Lonely Place, with Nicholas Ray and Gloria Grahame, 1950: "The film character's pride in his art, his selfishness, his drunkenness, his lack of energy stabbed with lightning strokes of violence were shared by the real Bogart."

The African Queen tows the actors and crew up the Ruiki River, 1951: "That raft itself became our stage," Huston wrote. "We could put cameras and equipment on it and move around . . . with as much facility as we'd have had on a studio floor."

232 South Mapleton Drive, 1950s: "I could put a down payment on an entire foreign country for the dough this joint set me back."

Bogart with Stephen, Leslie and Bacall, 1954: "I'll never live to see the little bastards grow up."

Nunnally Johnson, 1959: Johnson said that Bogart "never gets drunk. Just pumps in some Scotch, and stays a nice even glow all day."

Beat the Devil, with Peter Lorre, 1954: Lorre remarked: "It was a deliciously sardonic comedy, meant for art houses, and they opened it with a blood-and-thunder campaign. People just didn't get it."

The Caine Mutiny, with Van Johnson and Todd Karns, 1954: Bogart said: "Queeg was not a cruel man, he was a very sick man."

The Barefoot Contessa, with Ava Gardner, 1954: Bogart thought she was a North Carolina hillbilly who should never wear shoes.

Since Bogart had specifically dissociated himself from the Communists and was not a personal friend of any of the Hollywood Ten, there seemed to be no point, now that the press had turned against him, in destroying his career in order to uphold a principle that few others were now willing to defend. He had taken fifteen years to reach the top of his profession and didn't want to throw away everything he had. He therefore responded in a letter that Sokolsky printed in his *Daily Mirror* column of December 6, 1947. Bogart reaffirmed the constitutional principle that had originally inspired him to join the CFA. But he was forced to bend the knee, disavow his own behavior and admit that the high-minded excursion had been nothing more than a "foolish" expedition:

> My recent trip to Washington, where I appeared with a group of motion-picture people, has become the subject of such confused and erroneous interpretations that I feel the situation should be clarified.
>
> I am not a Communist.
>
> I am not a Communist sympathizer.
>
> I detest Communism just as any decent American does.
>
> My name will not be found on any Communist front organization as a sponsor for anything Communistic.
>
> I went to Washington because I thought fellow Americans were being deprived of their constitutional rights, and for that reason alone.
>
> That [the] trip was ill-advised, even foolish, I am very ready to admit. At the time it seemed like the thing to do.
>
> I have absolutely no use for Communism nor for anyone who serves that philosophy.
>
> I am an American.
>
> And very likely, like a good many of the rest of you, sometimes a foolish and impetuous American.

On December 15 *Newsweek* picked up the story and reprinted part of his letter to Sokolsky. It also quoted Bogart's admission that he had been politically naive and shamefully exploited by the very people he was trying to defend: "'We went in green and they beat our brains out.' . . . He thought he was defending the Bill of Rights, 'but in the shuffle we became adopted by the Communists and I ended up with my picture on the front page of the *Daily Worker.*'" A first-page headline, with photo, in the Communist *Daily Worker* of October 27, the day after he arrived in Washington, had indeed said: "Stars Fly East To Fight Probe: Bogart, Bacall, Lead 26 Notables."

Three months later, in March 1948, the darling of the *Daily Worker* followed up his letter to Sokolsky with a *Photoplay* article, "I'm No Communist." He began by explaining that the CFA had originally been supported by the liberal press, which suddenly turned against them and singled out Bogart as their main victim: "The *New York Times,* the *Herald-Tribune* and other reputable publications editorially had questioned the House Committee on Un-American Activities, warning that it was infringing on free speech. When a group of us Hollywood actors and actresses said the same thing, the roof fell in on us. In some fashion, I took the brunt of the attack. Suddenly, the plane that had flown us East became 'Bogart's plane,' carrying 'Bogart's group.' For once, top billing became embarrassing." He then reaffirmed his original principles, but clearly dissociated himself from the Communists and the Hollywood Ten: "I'm about as much in favor of Communism as J. Edgar Hoover. I despise Communism and I believe in our own American brand of democracy. Our planeload of Hollywood performers who flew to Washington came East to fight against what we considered censorship of the movies. The ten men cited for contempt by the House Un-American Activities Committee were not defended by us. We were there solely in the interests of freedom of speech, freedom of the screen and protection of the Bill of Rights. We were not there to defend Communism in Hollywood, or Communism in America." He concluded, as a regular fellow, by confessing that he had been tricked and by reaffirming his patriotism in words that unintentionally recalled his testimony before HUAC in 1940 ("I think Hollywood people are dupes in the most part"): "We may not have been very smart in the way we did things, may have been dopes in some people's eyes, but we were American dopes! Actors and actresses always go overboard about some things."[15] The flaw in his argument, of course, is that he claimed to uphold the principles of the Bill of Rights while admitting that they did not apply to actual or alleged Communists, a conclusion that resembled the views of the Right-wing members of HUAC.

While making *Key Largo* in February 1948, Bogart and his friends were questioned about the public imbroglio. Bogart cited his exploitation by the Communist press and repeated the "we were dopes" argument. Huston explained why Bogart needed security, Robinson said people lacked courage since Roosevelt's death and Bacall loyally defended her husband:

> "Roosevelt was a good politician," [Bogart] said. "He could handle those babies in Washington, but they're too smart for

guys like me. Hell, I'm no politician. That's what I meant when I said our Washington trip was a mistake."

At which John Huston intervened: "Bogie owns a fifty-four-foot yawl. When you own a fifty-four-foot yawl you've got to provide for her upkeep." Edward G. Robinson grunted: "The Great Chief died and everybody's guts died with him."

"How would you like to see *your* picture in the front page of the Communist paper?" asked Bogart.

"Nijah," Robinson said, sneeringly.

"The *Daily Worker* runs Bogie's picture and right away, he's a dangerous Communist," said Miss Bacall.

"Let's eat," said Huston.[16]

Bogart's recantations in December 1947 and March 1948 enabled him to get an FBI clearance and remove all threats to his career. He was not, like many others after 1947, forced to humiliate himself by testifying in public and to ruin the careers of his colleagues by naming them as Communists.

The response to Bogart's recantations ranged from vituperative attacks to sympathetic understanding. The harshest response came from two of the Ten and from one of the more radical performers who had flown with him to Washington. Lester Cole baldly stated: "Humphrey Bogart, frightened, led an exodus from the CFA, and many followed." Alvah Bessie, a militant Communist who had fought with the Abraham Lincoln Battalion in the Spanish Civil War, tried to explain Bogart's behavior and apology: "Humphrey Bogart almost immediately repudiated [the CFA], accused himself of being a dupe (and a dope), and—by this action (which was obviously the result of having the screws put on him by the producers)—provoked a panic that rapidly destroyed the Committee for the First Amendment itself." But since Bogart did not say he had been duped until December 6, about five weeks after he returned from Washington, he had not repudiated the CFA "almost immediately." Larry Adler was most severe. He emphasized Bogart's betrayal, which encouraged many others to defect: "The press attacked us and Humphrey Bogart caved in in the most demeaning, debasing way, saying that he was duped, didn't realize what he was doing, but he was sorry and knew the American people would allow him one mistake. And then Gene Kelly reneged, and Danny Kaye reneged, and Frank Sinatra reneged, and those of us who didn't stood out like carbuncles."[17]

Other members of the CFA, who had counted on Bogart to stand firm under pressure, were appalled when he abandoned them. Most felt, like

Evelyn Keyes, that his recantation was a cowardly sell-out. Marsha Hunt recalled that Bogart had been vehement and articulate about the behavior of HUAC, and had clenched his fist in anger about both the testimony of Jack Warner and the unfair treatment of Lawson. His recantation therefore came as a "body blow" that left his friends "thunderstruck."

It is easy for people who did not live through these times to condemn Bogart's behavior. His son Stephen recently agreed with his father's critics and remarked: "If he went to defend constitutional rights, then how was he misled or ill-advised?"[18] But this ignores Bogart's outrage after being duped by the Communists, his reluctance to jeopardize the company he had formed and his fear that he would lose everything he had worked so long to achieve.

Philip Dunne and John Huston, both friends of Bogart, were more sympathetic and discerning about the timing and his motives. Dunne said: "Bogey some weeks later understandably gave way to ferocious pressures and apologized for his actions." Huston, whose friendship with Bogart survived his defection, thought his statements were a sad mistake, but agreed with Dunne that "the pressures were terrible." Ring Lardner, Jr., the most fair-minded and perceptive of the Ten, recently wrote: "Both Phil Dunne and John Huston, who were mainstays of the Committee, reacted unfavorably to how contentiously some of us responded to the questions from HUAC members and counsel, and that may have been cited by Bogie as a reason for his defection." Arthur Miller, who courageously opposed HUAC in 1956, also saw the moral complexity of the issue. He said Bogart had been misled by the Hollywood Ten, who did not tell him that they were Communists, and feared the witch hunt would end his career. Miller now "hesitates to judge him in this two-edged story."[19]

Bogart himself was furious that he had been misled by the Ten, pushed to exaggerated prominence in the CFA and forced to publicize his patriotism as if he had been a "friendly" witness — only to be attacked by the very people who had maneuvered him into that false position. During a CFA meeting after their return to Hollywood, Bogart shouted at Danny Kaye: "You fuckers sold me out." Richard Brooks' novel *The Producer* provides another vivid portrayal of Bogart's difficult situation when a friend gives Steve Taggart, a potential victim of a congressional investigation, ironic advice about how to destroy himself: "Take an ad in the paper. Say you're behind Shea. Sign your name to it. Go ahead. Fly to Washington with him. Let those Congressmen put you on the stand and take you apart. You're a million-dollar investment. Throw yourself in the can and pull the chain." Later on, Taggart complains: "All you want to do is use me. . . . I stick my neck out and what do I get for it?"

The most interesting defense of Bogart came from Edward Dmytryk. He had left the Communist Party before receiving his subpoena, and was one of the Ten. Dmytryk said that the Soviet Comintern itself had tried to link the defense of the Ten with the quite unrelated issue of Negro rights in the South and—wanting them to be martyred—had instructed them to behave outrageously when called to testify. Dmytryk believed that Bogart had indeed been used and manipulated, and that the actor, after talking to George Sokolsky, acted wisely by swiftly dissociating himself from the Ten.

The artistic and political effects of the HUAC hearings were far-reaching and disastrous. In 1950 the Hollywood Ten took their case to the Supreme Court, but it had become more conservative after the death of two liberal justices and denied them a hearing. Though no one had ever proved that they were Communists, each of the Ten was sentenced to a year's imprisonment for contempt of Congress. At the same time, Parnell Thomas was sentenced to eighteen months for padding his payroll and wound up in Danbury prison with two of his victims, Lardner and Cole. Dmytryk served his jail sentence, but later appeared as a "friendly" witness, explaining: "I didn't want to be a martyr for a cause I didn't believe in."[20]

When HUAC reconvened in 1951, a mass of friendly witnesses were in a panic to get clearance and avoid the ever-increasing blacklist—which eventually affected about three hundred people. They confessed their political sins and were forced to incriminate their colleagues. They managed to save their skins and were able to work, but humiliated themselves and lost the respect of both inquisitors and victims. As a sense of fear and repression swept through the industry, screenwriters who refused to recant were ruined and forced into exile. Many of them worked under pseudonyms at greatly reduced fees and never got the credits they had earned. "The blacklist took all the best and brightest people out of Hollywood," said the writer Arthur Laurents, "ushering in the blandness, compromise and conventionality of much of the 1950s film culture," which provided a dull contrast to the biting political criticism in the Warners movies of the 1930s. If the Hollywood Ten had won their case, Joseph McCarthy might not have been able to dominate American politics in the 1950s. The director Joseph Losey, who left America for England, believed that "if one man had stood up and said 'I'm a Communist—so what? The Communist Party is not illegal and there are 90,000 people in the Communist Party,' it would have stopped the witch hunting."[21]

‹ V ›

BOGART'S CALAMITOUS involvement with the CFA did not dampen his taste for politics in the early 1950s. Spurred on by Bacall, he took part in two political campaigns and had his third confrontation with HUAC. In 1950 he actively supported Helen Gahagan Douglas, who had been an actress and singer, and was married to the actor Melvyn Douglas. Twice elected as a liberal Democratic congresswoman from Los Angeles, she had strongly criticized HUAC and in her bid for a Senate seat was defeated by Richard Nixon. In a typically vicious and unscrupulous campaign, he smeared her as a Communist. Just as Bogart had upheld his right to support Roosevelt in "I Stuck My Neck Out" in 1945, so in 1950 he once again defended an actor's right to engage in politics. His interview on CBS radio was quoted in the *Daily Variety* of November 6, 1950. At a time when the mood of the country had turned Republican, Bogart revealed that his celebrity had made him vulnerable to attack: "A movie star pays a tremendous income tax. . . . It's enough to buy an airplane. . . . That's another reason I have a right to say what's done with my money. Of course," he added ironically, "there are some Republicans who feel that a movie star should not have a right to engage in politics if he's a Democrat."

In the spring of 1951, when Bogart was on the way to film in Africa and HUAC resumed their investigation of Communist subversion in Hollywood, his role in the CFA — of which he had been cleared — once again came under scrutiny. That year, an anti-Communist newspaper named *ALERT* called Bogart and Bacall "swimming-pool proletarians." When the actor Larry Parks was called as a "friendly" witness on March 21, 1951, he said: "I don't recall ever attending a meeting with Humphrey Bogart."[22] But when Sterling Hayden testified on April 10, he incriminated Bogart.

Hayden, a marine captain in World War II, had joined the Communist Party in June 1946 and left it in December. He took part in the CFA's trip to Washington in October 1947. By his own admission, in early 1951 he was frightened and desperate to get work. But he could not obtain clearance until he had betrayed his friends and had been acclaimed as a patriotic hero by the Right. Hayden began by stating that "the people who lent their names and gave money to this Committee for the First Amendment, to the best of my knowledge, certainly had no idea that it was a Communist front, any more than I had." Hayden misled HUAC, as he knew that the CFA was *not* a "Communist front." When asked, "Who spearheaded the Committee for the First Amendment?" he identified Bogart and Bacall: "The first name that comes to mind is Humphrey Bogart. And his wife. . . . I know there was a gathering at Ira Gershwin's house at which a couple of hundred people were present. The spokesmen were John Huston and Phil Dunne."

Huston wrote that Hayden was "one of the few among [the infamous] who didn't try to excuse himself, or to justify his actions. At one time he had been an actual card-carrying Communist, but, under the pressure of the Red Scare, he changed his mind and decided that Communism was a danger to this country. He proceeded to name names—including that of his best friend. . . . He openly declared that he was ashamed of himself for what he had done, wrote a book which told about the episode." In his autobiography, *Wanderer*, Hayden frankly admitted his selfishness and cowardice, and bitterly concluded that "only a handful . . . denounced this abrogation of constitutional freedoms whereby the stoolie could gain status in a land of frightened people."[23] Hayden's testimony did not harm Bogart, who had already been cleared. But it was used to discredit other Hollywood stars and show that HUAC still had the power to humiliate and destroy more vulnerable actors.

The HUAC investigations of alleged Communist subversion in Hollywood exposed the polarities in American political life and intensified the long-standing opposition between studio executives and their employees. It discredited the industry and gave the impression of a deep-rooted Red conspiracy. It destroyed friendships, broke up marriages and ruined hundreds of careers. It brought in a secret blacklist, dispersed some of the most talented artists and weakened the tottering studio system. It also led, in the Eisenhower years, to many bland, smug films, with stars like Rock Hudson and Doris Day, that were devoid of significant content.

The blacklist began to crack in 1953 when Dalton Trumbo, writing under an assumed name, won an Oscar (accepted by his "front") for *Roman Holiday*, but didn't really break until 1960, when Trumbo got a screen credit for *Exodus*. Bogart, threatened but not seriously damaged, realized the perils of celebrity. But he went out of his way to work with blacklisted artists and actively supported Adlai Stevenson, who strongly opposed the Communist witch hunts, in the presidential campaign of 1952.

◇ 11 ◇

Mexico and the Florida Keys

1948-1950

⟨ I ⟩

IN 1946 Bogart, Warners' most popular and profitable actor, earned $432,000. Impressed by his power at the box office, Warners offered him a new fifteen-year contract. The sixty-seven-page document, effective January 1, 1947, stipulated that he would make one picture a year at Warners for a salary of $200,000, which guaranteed him $3 million in future earnings. He could reject two out of three of their stories, but had to take the third one or provide his own script. He could turn down any director except the five he specifically approved: John Huston, William Wyler, John Ford, Billy Wilder and Edward Dmytryk. After complaining for years about long hours, he could now stop working at the studio at 6 P.M. While on location he would get $1,000 a week for expenses, air fare for his family and salary for his hairdresser-secretary (Verita Peterson), who took care of his hairpiece, answered his mail and mixed his drinks. The contract also allowed him to form his own company and make his own films. It was valid for as long as he chose to honor it; he could cancel it, if he wished, after seven years. In Richard Brooks' *The Producer*, Bogart/Taggart says he has finally achieved independence because he has "two hundred thousand dollars in the bank. And a nonexclusive contract without options for one picture a year for fifteen years, and by that time I'll be too old for acting in pictures anyway." The contract gave him both financial security and the freedom to choose the movies he wanted to make.

After completing his most recent film, *The Big Sleep,* and while making his next one, *The Two Mrs. Carrolls* (shot between April and June 1945, but not released until 1947), Bogart married Bacall. By the time he had finished his next two films of 1947, *Dead Reckoning* and *Dark Passage,* he had bought the *Santana* and the big house in Benedict Canyon, done a Lux Radio Theater adaptation with Bacall of *To Have and Have Not,* and signed the long-term contract with Warners.

The Two Mrs. Carrolls (original treatment by William Faulkner) and *Conflict* have similar plots. In both pictures Bogart (recently divorced in real life) plays a man plotting to murder his wife so he can marry a more desirable younger woman, acted by Alexis Smith in both movies. *The Two Mrs. Carrolls* is an up-to-date version of Robert Browning's famous poem "My Last Duchess" (1842). In both works a cruel and egoistic man of taste, refinement and culture plans to destroy his innocent wife, whose portrait — an extension of himself — he proudly exhibits. In the poem the jealous duke has had his young wife murdered and displays her portrait while negotiating with an intermediary for a replacement. In the film Bogart, an American artist living in England, has already killed his first wife. He paints his second wife (Barbara Stanwyck) as "The Angel of Death," revealing her skeletal rib cage under a torn black dress. Once he has captured his wives in his paintings, they lose their reality and become his victims.

The film borrows the menacing English country house and the fearful wife, haunted by the death of her predecessor, from Hitchcock's *Rebecca* (1940). Bogart, a distant and improbable father, has a young daughter by his first marriage. Played by a sophisticated English girl, Ann Carter, she is the only convincing child in his films. Nigel Bruce as the doddering doctor and Anita Bolster as the peevish housekeeper are also first-rate. But the dialogue is stilted ("We mustn't lose each other ever, Sally") and the picture struggles through the awkward permutations of plot.

Bogart attempts to kill Stanwyck in order to gain the love and artistic inspiration of Alexis Smith. But he is blackmailed by the druggist who sells him the evil potion and must also murder him. Stanwyck discovers Bogart's plot, throws her poisoned milk out the window and fends him off after he crashes into her room to do her in. Using the same twitching hand gestures as in *The Petrified Forest,* Bogart seems ill at ease as a suave psychopath in an alien setting. When arrested, he pathetically explains: "I had to do this so I could go on with my work." After wittily asking the bobbies if they would like a glass of milk, he is led away in the quiet English manner. Howard Barnes of the *Herald-Tribune,* impressed by his acting, said Bogart "gives a brilliantly modulated performance as he changes from a dashing suitor to a Borgia-like Van Gogh."[1]

In the summer of 1945 Bogart made *Dead Reckoning* for Columbia with Lizabeth Scott. She later gave a somewhat misleading account of their work on this picture: "He set the pace. He would arrive on the set totally unprepared at nine. He would then proceed to learn his lines before his martini and lunch. Then he would work till five and leave, the scene completed or not. These were his rules and although I was equally the star of the picture, I abided by them, as did the crew, the director, the producer, and the studio. . . . He was extremely intelligent. . . . I knew [he] was a great star, and yet he didn't intimidate me when I met him. . . . He was very dear to me, very kind to me, and just a charming man."

Bogart never memorized his lines the day before a scene; he preferred to master them immediately beforehand in order to be as natural and spontaneous as possible. The twenty-two-year-old Scott was certainly not "equal" to him as a star, and he would never have been allowed to keep the entire company waiting every day until after lunch. All his colleagues emphasized his professionalism and patience while *others* struggled to master the scene. He used his star status to quit work at six, but always felt the need to mock himself and his profession. He thought it somewhat phony, even effeminate, to put on airs and make-up, impersonate an imaginary character and act vapid parts in the void of a studio. Though he had to work very hard at it, he also found acting "too easy," and felt puritanical guilt about enjoying many aspects of the job while achieving extraordinary success. He told Scott, as he had told Bette Davis: "I would have liked to be anything but an actor. It's such a stupid thing to be."

Dead Reckoning was directed by John Cromwell, who had also directed him on stage in both *Drifting* and *Swifty* in 1922. Bogart had great rapport with his old buddy, but Scott found Cromwell dictatorial. His most minute orders had to be followed and everything had to be done exactly his way. *Dead Reckoning* has some fascinating echoes of Bogart's three recent triumphs. When Scott, the same physical type as Bacall, first makes her appearance, we hear her husky voice before we see her. Then the camera travels slowly and enticingly up her body, from her long legs to her delicate face and long blond hair. Bogart introduces himself to Scott, as to Bacall in *To Have and Have Not,* by lighting her cigarette. He calls her "Mike" (as he called Bacall "Slim"), and sits enraptured at her nightclub table while she sings a sexy song. Though her metallic white dress, with gauntlet sleeves and tasseled belt, looks more like a science-fiction costume than the elegant outfits of Bacall, Scott also wears a beret, jacket and skirt in the later scenes. Bogart clinches the similarities between the two actresses by mentioning President Truman and telling Scott: "Maybe he'll even let you sit on his piano."

In *Dead Reckoning,* as in *The Big Sleep,* Bogart is beaten up and looks haggard (his temporal artery is now prominent on his forehead) while the heroine always remains immaculate. In both films Bogart does research in a library and escorts a lady, carrying her winnings, out of a gambling casino. The contrast between the suave Eddie Mars and his brutal hench-man Canino is repeated in Martinelli and the savage Krause. At the end of both films, the villain opens the door in the rain and is shot by the murderer who really wants to kill Bogart. The heroine of *Dead Reckoning,* like the author of *The Big Sleep,* is appropriately named Chandler.

The plot and characters of *Dead Reckoning* are clearly based on *The Maltese Falcon.* In the former Bogart, an ex-paratrooper, tries to clear his army friend who has been accused of murder and then mysteriously killed. Just as Spade must avenge the death of his partner, Miles Archer, so Rip Murdock (Bogart) tells Coral Chandler (Scott): "A guy's pal is killed, he ought to do something about it." He behaves like a detective in search of the real murderer, but (like Sam Spade) acts entirely on his own and in direct opposition to the flatfooted police. Martinelli, an educated villain like Joel Cairo and Kasper Gutman, insists, with polite and elaborate diction: "Brutality has always revolted me as the weapon of the witless." In both films Bogart is drugged by the suave criminal and then kicked by the heavy when he falls. Coral Chandler, like Brigid O'Shaughnessy, is a deceitful murderess who manipulates Murdock and tries to trick him into believing that someone else has committed her crime. But Scott cannot convey Mary Astor's ambiguously attractive evil. He ironically tells Chand-ler, as he had told O'Shaughnessy, "You're awfully good." At the end, he also forces Coral to confess the murder and tells her (as he had told Brigid): "You're going to fry."

The plot cracks along and has some fine moments. There's some effective business as a waiter's corpse is dumped in Murdock's hotel room, hidden by him in a laundry basket and then returned in the trunk of his car to the house of the murderer. When Murdock is knocked unconscious, images of a parachute jump flash through his mind; when Chandler is dying (in a hospital gown and bandages that recall her futuristic white outfit) the paratrooper compares death to "going out the jump door."

The hard-nosed, bitter, misogynistic dialogue follows the tradition of Hammett and Chandler. Murdock warns the police: "I always get even, lieutenant," and when a gangster steals a vital letter he snarls: "I'm a guy that likes to get his mail." The refrigerated morgue, where he tells the police "I think I ought to take a squint at your stock" and finds his friend's body charred "as crisp as bacon," is "the one cool spot" in the hot Gulf Coast town. Just before incinerating the gangster, he asks: "How would you like yourself, medium rare?" Referring to women stripped of their make-up, he remarks: "All females are the same with their faces washed."

In the most famous put-down lines of the film, he expresses a male fantasy by telling Chandler: "Women ought to come capsule size, about four inches high. When a man goes out for an evening, he just puts her in his pocket and takes her along with him, and that way, he knows exactly where she is. . . . And when it comes to that time of the evening when he wants her full-sized and beautiful, he just waves his hand and she becomes full-size." These startling lines, delivered in Bogart's cold satiric manner, express the idea, characteristic of 1940s *film noir,* that women are evil and dangerous unless carefully controlled by men. In *Dead Reckoning,* whose title refers to settling accounts for his dead friend, Murdock is able to control and expose the woman murderer.

Bogart is effective in this familiar role. He relaxes in the corner of a train by raising his knees and cupping his drink in his hands. When telling a general that his army friend has disappeared he nervously moves his fingers on the arm of the chair. In his hotel room he mocks the heavy southern accent of the telephone operator, paces the floor while thinking about what to do and pitches oranges into a soft chair to release his nervous energy. Drugged by Martinelli, he rubs his eyes to keep them open and then falls forward onto the floor.

He makes a comic attempt to hide by walking behind two fat ladies in the hotel lobby; stumbles a bit before asking a friend to crack Martinelli's safe; shows his teeth and puts a finger in his mouth when stopped by a cop for speeding. He looks sceptical when Scott offers a far-fetched explanation of the crime, widens his eyes and turns slowly toward her when she says they might possibly marry. He puts his fingers around her throat to keep a slight distance before kissing her; and when he begins to trust her, rests his hands protectively on her shoulders before their next kiss. Though Bogart seems to be an effortless actor, he actually uses a great many conscious techniques to make his character convincing.

In both *The Two Mrs. Carrolls* and *Dead Reckoning* the studios put Bogart into formulaic films. One was an unsuitable role, the other capitalized on his previous successes. He had come a long way since the 1930s, but still had to go through the familiar paces instead of being challenged by something new. He excelled at natural acting and a dark, sardonic tone; and longed to make movies which, unlike these stereotyped mysteries, were original and fresh.

In July 1946, while Bogart was making *Dead Reckoning,* the producer Jerry Wald wrote Jack Warner about the actor's next picture, *Dark Passage.* Stressing the difficulty of finding a suitable project, he said that Bogart (more flexible than usual because he wanted Bacall to appear in this film) was keen on the script by the writer-director Delmer Daves, who had co-authored the screenplay of *The Petrified Forest*: "I know you have continuous problems as to methods of getting Bogart to do a picture; and yet, here is one script that Bogart has read and likes. He approves of the director and will take any female star we suggest. . . . We had a lengthy lunch with Bogart and, outside of a few minor changes, he was ready and willing to do this script."[2]

The exteriors of *Dark Passage* were filmed on location in San Francisco, and shots of the city, Marin County, the bay and the bridges were used to create a realistic setting. It opens with an aerial view of Bogart's old haunt, San Quentin, and sirens sound as the protagonist, whom we do not see for the first hour of the film, escapes from prison in a barrel on the back of a truck. When he rolls off the truck he is coincidentally rescued and hidden by Bacall, the Good Angel who just happens to be driving by. Like her father, Bogart has been unjustly imprisoned for a murder he did not commit, and she wants to help him clear himself by finding the real criminal. "When I get excited by something," she tells him, "I give it everything I've got. I'm funny that way."

The title *Dark Passage* refers to the hero's difficult transition from imprisonment to freedom. In order to act freely, Bogart discovers a sleazy plastic surgeon who completely alters his appearance and prepares the face to meet the faces that he'll meet. As he goes under the anesthetic, not knowing what he'll look like when the operation is over, his fears are suggested in a montage of nightmarish images. The first-person camera stands for Bogart's point of view. The first time we see his head, he's swathed in bandages that cover everything but his eyes, nostrils, lips and ears. When the mummy-like wrappings come off, Bogart (not surprisingly) looks exactly like Bogart.

He finally discovers that Agnes Moorehead, who helped convict him, had also killed his wife and framed him after he rejected her advances. But during the confrontation that establishes her guilt she improbably stumbles and falls out of a window. Unable to prove his innocence, he must flee to Peru, where he arranges to meet Bacall. In the last "Peruvian" scene of the movie she rejoins him in a nightclub where clients consume tropical drinks and listen to Latin music, and men with pencil moustaches dance with ladies who wear flowers in their hair. In *Dark Passage* Bacall (in her own elegant apartment) is now proper and respectable rather than cheeky and déclassé. As Bogart's savior and reward she seems rather wooden and speaks slowly and unnaturally, like a teacher talking to a child. Without the cynical veneer and suggestive dialogue of her previous pictures, she fails to ignite a passionate spark.

The picture begins in a fresh and interesting way, but the experimental camera soon becomes tedious, the bandages cramp Bogart's style, and it soon lapses into a conventional thriller and love story. He is convincing in this film, as he would be in *In a Lonely Place,* when trapped and violent. In *Dark Passage,* as in *The Two Mrs. Carrolls,* the hero is accused of murdering his wife. Bogart was drawn to these pictures by his desire to escape from Mayo. The theme of *Dark Passage,* rescue and redemption through the help of a loving and generous woman, also suggests his liberation from Methot and marriage to Bacall.

⟨ II ⟩

THESE PREPOSTEROUS yet predictable films explain why Bogart frequently disparaged the movie business and his own part in it, and why he was so intrigued and excited by the prospect of making *The Treasure of the Sierra Madre* with John Huston. The project marked Huston's reentry into film-making after his adventures in war: he wrote, directed and (for the first time) acted in it. The film united several of Huston's passions: a Mexican setting, shooting on location, violent action during the revolutionary period and a rugged story of male adventurers. Much as Bogart preferred to quit work at six and go back to Benedict Canyon for a whiskey and soda, it seemed he had to suffer prolonged absence from home, bad food and extreme discomfort if he wanted to make a first-rate film.

One of the first American movies to be made outside the United States, it had a budget of $1,831,000 (of which Bogart got his first $200,000) and was filmed between mid-February and late July 1947. Apart from the mining scenes, which were shot in ten days near Kernville, in the Sequoia National Forest of central California, it was made in the mountainous country near San José de Perua, a few hours west of Mexico City. The remote little spa was off the main highway and at the end of a road leading nowhere.

On May 2 the unit manager sent the producer, Henry Blanke, a lively description of the bad grub and homely women at the Mexican watering hole: "This headquarters is as dull a spot you'll find this side of Forest Lawn. It is a mineral spa enlivened only with the creak of arthritic joints. The food, strangely enough, is poor and monotonous, but as no one ever seems to get very hungry the squawks aren't too loud. . . . The morale is as good as you'll find on any location trip where the few girls look like they've been raised on a steady diet of dog food. Bogey looks fine and is growing a fine new crop of hair." Bogart had lost most of his hair during hormone treatments, and threatened to take off his toupee when Walter Huston (playing the grizzled prospector, Howard) took out his false teeth to look more authentic.

The cast and crew spent their days working outdoors in the rough countryside, their nights bowling and drinking. After living in Mexico for several months, Bogart had learned only two Spanish words—Dos Equis, the name of a popular beer. The food provided by the hotel was almost inedible and sometimes made the company sick. Bacall occupied herself by shopping for canned goods and organizing alternative meals for everyone.

Huston idolized his father but mercilessly picked on his pretty new wife, the actress Evelyn Keyes. She joined them for several weeks and had no job to do on location. She felt like an intruder and never established meaningful contact with Bogart. When Huston attacked her Keyes envied Bogart's gentleness and devotion, his appreciation of Bacall's companionship and help. One evening Evelyn aroused Huston's wrath by wearing provocative clothing. She put on (she wrote) a print skirt "with a separate top that was—well, brief. Not much more than a glorified bra. . . . The trouble was when I leaned forward, my breasts bounced into view. John wasn't pleased. 'For God's sake, take that thing off,' he muttered. 'I don't want to see it on you again.'" When she put it on again a few nights later, "all he did was reach out, take hold of the brief top, and rip it in two. 'Put on something, honey,' he said, 'and let's go to dinner.'"[3]

Huston, a rugged athlete, drove the actors (including his father) relentlessly. Bogart agreed that the realistic setting enhanced the atmosphere of the film and said: "It's always better to shoot a hot-weather picture in a hot country. You get a different expression on your face." But he also resented the discomfort and felt that Huston had forced him to suffer unnecessarily: "John wanted everything perfect. I have to admire him for that but it was plenty rough on our troupe. If we could get to a location site without fording a couple of streams and walking through rattlesnake-infested areas in the scorching sun, then it wasn't quite right. . . . We'd stumble over rocks and stones and cactus and sagebrush. We'd dodge snakes and scorpions and things that must have been Gila monsters. The guy was a bundle of energy and I was a bundle of old, tired, left-over atoms." Walter Huston agreed that "acting is not supposed to be done outdoors." An old Mexican cavalryman, John Huston loved the colorful, barbaric country. In a press release written for Warner Bros., he recalled the recruitment of some all-too-eager horsemen: "I said my company would be willing to pay up to 40 pesos a day for trick riders. [The Mexican leader] said, 'For that amount they would let you shoot them in the arms and legs. Not to kill, you understand.' He waved a warning finger at me. 'No killing. We can't have any of that.'"4

While Huston indulged his taste for the more exotic aspects of Mexico, Bogart, whose boat was more important to him than his films, was terribly anxious to complete his work in time to race the *Santana* to Hawaii. He had spent a great deal of money on the boat, made elaborate preparations and sought assurance from the studio that he'd be able to go. On April 25, from the Hotel Reforma in Mexico City, he wrote Steve Trilling:

> I informed you at the beginning of the year I was planning to go into the Honolulu Race that starts on July 4th and asked you to arrange my schedule so that I could make it. The time is now drawing near, and I would like some sort of assurance from you that I will be able to make it. In case you don't understand my problems in regard to preparations for the race, and my anxiety, the following may help.
>
> I have already spent about $5,000 and will have to spend close to another five as soon as I am absolutely certain that I will be able to make it. There are seven men going with me as a crew, most of whom are planning to fly their wives over to see the finish, necessitating plane reservations, arranging leaves of absence from their business, etc. I am not asking you to rearrange schedules or in any way jeopardize the success of this picture, I only ask that the "Brains" get together and give me a pretty good idea as to when you think I will be able to get away.
>
> I would appreciate it very much if you would do this for me. As you are aware, we are progressing quite slowly here, but from what I hear the work has been good, so you must be pleased. . . .
>
> Regards, Bogie

Huston, whose priorities were quite different, had promised Bogart that they'd finish in time but didn't really give a damn about the race. When Bogart protested, Huston insulted and humiliated him. During the filming of this picture, Huston wrote:

> Bogie and I had our one and only quarrel. Bogie was very eager to get his boat, the *Santana*, into a race to Honolulu. The race

was soon to be run, so he was always trying to pin me down to a finish date. I refused to let Bogie's race schedule interfere with my picture, and told him so. Bogie sulked and became progressively less cooperative.

One day I was shooting a dialogue scene between Bogie, Tim Holt and Dad. I thought Dad could be better, so I asked them to do the scene again. Bogie asked, "Why?"

I didn't want to explain why.

"It has nothing to do with you, Bogie."

"Well, I don't see why you want to do it again. I thought it was good."

"Please! Just do it."

Bogie grumblingly did it again, and this time it came out all right. But that evening at the dinner table he started in on me again about the race. Suddenly I'd had as much as I could take. Bogie leaned across the table toward me to make a point, and I reached out and took his nose between my first two fingers and closed them into a fist. There was silence at the table.

Finally, Betty Bogart couldn't stand it. "John," she said, "you're hurting him."

"Yes, I know. I mean to." I gave one more twist, and let go.

Bogie came to me later and said, "John, for heaven's sake, what are we doing? Let things be with us as they have always been."[5]

For all Bogart's pleas, the picture wasn't finished until July 22 and he missed the yacht race.

During the stress and strain of work on location, Huston had to be the boss and pull his team into line. "Bogey the Beefer" lived up to his name, but may have felt he had gone too far with his complaints. In Huston's version of the story, *Bogart* offers to make up the quarrel. Though famous for his loss of interest in his own projects, Huston was deadly serious about this film and determined to make it as perfect as possible. Once in Mexico and out of Jack Warner's control, he took five and a half months and finished production twenty-nine days over schedule.

The Treasure of the Sierra Madre (1948) was based on the novel by B. Traven, a reclusive and mysterious German writer who lived in Mexico. He had corresponded with Huston about the story and was enthusiastic about his choice of Bogart for the central role. Though he wanted no personal publicity and refused to be photographed or interviewed, he could not resist coming to the set in the guise of his personal secretary, and was actually paid as a consultant.

The film opens in Tampico, on the Gulf of Mexico, in August 1924, as the oil companies are closing down. Expatriate laborers like Fred C. Dobbs (Bogart) are thrown out of work and forced to beg for money. Like Hemingway in *For Whom the Bell Tolls* (1940), Huston achieved realism by including Spanish dialogue that is made clear in the context of the film. The scenes in which masses of peasants dressed in black and white take the prisoners out to be executed and the hanging sickle that appears to announce the arrival of the Indians vividly evoke the menacing atmosphere of the country. In the early scenes Dobbs, lifting his belt and grimacing but humbly keeping his eyes down, keeps asking the same prosperous white-suited American for money. After his third request, the American (played by John Huston as if he were discussing the Honolulu race) tells him: "Go occasionally to somebody else. This is beginning to get tiresome." As a good-luck gesture, Ann Sheridan plays a silent part. When Fred C. Dobbs emerges from the barber shop with slicked-down hair, he catches her eye before she disappears into a house with furnished rooms.

With money from a lucky lottery ticket and back wages that the foreman had tried to steal, Dobbs and Curtin (played by Tim Holt) join up with an old prospector named Howard (Walter Huston) to seek gold in the Sierra Madre mountains. After weeks of searching they eventually find it and Howard dances a manic jig. They manage to bring the gold out of the earth while fending off the incursions of another prospector, Mexican bandits and friendly Indians who persuade Howard to cure their sick tribesmen.

Dobbs becomes suspicious and then paranoid about attempts to steal his share. When he accuses Curtin of searching for the gold he's hidden under a rock, Curtin says he's been looking for a Gila monster that has crawled underneath. He dares Dobbs to reach in and get his treasure. When he's too frightened to do so, Curtin levers up the rock with a piece of timber and reveals the monster belly-up on a pile of Dobbs' gold. Though Bogart never actually put his hand under the rock, Huston claimed (as with the tied-up scene in *Across the Pacific*) that he had played a devilish trick on his friend: "I got a camera clamp and I climbed underneath the set, which was made of the material which rocks are composed of in studios, and when Bogart put his hand in I put on the clamp while the cameras were running and he screamed, thought he had a Gila monster on his hand."

After madly shooting Curtin (who manages to recover, like the sick Indian boy who is revived by Howard), Dobbs delivers a fine soliloquy that recalls the guilt-tormented speeches of Shakespearean murderers: "Conscience. Conscience. What a thing. If you believe you've got a conscience, it'll pester you to death. But if you don't believe you've got one, what can it do to you?" A little later, just as he thinks he's reached a safe refuge, he sees the faces of the gold-toothed Mexican bandits, who have pursued him throughout the film, reflected in a pool of water. The leader (who has the same large protruding teeth as their mules) slashes him to death with his machete and strips the clothes off his body. But he ignores the gold-filled packs on Dobbs' burros, which wander off into the wind and wilderness. At the end of the film, Howard—laughing in the same way as he did when he first found the gold—explains: "The bandits thought there were bags of sand hidden in among the hides to make them weigh more. . . . They poured our goods out on the ground. The wind has carried all of it away. . . . It's a great joke played on us by the Lord or fate or by nature. . . . The gold has gone back to where we got it."[6]

Huston's characteristic moral fable, his theme that greed is the root of all evil, goes back to Chaucer's "Pardoner's Tale." In that poem, three rioters set out to find Death, but instead discover a heap of gold. Intending to cheat one another and possess the whole treasure, they slay each other and get nothing. The theme was also portrayed in Frank Norris' novel *McTeague* (1899). Driven once again by greed, the hero flees to Death Valley. In the desert, handcuffed to the man he has killed, he dies of thirst. Erich von Stroheim's film *Greed* (1925), based on Norris' novel, captured the desolation of nature and men.

Traven wrote Huston that the theme of his novel was the elusive and ephemeral nature of material objects: "No matter how hard you work, no matter how ferociously you fight, no matter how intensively you struggle for your existence you can never be sure of your gains or your property unless you have consumed it. Only what is in your tummy and what is in your brain is really yours." This idea is portrayed in the film when Howard, before setting out on his quest, describes the corroding effect of wealth: "You lose your sense of values and your character changes entirely. . . . I know what gold does to men's souls. . . . As long as there's no find, the noble brotherhood will last, but when the piles begin to grow, that's when the trouble starts."

Bogart, disheveled and depraved, suspicious and finally inhuman in this role, gave his most brilliant performance to date. James Agee, one of the best film critics of his time, wrote that "Bogart does a wonderful job with this character . . . miles ahead of the very good work he has done before." He was also wildly enthusiastic about the picture. He called it "one of the most visually alive and beautiful movies I have ever seen" and said the story was rich "in themes, semi-symbols, possible implications, and potentialities as a movie." He concluded by defining its meaning: "This is, after all, about gold and its effects on those who seek it, and so it is also a fable about all human life in this world and about much of the essence of good and evil."

Helped by Agee's influential review, *The Treasure of the Sierra Madre* was nominated by the Academy for best picture. Walter Huston won the Award for best supporting actor and, in an extraordinary triple father-and-son victory, John Huston also got Oscars for best screenplay and best director. Despite the Awards, the film was not, at first, financially successful. The stark location, the lack of women and love interest, the absence of a hero and the dark conclusion all had an adverse effect on its earnings. The commercial failure of this film was a great disappointment to Bogart. For years he had groaned about Warners' mediocre movies. Now, his fine performance in an unusual and well-made picture meant little to his audience. "Look what it did at the box office," he bitterly complained. "An intelligent script, beautifully directed—something different—and the public turned a cold shoulder on it. Critical praise doesn't pay the bills."[7] As he made plans to set up his own company, Bogart began to learn more about the difficulties of financing and the uncertainties of public taste.

‹ III ›

BOGART'S GOOD LITERARY TASTE was a crucial factor in his success as an actor. He formed friendships with many authors and chose to do films that were based on plays and novels by important writers: Robert Sherwood, Sidney Kingsley, Dashiell Hammett, Ernest Hemingway, Raymond Chandler, B. Traven and Maxwell Anderson, who wrote *Saturday's Children* in 1928 as well as *Key Largo* in 1939. Bogart also sought screenplays by Lillian Hellman, William Faulkner, James Agee and especially John Huston, who wrote seven of them, from *The Amazing Dr. Clitterhouse* (1938) to *Beat the Devil* (1954).

Richard Brooks' novel about Bogart and the film executive Mark Hellinger, *The Producer,* reveals his fascination with Bogart as actor and man. Bogart was also interested in Brooks' films. Co-author with Huston of Bogart's next picture, *Key Largo* (1948), Brooks later wrote the script and directed Bogart in *Deadline—U.S.A.* (1952) and *Battle Circus* (1953). Bogart admired his fiery personality and creative intelligence, and the rebellious ex-marine became, like Huston, a close friend.

Bacall explained that Brooks, "a fantastic fellow, full of extreme opinions," had beliefs that strongly appealed to her husband. Sounding like Bogart himself, Brooks swore "he would never own a foreign car, have a swimming pool, wear a tie—no bigger house, no falling into the Hollywood trap." Until his marriage to Bacall, Bogart had refused to acquire the visible signs of wealth beloved by movie stars. Now he called Brooks "the Angry Writer" and, since Brooks also liked to stir things up, cherished his unquenchable wrath. He played fiercely competitive games of chess with Brooks; he would argue with the nervous, troubled, moody and volatile man, work him into a rage and then say: "Look at him now. His eyes are getting big and red!" Brooks did, in fact, remain an outsider and lived in an unfashionable apartment south of Olympic Boulevard.

Brooks stood for uncompromising ideals that Bogart, despite his cynical remarks about "the business," truly valued. For Brooks, Bogart was a superb actor whose problems were typical of a film celebrity: the oppressive demands of the studio, the invasions of the public, press and gossip columnists (whom Bogart loved to tease), the attacks by Right-wing politicians, the difficulty of maintaining a marriage and stable personal life, the struggle with alcohol, the lure of money, the temptations of women and the illusions of being a star.

A great believer in authentic atmosphere, Huston worked with Brooks on the screenplay of *Key Largo*—interrupted by the CFA flight to Washington—in an out-of-season hotel in the Florida Keys. They hired Seminole Indians, Jay Silver Heels and Rodric Redwing, to play the Osceola brothers, who were named after an early nineteenth-century tribal chief. Since shooting *The Treasure of the Sierra Madre* on location had inflated the original budget by $600,000, Jack Warner insisted that *Key Largo,* apart from the opening shot, be filmed indoors at the studio in Burbank. It was made in three months from December 1947 to early March 1948, and certainly captured the mood of tropical menace. Discussing the special effects, John Brosnan wrote that a good deal of the action is "centered around a sea-front setting which includes a jetty extending out into the water, several launches moored nearby, and a large yacht moored in the distance. [But] the 'sea' is a studio tank and the launches vary in size from full-scale to miniature (the 'large' yacht is only a few feet in length) in an attempt to force the perspective and to create the illusion that the horizon is miles away. . . . The later scenes in the same film which supposedly take place on a launch at sea were also filmed in a tank, but in this case the horizon had been camouflaged with a studio-made fog which makes the whole thing much more effective."[8]

Making the film—which is more theatrical than cinematic—was difficult because Huston followed the stage presentation and had nine principal actors on the set. Frank McCloud (Bogart), a former army major, visits and consoles his wartime comrade's old father James Temple (Lionel Barrymore), who is confined to a wheelchair, and his young widow Nora (Lauren Bacall). McCloud tells the Temples that their son and husband had died in the battle of San Pietro, which Huston had actually filmed in his wartime documentary. As in *The Petrified Forest,* the place is taken over by a criminal—the notorious racketeer and counterfeiter Johnny Rocco (Edward G. Robinson)—accompanied by his girl Gaye Dawn (Claire Trevor) and his four henchmen. The plot concerns McCloud's movement from apathy to action as he slowly edges toward violence and then explodes. He confronts the gang, dispatches them on a boat trip to Cuba and returns to Key Largo to claim Nora Temple. The climax, lifted directly from the last chapters of Hemingway's *To Have and Have Not,* had not been used in Howard Hawks' film.

Key Largo triumphantly reunites Bogart, Robinson and Claire Trevor, who had appeared together in *The Amazing Dr. Clitterhouse.* After all their crossfires in the 1930s, when Bogart was the principal victim, it was finally his turn to kill Robinson—and survive. Robinson recalled their long association: "When I was the reigning star Bogie would be slain first, and I'd live another reel before I got it. As the years passed and Bogie became the reigning star and I was demoted to character roles, *I'd* get the bullet first and Bogie would live out another reel." Robinson understood how difficult his own long reign had been for Bogart. Like Davis and Cagney, he remembered Bogart's bitterness and praised his technical skill: "I loved Bogie. I knew his eccentricities and could handle them. He was frustrated he'd had to wait so long for recognition. In his last pictures he was getting so good as an actor—and so good as a man, too." In *Key Largo,* however, Robinson—with his fan, cigar, flashy clothes, guns, hoods, mistress and extreme behavior—steals the film. Bogart, never very effective as a crusading knight, is restrained and passive until the end of the film, while Robinson's powerful, colorful character is intriguingly evil.

"Lucky" Luciano, the real gangster and model for the head of the prostitution ring in *Marked Woman* (1937), had recently been tried and deported to Cuba, and now became the basis for Robinson's character. Robinson had originally been called Muriello (which was considered too close to Luciano) and then Johnny Rocco, after Little Rico (his first major role) in *Little Caesar*. Luciano's alcoholic mistress, Gay Orlova, who had loyally followed him to Cuba, appeared in the film as Gaye Dawn. Huston, who said he wanted to expose "the crustacean with its shell off,"⁹ first showed Rocco in a strikingly original scene—naked, smoking a cigar and sweltering in a bathtub. McCloud caustically characterizes him as "the master of the fix. When he couldn't corrupt, he terrified. When he couldn't terrify, he murdered."

The villainous Robinson—who wears two-toned shoes, a cowboy belt and a hideous tie—forces a kiss on Bacall and whispers suggestively to her (perhaps to get her back in the bathtub with him). He humiliates the drunken Claire Trevor by forcing her to sing for a drink, though her condition has clearly been caused by their bitter relations and the life she has been forced to lead. When her voice cracks in a pathetic performance, he snarls "you're rotten" and refuses to give her the drink. Sympathetic to her plight, Bogart defies Robinson and pours it out for her. Robinson bullies Trevor, but is terrified by the natural force of the hurricane which batters against the hotel and foreshadows the violence that will be turned against the gang. He has no response when Bogart ironically exclaims: "If it doesn't stop, shoot it."

On December 10, 1947, the day shooting began, one of the producers noted the weaknesses in the pace and dialogue: "You forgive Barrymore for his big talk because he is old and a kind of prophet. However, Bogart and Bacall . . . should talk in the idiom of normal, every day people. If Brooks will do this he will remove a rather irritating preachiness in the script." Barrymore, in a quavering voice, continued to ham it up. The wasp-waisted Bacall, who had little to do but look concerned, seemed stiff and ill-at-ease in the role of devoted helpmate. Just as Huston had forced Mary Astor to run breathlessly around the set of *The Maltese Falcon* and twisted Bogart's nose while making *The Treasure of the Sierra Madre,* so in *Key Largo,* to pump some real emotion into Bacall, he twisted her arm and made her wince.

At the end of the shooting Jerry Wald, concerned that Bogart might be overshadowed by Robinson if his character was too bland, wanted "to punch up his scenes in the different sequences throughout the picture." Bogart arrives in Key Largo sweating heavily, as he did in General Sternwood's greenhouse at the beginning of *The Big Sleep*. In a characteristic Huston touch he tells Claire Trevor, who's bet on a horse race, that he's been bred "by John, out of Helen."

In *Key Largo* Bogart says "I like the sea" and expertly ties up the boat (called the *Santana*). Huston wrote that "the action ending in the boat was something which would not only appeal to the star, Humphrey Bogart, who is a boat owner and has made one of his big successes in *To Have and Have Not,* but it would also show him in the kind of action which his fans expect of him." When Robinson forces Bogart to take the gang by boat from Florida to Cuba, Trevor, grateful for his sympathy, secretly slips him a gun. In the high-seas carnage, Bogart kills the gangsters, who have killed the sheriff's deputy. He suddenly swerves the boat so that one hood, leaning over the side to throw up, falls overboard. He shoots the second one and picks off the third as he comes up the passageway. Robinson kills the fourth when he refuses to confront Bogart on deck. Bogart then lashes the wheel and climbs on top of the pilot house. He refuses Robinson's bribe and gets even for all the fatal bullets in the 1930s by killing him as soon as he emerges at dawn from the bowels of the boat.

Huston told *Time* that he had "tried to make all the characters old-fashioned (the gangster's moll is out of the 1920s), to brand them as familiar figures, and to suggest they were ready to take over again." *Key Largo* derives its emotional intensity from its controlling idea: that after the war, Americans had to turn their attention to the grave social problems at home. The movie still has dramatic power because Bogart and Robinson are such effective and enthralling adversaries.

To Bogart, the returning soldier, Robinson, the gangster as Fascist, capitalizes on social apathy and personifies the evils he had fought against in the war. By killing them, he avenges the death of his friend and expresses the same themes of brotherhood and loyalty as in *The Maltese Falcon* and *Dead Reckoning.* As in *To Have and Have Not,* the Bogart character is inspired by Bacall's idealistic statement, "A cause isn't lost as long as one person is willing to go on fighting." He moves from egoistic indifference about the corruption of the world, "I fight nobody's battles but my own," to the fine rhetorical pronouncement: "We're fighting to cleanse the world of ancient evils, ancient ills."

James Agee, alert as always to Huston's achievement, said the film conveys "heat, suspense, enclosedness, the illusion of some eighteen hours of continuous action in two hours' playing time. The lighting is stickily fungoid. The camera is sneakily 'personal'; working close and in almost continuous motion, it enlarges the ambiguous suspensefulness of almost every human move."[10] It was a spectacular year for John Huston. In 1948 Claire Trevor won an Academy Award for best supporting actress in *Key Largo* at the same ceremony where Walter Huston and John Huston got Oscars for *The Treasure of the Sierra Madre.* Bogart gave another solid performance, holding center stage in the movie but reaping no honors himself.

IN THE LATE 1940s, after Bogart had signed his fifteen-year contract with Warners, the studios' iron hold on the production of movies began to weaken. John Huston explained the factors that contributed to the decline and fall of the old system:

> The studios were accused of being monopolistic and, under the anti-trust laws, were forced to sell off their own theaters. There were new tax structures; the advent of television kept many people away from the theaters; the growing power of agents to demand more in salaries and benefits for their actor clients escalated production costs alarmingly. Eventually actors —having been liberated from long-term contracts and the weekly salary—were asking astronomical sums for individual pictures, and were freelancing. Some formed companies and started exercising their own creative ideas.

At the same time, producers realized that making pictures in foreign countries not only provided realistic backgrounds, but also enabled them to reduce both costs and taxes. Leading actors, by forming their own independent film companies, could substantially reduce their taxes by taking a percentage of the profit from a movie, which would be taxed as capital gains, instead of receiving a salary and paying the much higher income tax.

In 1947 Maree and Bogart formed their own company and signed a long-term contract to make one picture a year with the veteran producer Mark Hellinger, "a colorful guy, who wore a [gangster-like] black shirt and white tie as his trademark." Bogart had liked and admired Hellinger, a well-known journalist and syndicated columnist for the New York *Daily Mirror*, since the 1920s. The erratic wise-guy, heavy drinker and congenial man-about-town, married to a former Follies dancer, had written Broadway plays and revues. He hung around with Damon Runyon types— prize-fighters, actors, chorus girls—knew all the big shots and was a pal of Walter Winchell. In 1937 he signed on with Warners as a story consultant, writer and producer. Hellinger wrote the original story of *The Roaring Twenties* and, as an associate producer (under Hal Wallis), had been closely involved with the day-to-day filming of *Brother Orchid, It All Came True, They Drive By Night* and *High Sierra*. Hellinger looked up to Bogart and treated him like a star before he became one.

Hellinger had been a war correspondent in the Pacific during 1943–45, and after the war had produced *The Two Mrs. Carrolls*. He thought of starring Bogart in Hemingway's *The Snows of Kilimanjaro,* and wanted Marlon Brando to play the young criminal in *Knock on Any Door*. To the young Bacall, Hellinger was a generous bon vivant with a flashy yet endearing style: "He was known for his capacity for drink and for getting everyone else drunk—he could drink a bottle of brandy and a bottle of seventeen-year-old bourbon on the same day and it would never show. He drove his big black Cadillac with the license plate MH1. . . . He knew many hoods. . . . Went to the racetrack. Was known for his extravagant tipping. . . . He never let anyone else pick up the check. . . . A sweet, vulnerable man—a good friend, loved by all." Bogart's plans to make movies with him came to an end when Hellinger suddenly died of a heart attack, in December 1947, at the age of forty-four.

In April 1948 Bogart, one of the first actors to create his own company, bought Hellinger's stock and film properties, and formed Santana Pictures with Robert Lord and Morgan Maree. Lord, a writer and producer at Warners since the early 1930s, became president of Santana. Three years younger than Bogart and educated at Chicago and Harvard, the quiet, scholarly Lord had worked for *The New Yorker,* won an Academy Award for the original story of *One Way Passage* (1932), written the screenplay for *Black Legion* (1937) and produced the first four Santana pictures. Jess Morgan described Lord as a short, frenetic kind of guy, as a typically insecure producer who was afraid he would fall from Bogart's favor. Lord always said hello to the office boys and remarked: "You never know when they'll be running the studio." Sam Jaffe, resentful that he hadn't been consulted when Lord replaced Hellinger, felt that Bogart had "selected a man who was far gone at Warner Bros., and they made a couple of bad pictures and the contract was over. But [Bogart] didn't seek advice. He hired the wrong people, he hired the wrong man, and this [forty-six-year-old] man was over the hill."[11]

Santana made five films in six years and released them through Columbia (not Warners), which provided the studio facilities for production of the pictures in return for a standard overhead charge of twenty-five percent of the cost. George Antheil, the American avant-garde composer, wrote the music for the first four pictures. The first two Santana films, *Knock on Any Door* and *Tokyo Joe* (both 1949), marked a descent from the heights Bogart had attained in the 1940s. The former, directed by Nicholas Ray, was based on a 1947 novel by the black writer Willard Motley. He had worked in the Federal Writers' Project in Chicago, became a victim of the Communist witch hunts, emigrated to Mexico and lived there until his death. The novel portrayed the disastrous effect of the penal system on young offenders, had sold 350,000 copies in its first three years and was a hot property.

The opening shootout (in which a criminal kills a cop), the Dead End Kids–type gang ("only suckers work"), the wisecracking dialogue (with the famous line: "Live fast, die young, and leave a good-looking corpse"), the seedy atmosphere of the lower-class world, the crusading lawyer (played by Bogart) who comes from the same slum as the gangster, the flat trial scenes and dull courtroom summation, the confession of murder and sentence to death, and especially the idea that society is largely responsible for breeding criminals ("Knock on any door and you may find Nick Romano") all seem like a familiar replay of Bogart's socially-conscious gangster pictures of the 1930s. Even the convict's love for the potentially redemptive woman recalls Bogart's ill-fated love for Lupino in *High Sierra*. The only difference, which is not developed, is that Nick shows signs of being a genuine psychopath. In the best scene of the otherwise predictable movie, Nick's wife tells him they're going to have a baby. Instead of responding with conventional tenderness and joy, he coldly tells her to get rid of it. After he loses his job and rejects the baby, his wife kills herself. Her suicide prompts Nick's breakdown and confession in court. It's difficult to understand why Bogart chose the inept John Derek to play Nick Romano or why he approved the weak script, which the "Technical Advisers" from the National Probation and Parole Association couldn't bring to life.

Bogart plays an ex–fighter pilot with bow tie and trench coat in *Tokyo Joe,* which imitates elements of *Casablanca* and *Across the Pacific.* After the war he returns to his nightclub (now in Tokyo), to a song associated with lost love and to a wife he had left in 1941. He finds she's being blackmailed, after making wartime broadcasts in order to protect their child, and foils a Communist plot to fly war criminals back to Japan. Bogart, improbable as a father on screen and in life, saves his child from the villains. After being wounded by the enemy, he returns to his wife and assures her: "I'll be fine for you this time."

The authentic Japanese footage, used as a backdrop, makes the studio setting seem even more fake. As in *Across the Pacific,* the Japanese (led by Sessue Hayakawa, who later played the cruel commandant in *The Bridge on the River Kwai*) are in this postwar film still treacherous, cruel and evil. They threaten his wife, kidnap his child and do awful things to Bogart. When their plot goes wrong, they commit hara-kiri. The Americans say: "I don't know, these goofy Orientals get me. . . . All these Japs look alike for my dough," and Bogart makes a propagandistic speech (worthy of Douglas MacArthur) about American achievements in Japan. Bogart backed the shallow adventure movie, but his heart wasn't in it. His heroic rescue is flat and predictable, and he seems to have walked through the part like a public figure playing a theatrical version of himself.

‹ V ›

BOGART WAS A MAN of fixed habits, and spent a great deal of time drinking in his favorite bars and nightclubs. Though he liked to provoke others to rowdy behavior, in public he rarely drew attention to himself. One notorious incident took place in New York on September 25, 1949 when he was drinking with a friend at the El Morocco nightclub at 4 A.M. Sitting between them were two giant toy pandas that Bogart had bought for his son Steve and named Jack and Harry after the Warner brothers.

Suddenly Robin Roberts—"a dark-haired and lush model, kittenish under the influence of 'quite a few drinks'"—approached his table and, "challenged" by the situation, tried to take away one of the toys. As she grabbed it (it's not clear whether she chose Jack or Harry), Bogart shouted: "Get away from me, I'm a happily married man, and don't touch my panda." He pushed her away and she fell on the floor. She later claimed that he had used excessive force and bruised her, and that she felt "hurt and humiliated." She charged him with assault and sued him for $25,000.

Though Bogart was mortified when he realized what he had done, he decided to fight the model in court. He jokingly told reporters that the panda belonged to his son and that the model had no right to grab it. "This is a free country, isn't it?" he said. "I can take my panda any place I want to. And if I wanna buy it a drink, that's my business." He preferred the company of pandas to actresses, who were always babbling about their latest movie. When asked if he'd been drinking, he axiomatically replied that everyone was drunk at 4 A.M. Bogart's lawyer (and Bacall's uncle) Charles Weinstein argued that Roberts' intrusion was a cheap publicity stunt, an attempt at polite blackmail by a "Hollywood-stricken female." Bogart, he held, was merely using sufficient force to protect his rightful property. The court accepted Weinstein's argument and dismissed the complaint for "lack of sufficient grounds."

Though Bogart's fans booed her as she left the Magistrates Court, the panda incident gave Roberts the greatest publicity break in her career. Bogart candidly summed it up by saying: "Partly I was loaded and partly it was a frame. A little tart wanted to get some money." El Morocco banned him for life, which meant in practice that he couldn't enter the premises until his next visit to New York. Bacall, annoyed by all the fuss, sardonically commented: "It's about time you got a little dignity. You know, you're pushing fifty." Warner Bros. (despite the wonderful plug for Jack and Harry) were distressed by the discreditable news stories about Bogart's "habits, opinions and conduct in public life." Invoking the dreaded morals clause, their lawyer wrote: "We desire to remind you that such news articles are extremely damaging to this company."[12] But the episode, which kept his name in all the papers, was not at all damaging to Bogart. It actually enhanced his image as a witty, wisecracking, hard-drinking bon vivant who got tough with predatory dames. He stood up for his rights and won his case.

Chain Lightning (1950), Bogart's next film for Warners, was made between April and July 1949. Originally titled *Jet* (chain lightning moves quickly in jet-like zigzags) and based on the test-pilot careers of Howard Hughes and Chuck Yaeger (who later became an astronaut), it is an up-to-date version of Bogart's first aeronautical movie, *China Clipper* (1936). The Warner files are filled with memos about cooperation from the air force, stock film of flights and technical information from the research department. In the movie, the pilots flip a lot of switches and cockpit chatter ("We've got to test the effect of atmospheric pressure on the discharge valve") replaces meaningful dialogue. Bogart, who looks like a giant frog in his new jet gear, mocks his own role by frantically shouting: "Get me out of this Buck Rogers monkey suit!"

In this conventional picture Bogart is a World War II ace ("The hard way, for Matt, is the only way") working for an ambitious plane manufacturer (Raymond Massey). He flies an unsafe jet over the pole from Alaska to Washington, D.C. to win a $30,000 bonus for himself and get an air force contract for the firm. But the development of a safe model, which the designer dies for, delays the sale of a new plane, which the ruthless tycoon demands. After landing the plane while out of fuel, Bogart tests the safety ejection for the sake of the dead designer. He also wins the devoted Eleanor Parker ("I did it for us"), whom he had courted in England during the war. As in *Casablanca, To Have and Have Not* and *Key Largo,* Bogart moves from cynical statements to brave acts. Otis Guernsey, Jr., writing in the *New York Herald-Tribune,* noted the faults of the picture, which even Bogart's professional performance couldn't save: "This is one of those films which cuts from the air to the anxious features of the heroine on the ground in a sort of maddening schizophrenia of love and aerobatics." Eleanor Parker's "performance is thoroughly consistent: not one bit of it is convincing. . . . Bogart plays through it all with a steady, skeptical aplomb of an experienced actor who has seen everything twice, and he is responsible for most of the meager conviction carried in this story."

‹ VI ›

BOGART WANTED Bacall to co-star with him in *In a Lonely Place* (1950), his first important film for Santana, but Warners wouldn't loan her out because he had refused to make and release his movies with their studio. The screenwriter Andrew Solt recalled the origin of the film, which was based on a mystery novel, set in Hollywood, by Dorothy Hughes: "I was asked to the Bogart house [in Benedict Canyon] to read the script to him. . . . When I finished reading there was a long silence. . . . Bogie took a long drag on his cigarette, holding it in the famous Bogart fashion. . . . Then he said 'It's okay. We'll make it as it is.'" But the biographer of Nicholas Ray, who directed the film, said that "of the 140 pages only four made it to shooting *without* revisions."

In this picture Bogart plays the screenwriter Dixon Steele, a character strikingly similar to himself. He twice orders Bogart's favorite ham and eggs. He reveals his ignorance of household matters by obstinately trying to straighten out a grapefruit knife and then hacks away at the fruit. His favorite restaurant is based on Mike Romanoff's, his agent Mel Lippman (Art Smith) on Sam Jaffe. Bogart asked Solt to write a part for Robert Warwick, who had appeared with him in the play *Drifting* (1922) and in the film *A Holy Terror* (1931). Warwick had helped him at the beginning of his career and had now fallen on hard times. He plays Charlie Waterman, a broken-down alcoholic actor who recites Shakespeare's sonnets in a deep theatrical voice as he puts the weary Steele to bed. An arrogant producer's brutal insult of the unfortunate Waterman recalls Bogart's humiliation and bitterness after his early failures in Hollywood; the loyalty and affection expressed in his scenes with Warwick reveal the finest side of Bogart's character.

Like Bogart, the hard-drinking Steele is embittered, caustic and aggressive, but also witty, honorable and loyal to friends. When he falls in love with Laurel Grey (Gloria Grahame) he regains his ability to write and becomes considerate, even tender. His violence (more astonishing, somehow, in a writer) and his inability to work recall the most difficult periods of Bogart's marriage to Methot; his belief that happiness is precarious suggests his fears about his marriage to Bacall. Louise Brooks wrote that this film "gave him a role that he could play with complexity, because the film character's pride in his art, his selfishness, drunkenness, lack of energy stabbed with lightning strokes of violence were shared by the real Bogart."

The characters in the film also reflect the broken marriage of Nicholas Ray and Gloria Grahame, who later married Ray's son by another woman. In order to maintain appearances after their separation, Ray, also a heavy drinker, slept in a dressing room on the set while making the movie, but the strain was apparent throughout the filming.

In the picture Steele hides his pathological streak of violence—the result of his traumatic experience in war—beneath a cool exterior. But his past behavior (brawling on the set, breaking his girlfriend's nose) and chance encounter with a hatcheck girl make him the prime suspect in a murder case. He had invited her home to tell him the plot of a trashy novel that he cannot bear to read but must somehow turn into a film script. His neighbor Laurel Grey tells the police that she saw the girl leave his apartment (when he introduces her to Mel Lippman he says: "My agent. My alibi") and he's released by the cops (the scenes at police headquarters were filmed at the Beverly Hills town hall). Dix and Laurel have some witty exchanges when he leans forward to embrace her and she seductively remarks of his face: "I said I liked it. I didn't say I wanted to kiss it." Overwhelmed by the strain of the investigation as well as by the pressure of work, he reverts to his old paranoid behavior and "has to explode sometimes." He crashes into a young man's car and beats him unconscious, then almost strangles Laurel as she tries to leave him.

More tender and feminine than Bacall's heroines, Laurel tries desperately to commit herself to the psychopathic Steele. Cook, typist, nurse-maid and lover, she stabilizes him, but is terrified of his aggressive rage. She both mothers him and shrinks away in fear. Realizing that his violence is closely connected to his deepest emotions, she confesses: "I love you but I'm afraid of you. . . . I can't live with a maniac." Though Steele is also in love with Laurel, he cannot express deep affection and his hate is much stronger than his love.

The screenplay often differs from the novel, but departs most strikingly at the end. In the book, Steele turns out to be a serial killer of women. In the film, the real murderer is caught and Steele exonerated. Though he's cleared of the crime, their love is destroyed by his mania and her fear. As he walks out of her life, through the courtyard where they first saw each other, she varies the lines he had spoken earlier and says: "I lived for a few weeks while you loved me. Goodbye, Dix." When he leaves her and returns to his lonely place in the world, we know he'll continue to slide into failure (exemplified by the has-been actor) and uncontrollable violence.

Bogart—wearing his now characteristic polo shirt and sports jacket—lowers his chin, raises his eyes and says "aha!" when rejecting the advances of his old girlfriend, and gives the same "aha!" to the hatcheck girl after convincing her that he only wants her to tell him the story. He looks bored and irritated when she relates the banal plot, and makes an impatient, open-palmed pushing motion while walking behind her and urging her out the door.

He shifts uneasily about as the police chief questions him, and smiles at his own wisecracks; he defiantly puts his foot on a chair as Laurel enters the office and smiles again when she boldly tells the cops: "I like his face." He's pleased by Lippman's anxiety, puts his hands on his agent's shoulders when denying the murder charge, and tenderly holds his face after losing his temper and slapping him. He grits his teeth while urging his policeman friend to act out the crime and squeeze his wife's neck harder, then withdraws a bit by shaking the wife's hand but not the friend's as he leaves their house.

Bogart's at his best when suddenly switching from gentleness to rage with Laurel. He seductively exclaims, "Ooohhh, come in," when she first appears at his door, clasps his hands nervously in her apartment, kisses her with unusual tenderness and wrestles playfully with her after completing a surge of work on the script. As they listen to a nightclub singer, he whispers something sexy in her ear. But when a cop who's been trailing him appears, he fiercely stubs out his cigarette and rushes away. Mocking a foolish response to his script, he places his hands on his chest and says in a stagey voice: "Haven't I read this somewhere before?" But when he discovers that Laurel's seen the police without telling him, he drives off like a madman; and when he learns that his agent and closest friend has taken his script without his permission, he lashes out viciously and knocks off his glasses.

Bogart is frightening in his portrayal of manic rage. Ray, who mentioned that Bogart valued spontaneity and would "go dry" after six takes, expressed admiration for his ability to merge his own character with the part he was playing: "He was much more than an actor: he was the very image of our condition. His face was a living reproach. . . . The quality of being and of acting at the same time was perhaps as true of Bogart as of anybody I've seen on film. He was always very well prepared—he knew what the scene was to be, he knew his action, and the details came naturally to him—but he wouldn't learn his lines until the last moment . . . [and] had a truly photographic memory."[13]

Thinking of his personal relations with Grahame, Ray also observed that in an earlier version of the script Dixon killed Laurel at the end: "it was all tied up into a very neat package. . . . And I thought, Shit! I can't do it, I just can't do it. Romances don't have to end that way. Marriages don't have to end that way, they don't have to end in violence for Christ's sake, you know. And let the audience find out and make up its own mind about what's going to happen to Bogie when he goes outside the apartment area. . . . In *In a Lonely Place,* at the ending of the film, you do not know whether the man is going to go out, get drunk, have an accident in his car or whether he is going to go to a psychiatrist for help. And that's the way it should be." The vulnerability of the hypersensitive hero, one critic has noted, "the paranoia, distrust and treachery that colour its portrait of Hollywood are surely linked to the mood prevailing in the United States during the anti-Red witch hunts."

In 1957 Bogart gave a typically frank appraisal of the first Santana films. He remarked that "*Knock on Any Door* was good, could have been better, and set us on our feet because it made money. We made it for $900,000 plus 25 percent overhead, but I couldn't afford that now. *Tokyo Joe* made money too. *Sirocco* was one we had to do. It stank, of course." Nathaniel Benchley, echoing Sam Jaffe's judgment of Santana's "bad pictures," offered the commonly accepted opinion that "it was faintly embarrassing, having split from Warners because he was tired of their trash, to be unable to come up with a truly distinguished picture." But Bogart did not leave Warners until 1953, after he had made four films for Santana. After the war had interrupted many careers and the Communist witch hunts had driven many writers out of Hollywood, good properties were especially hard to find. Billy Wilder observed more perceptively that no one can make five out of five good pictures, that two good ones out of five —*In a Lonely Place* and *Beat the Devil*—is an impressive achievement. Bogart made good money as well as good films with Santana, and in 1955 sold his interest in the company to Columbia for more than a million dollars. He hung the framed check on the wall of the den and proudly told a friend to "count those zeroes."[14]

✦ 12 ✦

Africa and
the Academy Award
1951-1953

⟨ I ⟩

NEITHER *The Enforcer,* Bogart's last film for Warners, nor *Sirocco,* his fourth for Santana, offered him much of a challenge. The first is a well-constructed gangster thriller, the second a poor man's *Casablanca,* and both show Bogart predictably being Bogart. Though he was amply paid, he publicly criticized both films.

The Enforcer (1951) was shot in only five weeks, in late July and August 1950, with a budget of more than a million dollars. The story was inspired by the recent investigations of Senator Estes Kefauver's crime committee and by the discovery of a killing service called Murder Inc. This organization took out "contracts" on "hits," and planned to escape capture by disguising the motive for the crime and eliminating the connection between killer and victim. The movie had a strong cast of male actors, unusual criminal characters and interesting twists of plot. The blubbery Zero Mostel gives a good performance as a frightened small-time crook. In his later pictures, Bogart went out of his way to work with actors and directors—like Art Smith, Zero Mostel, Lee J. Cobb, Fredric March and Edward Dmytryk—who had been persecuted by the House Un-American Activities Committee.

As in *Marked Woman* and *Knock on Any Door,* Bogart plays a crusading attorney, here named Martin Ferguson. *The Enforcer* refers both to Mendoza, the gang boss who enforces the murder contracts, and to the District Attorney who enforces the law, and the picture provides a classically satisfying struggle between good and evil. Ferguson must secure a witness who will testify against the head of the mob. But one of the mob warns

244

"I got a big turnover in friends" and kills every witness Ferguson finds. The fast-moving, shadowy, nocturnal film opens powerfully in a dark, wet courtyard as Rico (Ted DeCorsia), a captured criminal bargaining for clemency, has agreed to testify against the boss and is delivered to Ferguson under heavy guard. The police are dressed in black, Rico wears a white shirt; and they carelessly leave his room lit with the blinds up so the mob can take a shot at him. Rico then loses his nerve and exhibits a kind of grease under pressure. Convinced that he will also be murdered, he bashes a cop's head on a sink, tries to escape and falls off the ledge of a high building.

The taut double plot unfolds in a series of grim flashbacks that portray episodes in the murder case that Ferguson has to solve. In one scene Mendoza (Everett Sloane) hires Rico as a professional killer, telling him "I could use a man like you." Rico in turn recruits Big Babe Lazich (Mostel) and orders the nervous fat man to "burn that tent you're wearing and get yourself a suit." We also see startling images of the gang's ruthlessness and cruelty: a man thrashes madly about till he's tied up; a hand sharpens a razor and slits the throat of a potential informer. As Bogart observes: "Any outfit that has its own undertaker is operating on a pretty big scale."

The police are always one step behind the mob but Bogart, laconic and able as always, threatens a reluctant captive who's terrorized by both the gang and the law. Glancing at a nearby corpse, he casually says: "I think there's room for you in that basket." As the strands of the investigation come together, he realizes that the gang has killed the wrong woman. In an exciting climax he rescues the dead girl's roommate as the criminals close in for the kill. She is the only surviving witness of a crucial murder and will help Ferguson convict Mendoza.

The film is authentic and Bogart's performance unusually low keyed and restrained, but his gestures seem too pat and familiar. He stretches to suggest how long he's been waiting for Rico. When Rico arrives, he grabs his shirt and shakes him. When Rico falls off the ledge, he first looks down, then turns away sharply to avoid seeing the crash. He purses his lips, puts his fingers on his temple and broods about what to do when his key witness dies. During other tense moments he thoughtfully draws his thumb across his lower lip, impatiently slaps a sheaf of papers, rubs his brow as he hears the useless confession of the dead man, and bites his lower lip. When he realizes how to solve the crime he snaps his fingers excitedly, and pounds a microphone in his palm as he waits for a call.

Bogart had now reached the end of the line with Warners, and was no longer willing to be the obedient star who praises the studio, the film and himself. On October 16, 1950, the head of the East Coast office sent Jack Warner a frantic telegram complaining that Bogart had been heard in "21," "announcing in a loud voice to everyone within earshot what a lousy picture *The Enforcer* is. Ridiculous to try to arrange press interviews. He is only looking for trouble." But Warners' *Enforcer* was much better than Bogart's *Sirocco,* and his behavior was inspired more by his sour relations with the studio than by the supposed faults of the offbeat and often quite riveting film.

Bogart suggested some of the weaknesses of *Sirocco*—the conventional hero, stale dialogue and weak ending—as well as his boredom with the uninspiring project when he told Lillian Ross: "The role is a cinch. The role doesn't bother me. I've been doing the role for years. I've worn that trench coat of mine in half the pictures I've been in. What I don't like is business worries. . . . Santana has had eleven writers on *Sirocco* and none of them goons has come across with an ending yet."[1] The film takes place in Damascus in 1925 as Syrian revolutionaries try to overthrow the French Protectorate. The Levantine setting—tarbooshes and hookahs, bead curtains and belly dancers—is completely fake. The male actors are good (Mostel and Sloane reappear as a scheming Armenian and a French general), but all the French and Arab characters have strong American accents.

Bogart, who doesn't look very tough in a bow tie, operates a gambling casino and runs guns to the Arabs for money. After the sneaky natives blow up a restaurant and kill civilians, the French colonel (Lee J. Cobb) tells him: "You have no morals, no political convictions." Bogart gets involved in a love triangle with Cobb and his mistress (Marta Toren), who wants to leave Cobb and run away to Cairo with Bogart. Looking at his battered face, she thrills him by exclaiming: "What a man! You're so ugly. Yes, you are. How can a man so ugly be so handsome?" In the end Bogart, betrayed by the Arabs and arrested by the French, secures his release by arranging a meeting between the emir and the colonel to discuss a truce. After accepting French money to ransom the colonel, the emir tells him: "You're a dreamer and a fool." The screenwriter goons, giving up the struggle to make sense of this trite material, decided to end it all with a bang. Bogart, without even kissing Marta Toren, is killed by an Arab grenade.

‹ II ›

BOGART WAS TERRIBLY BORED with conventional movies, despite the high salary and profits. After several perfunctory performances he began to extend his range, sometimes returning to the lighthearted roles he had played in his youth on Broadway. Once again an ambitious project, written and directed by Huston, shot on location in acute discomfort, rescued him from predictable parts. *The African Queen* (1951) gave him a chance to display his wit and humanity, his fine grasp of character and comic timing.

Columbia and Warners had previously planned to make C. S. Forester's *The African Queen*—first with Charles Laughton and Elsa Lanchester, then with David Niven and Bette Davis, and finally with Paul Henreid and Ida Lupino. But none of these projects worked out. Warners would have shot the movie in a tank on the back lot in Burbank, with no real Africans in sight. But the flamboyant, luxury-loving Austrian-born producer Sam Spiegel, who always operated on the verge of bankruptcy, bought the rights from Warners. The director Joseph Losey described him as "a highly educated man and a very bright and not insensitive man. He is a megalomaniac and I think impossible for most directors to work with because he wants his films to be 'Spiegel' pictures."

Though he seemed like a caricature of a movie entrepreneur, Spiegel was adventurous and ambitious, able to tolerate extreme financial pressure and willing to give in to Huston's quixotic and very expensive decision to make the film in a remote and dangerous place. Spiegel arranged the precarious financing with the Woolf brothers' Romulus Films in England. The original budget was about £400,000. Bogart got $160,000 in deferred payments and 30 percent of the film's profits. The co-star Katharine Hepburn got $65,000 in cash, the same amount in deferred payments and 10 percent of the profits. The director Huston got $87,000 and half the profits. Spiegel and the Woolfs took financial risks and, using fine actors and director as their insurance, produced a masterpiece.

Bogart's mother had sparked his interest with tales about her art studies in Paris, which he had hoped to see during his naval service in World War I. But he was not very interested in foreign travel. Before he met Huston, he rarely went beyond the 120 miles between Beverly Hills and Palm Springs. But once under Huston's spell, he agreed to fly 12,000 miles into the Belgian Congo in central Africa. Bogart believed that his first two marriages had broken up because of separations from wives who pursued their own careers. He therefore insisted that Bacall travel with him to Africa, and they remained abroad for four and a half months.

When the couple left Los Angeles for New York and Europe in March 1951, the nursemaid Alyce Hartley brought the two-year-old Steve to the airport to see his parents depart. As soon as their plane took off, she had a cerebral hemorrhage and died instantly, still holding the child in her arms. Bacall's mother rescued Steve and took care of him. The Bogarts maintained their schedule, continued their journey and sailed to France on the *Liberté* on March 12. Bogart had lived for many years in the rather circumscribed world of the studio and Hollywood, where ordinary people allowed the stars to maintain their privacy. On the streets of Paris he was pleased to discover he was famous. Strangers would enthusiastically call out "Umfree Beaugare" and, making machine gun noises, pretend to shoot him down. Bogart and Bacall, like other wealthy American tourists, enjoyed the night life in Paris, London, Venice and Rome in that joyous time when Europe was recovering from the war and beginning to live again.

In early April 1951, just before leaving for Léopoldville, the Bogarts, with the aid of an American monsignor, had an audience with an even greater celebrity—the seventy-five-year-old Pope Pius XII. They were led through the Vatican Museum and the Sistine Chapel and into the gold-ceilinged throne room. Then, with ten others, they passed through five increasingly smaller rooms and formed a semi-circle. The Pope entered silently, dressed in white and wearing red velvet slippers. They knelt to kiss his ring; he blessed them and gave them a medal.

For once, Bogart seemed intimidated by the spectacle. He made no sarcastic remarks, no Jack Warner jokes about catching his act at the Palace, and was more pious than Pius. Assuming an uncharacteristically reverential tone, he told Louella Parsons: "I stood there deeply impressed, not only with his genuine spiritual radiance, but with everything about him—his appearance, his voice, his ability with languages."[2] When the Pope asked where he came from, Bogart, thinking Hollywood would sound rather tawdry, chose a more reputable residence and said: "San Francisco." Bogart professed the proper attitude in public, but in private his humble piety soon wore off. He later joked that the Pope, who had stared intently at Bacall and held her hand for a long time, might request an even more intimate audience with her.

Bogart had met Katharine Hepburn in London. Their relationship, so central to the film, developed into a close friendship during the difficult months in Africa and endured until his death. Brilliantly cast as the plain and pious Rose Sayer, she was (like Bogart) the child of a surgeon and a suffragette. As a girl she had visited her aunt at Lake Canandaigua, but had never met little Humphrey. She came from a family with a high number of suicides and had herself suffered a nervous breakdown. Married for a time, she had had affairs with the poet Phelps Putnam, the director John Ford, the producer Leland Hayward and the tycoon Howard Hughes as well as a long-term relationship with the married Spencer Tracy. Her mother had died just before she left for Africa, and she was unusually prickly and irritable when she reached Europe. Hepburn lived intimately with Bogart and Bacall for two months and observed them closely. She recalled their powerful physical bond and their enjoyment of quarrels that were followed by a delightful reconciliation: "She and Bogie seemed to have the most enormous opinion of each other's charms, and when they fought it was with the utter confidence of two cats locked deliciously in the same cage."

Though there were many African servants, Bacall made herself useful as laundress, chef and nurse. Bogart liked to see her play a domestic role, and would have been quite content if she had given up her career and stayed at home. She ironically said that when she "traipsed along to Africa . . . washed his clothes, cooked for the cast and crew, this suited Bogey down to the last tsetse fly. He was prouder of me then, this I know, than he ever is when he sees me on the screen. I was in a woman's place, wasn't I?" Bogart — recalling Mayo's angry query: "who's going to wash his socks?" — remarked of his wife: "I don't know what we'd have done without her. She Luxed my undies in darkest Africa." In the *Sunday News* of December 2, 1951, next to a photo of him sleeping in a hammock while Bacall hangs out the wash, Bogart wrote: "You think Baby would do this for me at home? Not on your life. I take her half way round the world, and suddenly she becomes the perfect housewife. In Hollywood she once washed a handkerchief — no kiddin'."[3]

Huston, the co-author as well as director, believed (as he had in Mexico) that the film would have more character and the actors would give better performances if they actually suffered hardships on location. He had scouted sites by plane in Kenya, Tanganyika and Northern Rhodesia and rejected Lake Victoria, which "looked like suburban Maidenhead" and was too pretty for a jungle setting. He finally chose Uganda and the Belgian Congo, where banking, communications and logistics were much more difficult to arrange than in British territory. But he liked the challenge of a primitive setting and wanted to be as far as possible from Spiegel's control. Huston, Hepburn, Bogart and Bacall, with a production staff of thirty-four British technicians, spent ten weeks (early April to mid-June) in Biondo, on the Ruiki tributary of the Congo, as well as in Butiaba on Lake Albert and in Murchison Falls, both in western Uganda.

The African Queen was mainly shot just beyond Stanley Falls, where Conrad had entered the heart of darkness in 1890, and Bogart's broken-down boat in the film looks rather like Conrad's "battered, twisted, ruined, tin-pot steamboat," the *Roi des Belges.*

Peter Viertel, who helped Huston write the final scenes, met the actors at Stanleyville airport. He broke the news that Huston, instead of politely waiting to welcome them, had left only an hour before to hunt elephant near the makeshift village that had been constructed for the cast and crew. Hepburn—extremely anxious about the unfinished script, the lack of funds and the slapdash preparations—thought "it was an utterly piggish thing to do and it makes me mad to think of it even now—goddamn—goddamn." While they were hanging around Stanleyville, a fire broke out on the motorboat they had hired to cross the river and the captain was seriously burned. Bogart, as cool and courageous as in his movies, promptly put out the fire with blanket and sand. A few days later, they crossed the Congo, took an eight-hour ride on a wood-burning train to the nearest town and traveled the final forty miles by car to Biondo.

Huston wanted a close jungle and narrow river for filming. The Ruiki, a thin winding waterway with trees and thick vines forming a canopy between stream and sky, was perfect. This was Bogart's first color film, and the exotic scenery looked spectacular. Biondo "was a romantic-looking place," Huston wrote, "huts all thatched with palms, little paths lined with bamboo and a dining room big enough to hold seventy-five people. We even had shower baths. . . . Most of the shooting was done on a raft made of planks laid across pirogues. . . . All in all, for a film where everything we needed had to be flown in or shipped in laboriously overland, things went quite smoothly. We lacked luxuries, but we had basic comforts."[4] Huston could not see the rushes in Africa. He sent the film to Nairobi and had it flown to London, and the Woolfs cabled back their favorable reaction.

Bogart, older and less adventurous than the others, was not enthusiastic about Africa. He would just as soon have stayed home and made the picture in the comfort of the studio. Unlike Hepburn, he never went hunting with Huston and preferred to remain in the isolated camp—reading, talking and drinking. "Bogey the Beefer," who called himself "a natural-born griper," disliked the unpleasant and sometimes dangerous conditions: the bad roads, intense heat, withering humidity, green mildew, foul water, malaria and dysentery, tsetse flies, stubborn mosquitoes and voracious red ants, poisonous snakes and wild boar, crocodiles and hippos swarming next to the boat. Huston tried to exaggerate the horrors, claiming that when game got scarce the hunters had secretly turned them into cannibals by supplementing their diet with human flesh.

Bogart stuck to canned pork and beans and asparagus during this time of "semi-starvation," which he found "rougher than a stucco bathtub." They played darts in the evening, went to sleep by ten and got up at five. Bacall made sure that everyone took their anti-malaria pills. But when they moved to a houseboat on the Nile in Uganda, the water filters didn't work. Hepburn had a severe bout of dysentery and often vomited between takes, the cameraman Jack Cardiff and many others succumbed to malaria, and nine crew members were sent back sick to England. Neither Bogart nor Huston got sick. Hepburn's theory was that they "had so lined their insides with alcohol that no bug could live in the atmosphere." Bogart's final judgment of the African journey was: "pretty awful, but I wouldn't have missed it."[5]

While Bogart was complaining about the food, the heat and the bugs, Hepburn got on his nerves by finding the whole experience quite glorious. He teased her mercilessly and once, while she was sleeping, placed a freshly-caught fish on her back. With characteristic frankness, he mocked her affectation, quirkiness, vanity, egoism and didactic monologues, and compared her to the lady politician she had played in a 1942 movie:

> She used to say that everything was "divine." The goddam stinking natives were divine. "Oh, what a *divine* native," she'd say. "Oh, what a *divine* pile of manure!" You had to ask yourself, "Is this really the dame or is this something left over from *Woman of the Year?*"
>
> She does pretty much as she goddam pleases. . . . She came in lugging a full-length mirror and a flock of toothbrushes. She brushed her teeth all the time and she habitually takes about four or five baths a day. She talks at you as though you were a microphone. I guess she was nervous, though, and scared of John and me. . . .
>
> To keep her happy, we rigged up a sort of Chic Sale dressing shack, floated it on oil drums, and towed it upstream to location every morning and back again every night. It was a clumsy, yawing barge which took a good two hours to drag each way. But Katie waited on the bank for her dressing room before she'd start work.

He also told the *Hollywood Reporter* that the Bryn Mawr graduate talked a blue streak and was terribly pleased with herself, but could also be sympathetic and kind hearted: "She won't let anybody get a word in sideways. She keeps emphasizing what a superior person she is. At first, I felt as though I was expected to kiss the hem of her skirt, or to lie down on my face in the dirt before her. One day, early in the morning, Huston and I were a little red-eyed from a hard night over a huge bottle. We asked Kate if she had anything that would open our eyes. She was marvelously sweet and naive. She fixed us coffee." Bogart was annoyed when Hepburn, a teetotaler who had struggled for years with Spencer Tracy's heavy drinking, ranted for hours about temperance and the evils of alcohol. He told her off for "always trying to cure the world's ills." He also was puzzled by her sharp, ambiguous retorts—to which Huston responded with a comradely phrase from Conrad's *Lord Jim*: "'You boys believe you're being awfully wicked, don't you?' she snorted. 'Well—you don't know what the word "wicked" means!' The two men looked confused. 'Now, what the hell is she driving at with *that* crack?' Bogie asked. Huston shrugged. 'I dunno —but I *think* she's one of us!'"[6]

Peter Viertel's fine Hemingwayesque novel *White Hunter, Black Heart* (made into a film with Clint Eastwood) describes the making of *The African Queen* and portrays the main characters in the Africa expedition. It focuses on John Wilson (Huston), famous for his skill at directing but notorious for his renegade overspending. More interested in hunting elephants than in finishing the picture, he is willing to stay in Africa indefinitely. Bogart's boat race wasn't important to Huston during the filming of *The Treasure of the Sierra Madre,* but his own obsession with elephant hunting had top priority during the making of *The African Queen.*

Bogart had gone hunting with his father as a child, disliked the idea of killing animals and would not allow Bacall to accompany Huston. In Viertel's novel Bogart appears as Philip Duncan, an insecure man with a rasping voice, "given to aggressiveness when not entirely sober, a not uncommon Hollywood trait." In Stanleyville everyone buys huge supplies of canned goods to be ready for any catastrophe. When Wilson, a great womanizer, fails to show up, Duncan tries to explain his absence: "Where's the ogre? Why wasn't he there to meet us? I bet he's shacked up with one of these black ladies and has forgotten all about us." Mrs. Duncan, who'd come to Paris with a mountain of luggage, is also sceptical about his motives and worried about his fondness for practical jokes. "I'm sure that bastard John is thinking up some horrible gag for us. He wants to get us off in some horrible hole, and then just stay and stay and watch us all suffer," she says. Hepburn is the domineering Kay Gibson, who is first dubious about the African location and then says: "I'd like to stay here for years and see it all." But, Philip Duncan notes, she is also concerned about the size of her part and his domination of the film: "She feels she's just a foil for me the way it is now. She just listens and I do all the talking."[7]

The company soon discovered that it was as difficult to film in Africa as to live there. Every morning five cars and trucks drove the actors three miles from Biondo to the banks of the river. Then the thirty-foot *African Queen*—which they had found in derelict condition on Lake Albert, repaired and transported 600 miles from Uganda to the Congo—pulled four rafts up the river. The first, Huston wrote, was "a replica of the *Queen*. That raft itself became our stage. We could put cameras and equipment on it and move around, photographing Katie and Bogie in the mock-up with as much facility as we'd have had on a studio floor. The second raft carried all of the equipment, lights and props. The third was for the generator. The fourth was Katie's, equipped with a privy, a full-length mirror and a private dressing room."

They would steam a fair distance up the Ruiki, turn the whole elaborate procession around and do most of the shooting while drifting downstream. But the technical difficulties, even when the crew was healthy, were enormous. Hepburn described how "the camera or lamps or whatever [were] caught by the overhanging shrubbery on the banks. Or we would . . . hit a submerged log and catch on it. Or the sun would go in. Or it would rain. The hysteria of each shot was a nightmare. And there was always the uncertain factor of Bogie and me and whether John thought we'd done a scene well. Or the engine on the *Queen* would stop. Or one of the propellers would be fouled by the dragging rope. Or we would be attacked by hornets. Or a stray pirogue would suddenly appear in the shot." When the rafts hit the river banks during sharp turns, Bogart the yachtsman barked out commands to the crew.

They also had difficulty with the leeches, needed for the scene in which the hero has to get out and pull the grounded boat through the murky water. Huston naturally wanted to use real six-inch bloodsuckers, acquired from a scarred leech-breeder, on Bogart's skinny frame; the terrified actor adamantly refused. The special effects man, Cliff Richardson, described how he solved the problem by pasting realistic-looking rubber ones on to Bogart: "At first they had real leeches which were supposed to be stuck on the back of a stunt man, but they wouldn't stick. They even arranged for a nurse to puncture his back in the hope that the blood would interest the leeches but that failed too. So I made a plasticine model of one of the leeches and from that a plaster mould was made. We cast the 'leeches' in rubber and inserted a small blood sac into each one. To stick them onto Bogart I used a waterproof adhesive. They had a hell of a job pulling them off but they worked like a charm."

Richardson had more trouble arranging the scene in which Bogart and Hepburn are attacked by swarms of mosquitoes. He had two thousand real insects specially bred by the Institute of Tropical Diseases, and planned to photograph them flying about in a glass-sided box. He would then superimpose these shots over the actual scene in the film. But the little beasties refused to cooperate and settled listlessly on the bottom of the box. Richardson said that they "eventually solved this problem by shooting through an aquarium filled with clear water which was vigorously stirred after throwing in a handful of tea leaves. The gyrating leaves together with the high-pitched buzz of mosquitoes on the sound-track proved quite successful"[8]—though the thick tea leaves look more like swirling butterflies than mosquitoes.

Huston posted an African night-watchman next to the boat, telling him to observe it closely and make sure nothing was stolen. One night, as he looked at it very carefully, it slowly sank to the bottom of the river. It took two hundred Congolese workers three days to haul it to the surface. In the midst of these disasters Sam Spiegel turned up, looking ludicrously out of place with his white shorts, knee socks, pot belly and huge cigar. Though desperately worried, he managed to survive all the chaos and hold the project together by wheedling more and more cash out of the backers.

‹ III ›

THE SCREENPLAY had been written in New York in the fall of 1950 by Huston and the novelist James Agee, who as a critic had been very keen about *The Treasure of the Sierra Madre*. Agee found it fascinating and exciting to write with Huston while watching that "particular intelligence and instinct at work. And so is learning from him . . . about good crafts-manship and taste and imagination." The story is simple but extremely effective. According to the *Daily Telegraph,* Forester's novel "was inspired by a little-known chapter in the East African campaign of 1915. In that year two armed motor-launches were shipped from London to Cape Town and carried 2,500 miles north by rail, thence 500 miles by jungle track and river and rail again, to the shore of Tanganyika. There they made short work of the German vessels that had been impeding operations."

Though the unusual color photography of scenery and animals must then have seemed spectacular, the film is not about Africa but about two people in Africa. Charlie Allnutt, the dissolute skipper of a decrepit river boat, and Rose Sayer, the strait-laced sister of an English missionary, are thrown together at the outbreak of World War I after her brother dies of a heart attack following the German raids on his compound. Allnutt, concerned about her welfare, stops by and rescues her from the now deserted mission house. Though Rose knows nothing about handling boats or navigating the river, she takes the upper hand. To avenge her brother's death, she persuades Allnutt to run a series of dangerous rapids. She intends to blow up the German gunboat that dominates the lake and blocks the invasion route of the British forces.

Bogart's personal relations with Hepburn in real life were strikingly similar to the relations of the characters in the movie. He was the hard-drinking cynic, she the preachy spinster. They suffered the same illnesses and dangers in the compound as in the film. They began with prejudice and suspicion, and endured many hardships. Confined in a narrow space and an isolated setting, they overcame mutual hostility and eventually became very fond of each other. Hepburn was—with Mary Astor, Ingrid Bergman and the early Bacall—one of Bogart's great co-stars. She felt he was well trained on the stage and (in her telegraphic style) called him "a generous actor. And a no-bunk person. He just did it. He was an actor who enjoyed acting. Knew he was good. Always knew his lines. Always was on time. Hated anything false."

Theodore Bikel, the Austrian-born actor and singer who played an officer on the German gunboat, described the unusual way that Bogart prepared to shoot the last scenes in England: "Rather than learning his lines the night before, he looked at the script in the early morning hours as we sat in the make-up trailer. Then, while the hair people put a small hairpiece on him, he repeated the lines to a script person a couple of times and then he was set for the rest of the day." Bogart explained that this more spontaneous method worked because he and Hepburn aimed for natural rather than dramatic speech: "we seldom learned our lines [verbatim] for *The African Queen.* Instead we just got the general idea and talked each scene out overlapping one another, cutting one another off, as people do in everyday conversation."[9]

Hepburn played her part with dour seriousness until Huston suggested how to make her character more comical and congenial. He reminded her that Eleanor Roosevelt always smiled when she visited soldiers in hospitals and told her, when condescending to Bogart's character, to imitate that ladylike "society smile." Hepburn effectively used the familiar gesture in an exotic context and felt his "awfully clever piece of direction" enhanced her performance. Huston—who didn't use a storyboard, a daily plan or a list of shots—was "the most laid-back director" Jack Cardiff had ever worked with. Nothing bothered him and he was always perfectly calm.

He even fished while shooting a scene and when Hepburn complained, said: "Honey, I'm listening. You're doing just great!"

Bogart told Cardiff: "Listen, Jack—you see my face. It's got a lot of lines and wrinkles on it. I've been cultivating them for years, and I like them. They are *me*—so don't try and light them out and make me look like a goddam fag." As Allnutt he has the same prominent front teeth, scruffy beard and ragged clothes as Fred C. Dobbs in *The Treasure of the Sierra Madre,* but his personality is completely different. He wears a convict-like striped shirt, red neckerchief, black-brimmed torn white cap, stained white trousers and canvas shoes. He is very nimble on the boat. Dobbs longs for a cigarette butt that is snatched up by a street urchin at the beginning of the Mexican picture; Allnutt's casually discarded cigar at the start of *The African Queen* stampedes the natives out of the Sunday morning service conducted by the Reverend Samuel Sayer (Robert Morley). Morley's scenes were shot in London, his African congregation was shot on location, and the two separate parts were convincingly spliced together.

The film begins as the German troops burn down an African village and drive out the natives; it ends as a German gunboat, struck by a homemade torpedo, suddenly explodes. There's a great deal of water in between the two fires (800 gallons were poured on Hepburn in the London studio). Allnutt's boat, in alternating scenes of crisis and calm, navigates the swirling river, slips past the German fort and sails into the lake to carry out its mission. The essence of the wonderfully comic film is the contrast between the two spikey, middle-aged characters. Isolated on the boat, they find it difficult to maintain the proprieties and clash bitterly as she condemns his character and spurs him into action, while he mocks her affected speech and resists her orders. After overcoming a series of increasingly perilous obstacles, each one bringing them closer together, they transcend their differences of class and character. As her brittle crust melts and reveals an emotional core, they fall in love.

The main conflict concerns Allnutt's sensible opposition to Rosie's madcap plan to sink the German ship. She tries to shame him, in her most patronizing schoolmarm manner, by asking: "In other words, you are refusing to help your country in her hour of need, Mr. Allnutt?" But he continues to ignore her commands, while fortifying himself with ample quantities of gin, and does a witty imitation of her high and mighty airs:

> "I mean we ain't goin' to do nothin' of the sort."
> "Why, *of course* we're going! What an absurd idea!"

"What an absurd idea! What an absurd idea! Lady, I may be a
born fool, but you get ten absurd idears to my one, an' don't
you forget it!"

When she calls him a liar and a coward, he lashes out with a caustic
analysis of her character. "'Oose boat *is* this, any'ow? 'Oo asked *you* aboard.
Huh? Huh? You crazy, psalm-singin', skinny old maid."

After this dispute, Rose, acting out Hepburn's real-life fury at Bogart's
drinking and needling, pours Allnutt's precious gin into the river and
throws the empty bottles overboard. When Rose and Charlie survive the
cataracts and gorges, she transcends her puritanical repression and reveals
her sexual awakening by confessing she had loved the excitement: "I'd
never dreamed that any—any mere—er—physical experience could be
so *stimulating.* . . . So *exhilarating.*" When they pass the last obstacle,
through a combination of his mechanical ability and her plucky imagination, he exclaims, "Can't 'ardly tell water from land—or for that matter,
day from night," and she replies: "The whole thing is like a fever dream,
isn't it?" In the thrill of the moment he embraces and kisses her. Though
she is transformed and responsive, he's shocked and appalled at first by
his own rash behavior. After their lovemaking, she serves him "breakfast
in bed." Filled with joy, he does an imitation of the hippos and monkeys
they see on the banks of the river.

The weakest part of the picture is the contrived conclusion. Charlie
loads his boat with explosives and intends to ram the Germans. But before
he can do so the boat is swamped and overturned during a storm on the
lake. They manage to swim away from their capsized craft, but are captured and taken aboard the enemy ship. As in *Casablanca* (where he
answers "Drunkard") and in *Passage to Marseilles* (where he answers "Eskimo"), an officer once again asks his nationality and he reluctantly replies:
"English." They are sentenced to death for spying, but the captain agrees
to Charlie's sentimental request to marry them before they are hanged.[10]
After a brief ceremony he exclaims: "I now pronounce you man and wife.
Proceed with the execution."

At this very moment the *Queen Louisa* runs into the abandoned
African Queen and is blown up. Charlie and Rose jump ship, swim toward
the shore and glide out of the last frame. Huston's script girl, Angela Allen,
noting his characteristic restlessness and inability to perfect his work,
observed that he was "bent on self-destruction. So frequently in his
pictures he made a wonderful film, but when it came to the end he did
something that kind of blew it. And he knew that he was doing it. . . . He

got too bored to think up a good end. It wasn't on a par with the rest of the film. It's a wonderful picture, but the end is a bore." Audiences, however, liked the upbeat conclusion. The picture cost $4 million to make and earned more than $40 million.

During his long career Bogart had developed a sophisticated and ambivalent attitude toward his profession and his role in it. He laughed at starstruck idolaters and disliked the spurious glamour of the film industry. He often attacked the blatant stupidity, the meretricious beauty and the fatuous egoism of his colleagues: "Most of the actresses in Hollywood are the dumbest broads in town and ninety percent have no sex appeal. . . . Most of the stars bore me—always blabbing about their latest movies." Accustomed to fame as a child, he mocked the inflated importance of the Academy Awards and in 1949 invented the Oscar for Animals. Pard, Bogart's unlucky dog in *High Sierra,* was a strong contender, but he gave the first two prizes to Asta, the wirehaired terrier in *The Thin Man,* and to the impressively stolid water buffalo in *The Good Earth.*

In March 1950, the year before he made *The African Queen,* he once again attacked the Awards and caustically commented: "It's about time someone stuck a pin in the Oscar myth and let out all that hot air contained in the Academy Awards. . . . The only answer [to who is best] would be to have everyone perform the same role. One year you could have all the actors play *Hamlet* and all the actresses do *Mildred Pierce"—* Joan Crawford's popular tearjerker of 1945. Richard Brooks' *The Producer* portrays another conversation in which Bogart attacked the Award:

> "I've got a great script for you to do," Matt told Taggart. "It's about coal."
> "I'm tired of looking filthy in pictures," said Taggart.
> "This'll get you the Academy Award," said Matt.
> "Skip the commercials," said Taggart.
> "On the level, baby. This'll get you the Award."
> "That's no incentive," said Taggart. "The best people never get 'em. Did Cary Grant ever get one? Did Chaplin? Did Bogart?" Taggart went on belittling Academy Award winners, his bitterness stemming from the fact that he had never won one.[11]

Bogart thought *The African Queen*—in which he was at once adventurous, comic and romantic—was his best film. It got four Academy Award nominations: for actor, actress, director and screenplay. After all his mockery and apparent disdain for the Award, he realized that he would very much like to win it. When the picture was completed, Sam Spiegel's publicist told Bogart that the public relations firm Cleary, Strauss & Irwin could help him get the Oscar. It was common, then as now, for actors to hire a company to campaign on their behalf. John Strauss came from the same background as Bogart and had gone to Exeter, but since he did not drink, his convivial partner Frederic Cleary seemed best qualified to handle their client. Anxious to maintain his persona, Bogart made it plain to Cleary that he didn't want anyone to know he was pushing for the Award. They decided on a subtle campaign that quietly planted favorable stories in the gossip columns instead of taking out big ads in the trade papers. John Strauss said that no one ever found out about it.

Bogart seemed to have been chasing the seven-pound, gold-plated brass statue (the same weight as his daughter Leslie, born in August 1952) for as long as Greenstreet had pursued the Maltese falcon. In "The Oscar Myth" he wrote: "I have been up for an Academy Award twice, and I struck out both times. The first time was in 1936, when I was nominated for a supporting award for playing Duke Mantee in *The Petrified Forest*." Though he had *not* been nominated in 1936 (no one on *Cosmopolitan* had bothered to check this), he had been nominated for *Casablanca* in 1943.

In March 1952 Nunnally and Dorris Johnson hired a limousine and, as the beams of the huge arc lights swept the night sky above Hollywood, accompanied Bogart and Bacall to the Awards ceremony at the Pantages Theater. Marlon Brando, who played Stanley Kowalski in *A Streetcar Named Desire,* was the favorite for best actor, but recognition for Bogart was long overdue. Though usually cool and detached on such occasions, he was obviously very excited that night, nervously moving his hands as he talked. When Greer Garson announced his name, he was ecstatic.[12] He walked stiffly across the stage and momentarily turned his back to the audience as he accepted the statue she held out to him.

After Claire Trevor had been nominated for *Key Largo* she asked him, "What do I say if I win?" Bogart, condemning the usual gushing response, urged her to "just say you did it all yourself and don't thank anyone." He planned to say the same thing if he' won. But when it came time to speak, he couldn't help thanking those he knew had made his fine performance possible. He said: "It's a long way from the Belgian Congo to the stage of this theatre. It's nicer to be here. Thank you very much. . . . No one does it alone. As in tennis, you need a good opponent or partner to bring out the best in you. John and Katie helped me to be where I am now."

The lives of the stars were psychologically and financially precarious. Recognition was gratifying, but also increased the anxiety of a nervous profession. Oscar winners (like Nobel Prize winners) paid dearly for their

Award by setting impossible standards for themselves. Bogart's triumph did not stop him from criticizing the Awards. "The way to survive an Oscar," he said, "is never to try to win another one. You've seen what happened to some Oscar winners. They spend the rest of their lives turning down scripts while searching for the great role to win another one. . . . Instead of 'making' a star, I think Oscar has the kiss of death." He felt that winners became too cautious, that "too many stars—and directors, too—win it and then figure they have to top themselves. They think every picture they do has to be of Academy Award caliber; they become afraid to take chances. The result: A lot of dull performances in dull pictures."[13]

‹ III ›

IN MARCH 1952 Bogart seemed to have everything. He was happily married, had a son and another child on the way, owned a yacht and his own independent film company, had achieved the highest recognition, and was one of the wealthiest and most successful actors in the world. Bacall now decided that it was time to acquire a mansion. She was tired of the remoteness and the rattlesnakes of Benedict Canyon, and wanted to live in a neighborhood where her children would have playmates. In June 1952, between the Academy Award and the birth of their daughter, Bogart bought for $165,000 a luxurious residence at 232 South Mapleton Drive in Holmby Hills, between Beverly Hills and Bel Air. He disliked changes of any kind and would have been content to remain in rustic Benedict Canyon, or even in garish Horn Avenue. But he now moved up to "where all the creeps live, all the millionaires."

The large, two-story, whitened brick "French colonial" house had shuttered front windows, a long tree-lined driveway and an acre of land behind a low wall. It had fourteen rooms, a marble veranda, two tennis courts and a four-car garage. The dining room was furnished, for a quarter of a million dollars, with French Provincial furniture and paintings by Andrés Segovia, Bernard Buffet, Raoul Dufy and Pablo Picasso. Bogart said of a misty blue-gray abstract painting that Bacall acquired in Paris: "To tell the truth, that hangover was so bad I thought the picture was a battle scene. It turns out it's supposed to be a harvest."

The oak-paneled den, where the family spent most of the time, was called the Butternut Room and had high windows that overlooked the garden and swimming pool below. There was a wall full of books, a fireplace and a bar, boat racing trophies and a model of the *Santana,* photos of themselves and their friends (including the one of Truman and Bacall). The plaid wallpaper was left behind in the canyon and a butler called Russell replaced Fred Clarke. A year after they moved in, a guest dropped a cigarette down the chute to the incinerator and caused a small explosion. Bogart, who didn't give a damn if the place blew up but forked out for it when he had to, cracked: "I could put a down payment on an entire foreign country for the dough this joint set me back, and I can't even set my drink down without having to go find one of those little fucking coasters!" He was grateful that Bacall never finished decorating the massive living room and took a jab at her pretensions when showing Hedda Hopper around the house: "This place is so elegant that I'll have to wear a black tie every night. When Betty showed me through the place she pointed out the suites for herself, the babies, the butler and the maid; then she showed me an oversized closet and said, 'That's your room.'"[14]

In the fall of 1952 Bogart actively supported Adlai Stevenson, who ran against Eisenhower as the Democratic candidate for president. Bogart was a registered Democrat and had been the Party's most steady and popular star for more than a decade. But he originally thought that Eisenhower was more tough and pragmatic than Stevenson, and was persuaded by Darryl Zanuck to attend a rally for Ike in Denver. Bacall soon convinced him to switch his allegiance from the Eisenhower-Nixon ticket to the more liberal and intellectual candidate. In mid-October they accompanied Stevenson during his campaign down the Pacific coast and on his final whistlestop train through the Northeast. Stevenson's staff gave a vivid account of the Bogarts' cheerful participation, immense popularity and enormous value to the campaign:

> "They were what really brought the crowds in more than the candidate," said Stevenson aide Bill Blair. "They would come out and make a few remarks of introduction. But once they went back in, the crowd would keep chanting for them. We'd get ready to introduce the candidate, or the local candidate, and the crowd would be chanting all the time 'Bogie and Bacall,' and you'd bring them out again, and then there would be wild cheers. The actors seemed to enjoy their appearances as much as the crowds did. They kept their humor even after a platform collapsed under them in New London, Connecticut." "It was a happy addition," said [Arthur] Schlesinger, one

of the governor's speechwriters. "Some stars have a reputation for making special demands all the time. They did not; they were very easy and relaxed. It was a novelty for them, which they were savoring. I think they had a good time."

The Bogarts were immensely loyal to Stevenson throughout his faltering and finally disastrous campaign: "Bacall and Bogart stayed with Stevenson through the end, joining him in Chicago for his final rally, and after flying back to California to vote, rushing back to Springfield (over Bogart's objections) to spend Election Night with the governor. When they arrived in Illinois, Bogart collapsed into his hotel bed with a virus. Bacall bundled him up and rushed over to the Executive Mansion for what turned out to be a wake."

Bogart's support for Stevenson was complicated by Bacall's passionate involvement with the candidate. John Barlow Martin's biography, though discreet on this subject, gives the impression that Stevenson was fond of Bacall but used her for political advantage while remaining emotionally aloof. In "I Hate Young Men," an article published in *Look* in November 1953, Bacall excluded actors from her list of distinguished and gentlemanly older men. She praised her favorites: Robert Sherwood, Nunnally Johnson, Alistair Cooke, Louis Bromfield and John Huston, and went overboard about Stevenson: "He is a man of complete integrity, of wisdom and humor. He seems to have it all—the ability to make you laugh at the most difficult moments, innate good sense and uncompromising convictions."

One Hollywood friend remembered Bacall "'mooning over' Stevenson at a party, while her husband . . . watched 'with amusement.'" But Bacall, who said she worshipped and adored Stevenson, could also make Bogart furious. When she wanted to stop in Illinois for a dinner party on the way back from New York to Los Angeles, Bogart shouted over the telephone: "'Absolutely not'—he wanted me to come home. I said it was perfectly harmless, it meant only two days more, and I had already accepted. He was in a rage and slammed down the phone. Somewhere in him was anxiety about my feeling for Adlai." Faced with an angry ultimatum from her husband, Bacall (as usual) did as she pleased and stopped in Illinois.

Nunnally Johnson noted that Bacall was seriously interested in Stevenson, but that he did not respond enthusiastically to her overtures: "Bogey claims that Betty wants to be the First Lady of the Land but that while the country may accept one divorced person in the White House, it certainly wouldn't stand for two. . . . Betty says that the only indication of a personal interest that she has been able to detect in Adlai so far was that during one conversation he carelessly rested his hand on her knee and let it remain there for an hour or so. This, she says, gives her hope."[15] Bacall continued to court Stevenson after Bogart's death, but never managed to snare him.

A much livelier engagement took place on November 4, 1953 just before the Bogarts attended the premiere of *How to Marry a Millionaire* with Marilyn Monroe. A photograph reveals Bacall's modest cleavage as Bogart turns away from her and looks with a professional glance down the tight, low-cut dress of the gushing Monroe. Nunnally Johnson, who wrote the screenplay of the picture, was impressed by Monroe's ability to drink with the boys and overwhelmed by her liveliness and beauty. He recalled that their little party consisted simply of "Bogart and Betty, old friends of ours, and Mrs. Johnson and myself. Marilyn entered with a request for a drink, a stiff one, bourbon and soda, and I provided her with same. Then even though it was to be a quick and early dinner she asked for another. And got it. At the time I knew nothing of her drinking habits but was beginning to admire her for her start anyway. And naturally neither Bogey nor I would have permitted her to drink alone. At dinner she was actually vivacious, her eyes sparkling, eager and laughing, so radiantly beautiful and attractive that I found myself beginning to like her."

In the spring of 1955 a group of Hollywood celebrities (Bacall's actor friends were more glamorous than Bogart's eccentric mavericks) gathered around the Bogarts and formed the original, self-consciously named Holmby Hills Rat Pack. At the core of this wealthy and convivial society were Frank Sinatra, David Niven, Judy Garland and her husband Sid Luft as well as Mike Romanoff and Swifty Lazar. It also included, on more expansive occasions, the writers George Axelrod and Charles Lederer, the songwriter Jimmy Van Heusen and the producer Charles Feldman. Their hedonistic aims were to relieve boredom and perpetuate independence. Rejecting the morality of the studio and the wholesome family values of the Eisenhower years, they met mainly to drink, gamble and carouse.

When Noel Coward came to Hollywood in the mid-1950s, he was swept up and entertained by the exclusive group, who amused their sophisticated English guest. Coward recorded in his diary: "Friday it was the Bogarts' turn. A barbecue party by the pool. Really great fun although it got a bit nippy and I was delighted to get indoors. The same familiar glamorous faces. . . . There have been a series of parties as usual, each one indistinguishable from the other, culminating last night in the Bogarts' Christmas Eve revel which was great fun and highly glamorous to the eye." Coward confirmed Swifty Lazar's description of a high-spirited but rather childish prank that took place at Sinatra's Palm Springs house on New

Year's Day in 1956: "Bogie, who always liked to stir things up, saw an opportunity that was too good to miss—he pushed me in the pool." After Swifty emerged, he pushed Bogart into the pool. When Bogart, looking at his ruined Cartier watch, asked: "How are we going to get this dry?" Swifty "casually tossed the watch into the blazing fire and said, 'Like this.'" He then replaced Bogart's timepiece with a Mickey Mouse watch. Coward (like Clifton Webb) appealed to Bogart's campy side, which he showed in *Stand-In, The Return of Doctor X* and *Beat the Devil*. They got on splendidly and Bogart told him: "I think you are wonderful and charming and if I should ever change from liking girls better, you would be my first thought."[16]

Despite all the glamour, their life was sometimes artificial and hermetic. They sealed themselves off from the outside world to protect their privacy and be free to behave in an uninhibited way, and tended to see the same movie people in the same blur of parties. Bogart's childhood friend Lee Gershwin—who was worth $25 million, lived like royalty and always played the grande dame—would exclaim, when traveling in Third World countries: "This is so much better than being bored in Hollywood, bored with Bogey and Betty and all the rest."

In the late 1940s Bogart and Bacall had done radio adaptations of *The Maltese Falcon* and *To Have and Have Not* in order to publicize and cash in on those films. Just before leaving for Africa in March 1951 they signed up for a weekly radio series, *Bold Venture*. A familiar mixture of *Casablanca* and *To Have and Have Not*, it ran for two years and earned them a total of $250,000. *Newsweek* wrote that "As Slate Shannon, Bogart is the proprietor of a small, quasi-respectable hotel, tenanted by a motley, shifting cast of characters. Instead of the Sam of *Casablanca*, there is a calypso singer named King Moses. There is Shannon's boat *Bold Venture*, ever ready to roar to the rescue of a friend or the search of an enemy. And there is Sailor Duval (Mrs. Bogart), described as Shannon's ward but played with sultry, sexy monotones."

In the early 1950s, as television began to rival radio and movies, Bogart made a number of appearances that increased his income and kept his image in the public eye. On October 25, 1953 (for example) "Baby Face" Bogart, parodying his gangster roles and mocking the absurd plots of his worst pictures, turned up on Jack Benny's show. Arrested by Benny, who tries to get him to confess, Bogart won't talk. But he alludes to Lucky Strike, the sponsor of the program, and puts in a plug for his latest film, *Beat the Devil*.

On September 3, 1954, he and Bacall appeared on Edward R. Murrow's *Person to Person*, which was filmed in their South Mapleton Drive house. On the videotape of this show Bacall seems ill at ease and keeps tucking in her already tucked-in blouse as she walks away from the camera. Bogart, casually dressed in a polo shirt and sports jacket, is relaxed and appealing. He discusses film and stage acting, whether he missed New York and wanted to return to the theater, how type-casting helps make stars, Bogart and Bacall's roles as the Tough Guy and the Look, the gold whistle based on their seductive scene in *To Have and Have Not* and the importance of making movies that appeal to a wide audience and earn money. Their small children (angelically dressed for bed and looking as if sent from Central Casting) also make a brief appearance. Five days later, the reviewer in *Variety,* praising the program, said: "the Bogarts' sequence moved fast, deftly and amusingly. The actor was himself, natural, while Miss Bacall, a little stagey, hammed it up a bit. The Bogarts, a literate, witty, engaging couple, indulged in entertaining chit chat about themselves, film and theatre, with some amusing crisscrosses of conflicting opinions on acting and living."[17]

But life on South Mapleton Drive was not as harmonious as it appeared on television. A year earlier, in the spring of 1953, Bogart's neighbors were up in arms. In addition to Harvey, the Bogarts now had two other boxers, George and Baby. They lived in one of the most expensive areas in the world, and many successful and wealthy people—the architect Welton Becket, the radio writer Cy Howard and Charles Correll of the *Amos 'n' Andy* show—all protested about the horrible noise of the barking dogs.

Art Linkletter described the unpleasant situation from a neighbor's point of view: "from the time they were let out of the house [at night] until dawn they'd race up and down the yard, barking the length of the yard (about half a block), at every automobile that passed. Bitterness grew and resentment increased when various neighbors tried to reason with Bogart, claiming that they had to get a night's sleep. Bogart was adamant. The way he saw it, the dogs were his property . . . and they could behave as they wished." Bogart even sent a telegram from Italy, where he was making *Beat the Devil,* declaring that he would "defend to the death the right of the boxer dogs to bark at night in Hollywood." When Cy Howard, whose work was disturbed, asked: "Couldn't you do something about them? Couldn't you have their vocal cords cut?" Bogart aggressively replied: "If anybody needs his cords cut, you do."

Finally, the neighbors filed suit. Cy Howard testified that Bogart, instead of responding to the problem, assumed his screen persona and defended his ill-behaved boxers. "They bark all day and they bark all night," Howard complained. "I don't think we should have to regulate our lives to suit these dogs. They jump over my fence and chew my dog. I caught one of them swimming in my pool. When I complained to Bogey all he did was play scenes from his three previous pictures." Threatened with legal action and bad publicity, Bogart was forced to back down. His lawyer promised that Bogart "would endeavor to see that the animals are kept in at night and efforts made to train them against barking."[18]

⟨ V ⟩

AFTER *The African Queen* Bogart appeared in two movies, *Deadline—U.S.A.* and *Battle Circus,* both written and directed by his close friend Richard Brooks. He was always polite and deferential to Bogart, but his erratic direction and sudden bursts of temper caused great difficulties on the set. Warren Stevens, who played the top reporter on Bogart's newspaper, recalled that they had rehearsed for a whole week before starting to shoot and that everyone had seemed quite happy. But Brooks suddenly exploded on the first take. He had changed his mind about how to do the scene and took all day to get exactly the shot he wanted. Stevens suspected that personal problems made him go beserk. Brooks was rude, unreasonable and hard on the crew, who once retaliated by dropping a dangerously heavy sandbag right next to where he was standing.

Stevens also had an exhilarating experience with Bogart. Starting in the late afternoon without a rehearsal, they shot a difficult scene in one take. Delighted that their performance had worked so well, Bogart exclaimed: "By God, we winged it!" Kim Hunter, who had just won an Oscar for best supporting actress in *A Streetcar Named Desire,* played Bogart's former wife in *Deadline—U.S.A.* She found him "straight on"—charming, open, warm and friendly—and said he usually rehearsed carefully before filming.[19]

Deadline—U.S.A. (1952), made for Twentieth Century–Fox, has a good plot and a fast pace. Bogart, a courageous editor, mounts one last crusade as his paper, owned by the stately Ethel Barrymore, is dying beneath him. Still in love with his ex-wife, he proposes remarriage and tries to revive their relationship. He's written a sensational story that exposes political corruption and murder, but needs concrete evidence to convict the crime boss. A petty crook tells Bogart that his showgirl sister was killed by the boss after refusing to give back the money she was holding for him. Before the hood can sign a statement, he is "arrested" by the boss's uniformed men. After they shoot him, he falls into the thrashing printing machines. The search for evidence and the murder of a crucial witness who falls to his death recall the opening scenes of *The Enforcer*.

The convincingly idealistic Bogart makes a stirring speech in court on the need for a free press. As the paper is about to fold, the showgirl's mother turns up with the girl's diary and the missing money. The plot lines move effectively together as Bogart publishes the story, saves the paper (as he had saved the studio in *Stand-In*) and wins back his wife. Triumphant at the end, he tells the vice boss: "As long as one newspaper will print the truth, you're finished!"

Deadline—U.S.A is an effective potboiler; *Battle Circus,* made for MGM in 1953, is embarrassingly bad. The title alludes to the constant movement of the circus-like tents of the Mobile Army Surgical Hospital (MASH) as the battle lines shift during the Korean War. Made before the war had ended, *Battle Circus* failed to portray the Korean conflict as MGM's enormously successful *Battleground* (1949) had portrayed World War II. Unlike its predecessor, it tried to appeal to every kind of audience and was an unhappy mishmash of conventional genres: "a war film, a combat film, an airplane film, a circus movie, a screwball comedy, a romance and a hospital movie."

The casting of opposite types, which was inspired in *The African Queen,* is disastrous in *Battle Circus.* Bogart is an army surgeon; the coy and wholesome June Allyson is a novice nurse. Allyson wins Bogart's love by disarming a battle-crazed Korean prisoner who threatens to blow them up with a hand grenade. She primly warns Bogart: "Major, you've got to stop creeping up on me," but he surprises her in a dark shower. The tent collapses, she falls in the mud and they kiss. When she asks, "Can't you say you love me?" he replies: "It's better to do it than to say it." Bogart, never much good as a flirtatious lover, seems stiff and awkward in the love scenes.

The movie, aiming at documentary realism, shows the doctor and nurse "slogging around in the mud and rain, surrounded by the enemy." But the cliché-packed picture (a hard-boiled American sergeant adopts a wounded Korean kid) limps along with no dramatic structure. In 1970 Robert Altman's darkly comic *M*A*S*H,* set in the same battle circus, was a great success. Its crude sexual jokes, blood-spattered surgical scenes and biting satire on the stupidity of the army fulfilled the potential of the story and gave a more realistic sense of the war. Only Bogart's $250,000 fee and need to keep up his "big house and big cars," which he had warned young actors to avoid, explains his appearance in this picture.

‹ VI ›

IN 1952, at the end of the great decade that stretched majestically from *The Maltese Falcon* to *The African Queen*, Bogart could look back on his career with considerable satisfaction. In a profession that glorified youth and beauty, Bogart — with sallow complexion and bloodshot eyes — seemed to flourish as he grew older. In a place where talent blossomed early and few stayed the course, he had endured. "I'm a professional," he said in the *Time* cover story of June 1954. "I've done pretty well, don't you think. I've survived in a pretty rough business." André Bazin, the distinguished French film critic, praised his skill as an actor and called him the archetypal hero of our time: "Bogart is, without doubt, typically the actor / myth of the war and post-war period. . . . He improved, became sharper, as he progressively wasted away."[20]

Bogart's last four films had been for Santana, Horizon, Fox and Metro. Sam Jaffe complained that Warners, after all his successes, "never prepared or bought a book or bought a play or had anything for Bogart." He could not agree on stories for himself or Bacall (who was also under contract with Warners and often on suspension), and had not made a picture for Warners since completing *The Enforcer* in August 1950. In November 1950 an amendment to his contract gave him less money in exchange for more freedom, allowed him to reject a single picture each year and dropped his fee from $200,000 to $160,000.

In May 1952, resentful of losing the leading role to Burt Lancaster in William Inge's *Come Back, Little Sheba* because Warners (as Jaffe complained) had failed to buy the property, Bogart used Hedda Hopper to express his dissatisfaction. He told her: "There will come a day of reckoning. In five years, when I have no hair or teeth, Warners will have to keep putting me in pictures." Shortly after this appeared in Hopper's column, Warners' lawyer Roy Obringer wrote him that the studio, upset by his cynical comments, were "at a total loss to understand your attitude in this matter." A month after Bogart's remarks, Warners' lawyers told the studio executives that there was absolutely no way to terminate his contract. In the fall, however, Bogart's lifelong dislike of Jack Warner and resentment of the studio boiled over and led to a final rupture. On September 23, 1953, with nine more years to go, he gave up the remaining guarantee of $1,440,000. He was released from his contract and after seventeen years left Warner Bros.

Bogart was not a great movie fan. He liked to keep his life and work separate; and except for his current picture and premieres, rarely discussed old films or went to new ones. But when he acquired his own movie projector and screen he would, just before his birthday, decorate the Christmas tree and show his own 16-millimeter print of the Fredric March–Janet Gaynor version of *A Star is Born* (1937). Though he had seen it many times before, he always cried through the film. If friends asked what he was weeping about, he'd reply: "I don't know. It just makes me cry."[21] The picture tells the story of how a young, innocent and beautiful actress becomes a star while her older, spoiled, egoistic husband —who had discovered her, nourished her talent and appeared with her in the film that made her famous—falls from stardom, cannot be saved by his wife and sinks into alcoholism, despair and suicide. Bogart clearly saw himself and Bacall reflected in this movie. Deeply disturbed by it and fearful of a similar fate, moved by the theme of mutability, the transience and loss of all earthly things, he obsessively and ritualistically watched it every year.

Bogart knew he had reached the top and already had everything Hollywood could give. Though he had long wanted to leave Warners, he couldn't help feeling a sense of loss at parting from the company where he had spent most of his career. He believed he could make better films and, unlike most established actors, was willing to take chances. Now on his own, he suffered the post-Oscar blues.

♦ 13 ♦

A Versatile Actor

1954

⟨ I ⟩

IN THE LAST PHASE of his career Bogart moved away from tough-guy parts and formulaic movies. He now took on an astonishing variety of unheroic roles—psychopathic writer, drunken skipper, inept con-man, paranoid navy captain, reluctant lover, washed-up movie director, down-and-out journalist—and finished strongly with some of his most original films. *Beat the Devil, The Caine Mutiny* and *Sabrina* all appeared in his miraculous year, 1954.

Beat the Devil, Bogart's last project with Huston and with Santana, is his most eccentric and puzzling picture. In September 1951 Huston asked him to buy the film rights of Claud Cockburn's novel (published under the pseudonym of James Helvick) for $10,000. It was not an especially promising property. But Cockburn, who had been a London *Times* correspondent in the 1930s, now lived near Huston in Ireland and needed the money. Bogart replied by telegram with his own proposal and a Swahili flourish ("How are you? I'm fine") that recalled their journey to Africa: "Have advised Morgan Maree purchase *Beat the Devil* at terms stated in your cable. Would you be interested in directing same for Santana partnership? Deal object to make a buck for both of us. *Habari. Mzuri* too. Bogart." The actor would try almost anything in order to work with his most talented friend. "The monster is stimulating," he had said in 1950. "Offbeat kind of mind. Off center. He's brilliant and unpredictable. Never dull. When I work with John, I think about acting. I don't worry about business." But after putting half a million dollars of his own money into *Beat the Devil,* he had plenty of business worries.

The pre-production phase inspired a lively and amusing exchange of letters. Huston had offered Bacall a part in the film, but she was pregnant at the time and unable to accept. In October 1952, just after their daughter was born and while he and Bacall were actively involved in the presidential election campaign, he wrote Huston: "Because I always open my wife's mail, I read your insidious and immoral proposals to my wife. It is perfectly safe to promise Miss Bacall a leading part in our picture as soon as you are perfectly sure that she is knocked up—by me, that is. I have therefore instructed Miss Bacall to disregard your blandishments and as your employer I implore you not to further fuck up my home, which has already been fucked up like Hell by [Adlai] Stevenson. . . . Miss Bacall supports wholeheartedly Governor Stevenson, up to the vomiting point."

The following month Huston, who loved custom-made clothes and was a bit of a dandy, suggested his conception of Bogart's character in the film: "It's important that Dannreuther should be a brand new Bogart. Not that old thing that's been haunting raincoats and snap-brimmed hats for God knows how long. I'd like to see you a very continental type of fellow. An extreme figure in a homburg, shoulders unpadded, French cuffs, Regency trousers, fancy waistcoats and a walking stick. The eyepatch is debatable." Bogart—who disliked wearing an elaborate rig, and as star and principal investor inevitably got his own way—sent Huston his frank appraisal of this idea: "As regards your brilliant conception of my wardrobe, may I just say that I think you're full of shit. May I suggest that *you* wear the costume that you describe and that I kind of go around in old tweeds. . . . As regards the cane, I don't have to tell you what you can do with THAT!"[1]

Postwar Italy offered filmmakers warm weather, a six-day work week and cheap labor. Huston and Bogart amused themselves by having both prostitutes and aspiring actresses sent down from Rome. Huston made *Beat the Devil* in Ravello—a town of curving streets and terraced vineyards, high above the Amalfi coast, south of Naples—from February to April 1953. Jennifer Jones earned $125,000, Peter Lorre $15,000 and Robert Morley £10,000. Since Bacall now had two small children and was making *How to Marry a Millionaire,* she remained in Hollywood while Bogart flew to Rome and drank at the Excelsior Hotel. On February 6, while driving down the Appian Way from Rome to Naples, his Italian chauffeur got into an accident that foreshadowed the car crash in the film. Though the picture was delayed while Bogart had his mouth repaired, Huston found the whole thing quite hilarious: "The driver couldn't make up his mind which road to take, so he went straight ahead, right over an island, through a heavy stone wall and into a ditch. I was up front, so I had a chance to brace myself, but Bogart was asleep on the back seat. . . . 'Chrith, no! Somethin'th happen t' my tongue!' He stuck his tongue out.

A piece of it was split over into a flap like a little trapdoor. Moreover, all his front teeth—actually a full bridge—had been knocked out." Bogart needed several stitches and a German doctor in Naples sewed up his "little trapdoor" without an anesthetic. "Bogie had guts," Huston said. "Not bravura. Real courage."

Disdaining hometown nepotism, Bogart had told a reporter: "I like making pictures away from Hollywood. You don't have those fat cat producers and their relatives under your feet all the time." But he also liked plain food and, returning to Italy for the first time since his USO tour of 1944, found conditions at the Hotel Palumbo in Ravello nearly as unpleasant as Africa. "Those dagos," he cracked, "throw everything but Mussolini in the soup." His evenings were enlivened by poker games with the photographer Robert Capa, who had been hired to do special photo layouts. The worst player in the world, Capa lost his salary every night. There were also visits from Orson Welles, George Sanders and Ingrid Bergman. The actress recalled that Bogart was concerned about her scandalous involvement with the Italian director Roberto Rossellini: "We had supper together with other friends and he was a little bit upset about my having left Hollywood. He felt sorry for me because he thought I had ruined my career by stepping away from the Hollywood scene and into Italian movies. . . . So I said to him, 'Well, I am a very happy woman and maybe that is just as important as being a box office success in America.'"[2]

Apart from Bogart's car accident and the difficulties of filming in Italy, Huston also had great trouble with the script. The first version of the screenplay, written by Claud Cockburn, was quickly discarded. The second draft was done by Peter Viertel, who had worked on *The African Queen,* and Anthony Veiller, who had produced *Chain Lightning.* Viertel wrote that Huston, unenthusiastic about their effort, "was thinking of abandoning the project and was concerned only with the damage this might do to his friendship with Bogey."

A week before shooting was to start David Selznick, whose wife Jennifer Jones was the co-star, suggested that Huston collaborate with the twenty-nine-year-old Truman Capote. The strikingly original writer, then living in Rome, agreed to work on the script for $1,500 a week. Capote, a flamboyant homosexual, shared a hotel room with Huston, which prompted Bogart to invent a number of scurrilous stories about them. Capote, much tougher than he looked, beat Bogart in several arm wrestling contests at $50 a throw. "At first you can't believe him, he's so odd," Bogart wrote Bacall, "and then you want to carry him around with you always."

Like Huston, Capote disliked the Viertel-Veiller script, a straightforward melodrama, and called it a "stinker." He said: "When I started, only John and I knew what the story was, and I have a suspicion that John wasn't too clear about it."[3] The movie, like most of Huston's work, portrays a grandiose quest that ends in tragicomic failure. The story concerns a quartet of inept crooks in search of uranium deposits in British East Africa. To get there they must "beat the devil" and surmount a series of diabolical obstacles: their ship breaks down and they are stranded in an obscure Italian port; they have a car accident; the *Nyanga*, the ship they sail on, explodes (an allusion to *The African Queen*); they are shipwrecked and captured by Arabs. There is also murder, deception and treachery.

The four symmetrically matched international crooks (the tall fat Morley, the tall thin Marco Tulli, the short fat Lorre, the short thin Ivor Barnard) are entangled with two oddball couples (Bogart and Lollobrigida, Jennifer Jones and Edward Underdown). Underdown suspects Bogart of being a fraud; Bogart knows Underdown, who plays a bogus English aristocrat, *is* a fraud. Each husband is in love with the other's wife, each wife with the other's husband. Jones beats Underdown in chess while flirting with Bogart, but he seems a dispassionate and uninterested lover. In the end Underdown, having survived an attempt to murder him aboard ship, disappears over the side, reaches Africa and acquires the uranium deposits that Morley's gang has been trying to get.

Capote and Huston (like the writers on *Casablanca*) were rarely more than two or three days ahead of the shooting schedule. They tried to establish the style of the picture by telling the actors what they planned to do. Then, writing frantically to keep up on the script, they wrestled with the complications of plot and characters. Despite the intense pressure and considerable confusion Capote, like Bogart, enjoyed working with Huston:

> At least one picture I wrote, *Beat the Devil,* was tremendous fun. I worked on it with John Huston while the picture was actually being made on location in Italy. Sometimes scenes that were just about to be shot were written right on the set. The cast was completely bewildered—sometimes even Huston didn't seem to know what was going on. Naturally the scenes had to be written out of sequence, and there were peculiar moments when I was carrying around in my head the only real outline of the so-called plot. . . . It's a marvelous joke. Though I'm afraid the producer didn't laugh.

Bogart was usually careful with his investments and said he wanted to "make a buck." But when Huston told him, as they began to shoot, that they still had no ending (and perhaps no middle either), he replied, with a crooked grin: "Why, John, I'm surprised at you. Hell, it's only money!" The more cautious Robert Morley observed: "It is debatable whether one should put money *into* a picture. It may be preferable merely to take it out." Morley caught the insouciant mood in Ravello by remarking that Capote "never seemed to manage to write very much on any one day, but then as we didn't film very much either, it didn't matter." The situation did not improve when Capote interrupted work and returned to Rome to visit his pet raven, which refused to talk to him on the telephone and seemed to be quite ill.

About a quarter of the film was shot in a London studio. As Morley telegraphed the English producer John Woolf: "We have now returned to our capital and we hope yours returns to you. But we rather doubt it." While in London in June 1953 Bogart saw the Coronation of Queen Elizabeth. As people waited stoically through the rainy night for the next day's ceremony, they recognized Bogart, who cheered them by signing autographs. Referring to the London restaurant where Woolf frequently took him to dinner, Bogart wrote on July 15, 1953: "Thank you for your foresight and understanding of that den of thieves, Les Ambassadeurs. I cannot possibly understand how I could have run up a bill in one day of 240, American. I couldn't have been that drunk." Then, enclosing a gift and alluding to Woolf's current girlfriend, he continued: "Enjoy yourself with that small piece of cashmere and when it is worn out or Mata Hari is worn out, let me know as I have another piece (cashmere that is) for you which I will send immediately air mail."[4]

Though the structure is weak and the film oddly static, the dialogue is clever. Bogart nonchalantly says: "It's my expectations that hold me together." When Jones suggests they run away, he replies that it would be too risky: "Doctor's orders are that I must have money. Otherwise, I become dull, listless, and have trouble with my complexion." And Lorre offers Bogart an aphoristic description of time: "The Swiss manufacture it. The Italians squander it. The French hoard it. The Americans worship it. But time is a crook." But these high points are not quite clever and comic enough to energize the film's meandering pace.

The main trouble, as Huston told Bogart, was that "it's hard to tell whether it's a drama, a comedy or an action picture"—and this difficulty was never resolved. It began as an international melodrama, became a campy comedy and turned into a take-off on movie clichés. *Beat the Devil,* in which all the characters are absurd, became a parody of Huston's *The Maltese Falcon,* where the uranium replaces the elusive bird. Though the picturesque setting could have been shot in color, Huston made the allusion clear by using black and white. Bogart and Peter Lorre (one of the crooks) had appeared in the earlier film. Robert Morley, an equally rotund but more genial villain, replaced the ailing Sydney Greenstreet. Ivor Barnard, the irrational and violent Major Ross, had the same function as the gunsel Elisha Cook, Jr. and the lying Jennifer Jones paralleled the treacherous Mary Astor. The wild card in this eccentric enterprise was, as W. R. Burnett had pointed out, the temperamental director: "If Huston really likes a property, there's no person who can put it on the screen better. But if he is not entirely sold on the thing he is doing, he can make a bomb."

Despite Huston's close friendship with Bogart and Lorre, the actors were a very mixed bunch who lacked the camaraderie of the Warners troupe in *The Maltese Falcon.* Lorre had had a rough time since *Passage to Marseilles,* his last picture with Bogart, who now helped to revive his career. He had divorced his first wife and married the young Kaaren Verne. Dropped by Warners in 1946, he had formed an independent company but found it difficult to get work. He was swindled by his lawyer and went bankrupt in 1949. He married for the third time and had a daughter in 1950, but that marriage would also break up in 1959. He had made no films since 1951, was still recovering from drug addiction and a long illness, and had to be treated delicately on the set. Lorre, whose dyed blond hair was a tribute to Capote, looked like an aged version of the writer.

Bogart found Jennifer Jones, who wore a blond wig in the movie, a "total kook." She asked him to rehearse a scene in her room and spent the whole time sitting on top of a tall clothes chest, peering down at him unnervingly. The Italian actors did not speak English and had to learn their lines phonetically. Gina Lollobrigida, whom Bogart called Low Bridge and The Frigidaire to suggest both her build and her name, was improbably cast as his wife. Her rival Sophia Loren remarked that Gina "is good playing a peasant but is incapable of playing a lady." The French actor Jean-Louis Trintignant, who worked with her on another film, said she "was a little stupid: she understood nothing of what she was doing and completely embarrassed the director." But no amount of intelligence could have helped in this case, and conditions became even more difficult when Huston's instructions had to be translated into Italian. Like many others in the cast, Gina had trouble understanding the comic and satiric aspects of the film. But she did her best and Bogart called her a professional: "she was always punctual, went to bed early, and arrived on the set groomed and alert."[5] Her direct bright eyes, tight waist and jutting chest provide a curious contrast to the narrowed glances and dreamy seductive look of

Jennifer Jones. But Jones at least seems to grasp what's happening; Lollobrigida flounces about as if she were acting in a different movie. Her clinches with Bogart look like the marriage of a weary gangster and a chirpy calendar queen.

Both script and actresses gave Huston problems with the censors, whose certificate was needed to exhibit the film at home and abroad. After he had seen an early version of the script, Joe Breen told Jess Morgan of Santana Pictures that it had to be altered so that the criminals were punished and adultery eliminated. They also had to reduce the kissing and fondling, and hide the women's breasts. Bogart sardonically recalled that "we had the problem in *Beat the Devil* of tucking Miss Jennifer Jones' breasts back into her dress to please the Breen office." Lollobrigida's breasts were a more formidable problem. Audiences paid money to see them, but they had to be tightly covered up.

Dissatisfied with the original script, Huston had instinctively turned it into a satirical comedy, exaggerating the physical incongruities of the cast as well as the grotesque excess of violence and disaster in the plot. But the restraints of censorship prevented him from completely transforming the material. It soon became clear, when sophisticated viewers found it incoherent, that the finished film was in big trouble. Bogart showed the film to a group of friends before its release, and in alarm wired Huston that they all "felt confused after the first ten minutes. Could not tell whether straight melodrama or comedy. We all think picture needs something to set mood. Have you any suggestions?" Huston agreed that "its off-the-wall humor left viewers bewildered and confused. . . . It was generally conceded to be a minor disaster, frivolous, self-indulgent, and all the rest of it."[6]

Feeling rather desperate, Bogart sought advice from the old pro Nunnally Johnson, who showed *Beat the Devil* to the expert film editors Gene and Marjorie Fowler. Gene confirmed that the audience was confused about the mood and style of the movie, which was "a real bomb." He tried to reedit it to emphasize its humor: "For the first six reels, I thought I was looking at a *Maltese Falcon*. And then suddenly it occurred to me, around reel seven, this was a very funny picture. And that was what the trouble was. It was not evident that it was a comedy. . . . So we recut the entire picture, moving the tail end sequence up to the beginning. And Nunnally wrote a funny line, as the main characters are being led away to jail in chains in the opening shot: 'Here are the smartest criminals in Europe.' In other words, 'It's okay to laugh.'"

When Huston showed the new version to the veteran director William Wyler, he finally said: "Well, John, that's the kind of movie that, when you've finished making it, you should make another one as quickly as possible." Peter Viertel "was amazed at how philosophically Huston had accepted Wyler's words. He had in all probability realized that *Beat the Devil* was doomed early on to be a failure." Peter Lorre attributed the failure not only to its confusing tone and structure, but also to its flat-footed marketing campaign: "It was a flop in New York. Why shouldn't it be? It was a deliciously sardonic comedy, meant for art houses, and they opened it with a blood-and-thunder campaign. People just didn't get it."[7]

The *Sight and Sound* reviewer identified the aims as well as the faults of the cryptic film, but missed its ironic wit: "*Beat the Devil* has the air of an expensive house-party joke, a charade which enormously entertained its participants at the time of playing, but which is too private and insufficiently brilliant to justify public performance. The script has some good lines, but meanders hopelessly and badly lacks a climax." John McCarten, writing in *The New Yorker,* was more sympathetic. He compared it to the novels of the most sparkling English stylist and called it "a sort of satire on melodramas dealing with international intrigue. . . . The whole affair is marked by an easy spontaneity, and every now and then it flashes with the kind of bright lunacy that used to be a conspicuous virtue of Evelyn Waugh."

Though Santana broke even on *Beat the Devil,* which later became a cult film and made money, Bogart was as disappointed as the audience. He believed that movies were a popular art and had to be intelligible. Though he still admired Huston, he thought he had fooled around with the script and let him down. Bogart had put a great many talented people in the picture and felt it should have been much better. Annoyed that he had paid for what turned out to be a gigantic private joke, he bitterly remarked that "only phonies think it's funny."[8]

⟨ **II** ⟩

BOGART CONTINUED to work outside Hollywood in the early 1950s and filmed most of *The Caine Mutiny* in Hawaii. The picture could not be made without the help of the U.S. Navy, which at first refused to cooperate on the ground that there had never been a mutiny in its history. The producer, Stanley Kramer, took his case before the Secretary of the Navy and Chief of Naval Operations in Washington, and also got the approval of several admirals in Hawaii. The director, Edward Dmytryk, who had been jailed as one of the Hollywood Ten, did not have clearance to enter the naval base at Pearl Harbor. The technical adviser, Commander James Shaw, a hero of the war in the Pacific, eventually secured this permission. After Kramer and Dmytryk convinced the brass that the movie would be creditable, they were allowed to use three tenders, two destroyers—the USS *Doyle* and the USS *Thompson*—an aircraft carrier and two thousand marines in landing barges. But certain crucial compromises had to be made. The reassuring statement "In its long and glorious history, there has never been a mutiny in the United States Navy" appeared on the screen at the beginning of the film; there was no mention of official assistance; and all negative references to the navy were toned down or eliminated. Herman Wouk's disastrous screenplay, based on his novel, was quickly abandoned. Once the new script was completed, the movie was shot in fifty-four days, right on schedule.

Bogart disliked "fat cat producers" and had some conflict with Stanley Kramer. Sceptical about the value of a producer's work, he defiantly asked him: "Suppose you didn't show up, what difference would it make?" When Kramer stood behind the camera and told Dmytryk what to do, Bogart warned him: "Look, pal. If you want to direct a picture, direct it; but I can only take direction" from one person.[9]

The Caine Mutiny is one of Bogart's dramatic triumphs, but the film itself breaks into three separate sections. The first part takes place before Bogart appears as Captain Queeg. It portrays the arrival in 1943 of the young Princetonian, Ensign Willie Keith (Robert Francis), aboard the sloppily-run *Caine,* his introduction to the straightforward executive officer Steve Maryk (Van Johnson) and to the devious peacetime novelist Lieutenant Keefer (Fred MacMurray). The second part begins about a quarter of the way into the picture as Philip Queeg, a fanatical spit-and-polish officer, takes command of the ship and quickly reveals his incompetence, cowardice and paranoia. He cuts his own line during target-towing practice, retreats under fire while landing marines at a beachhead and conducts a manic search for a missing can of strawberries. When Queeg loses control of the ship during a typhoon (artificially created in the studio), Maryk, incited by Keefer, takes over command and is later charged with mutiny. During the court martial in the third part of the film, Barney Greenwald (José Ferrer) ruthlessly exposes Queeg's madness and forces him to crack up on the stand.

The genial but shifty Keefer, who backs out when Maryk goes to tell Admiral Halsey about Queeg's irrational behavior (the scene on the carrier, in contrast to the *Caine,* shows the navy at its best), saves his skin by blaming Maryk at the trial. All Queeg's blunders are recounted, less dramatically, during the court martial. Queeg is first portrayed as a "tired man whose nerves are shot," then clearly revealed as a paranoid rather than ambiguous character, as he is in the novel and the play.

Dmytryk confessed that the film was a "disappointment" and insisted it "could have been a classic" if it had been longer. But length was not the real problem of this promising but fatally flawed picture. The music by the Warners workhorse Max Steiner ranged from the insistently corny ("Anchors Aweigh") to the blatantly martial. Like all the superfluous scenes in Bogart's best action films — from the love for the crippled girl in *High Sierra* to the letter from the dead man's wife in *The Treasure of the Sierra Madre* — the sentimental romance between Ensign Keith and his girlfriend nearly ruins the picture.

During a tirade at the party following the trial (an epilogue to the main story) Greenwald, who has never served at sea, expresses regret about destroying Queeg's career. He condemns the crew for not helping the captain when he was in trouble and praises him for defending America in the early years of the war. Echoing Kipling's "makin' mock o' uniforms that guard you while you sleep," Greenwald insists that they owe Queeg gratitude for doing "the dirty work" and "standing guard on this fat dumb happy country of ours," while "the Nazis were eating up Europe." In this dramatically weak speech, punctuated by the cliché of throwing wine in Keefer's face, Greenwald shifts the emphasis from criticism of an incompetent psychopath to sympathy for a sacrificial commander. But the speech had to be tailored to secure the essential cooperation of the navy.

In June 1953 Bogart, concerned about these damaging compromises, sought Huston's advice about the screenplay as he had sought Nunnally Johnson's help with *Beat the Devil*. Huston sent an acute analysis of its defects, with positive suggestions for improvements. He said Willie Keith's strained relations with his snobbish mother and romance with a nightclub singer who wasn't good enough for his wealthy family were trite; the sloppy but sympathetic Captain DeVries, the original skipper of the *Caine,* who becomes Keith's new commander at the end of the film, should actually demonstrate his capability and seamanship; Keefer should be made into a well-developed character instead of a "caricature of the cowardly intellectual"; and the pat, obvious ending should be eliminated. Unfortunately, none of Huston's ideas were used and these faults remained in the final version. Critics later pointed out the logical inconsistencies and glaring defects: "The first part of the film convincingly demonstrates Captain Queeg's cowardice and incompetence and presents the mutiny as the only way to save the ship during a typhoon. The film then executes a complete turnabout: the defense lawyer who has proven Queeg's incompetence now attacks the crew for not supporting Queeg when he really needed them.

Yet at no time have the men failed in their duties and responsibilities: it is only their captain, too paranoid to command the ship adequately, who has failed."[10]

Bogart's acting improved as he took on more demanding roles, and *The Caine Mutiny* was redeemed by the brilliant performance of the old navy hand. He invented the business of buttering and rebuttering a piece of toast in the wardroom in order to reveal Queeg's agitated state of mind. He gave Queeg a certain stature, even sympathy, and showed him clinging desperately to a job he was no longer able to do. Bogart believed that "Queeg was not a sadist. He was not a cruel man, he was a very sick man. His was a life of frustrations and insecurity. His victories were always small victories. He made the men stick their shirttails in and he cleaned up the ship. . . . In peacetime Queeg was a capable officer, but he could not stand the stress of war."

Since Queeg seems to be in control of himself during most of the court martial, his sudden crack-up is intensely dramatic. The click of the rolling steel balls in his nervous hands, the merciless close-up of his lined face and pouchy eyes, and the pathos of his monologue are much more effective in the film than in the play. "Aha, the strawberries. That's where I had them," Queeg exclaims during the trial. "They laughed at me. But I proved beyond a shadow of a doubt and with geometric logic that a duplicate key to the wardroom icebox did exist. I'd have produced that key if they hadn't pulled the *Caine* out of action." In the midst of his psychological disintegration, as he suddenly realizes that he's said too much and given himself away, the shocked judges stare at him with pity.

Bogart had already given a fine performance of suspicion and paranoia in *The Treasure of the Sierra Madre* and *In a Lonely Place,* and the breakdown scene in *The Caine Mutiny* is one of the greatest moments in his films. His performance, matched only by José Ferrer's in this movie, made the other actors seem rather weak. In September 1953, a few months after seeking Huston's advice about the script, Bogart told him that he was "rather well satisfied with [his] performance as Queeg, but didn't think too highly of Van Johnson and MacMurray."

On June 7, 1954, three months before the film was released, a drawing of Bogart as Captain Queeg—wearing an officer's baseball cap and smoking a cigarette, with a stormy sea in the background—appeared on the cover of *Time* magazine. *The Caine Mutiny Court Martial,* starring Lloyd Nolan as Queeg and Henry Fonda as Greenwald, was still running on Broadway when the film version appeared and also helped publicize it. The reviews and the profits were both excellent. The *Hollywood Reporter* called Bogart's "infinitely pathetic performance a high point in the history of screen acting." The film cost $2,414,000 and grossed $11 million. For the third time Bogart was nominated by the Academy for best actor of the year. He had beaten Marlon Brando, in *A Streetcar Named Desire,* in 1951; but in 1954 Brando and *On the Waterfront* beat Bogart and *The Caine Mutiny* for best actor and best picture. Bogart did, however, win the Golden Lion for best actor at the Venice Film Festival. When Spencer Tracy ribbed him by saying, "Hey, you're not an actor," he pulled out the fine reviews of *The Caine Mutiny* and said: "Just look at these."[11]

< III >

EDWARD DMYTRYK admired Bogart and had pleasant memories of their work together. Dmytryk got along perfectly with him and wrote that "his performance was superb. His transition from self-control, to petty truculence, to paranoia, then back to full awareness in the court-martial scene, is one of the finest I have ever witnessed. . . . No one could possibly have worked harder, stayed more sober, or been more cooperative than Bogey." Bogart's relations with the director, writer and stars of his next project, *Sabrina,* were exactly the opposite. The film was sunny and charming, but making it was the most contentious and acrimonious experience of his entire career.

Billy Wilder, the director, had originally wanted Cary Grant to play the financier Linus Larrabee, who unexpectedly courts and wins Sabrina Fairchild, his chauffeur's daughter, played by the twenty-four-year-old Audrey Hepburn. But Grant was committed to another picture. Only a week before shooting was to begin at Paramount, Wilder recalled, he had actors, sets and crew, but no male star and was "really up against it." Wilder had the innovative idea of casting Bogart in a romantic part that would be very different from his usual hard-boiled roles. He believed that Bogart could play an older man who was not at all amorous at the beginning but gradually falls in love.

Bogart was never enthusiastic about the part. Samuel Taylor's play *Sabrina Fair* (the basis of the film) had not yet opened and become a success on Broadway, so no one quite realized how good the movie version could be. Wilder and his young co-author Ernest Lehman went to Bogart's house with only half the first draft actually written. Bogart was not pleased that Wilder had originally wanted Grant and had doubts about playing the stuffed-shirt Linus while the handsome William Holden, as his brother and rival, David, got all the best scenes. Wilder promised to take good care of Bogart during the filming, but did not have to persuade him to accept the part. Sam Jaffe and Swifty Lazar, who thought his career would be enhanced if he could play high comedy, talked him into it. Ironically quoting Louis Mayer's dictum, "you must take the bitter with the sour," Bogart said, "All right, I'll do it." Wilder felt he did it mainly for the money.

Sabrina, made in seven weeks in October and November 1953, had a budget of $2,239,000 (about $65,000 a day). Bogart's contract for this film (as well as for *We're No Angels* and *The Desperate Hours,* both 1955) stipulated that he would earn $20,000 a week for ten weeks and $3,333 a day for retakes after that time. He got first-class air fare and a hotel suite in New York, a stand-in and a hairdresser (Verita Peterson) at $300 a week. Just as Edward G. Robinson had always killed Bogart when he was the higher paid star at Warners, so, Wilder said, "of course Bogart gets the girl [in *Sabrina*]. That's because he's getting [two] hundred thousand for the picture, and Holden is getting a hundred and a quarter."[12]

Wilder complained that the star, who had approval of the script, gave him a rough time. Bogart decided that Lazar had given him a "bum steer," and forced Wilder to recast the part and do a lot of rewriting. Several colleagues felt "he was unstable, edgy, still somewhat paranoid [after playing Queeg and] drinking more than was good for him." All this put him on a collision course with his co-stars and with Wilder, whom he had specifically approved in his last Warners contract.

Bogart and Bacall stayed at the St. Regis while filming location shots on Wall Street and the French Line docks. *Sabrina* was also shot on an estate in Glen Cove, Long Island, to suggest the wealthy, glamorous, lavish and hedonistic life of the characters, and give them (as in *Dark Victory*) a "Jay Gatsby look." There was tremendous tension, as in *Casablanca* and *Beat the Devil,* because the writers could scarcely keep up with the camera and wrote most of the script the day before it was shot. Bogart's agent warned Wilder that he was "very unhappy" and was "going to walk."[13]

The previous year Holden and Hepburn had won Oscars, he for *Stalag 17,* she for *Roman Holiday.* Wilder was very friendly with both of them and they formed a clique, hanging around with each other, meeting for drinks at the end of the day and seeing each other socially off the set. Wilder and Holden disliked Bogart and didn't ask him to join their parties because they thought he would spoil their fun. They made him feel like an outsider, even an outcast. By the time they realized he was offended, it was too late to invite him. Though Bogart returned their animosity and didn't want to join their little group, he disliked being excluded and resented the conspiracy against him. Used to filming with Warners or with Santana, where he was treated as a great star, he felt out of place at Paramount, where the whole crew were more sympathetic to Wilder. When Lehman gave copies of the finished script to Wilder, Holden and Hepburn, but forgot to bring one to Bogart, he called Lehman a "City College bum" and (as Hawks had done with Bacall) made an insulting crack about sending him back to Monogram where he belonged.

Bogart reserved his most bitter vitriol for Wilder. When the director added a line to the script, Bogart asked if his eight-year-old daughter had written it. He also suggested that the film was trivial, banal, even stupid. He knew how to put the knife in, mocked Wilder's German accent and spoke of Wilder (who is Jewish) as if he were a Nazi. "'Hey, Vilhelm,' Bogie said in a nasty tone, 'vould you mind translating that into English? I don't schpeak so good the Cherman, *jawohl*.'" He also told the press that the director was overbearing and authoritarian: "Wilder is the kind of Prussian German with a riding crop. He is the type of director I don't like to work with. He works with the writer and excludes the actor. . . . But the picture is a crock of crap. I got sick and tired of who gets Sabrina."[14] Wilder said that he "took it, played it and bitched"—until it became a success.

Wilder was annoyed that Bogart always exercised his contractual right to stop work at exactly 6 P.M. Even if the shot took three hours to light and was all set up, he would deliberately enrage the director by walking out instead of staying on for ten minutes more to finish it. Though Wilder disliked Bogart's unconventional methods, he had to admit that he was a consummate professional: "Bogart is a strange mixture of the laziest and the most conscientious actor. He is an extremely competent s.o.b. He comes on the set on time, but completely unprepared. But by the time the lights are set and, having looked at the particular scene about to be shot for a few minutes, he knows his lines. He never blows them. . . . He doesn't study a script at home at all. He may have a vague conception of what the script is about, but that's all. . . . He gives it to you in short spurts and it looks like a whole thought out conception when it comes out."

Bogart felt Wilder had not kept his promise to take good care of him. Audrey Hepburn had made a great splash in *Roman Holiday*. Wilder, entranced by Hepburn, knew that everyone in the audience wanted to see her strikingly beautiful face and favored her in every scene. Bogart considered her an amateur, thought she had an overblown reputation and resented her instant success. As with Katharine Hepburn in Africa, he also mimicked and bullied Audrey. It was impossible for her to memorize her part because the new pages of script were not delivered until she arrived on the set in the morning. Bogart, an old pro, quickly mastered his lines and got angry when she blew hers. He told her to stay home and study her part (as Lollobrigida had done in *Beat the Devil*) instead of going out with Holden every night and remarked that: "she's all right if you don't mind a dozen takes." The sweet-tempered Hepburn tried to avoid the land mines and stay out of the conflict, but noticed that Bogart seemed nervous in their love scenes. His unusual scenes with Hepburn worked in *Sabrina*, however, as they had not worked in *Battle Circus*. *Sabrina*'s script was excellent and Hepburn, nominated for another Oscar, was an infinitely better actress than Allyson.

Holden had appeared with Bogart in *Invisible Stripes* (1939) and the two men had never got on well. A conservative Republican with a puritan streak, Holden was notoriously critical of Hollywood parties and nightclubs. Bogart openly criticized Holden's acting, as he had criticized Raft's and Lupino's. When Holden heard about these caustic remarks he threatened to kill Bogart and took every opportunity to attack him in the press. In a 1956 interview Holden, scarcely a teetotaler or a model of probity himself—he drank heavily, was very shaky and often blew his lines—made a pompous pronouncement about Bogart's drinking friends and social life: "It's terribly important for people to realize that their conduct reflects on the way in which a nation is represented in the eyes of the world. . . . It might sound stuffy and dull, but it is quite possible for people to have social intercourse without resorting to a rat pack and even to drink or do anything without resorting to a rat pack."[15] He called Bogart "an actor of consummate skill, with an ego to match," and frankly confessed: "I hated that bastard. He was always stirring up things in ways he didn't have to."

Bogart had affairs with Methot during *Marked Woman* and with Bacall during *To Have and Have Not*. He tolerantly observed the affairs of Bette Davis and George Brent while making *Dark Victory* and of Mary Astor and John Huston while shooting *The Maltese Falcon*. But he was outraged by the married Holden's affair with the young Audrey Hepburn, which made her rejection of Holden for Bogart in the movie more piquant and ironic. He not only disliked the actors, but also felt their love life was interfering with her work.[16]

Considering all the problems and the extreme tension on the set, it's amazing that *Sabrina* turned out so well. Hepburn plays the naive and childlike Sabrina, who falls hopelessly in love with the dashing younger son, David. When he refuses to take her seriously, she tries to commit suicide in the closed garage by turning on the engines of the cars. She is saved by the boring old stick Linus, the older brother, who wears a three-piece suit, with tiepin, watch chain and furled umbrella, and runs the family's financial empire. Sabrina is sent to cooking school in Paris and trained by the Baron (Marcel Dalio, the croupier in *Casablanca*), who buys her a magnificent wardrobe. Their friendship stimulates her interest in older men.

She returns to Long Island two years later as a sophisticated young lady with a French poodle named David. She is still determined to marry David Larrabee, who eagerly responds to her flirtations. Wilder wanted Linus to sleep with Sabrina in the picture to show that he loved her; Lehman resisted this and kept them on a romantic level. Wilder wanted David to recognize Sabrina when she returned transformed from Paris; Lehman thought it would be better to delay his recognition during their witty conversation as he drove her from the train station to the estate. But David is now engaged to a wealthy young lady, who quips: "we drained the indoor pool to make room for the wedding presents." The fiancée's father is elegantly played by Francis X. Bushman, the popular silent film star who had appeared in the original *Ben Hur*. The debonair Larrabee père, who struggles to pry olives out of jars for his martinis, resembles a naughty old fellow in one of Peter Arno's *New Yorker* cartoons.

David's dynastic alliance is vital to the business interests of the Larrabees. Linus reluctantly and rather stiffly courts the girl himself, and actually kisses her before David does. He puts on his freshman beanie and Yale sweater, and takes her sailing (as Bogart did with many of his girls). On the boat he confesses that he too is emotionally vulnerable. Hepburn, who wears white with David and black with Linus, says: "It's so strange to think of you being touched by a woman." The shift in Sabrina's love — as Linus' grumpy persistence defeats David's shallow charm — is extremely well done. As he gradually thaws out, she falls in love with Linus and tells him: "It's me that's bothering me." David gives her up when he realizes that Linus, who can't continue to deceive the still-innocent girl, loves her more than he does. In the end, Linus hitches a ride on a tug called the *Maud Larrabee* (named after Bogart's mother), joins Sabrina on the ship to France and marries her himself.

Sabrina, a gentle satire on adolescent love and the mores of the leisure class, is a witty and sophisticated romantic comedy. It portrays the susceptibility of middle-aged men to love, and the power of youth and beauty to cross the boundaries of class. In *Stand-In* Leslie Howard had also played the cold financial genius who finally finds love, but Bogart never got over his initial hostility to the role. He disliked wearing a starched collar and homburg (though he had worn one in *Kid Galahad*) and playing a Wall Street tycoon. He felt he was deliberately miscast, had wanted Bacall for Audrey Hepburn's part and thought the plot, in which he stole the young girl from Holden, was absurd. Despite all his misgivings and conflicts, however, Bogart delivered the lines in his wry, sardonic manner. As Wilder had predicted, his gravity gave depth to the light-hearted film.

♦ 14 ♦

The Desperate Hours

1954-1956

⟨ I ⟩

Beat the Devil, The Caine Mutiny and *Sabrina* provided original parts that, in different ways, had challenged Bogart's ability as an actor. He was not to be so lucky again. The characters he portrayed in his last movies were weaker versions of roles he had done far better in the past. The movie director in *The Barefoot Contessa* and the journalist on the skids in *The Harder They Fall* recall the deteriorating Dixon Steele in *In a Lonely Place*. The essentially good criminals who act like naughty boys and then return to prison in *We're No Angels* hark back to his second movie, *Up the River*. The gunman waiting for his girl to bring the money, holding hostages and pursued by the police in *The Desperate Hours* echoes *The Petrified Forest*. Work on these films coincided with the insidious progress of his fatal disease, and he needed considerable courage to complete them.

Much as he preferred working in Hollywood, where he could live at home, lunch at Romanoff's and sail to Catalina on weekends, Bogart returned to Rome in January 1954 to work on *The Barefoot Contessa* with the writer-director Joseph Mankiewicz. Once more he settled into the luxurious Hotel Excelsior, with Verita now in attendance. Every morning they were picked up by a manic Italian driver for the forty-five-minute sprint to the Cinecittà studios or to outdoor locations around the city. After his previous accident at the hands of an Italian, he was nervous and constantly urged the driver to slow down. Bogart discovered George's, a restaurant near the hotel with an English-speaking bartender and familiar American food. George's and the downstairs bar in the hotel became his nightly hangouts. One evening William Faulkner, a congenial drinking companion since the days of *To Have and Have Not,* turned up and they had dinner together.

Mankiewicz was the last of Bogart's great directors. He had recently won two Oscars two years in a row, for best screenplay and best director of *A Letter to Three Wives* (1950) and *All About Eve* (1951), and was one of the most admired men in Hollywood. According to Warren Stevens, who played Kirk Edwards (the boorish tycoon, modeled on Howard Hughes) in *The Barefoot Contessa,* Bogart had great respect for Mankiewicz. He discussed the essence of every scene with the actors before filming and gave Bogart careful guidance rather than "hard direction." Mankiewicz (like Hawks) remembered the tension between them, in the beginning, as each tried to establish dominance. With a new director and unfamiliar setting, Bogart was careful to protect his own interests. "Bogie wanted you to be afraid of him a little," said Mankiewicz. "He made perfectly sure that you knew he was going to be an unpredictable man. . . . I caught on to that and I played my own little game of keeping him off balance by never giving him his opportunity. You forestall it by kidding him out of it."

The press agent for *The Barefoot Contessa,* David Hanna, noted that Bogart maintained as always his punctuality and high professional standards: "he arrived on the dot, was made up and ready exactly on schedule, never faltered when it came to lines, took direction quietly with a minimum of discussion." But his racking cough — a dangerous yet untreated symptom that began in the early 1940s — caused by chain-smoking and inhaling two packs of Chesterfields every day, led to serious problems on this and subsequent films. Warren Stevens recalled that though Bogart "coughed like mad" before and after work, it didn't seem to interfere with the filming. But Edmond O'Brien (who won an Oscar for his role as the sweaty, sycophantic press agent) remarked that Bogart could not always control his coughing fits: "many takes were printed simply for the lines Mank could get between the coughs."[1]

Ava Gardner played Maria Vargas, the barefoot contessa, a poor Spanish dancer modeled on Rita Hayworth. She is "discovered" by Kirk Edwards, and transformed first into an unhappy movie star and then into the even more unhappy wife of an Italian count. Bogart resented Ava's entourage and, alluding to her habit of going barefoot in the film, said she was a North Carolina hillbilly who should never wear shoes. She had recently left Frank Sinatra, and Bogart disapproved of her current affair with the dazzling Spanish bullfighter Luis Miguel Dominguín. "Half the world's female population would throw themselves at Frank's feet," he told her, "and here you are flouncing around with guys who wear capes and little ballerina slippers."

Maria has several lovers and an aristocratic husband. But she is most deeply (though not sexually) attached to the down-and-out alcoholic movie director Harry Dawes (Bogart) and helps to rescue his career. Their scenes have a certain tenderness when he tries to protect her from exploitation and when she confesses that her war-wounded husband (Rossano Brazzi) is impotent. But Bogart does not spark Gardner into an exciting performance. He disliked her, thought she was not a good enough actress for the difficult part and did not attempt to hide his feelings. He complained about her lifeless response in their scenes and sometimes gave her the wrong line (as he had done with Bacall) in order to get a better take. Gardner loved Europe and thought Bogart provincial because he "hated Italy and lived on ham and eggs and steak whenever he could." She later recalled that he had helped her as an actress, that "he certainly knew a lot more acting tricks than I did, and didn't hesitate to use them. I have to admit he probably forced me into a better performance than I could have managed without him."[2]

The Barefoot Contessa repeats, less successfully, many of the characteristic traits of *All About Eve*. Both slow and talky stories are told through a series of flashbacks and multiple narrators. Both provide an inside view of the theater and movies, and portray the rise and fall of a star. Both have a sweating producer and a sweating PR man, and caricature a ruthless villain (George Sanders and Warren Stevens). Both films lose vital dramatic possibilities by narrating instead of actually showing dramatic scenes like Maria's brilliant flamenco dancing and successful film test.

Mankiewicz also borrows some effective motifs from another movie. Just as the name Harry Dawes recalls Harry Lime, so Maria's rainy funeral in the statue-filled Roman cemetery, which opens *The Barefoot Contessa,* echoes the funeral in the Viennese cemetery that concludes *The Third Man* (1949). In the flashback that follows the funeral we see Maria's meteoric career and Dawes' Faustian bargain, during which he trades personal integrity for wealth and fame. After Maria leaves Kirk Edwards for another millionaire, Alberto Bravano (based on the playboy son of the Bolivian tin magnate Simón Patiño), the movie breaks in half. It shifts from Rome to the French Riviera, introduces a new set of characters and assumes a different tone. After she takes a gypsy lover from her own class, the Italian count rescues Maria from Bravano. The count brings her to his villa and they marry, but he does not reveal until after the wedding that a war wound has made him impotent. Maria, surrounded by wealth and luxury, is isolated and frightened. Bravano, who captured but failed to seduce Maria, had taunted her that she was not a woman. Now she is shattered by the revelation that her husband is not a man.

The self-consciously literary film, trying to hit too many targets, draws on the relations of the impotent man and unfulfilled woman in Hemingway's *The Sun Also Rises* (1926) and in D. H. Lawrence's *Lady Chatterley's*

Lover (1928). In Hemingway's novel Jake Barnes' war wound, which destroys his sexual capacity without eliminating his desire, leads to tender and tragic relations with Brett Ashley. The count's wound, by contrast, leads merely to courtly behavior and cruel deception. Lawrence's impotent aristocrat urges his frustrated wife to produce a son and heir with a lusty young man. The count also wants a son to carry on his noble line, but when he discovers that Maria is pregnant by her gypsy, he jealously kills her.

Bogart's six major scenes with Gardner establish and develop his protective attitude toward her. In her dressing room in the Madrid café he boldly peeks under a curtain to find her standing barefoot with her lover. Though she's angered by his intrusion, he soon wins her over as they joke and laugh together about the lover she likes to call her "cousin." Despite her stunning figure and low-cut blouse, Bogart always looks at her face. His honest concern contrasts with the predatory exploitation of Kirk Edwards and his sleazy press agent. Bogart squirms and looks exasperated when the agent, to impress Maria, praises his talent and Edwards' generosity, and he's the only man who stands up when she leaves their table. In the next scene, he follows Maria home to persuade her to accept their offer to make her a star. He listens patiently when she speaks, looks at her intently as if trying to gauge her prospects, and speaks slowly to suggest thoughtfulness and gravity. When she leaves her shoes behind, he carefully picks them up and carries them away. At her party in Hollywood, Bogart looks down with embarrassment when a vulgar woman questions Maria about her lovers, and makes a sincere plea for her to remain there to continue her spectacular career.

When they meet in Italy just before her wedding, his steady gaze shows his deep affection for her as she pours out her idealized love for the count who has not yet become her lover. Fearful that her fairy tale may be shattered, he asks: "Are you happy?" Then, lowering his voice, he hesitantly concludes: "Then I am happy." At her wedding party, he again conveys his doubts by taking a deep breath and looking down while trying to warn her of the dangers ahead. When they meet in his hotel room three months later, he's clearly concerned about her latest revelation. Angry at her infidelity, he clasps his hands together in a rare dramatic gesture and tries to convince her that the count will not accept her lover's baby as his own. He looks out the rainy window as she drives away to her doom, and in the final scene takes the shoes off her dead body. The film sags when Bogart is absent and revives when he reappears. He adds an element of virility that the count lacks, and enhances the display of Gardner's flamboyant character with his own quiet reserve.

The Barefoot Contessa—a sort of Star Is Stillborn—satirizes the glamour of stardom and glory of war, the joyless and impotent wealth of phoney international "society." But it depends on cinematic clichés—the count slaps Bravano's face and carries his wife's dead body in the rain—to convey its ideas. Its portrayal of the movie world is not as witty as *Stand-In* or as incisive as *In a Lonely Place*. Bogart's performance as a caustic, disillusioned yet sympathetic observer of Maria's troubled life is authentic and convincing. He breathes some harsh realism into a hothouse film that gets carried away with technicolor scenery, Spanish dancing and decadent Italian aristocrats.

‹ II ›

VERITA PETERSON had accompanied Bogart, as his contract specified, on *The African Queen* publicity tour to New York, Chicago, Houston, Salt Lake City and Las Vegas in 1951. In their Chicago hotel he told her: "I've got to have some Scotch and soda up here. I can't take this city cold sober." Surveying Salt Lake City from a hotel window, he found the Mormon teetotalers even more alien and terrifying: "the whole city is sober—the whole state, even. Can you imagine that? We're surrounded by sober!" Ernest Lehman, co-author of *Sabrina*, found Verita quite sexy and noted that the two were very close. Bogart confided in her and she knew him very well. If he needed a forbidden drink on the set, she would place a handkerchief over his whiskey and carry it over to him. Verita had stayed home when Bacall went with Bogart to Mexico and Africa. But in January 1954, when Bacall remained with the children in Los Angeles, Bogart took Verita to make *The Barefoot Contessa*. In the romantic setting of Rome they resumed the love affair that had begun when he was married to Mayo in 1942.

Bacall—carrying a coconut cake across the ocean as a peace offering from Sinatra to Gardner (Ava, in love with Dominguín, didn't want Frank or his cake)—joined Bogart in February. She dislodged Verita from his hotel room and disrupted their intimacy off the set. Verita considered Bacall a "pretentious, opportunistic interloper" who had moved into her territory and stolen Bogart away from her while she was trying to get a wartime divorce. She loved to record Bogart's cracks about his wife. Bogart said that he wouldn't have time to spend all the money in his large expense account, "but Baby will be here in a couple of weeks, and she'll go through this stuff faster than the government can print it." Sure enough, Bacall "drove Bogart to distraction with her shopping" in Rome. Warren Stevens took a car trip with the Bogarts and Verita after the film was completed. Though Bacall had just arrived, Bogart loyally insisted that Verita go with them. Bacall must have been jealous, but she held all the cards. Stevens saw no tension between the two women, who seemed to get along very well. Though Bogart had fallen romantically in love with Bacall, Verita drank with him, enjoyed sailing and was more of a pal than his wife.

The travelers stopped in Florence, but Bogart, claiming that "all places look alike," had no interest in the sights. According to Verita, he headed instead for the bars. Stevens, however, recalled that they went shopping on the Ponte Vecchio and did some sightseeing in Florence. Bogart saw the paintings in the Uffizi, Verita and Bacall giggled at the massive naked-ness of Michelangelo's *David*. They were the only guests at the Albergo Splendido in Portofino on the Italian Riviera, and during the heavy February rains Bogart taught Stevens how to play chess. In Genoa, the birthplace of Columbus, they were entertained by the conservative mayor. Unable to resist needling Stevens, Bogart jokingly told the mayor that Stevens was a Communist. Upset and angered, Stevens walked to the end of a jetty to cool off and gazed out to sea. Bogart followed him and, trying to placate his sensitive companion, looked out at the water and said: "I know! The world is round!" Bogart liked to be provocative and then use all his charm to win back his friends' affection.

Bogart once told a journalist that he got his scar when Verita bit him on the lip. In New York in 1954, when Verita was lunching with Bogart at the St. Regis Hotel, the gossip columnist Earl Wilson leaned over and asked him who Verita was. Just as he had once shocked his yachting friends when introducing Mayo, Bogart now grinned at Wilson and said: "Oh, she's my mistress."[3] Verita was so discreet that the ravenous gossip columnists never learned of their affair, but Bogart sometimes teased journalists by openly acknowledging it. Like Poe's purloined letter, no one noticed it, or was able to use it against him.

< III >

We're No Angels (1955), which followed the adventure comedy of *The African Queen* and the romantic comedy of *Sabrina,* was based on a French farce. Paramount's reader liked the play and emphasized its potential as a film: "This is a delightful comedy which has had considerable

success in Paris. Typically French in its mixture of cynicism and sentiment, it is well constructed with some good dialogue, and its strongest
suit is its characterization. It has a flavour of [Jean] Anouilh, but is kinder
and has more heart. Delicately handled, it would have film possibilities of
a specialist type." Julius Epstein did the first version of the screenplay,
originally called *Angels' Cooking* (a literal translation of the French *La
Cuisine des Anges,* 1952), but did not get screen credit.

With Bogart and Aldo Ray, Peter Ustinov played one of three escaped
convicts, wearing homespun prison uniforms, who take refuge with a
draper's family in Cayenne, French Guiana, on Christmas Eve, 1895.
While making the film Bogart invited the actor to dinner, just after
Ustinov's daughter was born, and made a deflating wisecrack that revealed
he could be more comical off screen than on:

> His face, so human and involuntarily kind, turned into the
> disenchanted mask he was known by. . . .
>
> "Congratulations, [Bogart said] and all that usual crap. I
> can just hear in my head the noise those women in the living-
> room are going to make when you tell them." And, [Ustinov
> wrote] holding a tray of drinks, he did a wonderfully overdrawn
> imitation of a roomful of women greeting the news of a child-
> birth. "Aaaoow—."
>
> We went into the living-room together. Bogie said he had
> an announcement to make, and spoke in the dead tones of a
> ring-side announcer. "Peter's just become the proud father of
> a baby girl. Both mother and child are doing well."
>
> "Aaaaooow—."
>
> Bogie gave me the filthiest of his enviable repertoire of
> filthy looks, while he dispensed his martinis. I recognized that
> his imitation was not overdrawn at all.

Ustinov later compared Bogart to "a sad, wrinkled pedigree dog" and
Bacall to "a dish full of condiments."

This picture also revealed the generous side of Bogart's character. He
often hired colleagues who had been blacklisted or had even named
names, and had assisted Marcel Dalio, Robert Warwick and Peter Lorre
when they were down. In *We're No Angels* and *The Left Hand of God* he
also helped two good actresses who had serious personal problems and
found it difficult to get work. In 1951 Walter Wanger, who had produced
Stand-In and was married to Joan Bennett, shot her lover (who was also
her agent) and was sent to prison. Jack Warner, shocked by the scandal,

said Wanger and Bennett could never again work at his studio. Bogart invited the Wangers to dinner at his home and revived her career by insisting (as Leslie Howard had once done for him) that she appear in his film. Bennett later paid tribute to his kindness: "The indomitable Humphrey Bogart stood up to be counted as one of my staunchest supporters. Paramount was planning *We're No Angels* starring Bogart, and in the face of vigorous opposition, he told the studio heads he wouldn't do the film unless I played the principal female role. In Hollywood, he fought not only his own battles but everyone else's, and he made the stand to show what he thought of the underground movement to stamp out Joan Bennett."[4]

We're No Angels, made in six weeks in June and July 1954, had a budget of $1,685,000. Bogart got his usual $200,000, Ustinov $40,000 and Aldo Ray $35,000. Bogart rehearsed for three days and worked for thirty-six days of the shooting. In this movie, as in *Passage to Marseilles* (both directed by Michael Curtiz), Bogart plays a Frenchman who escapes from Devil's Island. (He *leaves* for Devil's Island, a favorite locale in Hollywood films, at the end of *To Have and Have Not.*) Moved by the Christmas spirit, shamelessly exploited in the movie, the kindly convicts perform a series of good deeds. Using a poisonous pet viper to dispatch a greedy uncle and his nephew, they divert the uncle's money to the needy family and match the pretty daughter with a white-uniformed French officer who "looks like a glass of milk." After completing their mission, they happily return to prison—which seems more like a tropical resort than a penal colony. This labored farce lacks Curtiz' characteristic pace and the feeble jokes ("We'll cut their throats after we wash the dishes") are as flat as a collapsed soufflé. The arch fable does not give Bogart (always weak on whimsy) much scope, but allows him to do a light-hearted take-off of his convict roles.

In *We're No Angels,* Bogart had parodied the Three Wise Men who follow the star to Bethlehem. In *The Left Hand of God* (directed by Edward Dmytryk for Twentieth Century–Fox and released in 1955), he spends most of the movie impersonating a dead priest in order to escape the bondage of a Chinese warlord, ponderously acted by Lee J. Cobb with a shaved Yul Brynner head. A pilot in four previous pictures (the Warner Brothers were almost as aeronautical as the Wright Brothers), Bogart now plays Jim Carmody, an American airman shot down in China during World War II. The first version of the screenplay was written for RKO by William Faulkner, who had co-authored the two Hawks-Bogart films and written the treatment of *The Two Mrs. Carrolls.* After winning the Nobel Prize in

1949 his salary had gone up from $300 to $2,000 a week. Though Faulkner failed to animate the inert story, Fox paid RKO $110,000 (including $10,000 in legal fees) for the script and rights.

Darryl Zanuck, the head of Fox, carefully supervised all the stages of the film. In March 1954, a year before the shooting began, he told one of the writers that when Bogart first arrives at the Chinese mission the audience should assume he's really a priest and gradually learn that he's only pretending to be one. His personal background and feud with the warlord, Zanuck felt, had to be clearly established. Just before the movie went into production Zanuck, unhappy with the depiction of Bogart's character in the first version of the script, told the producer Buddy Adler: "I believe we should take more advantage of the Humphrey Bogart type. Carmody in his dialogue is written a trifle too much like a straight leading man. He should be more cynical, hard-boiled and a trifle more bitter. The great value of the story is that you take a cynical, hard-bitten, tough guy and compel him to impersonate a priest."

The film was shot in thirty-one days, in March and April 1955, with retakes and additional scenes completed later in June. Bogart got $250,000 ($50,000 more than usual), Gene Tierney $100,000. Bogart, who first appears on a broken-down mule, had to do a good deal of horseback riding in the film. He was recovering from a slipped disc, but did not complain about his pain. He continued to chain-smoke his Chesterfields, would break into paroxysms of coughing for several minutes at a time and often held up the shooting.

Bogart could always be relied upon to play a hard-boiled type. Now, in a Pat O'Brien role, he turns up in a clerical rig at a spanking-clean Chinese mission, the outline of his revolver showing beneath his cassock. But all Zanuck's tinkering with the script could not make him credible in this bogus version of what could have been called *The Bad Earth*. (The fake Oriental "mountains" seem lifted from the Paramount logo.) Bogart reaches a low point in his career when he leads a group of pigtailed Chinese children in a sentimental version of "My Old Kentucky Home." The hard-nosed Zanuck, who thought he knew what the mass audience liked, felt this was "very moving and very touching."

Bogart, a wolf in priest's clothing, delivers a sermon in impeccable Mandarin and quotes St. Paul to a Protestant minister: "I'm fresh out of faith, hope and charity, Reverend." He also sanctimoniously tells a peasant whose wife has just died in childbirth: "I think she's now with Someone who loves her as much as you do." Offering religiosity instead of religion, the movie neither emphasizes the ironic aspects of Bogart's impersonation nor exploits the dramatic potential of Tierney's forbidden love for a "priest." The audience could get more authentic atmosphere by sending out for Chinese food.

When Bogart is recaptured by Cobb, he gains his freedom by rolling dice with his former master and saves the village from the evil bandits. After making his peace with the local bishop, he clears the way for an unfettered reunion with the high-cheekboned, high-breasted Tierney. One critic observed that *The Left Hand of God* offers "a quaint variation of the standard western theme. . . . The hardfaced, gun-toting stranger rides into town and endears himself to the local populace before the evil land-baron muscles in to hold the town for ransom. In a showdown the stranger wrests the township from the badman's clutches." The *Hollywood Reporter* noted that Bogart, doing his best with a weak role, "manages to be inspirational without being preachy, a rare thing in religious pictures."

Just as Bogart had insisted on working with Joan Bennett after she'd been blacklisted by scandal, so he also agreed to work with the unstable Gene Tierney. She had a retarded child who was placed in an institution, and had been incapacitated by several nervous breakdowns. Shakily emerging from a sanatorium, her eyes seemed strangely wandering and unfocused. Zanuck wanted to give her a break, but Bogart had the right to reject her as co-star. Though usually critical of actors who were unprepared and made mistakes, he was as patient with Tierney's mental illness as he had been with Pat Bogart's and Mayo Methot's, and helped her complete the picture. Tierney later described her own unstable condition and expressed gratitude for Bogart's solicitude and sympathy:

> By the time I finished *The Left Hand of God,* with Humphrey Bogart, I was so ill, so far gone, that it became an effort every day not to give up. . . . The picture was the fourth I had made even as I felt my mind begin to unravel. I could not hold thoughts. I had no appetite. I felt scared for no reason. . . . [Bogart] recognized the signs, went to the studio bosses and warned them I was sick and needed help.
>
> They assumed that I was a trouper, was aware how much had been invested in the film and would not let them down. They suggested that Bogart be kind and gentle. He was nothing less. His patience and understanding carried me through the film. We did not know then that he was himself terminally ill with cancer.[5]

‹ IV ›

AFTER THREE technicolor movies, Bogart went back to the sharp contrasts and shadowy style of black and white photography, and to the tough characters and stark realism he had perfected in the 1930s. Bogart and Spencer Tracy wanted to appear together in *The Desperate Hours* (1955), but they could not agree on who would get top billing. Fredric March, who was paid $75,000, took over Tracy's role. Set in Indianapolis and based on the successful novel and play by Joseph Hayes, the film was shot in two months, from October to December 1954, on a budget of $2,388,000. On October 28 the unit manager reported a series of typical technical problems: a ten-minute delay due to buckled film, a fifteen-minute delay due to cable failure and a twenty-minute delay due to power pack trouble. In November, as Bogart was talking on the set to Eleanor Roosevelt (Katharine Hepburn's model in *The African Queen*), a 1,000-watt seal-beam spotlight suddenly exploded. Shielding the nine-year-old Richard Eyer (who played the son of the family taken hostage by Bogart and his gang), he was cut by pieces of flying glass.

Bogart had always been ill at ease with small children. He found it hard to relate to the kids who appear in his movies and never acts as naturally with them as he does with adults. He kidnaps a kid and his mother in *Three on a Match,* has a stereotyped son in *Black Legion* and a cute little daughter in *The Great O'Malley.* He murders the mother of his English daughter in *The Two Mrs. Carrolls* and rescues his daughter from the Japs at the end of *Tokyo Joe.* In *The Desperate Hours* he threatens to murder the boy (a typically cute child, rather like the kid in *Black Legion*) as he had done in *Three on a Match.*

The Desperate Hours, directed by William Wyler, who also did *Dead End,* recycles the plots of several earlier films. It has the same innocents-taken-hostage and evil-defeated theme as *Key Largo,* and was also based on a Broadway play and filmed with a stagey setting. In *We're No Angels* three comic escaped convicts invade a household and act benevolently; in *The Desperate Hours* three evil escaped convicts, led by Glenn Griffin (Bogart), invade a household and threaten to kill the family.

A fatal weakness in the later film, which minimizes the inherent sadism and violence, is that the criminals threaten but never actually harm the sacrosanct family. The unspeakably crude Sam Kobish (played by Robert Middleton) is easily tricked by Dan Hilliard (Fredric March). Glenn Griffin's handsome younger brother Hal (Dewey Martin), though lusting after the daughter of the house, behaves like a perfect gentleman.

Griffin snarls: "If I see a single light go on—the kid gets it. . . . If you pull anything, Hilliard, I'll let you watch me kick the kid's face in," but patiently tolerates the antics of the irritating little boy.

After Hal flees and Kobish is shot, Hilliard recovers his courage and faces down Griffin by telling him: "I got it in me. You put it there." He tricks Griffin by giving him an unloaded gun (the old Bogart would have checked for bullets) just before the climactic shootout. In *The Big Shot* and *To Have and Have Not* Bogart had escaped by shooting out the lights of a prison stage and a Vichy patrol boat. Griffin now shoots out the searchlight of the cops who have surrounded the house. But, slipping out unarmed and trying to escape through the police cordon, he is inevitably shot down.

The studio's publicity pamphlet boasted that "Bogart is back in the type of role that made him famous!" But if *The Petrified Forest* and *Dead End*, filmed in the 1930s, had seemed too constricted and close to the stage versions, *The Desperate Hours* lost the theatrical intensity of the original play. Paul Newman, who played Bogart's role opposite Karl Malden on Broadway, observed that "they made a lot of mistakes in the movie. They let it go outside of the house. . . . That whole sense of confinement and oppression was lost."

On May 30, 1955, six months after completing *The Desperate Hours,* Bogart recreated the stage and film versions of *The Petrified Forest* in a ninety-minute television adaptation on NBC's "Producer's Showcase." As in the theater, there were long rehearsals and a live performance. Henry Fonda took Leslie Howard's role, Bacall had Bette Davis' part, and each of the actors earned $50,000. It was directed by the talented Delbert Mann, who had just won an Academy Award for *Marty.* Bogart had a terrible hacking cough during rehearsals, but on the live telecast—when mistakes could not be corrected—he was flawless.

Bogart was as generous with Bacall in 1955, when her career was in the doldrums, as he had been a decade earlier in *To Have and Have Not.* According to Delbert Mann, he was mainly interested in "showcasing" Bacall. She had no theatrical experience, was extremely nervous and risked disaster. But Mann was pleased with her performance, which helped start her successful Broadway career. The play had been shortened by an hour and Bogart's role had, with his consent, been cut. He didn't ask for more lines and when someone suggested that his part be increased, said: "We don't need that. Leave it out." Though rather old for the part, now slower and more weary, he was as effective as he had been in the original stage and film versions. But the sophisticated Bacall, miscast as Gabrielle, was much weaker than the fresh and childlike Bette Davis. The whole production, which stressed Bacall's romance rather than Bogart's violence, seems talky, static and melodramatic, and lacks the dynamic connection of the three main characters in the film.

The producer Harry Sosnick remembered that Bogart maintained a fine line between discipline and hedonism: "The entire *Petrified Forest* takes place in a roadhouse, and a lot of it is done sitting around a table, Fonda and Bogart, with liquor bottles. They had colored water in the bottles all during the day, but at 5 o'clock, those bottles had to have real liquor, and there was hell to pay if the stagehand forgot to put them up. He was very temperamental about that." When told that his first and only dramatic performance on television had the largest viewing audience in history, Bogart coolly replied: "I don't give a damn if the whole world watches."[6]

The reviews were extremely favorable and praised Bogart's masterful —and slightly self-parodic—performance. *Variety* said: "This is Bogart in the type of role that cues comics to caricature takeoffs. Here he's at his best, a tough gunman capable of murder, snarling delight at the way his captives must abide by his orders, and animal-instinctive in the ways of self-preservation." The *New York Times,* confirming this judgment, was even more enthusiastic: "Mr. Bogart has been so identified with the part that he virtually has made it his own. Last night, in what was his debut on a live television drama, he was cold, vicious and convincingly peremptory. Few actors can suggest so much evil so quietly."

During rehearsals in Hollywood, where the program was made, the Bogarts gave a big party for the New Yorkers on the staff and invited a lot of celebrities. Henry Fonda, who had had a non-speaking part in *I Loved You Wednesday,* was overcome by a battery of Frank Sinatra's potent grasshoppers: "Bogie and Frank carried me back to the Beverly Hills Hotel, undressed me, and put me to bed. I do recall thinking, 'I should be embarrassed, but I ain't. I'm too drunk.'"[7]

In his last film, his best since *The African Queen,* Bogart played with complete conviction the kind of man he always feared he might become: a professional who had fallen from eminence to degradation. In 1937 he had made the boxing movie *Kid Galahad,* which also emphasized the racketeers' control of prizefighting, and now went to the fights at Madison Square Garden to prepare for *The Harder They Fall* (1956). The film was closely based on the career of Primo Carnera. The 6'6", 260-pound Italian had been the world heavyweight boxing champion in 1933, but was defeated by Max Baer the following year and left penniless after two successive knockouts in 1936. He later appeared as a heavy in several Hollywood movies. George Raft's biographer called Carnera a "pathetic giant reputed to have earned [a gangster's] combine a million dollars before the duped fighter, a man broken down physically, emotionally and financially, was finally told to go home after he was almost killed in the ring by a vicious slugger and honest champion Max Baer." In the film Mike Lane, who played Toro Moreno and would later appear in *Frankenstein 70* with almost no make-up, is beaten by the real Max Baer in the most realistic and brutal boxing scene ever shot. Moreno, who has a naive faith in the system, his bosses and his dangerously limited ability as a boxer, winds up looking like a Francis Bacon painting of raw meat.

Bogart is superb as the weary, disillusioned ex–sports columnist Eddie Willis. Out of a job and desperate for work, he agrees to publicize the Argentinian giant with "a powder-puff punch and a glass jaw" for the corrupt fight promoter Nick Benko (Rod Steiger). After a series of profitably fixed fights, Moreno is savaged by Baer. Then—in a cruel and magnificent scene—he's told that his net earnings during all that time amount to a total of $49. Disgusted with Benko, Willis gives Moreno his $26,000 share of the proceeds, puts him on the plane to Argentina so he can escape from another murderous tour and decides to expose his corrupt boss. Philip Yordan, who wrote the screenplay based on the novel by Budd Schulberg, described Bogart's dissatisfaction with his role: "Steiger's part was the picture. Bogart had a contract with Columbia, so he had to do the picture, and he had no role. He raised hell and gave me a bad time. He behaved very badly on the picture because it wasn't his picture. . . . He was supposed to be playing a weak man who sold out. He didn't want to play that."

Bogart's character, who doesn't in fact sell out at the end, was much better than Yordan suggested. But there was considerable tension between him and Steiger, who had the better part and stole the film as Edward G. Robinson had done in *Key Largo*. Steiger's intense and introspective, egoistic and neurotic Method acting—which encouraged performers to respond as much to their own deepest feelings as to the requirements of the text (Steiger called this "not what the character would do, but what *you* would do if you were the character")—was the antithesis of Bogart's more restrained and natural style.[8]

Steiger had been trained in the Actors Studio in New York, whose Method involved physical exercise on the set and "a great deal of muttering to himself." Bogart complained that "he couldn't work with Steiger, whose mumbling of his lines made Bogart miss his cues. 'Why the hell,' he asked, 'don't they learn to speak properly? Words are important. This scratch-your-ass-and-mumble school of acting doesn't please me.'" He also warned a friend: "Don't ever play an eating scene with them, because they spit all over you." When Nunnally Johnson remarked that Steiger must have been a great nuisance to work with, Bogart revealed his method of handling him: "Well, he's all right, if you'll be patient and wait for the cue. If he's got a line like, 'Hey you, come here,' that's the way it's written in the script, he'll say, 'You, you, you—here, I mean you, you, come here, come here, here'—there's an awful lot of that goes on. But if you wait, eventually he'll get around to saying, 'Hey you, come here.' And you can go ahead with it." Yet Steiger was an impressively powerful actor who could express his rage through the inflection rather than the volume of his voice. Though Bogart hated "emoting" and loved to needle his rival, he also confessed that Steiger's passionate performance was "blowing me off the screen."[9]

Bogart's mockery was intensely irritating, but Steiger later ignored their bitter disputes. Instead, he emphasized Bogart's professional standards and personal courage as well as the eyes that reflected his fatal illness:

> I had a part that was better than his, on paper. We discussed it together, and he used to kid me, "Oh, you son-of-a-bitch, you know you're killing me." I'd say, "Gee, Bogie, that's the way it's written, really." . . .
>
> Bogart was made out of tougher stuff. When I did the last film with him—*The Harder They Fall*—he died after that. He had cancer through that whole film, and not one of us ever knew this man was ill. . . . Once he didn't like one or two scenes because he had "a watery look in his eye," and that remark stuck with me when he died. . . . I don't know if it was because it was his last film or tears of pain. . . .
>
> Mr. Bogart was a gentleman. He was a man of honor, which is hard to find today in this business. . . . I think the most important thing about him was that he was a very courageous human being. I enjoyed working with him, and he was very kind to me.

The film opens as three cars suddenly converge for a sleazy meeting at a New York gym and Willis (who immediately lights a cigarette) agrees to promote for Benko the fragile giant who lacks the killer instinct. Willis is tormented by conscience as he sells out; his wife, who as always stands for decent values, criticizes his behavior and reinforces his guilt. Torn between loyalty and corruption, the only good man among the hoods, Willis opposes Benko even as he submits to him. As the impotent rage of Bogart's character boils into action, his personal hostility to Steiger sharpens and intensifies his performance.

The picture has the same fast pace and crisp, memorable dialogue as *The Maltese Falcon* and *Casablanca*. When Willis' guests turn up at a publicity party, he jokingly calls them "freeloaders"—just as Bogart did with his own friends. When discussing where to have the opening fights, Willis suggests: "Send him to California. They like freak attractions there." Having lost his self-esteem, he confesses to Moreno: "I did this for the money. Same as you." In one of the many agonizing scenes, Willis humiliates himself by begging his broadcaster friend not to reveal that the fights are fixed.

Steiger's Nick Benko is a riveting portrait of utter ruthlessness. After Moreno's manager is sent back to Argentina, Benko takes complete control and the boxer becomes his helpless victim. When his assistant wants to order sandwiches during a hospital visit to a mortally injured boxer, he snarls: "What's the matter? You're trying to make a picnic of this?" He believes all human beings are expendable ("Fighters come and go. Managers stay on forever"), and moves from the hypocritical "nobody gets hurt" to the savage "I don't care what happens to him, but get him in the ring." At the sad end of the picture Willis is corrupted and Moreno, beaten to a pulp, is brutally discarded. Willis must purify himself by giving away the tainted money he has earned. Though Benko (like the criminal at the end of *Deadline—U.S.A.*) will not meekly submit to exposure and destruction, the morally revived Willis must now risk his life to stop him.

The Harder They Fall extends the tradition of boxing films that runs from *Body and Soul* (1947) and *The Champion* (1949) to John Huston's seamy *Fat City* (1972). The producer, Jerry Wald, said the studio loved the film, but the audience didn't like it because it dealt only with one emotion: "sheer brutality."[10] But the movie has a moral dimension that transcends its subject matter and also deals with more significant themes: friendship, loyalty, conscience, trust, idealism and the desire to cleanse the world of evil. It portrays (like *The Barefoot Contessa*) a Faustian pact in which Willis trades his integrity, his very soul, for material reward. Benko, who exploits other men's work and blood, is a modern devil. The broken-down Willis seems a perfect tool for Benko, but ultimately becomes the modern anti-hero who has to fight him. Bogart was perfectly suited to play the ambiguous and difficult role of a weak man who tries to preserve a shred of his own dignity and finally refuses to give in to evil.

Bogart had not sold out or compromised his professional principles and had reached the end of an immensely distinguished career with his personal and artistic integrity miraculously intact. Neither arrogant nor materialistic, he liked plain living and retained his old-fashioned gentlemanly values. He was devoted to his family, loyal to friends, generous to those fallen on hard times. Formidably direct and honest, he kept his built-in shit detector finely tuned. Remarkably sane and modest for an actor, he rejected the flattery of courtiers and toadies. He got along without a personal astrologer, didn't need anyone to massage his back or ego and survived twenty-five years in Hollywood without a drug problem, a nervous breakdown or a psychiatrist.

✦ 15 ✦

A Respectable Disease

1956-1957

⟨ I ⟩

PERSISTENT COUGHING began to interfere with Bogart's work on *The Barefoot Contessa* in January 1954. They lasted for as long as thirty minutes, and left him exhausted and gasping for air. During these spasms he would instinctively touch his breastbone. Underneath, it turned out, was the fatal site of his disease. He had once completely lost his voice in Europe and had a skin cancer removed from the top of his ear. But he ignored the danger signs, refused to have a check-up and insisted, "There's nothing wrong with me."

When Bogart told Greer Garson that orange juice burned his throat, she was disturbed by the symptoms and urged him to seek medical advice. At Mike Romanoff's Valentine's Day party in February 1956, Amanda Dunne noticed that he couldn't swallow and didn't eat. She told him that her brother had had the same problem and that the cause had been psychological. Bogart, much relieved, asked, "Then it wasn't cancer?" and promised to see a doctor immediately. But the throat and lung cancer specialist he consulted, Dr. Maynard Brandsma, found nothing on the X-rays. He merely put him on a diet and told him to cut down his drinking and smoking. This allowed the disease to continue its rampaging course.

Bogart had never been seriously ill before. In his mid-fifties, he could reasonably expect to live for another twenty years. But in late February 1956 he was horrified to learn that he had cancer of the esophagus, the tubular canal that leads from the throat to the stomach. His drinking and smoking had certainly increased the chances of getting the disease, which is difficult to detect. Symptoms do not appear until the cancer has penetrated the nearby lymph nodes and from there spread dangerously through the body. Then, as now, the prognosis is poor and victims have a very high fatality rate.

Echoing Duke Mantee's most famous line in *The Petrified Forest* ("it looks like I'll spend the rest of my life dead"), Bogart told Bacall: "I've never spent much time with doctors. Now I'll probably spend the rest of my life with them." Bacall's mother moved into their house on South Mapleton Drive to help care for Bogart, and Bacall nursed him as faithfully as Maud had once nursed Belmont. Shocked by the illness that seemed a betrayal, a judgment and a curse, he hovered (like most patients) between realistic acceptance and hopeful self-deception. "We can't kid ourselves. We know what this stuff is all about, don't we?" he told Verita. "If you've got this damn stuff, you've had it. They'll probably cut my throat from ear to ear." Reacting angrily to the stigma attached to cancer, he also used the past tense and remarked: "Why shouldn't I say I had cancer. It's a respectable disease. It's nothing to be ashamed of." Ignoring its seriousness, he concluded: "It's no worse than gallstones or appendicitis."[1]

Maynard Brandsma referred Bogart to the Irish-born Dr. Michael Flynn, who did the biopsy and diagnosed the tumor—nine inches from Bogart's incisor tooth and in the middle of the chest—precisely where he felt the pain. To fortify himself in the hospital, Bogart brought in a pile of detective stories, a chess set and two bottles of whiskey. The chest surgeon, John Jones, performed the long, difficult nine-and-a-half-hour operation at the Good Samaritan Hospital on Wilshire Boulevard on February 29, 1956.

The esophagus is hidden inside the body and there is normally no need for anyone to come near it. But the surgeon, in the most frightening way, now opened Bogart's body, uncovered the damaged tissue and cut it out. Entering through his neck and chest, Dr. Jones removed a rib and most of the esophagus. After excising the tumor, he detached and sewed the jejunum (a portion of the small intestine, attached to the stomach) to the remaining upper tab of the esophagus. Since the lack of muscle control in this newly created tube channeled food directly into the stomach, the surgeon also cut the vagus nerve, which controls acid production, so that Bogart could digest his food without feeling nauseated.[2]

The cancer, not confined to the esophagus, had spread to the neighboring lymph nodes, which also had to be removed. Bacall (though not Bogart) knew he was doomed and could live for only a year or two at most. In fact, he lived for only ten and a half more months. But she planned for the future, decorated the house and continued to work in films, carrying on their normal life and rather desperately maintaining the fiction that he would recover. It was one of her finest performances.

In March 1956, during his three weeks in the hospital, a violent spasm of coughing tore open his stitches and blood poured out of his stomach.

In April and May Bogart had radiation treatments to retard the progress of his fatal illness. Every day for eight weeks, at the Los Angeles Tumor Institute, he was subjected to a machine that produced a million volts of radiation. The radiation was followed by a cobalt treatment, in which a radioactive substance was placed next to the tumor to destroy malignant cells. Bogart knew it was "the last resort in cancer treatment." This radiation therapy made him feel even more nauseated. He lost his appetite, couldn't eat and began to lose weight—inexorably slipping from a slim 155 to a ghastly 80 pounds. The slow destruction of his body, the increasing pain and humiliation of his illness, the diminution of his health and hope, exposed his physical and psychological nakedness and made him recognize his lonely vulnerability. Drawing on his deepest resources, he faced his radical treatments (a modern form of torture) with impressive fortitude.

⟨ II ⟩

BOGART WAS NOT TOLD that his condition was terminal and never discussed his impending death with Bacall. During these agonizing months he tried to keep his spirits up by making plans to resume his film career. "Bogie's main thought and yearning throughout his illness," Bacall wrote, "was only for work. If he could just work, he knew he would be well." Or, to put it another way, if he could work, it meant that he *was* well. He bought the rights to John Marquand's novel about an army officer, *Melville Goodwin, USA,* which he wanted to make with Bacall, and CBS bought Scott Fitzgerald's final novel, *The Last Tycoon,* for them to do on television. John Huston, as early as 1953, had wanted him to star in a movie version of Kipling's "The Man Who Would Be King." But after the torments of the Congo, Bogart didn't want to go to India. In 1956, when Bogart's last film was released, Huston told one of his backers that the Kipling story (which Huston finally made with Sean Connery and Michael Caine in 1975), "has been called off for another year. There are various reasons, but the most important is Bogey's illness."[3]

Harry Cohn, the head of Columbia, had released Santana's films and then bought the company. He was one of the most unpleasant men in Hollywood, but Bogart admired his energy and got on well with him. Cohn repeatedly announced that Bogart would appear in *The Good Shepherd,* based on the best-selling novel by C. S. Forester, who had written *The African Queen.* Cohn phoned Bogart every week, emphasized what a great part it was and told him that they were ready to start rolling as soon as he was well. Bogart confided to a friend: "Tell you why I think I'm going to beat this rap. It's Harry Cohn. He keeps calling me about going to work. Now you know that tough old bastard wouldn't call if he thought I wasn't going to make it."

Walter Wanger interested Bogart in a gangster-revenge movie, *Underworld USA* (made in 1960 with Cliff Robertson). Though he knew the actor was gravely ill, he told a colleague that Bogart "likes to be involved. He needs to have something to look forward to. And who knows — he may recover." When Sam Jaffe gave up hope and stopped offering scripts for him to consider, Bogart got angry and exclaimed: "You haven't brought me anything."[4]

Unwilling to change the habits of a lifetime just to please his doctor, Bogart kept smoking till the end, though he cut his consumption down to one pack a day. Since alcohol helped to kill the pain, he also drank as much as ever. Nicholas Ray, who directed two of Bogart's films, mentioned his unshakeable habits and fatalistic attitude: "Bogie knew he had cancer, but wouldn't stop smoking—or drinking. . . . I loved Bogie so much I even bothered to convert him from Ike to Adlai, but I couldn't take the damned Chesterfield from his mouth, and Adlai became Betty's adventure. Reforms with Bogie had little longevity, but what the hell, he knew he was going to die. After his first operation one could hear the Romanoff sanddab hit the bottom of Bogie's stomach, so he softened the creature's fall with a pool of Scotch and beer, and settled a haze of Chesterfield smoke around it."

Even when ill, Bogart was still feisty and amusing. When a friend's daughter turned up with her new husband in tow, he caustically told him: "I've forgotten your maiden name." Warren Stevens recalled that toward the end, when Bogart was very sick, Bacall phoned and said Bogart would like to have lunch with him. Stevens booked a booth at Romanoff's. Bogart appeared, sipped Scotch and water, and said he was as "emaciated as a Buchenwald prisoner." While they were talking, John Huston stopped by and sat down, then Peter Lorre, then the actor Alan Jenkins and several other friends. Bogart had carefully planned the whole episode so that Stevens would be stuck with the bill. He thought it was the funniest thing in the world, and Stevens was delighted to be the victim of such a lively gathering.[5]

Bogart was well enough to appear on the Ed Sullivan television show, dedicated to Huston, on July 1, 1956. But the gossip writer Dorothy Kilgallen, with astonishing insensitivity, exposed him when he was helpless and refused to let him die in peace. Acting on a tip from one of his private nurses, she claimed in her column that Bogart had been moved to the eighth floor of Memorial Hospital and was fighting for his life. Furious about this cruel fantasy, Bogart arranged for Joe Hyams to print his rejoinder in the *New York Herald-Tribune*: "I have read that both lungs have been removed; that I couldn't live another half-hour; that I was fighting for my life in a hospital that doesn't exist out here; that my heart has stopped and been replaced by an old gasoline pump from a defunct Standard Oil station. I have been on the way to practically every cemetery you can name from here to the Mississippi—including several where I am certain they only accept dogs. All the above upsets my friends, not to mention the insurance companies." Just before the end he told Hyams: "I'm down to my last martini. The only thing I'm fighting is to keep my head above the press."

Privately, Bogart continued the struggle. During a temporary respite he told Verita: "I'm better today. Don't I look better?"—and then warned her: "Don't give up on me." Huston also emphasized Bogart's urge to live and willingness to endure the ghastly procedures. Like the disease, they made him "sick as a dog." "We all knew he wasn't going to live, but he was still having those goddamn treatments. They wouldn't give up the ghost. We had a drink and Bogie said, 'Look fellas, come clean. Am I gonna make it or not? Tell me the truth.' And Morgan Maree said, 'Of course you are, Bogie. We're not kidding you.' Lying through his teeth. Which was all right. Bogie looked relieved and prepared to go on with it. He didn't want to know. And Betty didn't want him to read in the paper that he was going to die, so everyone who knew him put the best face on they could."[6]

On November 26, nine months after the operation, Bogart, thirty pounds underweight and with severe pain in his left shoulder, reentered the hospital. The official diagnosis was "nerve pressure" caused by scar tissue on his throat. In fact, the operation and subsequent treatments had not worked and (though he was not told) the devastating cancer had recurred. Now the chemical, nitrogen mustard, which resembled the mustard gas in World War I, was injected into his body to suppress the reproduction of malignant cells. In December he was allowed home again, this time to die. Just before Christmas Brandsma told Bacall: "I'm sure you'd rather know the truth, wouldn't you? I'm sure you know it already. Bogie cannot last much longer. We don't know how he's lasted this long. The nitrogen mustard didn't work. . . . I've done everything I know how to do—I'd hoped I'd gotten it all, but clearly I didn't."

In contrast to the cowardice he had shown in the past when threatened with physical violence, Bogart met death with bravado and panache.

During his last months he would stay in bed for most of the day, and at five o'clock his nurses would shave him and dress him in gray flannel trousers and a scarlet smoking jacket. At the cocktail hour he would slowly make his way downstairs to greet his daily guests. When he could no longer walk, the butler would lift him into a wheelchair and push it into the dumbwaiter, normally used to transport meals from the kitchen to the bedroom. The top boards were now removed and, sitting on a little stool, he would be lowered down to the kitchen and wheeled into the den. Friends had to steel themselves for the visit, which meant a great deal to him but was heartbreaking for them. They would discuss what they had been doing and who they'd been seeing, try to distract him with the latest gossip and news of the day.

His inner circle at the end included John Huston, Nunnally Johnson, Swifty Lazar, David Niven and Frank Sinatra. Dr. Flynn often stopped by to check up on his patient and check out the celebrities. Spencer Tracy and Katharine Hepburn appeared almost every night at about 8:30, after the other guests had left and Bogart was back in bed. The novelist John O'Hara reported that Bogart, the author of "Why Hollywood Hates Me," was "stunned by the fact that a lot of people really liked him." Toward the end of 1956 Nicholas Ray phoned Bacall and asked if he could see the invalid. She answered: "'He's unconscious right now. How long will you be away?'—'About six months.' 'He will be dead by then,' she told me."[7]

Several people close to Bogart have left vivid and moving accounts of his endgame. During Dorris Johnson's last visit he ate a few chips and nuts and still wanted whiskey, but his voice was harsh and his whole being weak and haggard. Billy Wilder, who also noted that Bogart drank and smoked till the end, felt "he was brave and he could take it." Richard Brooks emphasized his gallows humor and said he kept needling all the way to the grave: "He was genuinely tough and he was honest. A couple of weeks before he died he was still having guests and seeing friends in the afternoon. I went out to see him one day and found him sitting there as usual, drink in hand. After a while, he had a terrible coughing fit and he started vomiting blood. It was an awful thing to see. I got up and started to leave the room till it was over. And Bogie looked up at me and said, 'What's the matter, Dick, can't you take it?'"

Maynard Brandsma, who had seen many patients die, praised his stoicism and courage: "He went through the worst and most agonizing pain any human can take. I knew this and when I'd see him I'd ask, 'How is it?' Bogie would always answer simply, 'Pretty rough.' He never complained and he never whimpered. I knew he was dying and during the last weeks I knew he knew it too." The director George Cukor added: "I saw him twenty-three days before he died. He couldn't come downstairs anymore and he was heavily sedated. He kept closing his eyes. Still, he'd be telling jokes and asking to hear the gossip."[8]

Bogart's illness put a tremendous strain on Bacall and transformed her glamorous life into a nightmare. She had to care for him and also live with the secret of his impending death. In 1942 he had infuriated Methot by calling Ingrid Bergman "the only lady in Hollywood." Toward the end of his life, when a friend reminded him that Bacall had rarely gone out at night since his operation, he used the same old-fashioned word to describe her. "She's my wife and my nurse," he said. "So she stays home. Maybe that's the way you tell the ladies from the broads in this town."

Bacall had not slept with anyone before Bogart and, as she suggested in her article "I Hate Young Men," tended to get serious crushes on older admirers. Her infatuation with Adlai Stevenson during the 1952 presidential campaign had caused furious quarrels with Bogart, and he told Huston that Stevenson had "fucked up" his home "to the vomiting point." In the early 1950s Bacall also had a passionate flirtation with Leonard Bernstein. Bogart went off on his boat, leaving them alone together. He tried to discourage her by contrasting himself with Bernstein and by wisely warning her not to get too deeply involved with the musician: "He's not like us. You could never keep up with him. He's got places to go and things to do. He's a genius. . . . Lenny has too many things to do in his life to be a satisfying mate. You'd probably have a great time for a weekend but not for a lifetime." Bacall remained emotionally entangled with Bernstein and later wrote, while distorting Bogart's attitude, in her most gushing schoolgirl style: "He was ravishing to look at, with enormous vitality, energy, and a great sense of fun. Bogie and I were dazzled by him. . . . He and I were very much attracted to each other. . . . When he knew Lenny was coming to town, Bogie said, 'Oh, I can't take that sitting on the floor, playing the piano all night, I'm going on the boat!' . . . I used to think that if we had been free souls, Lenny and I might have run off together."[9]

When they were first married Bogart, fearing she might find someone else and leave him, had told her: "Don't do anything behind my back," don't do "anything dishonest." Stevenson had not responded to her overtures and she had probably not become sexually involved with him. In any case, as Bogart told her, these cultured men lived in a completely different world from Bacall's hermetic, luxurious and self-indulgent life in Hollywood. When she fell in love with Frank Sinatra, marriage became a distinct possibility. But she could not reveal her feelings and plans for the future to her dying husband.

Sinatra, a leading member of the Rat Pack, was Bogart's close friend.

When they first met at the Players Restaurant on Sunset Strip, Bogart, as if speaking a line from one of his film scripts, said: "They tell me you have a voice that makes girls faint. . . . Make me faint." Bogart could use insulting nicknames for Sinatra (as he did with his skipper Carl Petersen) without giving offense and often called Sinatra "the Dago." Both men were outspoken, defiant and reckless of their reputation. Sinatra admired Bogart's background, sophistication and integrity, and tried to model himself on his older friend. Earl Wilson wrote that "Sinatra the actor liked to have people compare him with Bogart, both as a performer and person. Bogart was a 'natural' too, one of the 'No Crap' school of stars without affectations or pretensions, a man who would use four-letter words if they seemed to be the ones needed at the moment, and in Bogart's conversation, they often were." Steve Bogart called Sinatra "as devoted as a son." In the early 1950s Bogart noted, with considerable irony: "I think Betty and I must be parent substitutes for him, or something. He's always around here."

Bacall—speaking euphemistically of her relations with Sinatra and noting that the sexual side of her marriage had inevitably deteriorated—admitted that Bogart became jealous of Sinatra during his illness "partly because he knew I loved being with [Frank], partly because he thought Frank was in love with me [and she with him], and partly because our physical life together . . . had less than flourished with his illness." She also confessed that she wanted Sinatra to compensate for her sick husband: "He was then at his vocal peak, and was wildly attractive, electrifying. . . . He represented physical health—vitality. . . . Part of me needed a man to talk to, and Frank turned out to be that man."[10]

Like Bacall, Sinatra loved luxury, was a lavish spender and tried to live up to his glamorous reputation. In his memoirs David Niven gave a romantic description of how, during a party on July 4, 1955, boats gathered rapturously around Sinatra's rented yacht while he entertained the spellbound spectators: "He sang till the moon and stars paled in the predawn sky. Only then did he stop and only then did the awed and grateful audience paddle silently home." But Richard Burton—whom the Bogarts had "discovered" when he was acting Shakespeare on the English stage and befriended when he came to Hollywood—gave a more accurate and amusing account of what really happened that night. Burton revealed in his diary that Bogart disliked Sinatra's narcissistic performances as much as he did Bernstein's. "Bogie and I went out lobster-potting," he noted, "and Frankie got really pissed off with Bogie. David Niven, who describes himself as bewitched all through the night, was trying to [distract Sinatra by setting] fire to the *Santana* at one point, because nobody could stop

Frankie from going on and on. . . . Bogie and Frankie nearly came to blows next day about the singing the night before and I drove Betty home because she was so angry about Bogie's cracks about Frankie singing. At that time Frankie was out of work and was particularly vulnerable and Bogie was unnecessarily cruel."

Six months later, during a New Year's Eve party at Sinatra's Palm Springs house, Noel Coward, noting Sinatra's characteristic mixture of vulgarity and glamour, observed that Bacall was openly jealous of his girlfriends. Frankie, as usual, "has a 'broad' installed with whom he, as well as everyone else, is bored stiff. She is blonde, cute and determined, but I fear her determination will avail her very little with Betty Bacall on the warpath."[11]

When Bacall and Sinatra began their public affair after Bogart's death, Louella Parsons, putting her characteristically sentimental spin on events, wrote that "it was part of Frank's friendship with Bogart 'to see that she didn't mourn in loneliness.'" But Sinatra, who had a strange notion of friendship, began to assuage the loneliness of his "parent substitute" well before she became a widow. Bacall, whom Sinatra later treated like a "broad" and discarded when he was fed up with her, did not always "stay home." Her biographer states that Sinatra was a notorious sexual predator and that Bogart knew of their involvement but was too sick to do anything about it: "Frankie boy liked to pal around with the wives of some of his cronies. . . . Bogey didn't seem to care. Maybe he knew he was in bad shape and maybe even dying."[12]

Nicholas Ray, comparing Gloria Grahame and Lauren Bacall, emphasized that "each was promiscuous." Another close friend of the Bogarts categorically said: "Everyone knew that Bacall was having an affair with Sinatra while Bogart was still alive." Verita, who insisted "I was there and saw it," remembered Bacall getting all dressed up to spend a weekend in Palm Springs with Sinatra. Bacall would exclaim, "Frank's so wonderful," while Bogart stayed home by himself. Kitty Kelly reported a friend remarking that "everybody knew about Betty and Frank. We just hoped Bogie wouldn't find out. That would have been more killing than the cancer."[13]

Bacall, then in her early thirties, had remained faithful to Bogart until she fell in love with Sinatra, whose attentions coincided with Bogart's physical illness and sexual decline. She knew Bogart was dying and she was eager to marry Sinatra, who could offer her a much more romantic and exciting life. Impatient, egoistic and demanding, he was not willing to wait for a whole year to sleep with her. Fearful of losing him, she gave in. In March 1958, fourteen months after Bogart's death, Parsons announced the Bacall-Sinatra engagement and forthcoming marriage. But Sinatra, resenting the pressure to marry, publicly and humiliatingly dumped Bacall. A few weeks later, she left with her children for a year in London.

‹ III ›

BOGART WAS STOICAL in the final stage of his illness. During his last month he had to cancel his birthday party, and could no longer hold a phone or raise a glass. He had trouble breathing and needed two large green oxygen tanks to give him air. A suction machine removed from his lungs the mucus that could have caused pneumonia. He had never complained and still clung to life, but now reached the very end of his physical resources. For the first time, when Bacall brought in the dreaded machine, he begged her, "Please, no more." Huston, who had praised his "guts" after the car accident near Naples, expressed admiration for his friend: "No one who sat in his presence during the final weeks will ever forget it. It was a unique display of purely animal courage. After the first visit—it took that to get over the initial shock of his appearance—one quickened to the grandeur of it, expanded, felt strangely elated, proud to be there, proud to be his friend, the friend of such a brave man." Just before his death, Huston wrote, "the cords of his neck stood out, and his eyes were enormous in his gaunt face. Betty decided not to tell Bogart the truth of his condition"—though the truth was inescapably and horribly evident.

He didn't want his little children to remember him in this state, and asked Bacall not to let them see him anymore. When Sam Jaffe's wife, Mildred, came to visit after an absence of several weeks, she was shocked by the change and could not help gasping at his appearance. Bacall, upset by her behavior, told her she had to control her feelings if she wanted to see him. Swifty Lazar, terrified of illness, could no longer face his dying friend. "I guess I'm a goner," Bogart said. "Swifty's stopped coming around." On January 3, 1957, under a headline that misdiagnosed his disease but announced he had shrunk to half his normal weight—"Down to 80 Pounds, Bogart Fights for Life against Throat Cancer"—the New York *Daily News* reported that "he is under heavy sedation and is in a deep coma much of the time." Gloria Stuart, who had known him since his early years in Hollywood, saw him only two days before the end. Still struggling to understand what had befallen him, he asked her the unanswerable "Why me?" and then remarked with characteristic coolness: "To hell with it."[14]

Bacall had been sleeping in a separate bed so that she would not disturb him. But on Saturday January 12 he asked her to sleep with him. She could not help noticing the relentless odor of decay and felt death was palpable. "I was awake most of the night," she vividly wrote, "and could see his hands moving over his chest as he slept, as though things were closing in and he wanted to get out. . . . That's what happens just before one dies. People feel claustrophobic—it seems as though everything is closing in. And everything is. It's their last fight—the restlessness—the thrashing." The following day he told the doctor: "last night was the worst night of my life—I don't want to go through that again." Bacall's experience was strikingly similar to Frieda Lawrence's with her dying husband. At the very end of his life, when the tubercular D. H. Lawrence asked Frieda for warmth and comfort, she tried to revitalize him with her own health and energy: "All night I was aware of his aching inflexible chest, and all night he must have been so sadly aware of my healthy body beside him. . . . He was falling away from life and me, and with all my strength, I was helpless."

The next morning, as Bacall was taking the children to Sunday school, Bogart spoke his last words to her—"Good-bye, kid. . . . Hurry back"—and drifted into a coma. At 2:25 A.M. on Monday January 14, 1957, three weeks after his fifty-seventh birthday, the nurse woke Bacall to tell her that he had died in his sleep. The cause of death was carcinoma of the esophagus. Bacall immediately called David Niven and said: "My darling husband is gone."[15]

Bogart died in middle age and at the peak of his career. He also, as Nunnally Johnson said, "died patiently, and I suppose bravely. Nothing else he could do. He just seemed to shrivel up. You'd go there to see him, he was maybe ten pounds smaller, and it was heart breaking." The English critic Kenneth Tynan, a great admirer of Bogart's work, found it hard to accept the death of a man who had always survived destruction to be reborn into another role: "We had watched him die so often, had seen him so regularly sacrificed on the altar of the motion picture code, that we had come to think of him as indestructible." That Monday afternoon Dorris Johnson picked up the eight-year-old Steve and the four-year-old Leslie from school and brought them back to her house. Fascinated by all the publicity, Steve solemnly said: "My daddy died, you know. Could I see TV, 'cause they're talking about my daddy." Leslie had a bad attack of asthma after his death, but now cannot remember his touch.

Bogart's will, drawn up on June 6, 1956, left most of his estate to his family. Morgan Maree was co-executor, along with the Security–First National Bank of Los Angeles, and Bacall was trustee for the children. He bequeathed $1,500 to his secretary Kathy Sloan and $2,000 to his cook May Smith, and established the Humphrey Bogart Foundation for cancer research. He left Bacall all his personal property—including clothing, jewelry, furniture and cars—and more than a million dollars: half in trust for his wife, the other half in equal trust for his children. He told a journalist that everything left to Bacall "is tied up in an ironclad trust fund. No fortune hunter is going to get a crack at it."[16]

Bogart's memorial service took place at All Saints Episcopal Church in Beverly Hills on the morning of January 17. During this public event —which resembled a Hollywood premiere or an Oscar ceremony—650 people gathered inside the church and 3,000 waited outside to see the procession of celebrities. Since Bogart was the first great star of his generation to die (followed by Flynn in 1959, Gable in 1960 and Cooper in 1961), the turnout was spectacular. The stars, writers, directors and producers—who came to pay their respects to a distinguished actor and to be seen paying their respects—included several who had not known Bogart well: Charles Boyer, Charles Brackett, Gary Cooper, Marlene Dietrich, Joan Fontaine, Tony Martin, James Mason, Gregory Peck and Danny Thomas as well as many friends and colleagues: Richard Brooks, Harry Cohn, Howard Duff and Ida Lupino, Errol Flynn, Leland Hayward, Katharine Hepburn and Spencer Tracy, Nunnally Johnson, Danny Kaye, Dick Powell, Ronald Reagan, David Selznick and Jennifer Jones, Jack Warner, Billy Wilder and William Wyler.

Bogart was notably absent from his own funeral. He had wanted his ashes strewn in the Pacific, but it was then against the law. While the service was taking place in Beverly Hills, he was cremated, along with the gold whistle that commemorated his love affair with Bacall in *To Have and Have Not*. His ashes were set in a marble wall behind locked doors in the Columbarium of Eternal Light, in the Gardens of Memory, in the Court of the Christus in Forest Lawn cemetery in Glendale. Bogart had called that garish graveyard of the stars, satirized by Evelyn Waugh in *The Loved One*, "a Disneyland for stiffs."

David Niven acted as chief usher at the appropriately traditional service. He and Bogart's Jewish friends, Mike Romanoff and Swifty Lazar, were pallbearers, though there was no pall to bear. A glass-enclosed model of the *Santana* stood on the altar where the coffin would normally rest. The congregation heard music by Bach and Debussy. The minister read the Ten Commandments and the Twenty-third Psalm, which concludes: "Surely goodness and mercy shall follow me all the days of my life: and I

will dwell in the house of the Lord for ever." He also recited the great sea
images of Tennyson's "Crossing the Bar":

> Twilight and evening bell,
>   And after that the dark!
> And may there be no sadness of farewell,
>   When I embark;
>
> For though from out our bourne of Time and Place
>   The flood may bear me far,
> I hope to see my Pilot face to face
>   When I have crossed the bar.

Bogart and Nunnally Johnson had had much in common. Both were
heavy drinkers, divorced, married to much younger wives and with small
children of the same age, and their friendship deepened as they grew
older. A week after the funeral Johnson wrote a drily honest account of
the ceremony that piquantly recalled Bogart's quick, irascible temperament and gregarious life in restaurants and bars: "Niven, Romanoff,
Leland Hayward, Irving Lazar, looking like the upper third of Yul Brynner,
and I were ushers. We did nothing but stand back and let them come in.
We were supposed to seat the gentry in certain choice locations and the
peasants otherwise, but I couldn't tell the gentry from the peasants, and
neither could any of the other ushers. . . . I think there was genuine grief
for Bogey's passing. There are a lot of people who still detest him, people
he had deliberately affronted, and God knows he could do that viciously,
but there were many more who were drawn to him because he was a lively
fellow. I myself feel the loss deeply. It must have been some twenty years
ago that I first ran into him, in a saloon, and his first words to me were
to get the hell out of here, [go] back east. As you know, he was never slow
to offer advice, even to strangers. But between us we knocked off a lot of
bottles together over the years and I'll miss him."

John Huston's brilliant eulogy, the most moving and memorable part
of the service, made many people weep for the extraordinary man they
had lost. Like Johnson, he emphasized Bogart's lively attacks on compla-
cency and his generosity of spirit:

> In each of the fountains at Versailles there is a pike which
> keeps all the carp active, otherwise they would grow over-fat
> and die. Bogie took rare delight in performing a similar duty
> in the fountains of Hollywood. . . . His shafts were fashioned
> only to prick the outer layer of complacency, and not to pene-
> trate through to the regions of the spirit where real injuries are

done. . . . Bogart's hospitality went far beyond food and drink. He fed a guest's spirit as well as his body, plied him with good will until he became drunk in the heart as well as in the legs. . . . He got all that he asked out of life and more. We have no reason to feel any sorrow for him—only for ourselves for having lost him. He is quite irreplaceable. There will never be another like him.[17]

EPILOGUE

The Bogart Cult

⟨ I ⟩

UNIVERSALLY KNOWN in his own day, Bogart has remained a lively figure in the imaginative life of our time. He stands for sexy masculinity and moral values—a contemporary blend of cool courage and detached idealism, self-sacrificing yet self-protective. Bogart's best movies embodied these ideals and were popular when they first appeared. They took on a new life when his extraordinary film cult began at the Brattle Theater (in Harvard Square in Cambridge, Massachusetts) in the summer of 1956 and was continued by cycles of films at the New Yorker Theater on Broadway and at the Eighth Street Playhouse in Greenwich Village. In January 1960 the Brattle began to have regular Bogart programs for three weeks each year. When *Casablanca* (the all-time favorite) was shown, students dressed in trench coats and fedoras shouted out lines of memorized dialogue as Bogart spoke them on the screen. By 1964, 15,000 spectators had seen forty-seven showings of fourteen Bogart films. The Brattle still has a Blue Parrot room (named after Sydney Greenstreet's café in *Casablanca*), in which a jukebox endlessly plays "As Time Goes By." The Casablanca Café, next door to the Brattle, has two large murals of the film.[1] During the 1964 festival a swooning Radcliffe student, defining Bogart for her own generation, called him "the ultimate man. He's so rugged. So absolutely unattainable. The essence of cool." Bogart's rebellious screen image led college students from the conservative Eisenhower years to the revolutionary politics of the 1960s.

The Bogart cult also took off in France. François Truffaut, who planned to film a remake of *Casablanca*, explained why he finally abandoned the project: "I am aware that American students have created a cult of the film, principally its dialogue, which they know by heart. There can be no doubt that most actors would feel as intimidated as I do and I cannot imagine Jean-Paul Belmondo and Catherine Deneuve being willing to step into the shoes of Humphrey Bogart and Ingrid Bergman."[2] But Albert Camus was delighted to take that step. In photographs of the French novelist—with trench coat, lined face and cigarette drooping from the side of his mouth—the Existential writer looked like the actor the French had called an Existential man. Interviewed by *Vogue* during a trip to America, Camus was pleased to be compared to the young Bogart. Wearing a tuxedo for the Nobel Prize ceremony in 1957, he was again gratified when admirers noted the resemblance. Bogart's *film noir* heroes were the popular equivalent of the characters in Camus' novels. Both considered (in different ways) the question of moral responsibility in an evil world and portrayed archetypal heroes trying to work out their own destiny.

Jean-Luc Godard's *Breathless* (1960) was the first film to pay tribute to Bogart's screen persona. At the beginning of the movie Jean-Paul Belmondo stops at a theater on the Champs-Elysées and stares at a poster of Bogart's last picture, *The Harder They Fall*. Wearing Bogart's trademark hat, imitating his gestures and mannerisms, Belmondo plays with his cigarette, draws his thumb across his upper lip, twists his mouth into a mean grimace and rapturously whispers the magic name—"Bogie!" Playing a thief and murderer, with Jean Seberg as his elusive Bacall, Belmondo exclaims: "I always fall for the wrong dames." Defiant, bold and reckless, he romanticizes his life as a cheap crook by identifying with Bogart, acts out his state of mind and lives dangerously because he knows he won't live long.

By the late 1960s the Bogart myth had been so absorbed into the national consciousness that it was time to turn it upside down. In Woody Allen's delightfully funny *Play It Again, Sam* (1972), based on his Broadway play of 1969,[3] Allen plays Allan Felix, a neurotic highbrow film critic who is obsessed with Bogart. Set in San Francisco, the picture opens with clips of the actual airport scene from *Casablanca*. Felix lives in an apartment decorated with photographs of Bogart and posters of *Across the Pacific*. He has a chess set, quotes books on Bogart and watches *The Big Sleep* on the late show. After his wife leaves him, the ghost of Bogart (expertly played by Jerry Lacy) appears. Self-consciously identifying with this "perfect image," Felix complains that his "sex life has turned into the Petrified Forest" as a romantic "Bogart" offers him sophisticated advice about how to handle women. Alluding to his own films, "Bogart" suggests several effective approaches: "The only thing a dame understands is a slap on the mouth or a shot from a .45. . . . The world is full of dames. All you got to do is whistle." After the timid Felix fails hopelessly on his first date, "Bogart" exclaims: "Well, kid, you blew it." But he reappears during moments of sexual crisis to urge Felix on to greater efforts.

The film is cunningly structured so that *Casablanca,* which provides a nostalgic and heroic frame of reference, is reprised at the end. In the final scene Felix gives up his girl (Diane Keaton), who wears the same style of hat worn by Ingrid Bergman, so she can fly off—not to Lisbon to help a noble hero of the Resistance—but to Cleveland with her crass and irritating husband. Sacrificing his love, as Bogart did, with a speech that echoes Rick's final words to Ilsa ("If that plane leaves the ground and you're not with him, you'll regret it"), Felix reveals that he's more devoted to the movie than to his own feelings. Though he can't be Bogart, he can imitate him, and actually enjoys giving up the girl so he can make the deliberately anti-heroic gesture: "It's from *Casablanca.* I waited my whole life to say it!" The film ends as "Bogart" remarks: "Here's looking at you, kid" and Dooley Wilson sings "As Time Goes By."

Bogart reappeared in several other movies based on his film persona. His name became an amusing verb in Milos Forman's *Taking Off* (1971) when a kid, dragging too long on a joint of marijuana, is warned: "don't bogart the roach!" In the rather flat-footed *Gumshoe* (1971), Albert Finney, a Liverpool vaudevillian who's seen too many Bogart movies and dreams of becoming a private eye, gets hopelessly involved in a murder case. In *The Man With Bogart's Face* (1980), an inept private dick who's had plastic surgery to resemble his idol (an allusion to *Dark Passage*), gets several jobs because he looks like Bogart. He too becomes implicated in a *Maltese Falcon*-like case. In *The Usual Suspects* (1995), a clever movie that borrows its title from *Casablanca,* the men rounded up to form a police line-up are not innocent street-dwellers, but daring crooks who commit a devastating crime.

Bogart inspired fiction as well as films. Mignon McLaughlin's "The Woman Who Dreamed About Humphrey Bogart," published in the popular magazine *Good Housekeeping* in October 1947, reveals that Bogart had seeped into the consciousness of American women. He not only appeared in the heroine's dreams, but "also made violent love to her . . . and she violently responded." Later in the story he suddenly changes from hero to villain: "Humphrey Bogart was blithe and gay no longer; he had turned possessive, arrogant, demanding. He insisted that she leave her husband and run away with him." In this story Bogart represents the woman's romantic longing, moral conscience and suppressed though violent hostility to her husband.

The most perceptive imaginative work on Bogart is (we have seen)

Richard Brooks' *The Producer* (1951). Based on the real person behind the screen image, the novel gives a fascinating sense, as the producer battles the studio, of how a movie is actually planned and made. It portrays the inevitable compromises and betrayals, the political issues and personal loyalties, the struggle for morality and integrity.

In poetry, Charles Bukowski in "Bogart in the World of the Dead" and John Berryman in the ninth "Dream Song" identified with the suffering Bogart persona, a hero to both lowbrows and intellectuals. Berryman's alter ego, Henry, alludes to Bogart's death by a police sharpshooter after he's retreated to the hills at the end of *High Sierra:*

> A mild crack: a far rifle. Bogart's duds
> truck back to Wardrobe. Fancy the brain from hell
> held out so long. Let go.

In "Bogart," the first story in his early book *Miguel Street* (1959), V. S. Naipaul writes that when *Casablanca* opened in Trinidad, "Bogart's fame spread like fire through Port of Spain and hundreds of young men began adopting the hard-boiled Bogartian attitude." The main character, who keeps disappearing and mysteriously turning up again, adopted an American accent, "drank and swore and gambled with the best. . . . He bought a hat, and pulled down the brim over his eyes. He . . . [stood] against the high concrete fence of his yard, hands in his pockets . . . and an eternal cigarette in his mouth." When he's arrested for bigamy, the cop warns: "Don't act tough, Bogart." The comic irony of the story is achieved in the contrast between the plump, oily, languorous antihero and the film persona he rather desperately tries to adopt.

Robert Coover's story "You Must Remember This," published in *Playboy* of January 1985, adds a sexual element to Rick and Ilsa's love scene when she comes to his room to get the letters of transit in *Casablanca*. He satirizes Rick Blaine's final renunciation and replaces political idealism with multiple orgasms. Coover projects his own vivid and elaborate fantasies onto the lovers in the film, who realize, despite her stupendous sexual response ("where she is going he cannot follow"), that they can't remain together. In Coover's deflation of romantic self-sacrifice, Rick has "made a balls-up of things with his complicated moral poses and insufferable pride."[4]

Bogart's name still has powerful commercial value. In Germany, a shady Bogart figure, smoking a cigarette and dressed in a snap-brim hat and trench coat, was used to advertise Venetian blinds. In 1971 Pan American Airways used the famous shot of Bogart at the end of *Casablanca* to sell flights to Morocco. Fifteen years later, an ad for Lufthansa once again used the airport scene from that film. In the 1990s the Curtis Management Company, which controls the posthumous use of his name and image, sold the rights to use Bogart in advertisements for an athletic apparel company, a real estate development firm, prints by the Accessory Warehouse, a promotional banquet for Hyundai cars, the MGM Grand Hotel in Las Vegas, Four Roses bourbon in Spain and GAP clothing ("Bogart wore khakis") with a photograph of the actor aboard the *Santana*.[5]

‹ II ›

AFTER BOGART'S DEATH Bacall, like Queen Victoria, lived in the great void left by her husband. She sold the *Santana*. She sold the vast South Mapleton Drive house, so full of morbid memories, to the producer Ray Stark and rented a smaller one in the same neighborhood. She auctioned off many of her possessions — "Antique and Period Furniture, Knabe Grand Piano, Persian Rugs, Paintings, Objets d'Art" — and donated the proceeds to the Charities Committee of the Motion Picture Industry. She lived for a time in London, then moved to New York and took a large apartment in the Dakota on Central Park West.

Two years later, in July 1961, Bacall married the New York actor Jason Robards, who looked somewhat like Bogart, had a similar name and shared his fondness for Scotch. Their son Sam was born that November. The astonishing surge of interest in Bogart in the 1960s forced Robards into rivalry with his predecessor and put a great strain on their marriage. "I'm certain that it's very tough on Jason's ego," Bacall said, "and I hope he understands." When Robards' heavy drinking led to a divorce in 1969, she seemed to be possessed by the spirit of her dead husband. His films, image and influence were still pervasive: "Bogey has taken over my life all over again. My brain is full of him — more acutely than when he died. [Twelve] years have gone by, but I'll never get away from him — and I don't think that's bad." Robards, laconically but bitterly, said: "I am tired of being Mrs. Bogart's Second Husband." Bacall's film career continued to decline after Bogart's death, but she finally achieved success with brassy Broadway musicals, *Cactus Flower* (1965) and *Applause* (1970).

Bacall said their children, who scarcely knew their father, were "screwed up due to childhood traumas." But they managed to lead fairly ordinary lives. Leslie, a New Age child, was married in a ceremony conducted by a Tibetan lama. Trained as a registered nurse, she is now a yoga therapist in Los Angeles. Steve drifted through two prep schools and three universities, sinking under the burden of his parents' fame. He sold insurance in Connecticut, divorced and remarried, moved to Ridgewood, New Jersey, and became a television news producer. In 1995 he published (with an unacknowledged ghost writer) a derivative and self-pitying memoir of his father. Just as Mary Pickford had once exclaimed: "If you ever dare to make me a grandmother, I'll kill you," so Bacall, who didn't want to seem old, was extremely annoyed when Steve had children. Referring to Dorris Johnson's grandchildren, she incredulously asked her: "Do you really like all those kids?"[6]

Bogart came from a strong theatrical background and, after the gradual growth of his screen persona, hit his stride in the early 1940s. He had great presence and charisma with the camera as well as a distinctive appearance and manner. He was deliberately restrained and had a laid-back quality that has remained extremely popular. He knew his business on camera, was economical of movement, speech and emotion. He took a long time to achieve fame and was a star for less time than most of his leading contemporaries. Like Cooper and Gable, the only ones to equal his rare achievement, he is considered an even greater actor today than he was during his lifetime.

The critic Richard Schickel, comparing Bogart to his peers, wrote that he appeared in more films "that are unarguably central to the history of the American cinema, whether it is regarded as an art form or a social force or both." Truman Capote paid tribute to Bogart's skill and endurance, calling him "an actor without theories . . . without temper but not without temperament; and, because he understood that discipline was the better part of artistic survival, he lasted, he left his mark."[7] In August 1993 *Entertainment Weekly*, with Bogart on the cover, voted him the "greatest movie legend of all time." His appeal remains universal and he will always be remembered for his finest scenes: his cool rejection of the duplicitous Mary Astor in *The Maltese Falcon,* his idealistic renunciation of the devoted Ingrid Bergman in *Casablanca,* his condemnation of the irritating Katharine Hepburn as a "crazy, psalm-singin', skinny old maid" in *The African Queen* and his sudden crack-up in *The Caine Mutiny.*

Notes

Bogart's Plays and Films

Bibliography

Index

Notes

Prologue: Bogart and Hemingway

1. Quoted in Stephan Talty, "Young Bogart," *American Film*, 16 (April 1991), 41; Ernest Hemingway, "Soldier's Home," *Short Stories* (New York, 1953), pp. 151–152; Jeffrey Meyers, *Hemingway: A Biography* (New York, 1985), p. 212. The childhood photographs appear in this book and in Carlos Baker, *Ernest Hemingway: A Life Story* (New York, 1969), no. 7. When I told *my* mother that I was working on a life of D. H. Lawrence, she exclaimed: "I'm so glad you're not going to write another book about a man who hated his mother." I replied: "Mom, Lawrence *killed* his mother!"
2. Hemingway may not have written the quote Bogart attributed to him. The real source is Jules Verne, *Twenty Thousand Leagues Under the Sea* (1870), trans., intro. and notes by Emanual Mickel (Bloomington, Ind., 1991), p. 163, in which Captain Nemo exclaims: "Live — live in the bosom of the waters! Only there can one have independence! There I recognize no masters! There I am free!"
3. Otto Friedrich, *City of Nets: A Portrait of Hollywood in the 1940's* (New York, 1986), p. 83; Hemingway, "The Killers," *Short Stories*, pp. 280, 281, 285; 280; 283; Hemingway, "The Gambler, the Nun, and the Radio," *Short Stories*, p. 469.
4. Raymond Chandler, *The Big Sleep* (1939; New York, 1950), p. 72.

1. Childhood, Andover and the Navy

1. Ezra Goodman, *Bogey: The Good-Bad Guy* (New York, 1965), p. 58; William Rothenstein, *Men and Memories: A History of the Arts, 1872–1922* (1931; New York, 1934), p. 36; W. A. Swanberg, *Dreiser* (1965; New York, 1967), p. 142. For more about Maud, see William Bangs, "An Illustrator of Child Life," *Quarterly Illustrator*, 2 (January–March 1894), 31–36; Beryl Rinehart, "Maud Humphrey and Her Work," *Hobbies*, 77 (February 1973), 144–145; *Who Was Who in American Art*, ed. Peter Falk (Madison, Conn.,

1985), p. 299; *Dictionary of Women Artists,* ed. Chris Pettays (Boston, 1985), p. 357.

2. Humphrey Bogart, as told to Kate Holliday, "My Mother: I Never Really Loved Her" (July 1949), *McCall's,* 103 (April 1976), 42. In the 1930s, reference books and Warner Bros.' publicity pamphlets listed Bogart's birthday as January 23, 1899. But his school records at Andover and his personnel records in the Navy Archives confirm that he was born on Christmas Day, 1899.

3. Richard Gehman, *Bogart* (Greenwich, Conn., 1965), p. 80; Joe Hyams, *Bogie: The Biography of Humphrey Bogart,* introduction by Lauren Bacall (1966; New York, 1967), pp. 23–24; Joe Hyams, *Bogart and Bacall* (1975; New York, 1976), p. 10.

4. Jonah Ruddy and Jonathan Hill, *Bogey: The Man, the Actor, the Legend* (New York, 1965), p. 15; Hyams, *Bogie,* p. 24.

5. Karen Choppa and Paul Humphrey, *Maud Humphrey: Her Permanent Imprint on American Illustration* (Atglen, Pa., 1993), p. 90; Zelda Fitzgerald, "The Girl the Prince Liked," *Collected Writings,* ed. Matthew Bruccoli (New York, 1991), p. 311; Frank Hamlin, "Summers at the Lake," *My Time* (1985), unpublished memoir, courtesy of Mr. Hamlin; Humphrey Bogart, "The *Santana* and I," *Hollywood in the 1940s: The Stars' Own Stories,* ed. Ivy Wilson (New York, 1980), p. 33.

6. Trinity School, *Upper School Handbook* (1995–96), p. 3; Trinity School, *Yearbook* (1917–18), pp. 15–16; Clarence Bruner-Smith, "A Short History of Trinity School," *Trinity Alumni Review,* Winter 1995, p. 4; Gehman, *Bogart,* p. 83; Interview with Clarence Bruner-Smith, New York, October 1, 1995; Talty, "Young Bogart," p. 43.

7. Andover Academy, *Catalogue* (1995–96), p. 11; Henry and Katherine Pringle, "America's Oldest Private School," *Saturday Evening Post,* 220 (September 27, 1947), 101; John Mason Kemper, *Phillips Academy at Andover: A National Public School* (New York, 1957), p. 8.

8. "Andover: A Study in Independence," *Fortune,* 29 (May 1944), 167–168; Gehman, *Bogart,* pp. 84; 84–85. Dr. Bogart actually wrote "not go to college." But, since the context of this statement (Dr. Cole thinks "he can do this") is consistent with Humphrey going to Andover so that he could attend Yale and become a doctor, the "not" must have been a slip of the pen that expressed his fears about his son's academic ability.

9. Frederick Allis, *Youth From Every Quarter: A Bicentennial History of Phillips Academy, Andover* (Andover, Mass., 1979), p. 427; Hyams, *Bogie,* p. 31; Gehman, *Bogart,* pp. 85; 85–86; 86.

10. Letter from Alfred Stearns to Belmont Bogart, April 2, 1918, Andover Archives; Gehman, *Bogart,* pp. 87; 87, 90; J. R. A. of Andover to George Frazier, May 23, 1949, Andover Archives.

11. Nathaniel Benchley, *Humphrey Bogart* (Boston, 1975), p. 16; Verita [Peterson] Thompson, with Donald Shepherd, *Bogie and Me: A Love Story* (New York, 1982), p. 91; John Scott, "Realist Denies He's Rowdie with Softie," *Los Angeles Times,* January 28, 1951, 4:3; Ruddy, *Bogey,* p. 213; Claude Fuess, Oral History, p. 14, Columbia University.

12. Hyams, *Bogart and Bacall,* p. 17; Hyams, *Bogie,* p. 32; Paul Michael, *Humphrey Bogart: The Man and His Films* (Indianapolis, 1965), p. 14; Gehman, *Bogart,* p. 90. Despite this letter, Humphrey was not listed among the Andover alumni who served in World War I.

13. Alfred Stearns to the Commanding Officer, Naval Aviation, Pelham Bay, October 4, 1918, Andover Archives; Franklin D. Roosevelt, Preface to Joseph Husband, *On the Coast of France: The Story of United States Naval Forces in French Waters* (Chicago, 1919), p. xv; William Sims, "Transporting Two Million Soldiers to France," *The Victory at Sea* (Garden City, N.Y., 1920), p. 366; Vice-Admiral Henry Wilson, *Account of Operations of the American Navy in France during the War with Germany* (n.p., 1919), p. 139.

14. Goodman, *Bogey,* p. 116; Benchley, *Humphrey Bogart,* p. 19; Louise Brooks, "Humphrey and Bogey," *Lulu in Hollywood* (New York, 1983), p. 59; Letter from the National Personnel Records Center, Navy Records Branch, to Jeffrey Meyers, July 26, 1995; Alistair Cooke, "Humphrey Bogart: Epitaph for a Tough Guy" (1957), *Six Men* (1977; London, 1978), p. 130.

2. Broadway and Failure in Hollywood

1. Kirsten Baskette, "Hollywood's Trigger Man," *American Magazine,* 135 (June 1943), 64; *The Man Called Bogart,* in "Hollywood and the Stars," United Artists TV, September 11, 1963; William Brady, *Showman* (New York, 1937), p. 277.

2. Clifford McCarty, *Bogey: The Films of Humphrey Bogart* (New York, 1965), p. 8; Goodman, *Bogey,* p. 40; Michael, *Humphrey Bogart,* p. 14.

3. Clive Denton and Kingsley Canham, *The Hollywood Professionals: King Vidor, John Cromwell, Mervyn LeRoy* (London, 1976), p. 104; Michael, *Humphrey Bogart,* p. 14; Goodman, *Bogey,* p. 30.

4. *New York Times,* October 17, 1922, p. 14; Samuel Leiter, ed., *The Encyclopedia of the New York Stage, 1920–1940,* 4 vols. (Westport, Conn., 1985), p. 887; Bogart, "My Mother," *McCall's,* p. 42.

5. F. Scott Fitzgerald, "May Day," *Stories,* ed. Malcolm Cowley (New York, 1951), p. 107; Edmund Wilson, *The Sixties,* ed. Lewis Dabney (New York, 1993), p. 48; Ruddy, *Bogey,* p. 71.

6. Goodman, *Bogey,* p. 39; Hyams, *Bogart,* pp. 39–40; Humphrey Bogart, "Why Hollywood Hates Me," *Screen Book,* 22 (January 1940), 66; *New York Times,* September 2, 1924, p. 22.

7. Brooks, *Lulu in Hollywood,* pp. 60, 59; Russel Medcraft and Norma Mitchell, *Cradle Snatchers* (New York, 1931), pp. 49, 70; Nunnally Johnson, Oral History, Second Interview, p. 1, Columbia University; Margaret Mayo, *Baby Mine* (New York, 1924), pp. 12, 16, 23.

8. Interviews with Cynthia Lindsay, Malibu, California, September 17, 1995 and March 7, 1996; Thompson, *Bogie and Me,* p. 24; Ruddy, *Bogey,* p. 81; Brooks, *Lulu in Hollywood,* p. 65.

9. Mary Mullett, "A Star at 22 — But After 17 Years of Preparation," *American*

Magazine, 96 (September 1923), 138, 142; Obituary of Helen Menken, *New York Times*, March 28, 1966, p. 33; Mullett, "A Star at 22," p. 138.

10. Mullett, "A Star at 22," p. 34; Obituary of Helen Menken, *New York Times*, March 28, 1966, p. 33; Brooks, *Lulu in Hollywood*, p. 66; Jonathan Coe, *Humphrey Bogart: Take It and Like It* (New York, 1991), p. 19.

11. Grace Mack, "Meeting Up with a New Menacing Man," *Motion Picture*, 52 (January 1937), 88; "Miss Menken Asks Divorce," *New York Times*, November 13, 1927, p. 7; Benchley, *Humphrey Bogart*, p. 39; Richard Brooks, *The Producer* (New York, 1957), p. 158; Hyams, *Bogie*, p. 25. For more on Menken, see Ada Patterson, "Helen Menken: Philosopher and Player," *Theatre Magazine* (New York), 37 (May 1923), 26, 56.

12. Interview with Frank Hamlin, Naples, New York, December 2, 1995; Frank Hamlin, "Summers at the Lake," p. 22; Interview with Jeanie Sims, London, July 27, 1996.

13. Bogart, "My Mother," *McCall's*, p. 42. In this article Bogart erroneously states that while he was in the navy the snobbish Maud "sold the West End Avenue house because she decided that all the better people resided on the east side of the city. She had social aspirations for my sisters, so they moved over to 56 Street near the river" (p. 42). Reference books reveal that the house—on 103rd Street, not West End Avenue—was sold, six years after Bogart left the navy, when his father retired at the age of sixty in 1925. By that time, Pat Bogart had fulfilled her social aspirations and married Stuart Rose (Kay Bogart never married). Benchley, *Humphrey Bogart*, p. 49, gives the address of the Bogarts' new apartment as 79 East 56th Street, which is off Park Avenue, not near the river.

14. Interviews with Verita Peterson Thompson, Daytona Beach, Florida, August 20, 1995 and New Orleans, February 24, 1996; Gladys Hall, "I Think It's Fine," unpublished memoir, Herrick Library, Academy of Motion Picture Arts and Sciences, Beverly Hills, California; Brooks, *The Producer*, pp. 62–63; Benchley, *Humphrey Bogart*, p. 32.

15. Maxwell Anderson, *"Saturday's Children,"* in Burns Mantle, ed., *The Best Plays of 1926–1927* (New York, 1928), pp. 88, 92; Ruth Gordon, *My Side: An Autobiography* (New York, 1976), p. 230; *New York Times*, January 12, 1929, p. 14; Larry Johnson, *It's a Wise Child* (New York, 1937), pp. 28, 111; Ruddy, *Bogey*, p. 28. Here again Bogart (or his biographer) got the facts wrong. *The White Sister*, starring Clark Gable (not Ronald Colman), appeared a few years later in 1933.

16. Robert Sklar, *City Boys: Cagney, Bogart, Garfield* (Princeton, 1992), p. 12; Humphrey Bogart, "Bogart on Hollywood," *Look*, 20 (August 21, 1956), 98; Goodman, *Bogey*, p. 118.

17. Michael, *Humphrey Bogart*, p. 15; Coe, *Humphrey Bogart*, p. 24; Bernard Rosenberg and Harry Silverstein, eds., *The Real Tinsel* (New York, 1970), p. 187.

18. Howard Taubman, *The Making of the American Theatre* (New York, 1967), p. 204; Bogart, "Why Hollywood Hates Me," *Screen Book*, pp. 69; 66; 69;

Humphrey Bogart, "Listen to Me, Kid," *Photoplay,* September 1949, p. 83; Sklar, *City Boys,* p. 57; John Van Druten, *After All* (London, 1929), pp. 70–71.

19. *The Letters of Nunnally Johnson,* ed. Dorris Johnson and Ellen Leventhal, introduction by Alistair Cooke (New York, 1981), pp. 7–8; Benchley, *Humphrey Bogart,* p. 54; Elia Kazan, *A Life* (New York, 1988), p. 89; Joshua Logan, *Movie Stars, Reel People and Me* (New York, 1978), p. 22.

20. Luigi Chiarelli, *The Mask and the Face* (London, 1927), pp. 13, 55. When *Midnight* was reissued in video, for commercial reasons the name was changed to *Call It Murder* and the titles altered to make Bogart, who actually had eighth billing, seem to be the star in what was anachronistically called a "classic film noir murder melodrama."

21. Choppa, *Maud Humphrey,* p. 91; Goodman, *Bogey,* p. 201.

3. *The Petrified Forest* AND WARNER BROS.

1. Belmont's obituary notice in the *Journal of the American Medical Association,* 103 (October 20, 1934), 1249, mistakenly states that he was sixty-two; Talty, "Young Bogart," p. 45; Bogart, "Why Hollywood Hates Me," *Screen Book,* p. 69; Arthur Hopkins, *Reference Point* (New York, 1948), pp. 61–62.

2. Louis Bromfield, "Bogie," *Photoplay,* 18 (March 22, 1941), 94; Blanche Sweet, Oral History, p. 126, Columbia University; Michael, *Humphrey Bogart,* p. 16; Walter Meserve, *Robert Sherwood: Reluctant Moralist* (New York, 1970), p. 104; Ruddy, *Bogey,* p. 34; *New York Times,* January 8, 1935, p. 26.

3. Charles Higham, *Warner Brothers* (New York, 1975), p. 2; *Hollywood Reporter,* September 16, 1932, p. 3; Neal Gabler, *An Empire of Their Own: How the Jews Created Hollywood* (1988; New York, 1989), pp. 121, 120.

4. Interview with Billy Wilder, Beverly Hills, September 12, 1995; Interview with Delbert Mann, Los Angeles, September 5, 1995; Lauren Bacall, *By Myself* (New York, 1978), p. 195; Casey Robinson, in *Backstory: Interviews with Screenwriters of Hollywood's Golden Age,* ed. Pat McGilligan (Berkeley, 1986), p. 296. For more on the studio, see "Warner Brothers," *Fortune,* 16 (December 1937), 110–113, 206–220.

5. Robert Sklar, *Movie-Made America* (New York, 1975), pp. 230, 232; Clause 20 in Bogart's contract of December 10, 1935, Warner Archive; Anthony Powell, *Miscellaneous Verdicts* (London, 1990), p. 213; Brooks, *Lulu in Hollywood,* p. 58; Hal Wallis and Charles Higham, *Starmaker: The Autobiography of Hal Wallis* (New York, 1980), p. 49.

6. Leonard Leff and Jerold Simmons, *The Dame in the Kimono: Hollywood Censorship and the Production Code from the 1920s to the 1960s* (New York, 1990), p. 7; see also 284–286. See Murray Schumach, *The Face on the Cutting Room Floor: The Story of Movie and Television Censorship* (New York, 1964) and Richard Randall, *Censorship of the Movies: The Social and Political Control of a Mass Medium* (Madison, 1968).

7. Robert Warshow, "The Gangster as Tragic Hero" (1948), *The Immediate Ex-*

perience (New York, 1970), pp. 131–132; Laurence Quirk, *Fasten Your Seat Belts: The Passionate Life of Bette Davis* (New York, 1990), p. 115; Charles Higham, *Bette: The Life of Bette Davis* (New York, 1981), pp. 51, 73; Humphrey Bogart, "The Role I Liked Best," *Saturday Evening Post,* 219 (December 14, 1946), 136.

8. Humphrey Bogart, "The Oscar Myth," *Cosmopolitan,* March 1950, p. 165; Ruddy, *Bogey,* pp. 42–43; David Shipman, *Movie Talk* (New York, 1988), p. 17.

9. Whitney Stine, *"I'd Love to Kiss You": Conversations with Bette Davis* (New York, 1990), p. 160; "Bogart on Hollywood," *Look,* p. 98; Goodman, *Bogey,* p. 117; Sklar, *City Boys,* p. 73.

10. Nora Johnson, *Flashback: On Nunnally Johnson* (Garden City, N.Y., 1979), p. 160; David Shipman, "Humphrey Bogart," *The Great Movie Stars: The Golden Years* (New York, 1970), p. 73; Kenneth Tynan, "Humphrey Bogart" (1966), *Profiles,* ed. Kathleen Tynan and Ernie Eban (London, 1989), p. 199; Arthur Schlesinger, Jr., "When Movies Really Counted," *Show,* 3 (April 1963), 125.

11. *Black Legion* file, April 16, 1938, Warner Archive, Doheny Library, University of Southern California. For a discussion of the Black Legion, see, for example, "Black Legion Thug Confesses Murder," *New York Times,* June 4, 1936, pp. 1, 15 and Paul Ward, "Who's Behind the Black Legion?" *Nation,* 142 (June 10, 1936), 731.

12. "Black Legion," *New York Herald-Tribune,* January 16, 1937, p. 46; Graham Greene, *The Pleasure Dome: The Collected Film Criticism, 1935–1940,* ed. John Russell Taylor (London, 1972), p. 151; Stine, *Conversations with Bette Davis,* p. 134.

13. Otis Ferguson, *Film Criticism,* ed. Robert Wilson (Philadelphia, 1971), p. 181; Jan Herman, *A Talent for Trouble: The Life of Hollywood's Most Acclaimed Director, William Wyler* (New York, 1995), p. 170; "William Wyler," *Directors at Work,* ed. Bruce Kantor, Irwin Blacker and Anne Kramer (New York, 1970), pp. 435–436; Axel Madsen, *William Wyler* (New York, 1973), p. 137.

14. Sidney Kingsley, *Dead End* (New York, 1936), p. 86; Peter Roffman and Jim Purdy, *The Hollywood Social Problem Film: Despair and Politics from the Depression to the Fifties* (Bloomington, Ind., 1981), p. 140; Association of Producers to Jack Warner, May 27, 1932, Warner Archive.

15. Madsen, *William Wyler,* p. 156; Greene, *The Pleasure Dome,* pp. 180–181.

16. Roy Hoopes, *Cain: The Biography of James M. Cain,* 2nd ed. (Carbondale, Ill., 1987), p. 275; Ruddy, *Bogey,* p. 32; *Los Angeles Times,* June 22, 1937. Mary Philips died of cancer in Santa Monica, California, in 1975.

17. Dore Schary, *Heyday* (Boston, 1979), p. 319; Interview with Jess Morgan, Los Angeles, September 5, 1995; Obituary of Morgan Maree, *Los Angeles Times,* December 1, 1985, 2:16. See also, *New York Times,* November 27, 1985, 4:23.

18. Thompson, *Bogie and Me,* p. 158; "Survivor," *Time,* 63 (June 7, 1954), 72.

19. Ruddy, *Bogey*, p. 45; "Bogart on Hollywood," p. 100; Coe, *Humphrey Bogart*, p. 38; Rex Lease and Kenneth Harlan, eds., *What Actors Eat — When They Eat* (Los Angeles, 1939), p. 26; Brooks, *Lulu in Hollywood*, p. 59.

4. Strife with Mayo

1. For Methot's obituaries, see the *New York Times*, June 10, 1951, p. 93 and the *Los Angeles Times*, June 10, 1951; Hyams, *Bogart and Bacall*, p. 78; Interview with Dorris Johnson, Beverly Hills, California, September 7, 1995; Hyams, *Bogie*, pp. 60–61.

2. Meyers, *Hemingway*, p. 82; David Niven, "Bogie," *Bring On the Empty Horses* (New York, 1975), p. 215; Hyams, *Bogie*, p. 65; George Frazier, "Humphrey Bogart: He Has a Hard, Unhappy Face and a Hard but Happy Life," *Life*, 16 (June 12, 1944), 55.

3. Peggy Slater, with Shelley Usen, *Peggy: An Affair with the Sea* (Santa Barbara: Edens, 1992), p. 90; Carlisle Jones, "World War I Navy Service Fitted Bogart for Modern Sea Picture," *New York Herald-Tribune*, May 16, 1943, 6:3.

4. Baskette, "Hollywood's Trigger Man," p. 63; Hyams, *Bogie*, p. 20; Thompson, *Bogie and Me*, p. 33; Brooks, *Lulu in Hollywood*, p. 66.

5. There is almost no record of Bogart's personal relations with these literary figures. There are no Bogart letters in the papers of Sherwood at Harvard and Bromfield at Ohio State, nor in the published correspondence of Thurber, Faulkner and O'Hara; no references to Bogart in the biographies of Robert Benchley and Dorothy Parker.

6. Goodman, *Bogey*, p. 91; Sam Jaffe, "An Oral History," pp. 208, 247, Herrick Library; Ruddy, *Bogey*, p. 50.

7. Bogart's correspondence includes one letter to Andover about his room and expenses at school (Gehman, 84); one letter to Lyman Brown about his divorce from Helen Menken (Benchley, 39); three letters to the writer Eric Hatch describing his boat, refusing an invitation and pretending to be a gushing fan (Benchley, 73, 82 and 84, and in the Boston University Library); four long telegrams to Hal Wallis and Jack Warner soliciting or rejecting roles (Sklar, *City Boys*, p. 114, Rudy Behlmer, *Inside Warner Bros., 1935–1951*, New York, 1985, pp. 127, 143, and in the Warner Archive); six to Lauren Bacall during their courtship and one while making *Beat the Devil* (Bacall, *By Myself*, pp. 114–119, 231); one to Steve Trilling about finishing a film in time for the Honolulu boat race (Warner Archive); four to John Huston about *Beat the Devil* (in Lawrence Grobel, *The Hustons*, 1989; New York, 1990, pp. 396–397, 412 and Herrick Library); and two to the producer John Woolf, in the Woolf Papers in London. These lively and enticing letters make one wish for more.

8. Letter from Eric Hatch to Howard Gotlieb, Curator of Rare Books at Boston University, November 1, 1970, Boston University Library; Letter from Humphrey Bogart to Eric Hatch, [November 1940], Boston University; Benchley, *Humphrey Bogart*, pp. 82, 84.

9. Alistair Cooke, "Humphrey . . . Guy," p. 136; Aljean Harmetz, *Round Up the Usual Suspects: The Making of "Casablanca"—Bogart, Bergman, and World War II* (London, 1993), p. 344; Peter Bogdanovich, "Bogie in Excelsis," *Pieces of Time* (New York, 1973), p. 38.

10. Hortense Powdermaker, *Hollywood: The Dream Factory* (Boston, 1950), p. 29; Bogart, "Why Hollywood Hates Me," *Screen Book*, p. 66; Charles Francisco, *You Must Remember This. . . . The Filming of "Casablanca"* (Englewood Cliffs, N.J., 1980), pp. 77–78.

11. Alan Frank, *Humphrey Bogart* (New York, 1982), p. 24; Bogart, "Why Hollywood Hates Me," *Screen Book*, pp. 66, 68; Earl Wilson, *The Show Business Nobody Knows* (Chicago, 1971), p. 276; Truman Capote, "Humphrey Bogart," *The Dogs Bark* (New York, 1950), p. 374.

12. Hyams, *Bogie*, p. 104; Interview with Jess Morgan; Cameron Shipp, "The Adventures of Humphrey Bogart," *Saturday Evening Post*, 225 (August 2, 1952), 33; Nicholas Ray, *I Was Interrupted*, ed. Susan Ray (Berkeley, 1993), p. 159.

13. Richard Lingeman, review of Hyams' *Bogie, New York Times Book Review*, September 25, 1966, p. 16. See Richard Avedon and Truman Capote, *Observations* (New York, 1957), p. 121; Brooks, *The Producer*, p. 64.

14. Mack, "Meeting Up with a New Menacing Man," p. 34; Sylvia Thompson, *Feasts and Friends* (San Francisco, 1988), p. 27; Interview with Dorris Johnson.

15. Sheilah Graham, "Bogie," *Confessions of a Hollywood Columnist* (1969; New York, 1970), p. 303; Cole Lesley, *The Life of Noel Coward* (1976; New York, 1978), pp. 394–395.

16. Benchley, *Humphrey Bogart,* pp. 5; 16; Jaffe, "Oral History," p. 209; Interview with Dorris Johnson; Armand Deutsch, *Me and Bogie* (New York, 1991), pp. 212–213; Edward Dmytryk, *It's a Hell of a Life but Not a Bad Living* (New York, 1978), p. 198.

17. Jaffe, "Oral History," p. 246; Interview with Gloria Stuart Sheekman, Los Angeles, September 4, 1995; Humphrey Bogart, "Bogart: Neuroses: Methot," *Herald Express*, c. 1942, clipping at University of Southern California; James Wong Howe, Oral History, p. 10, Columbia University.

18. Interview with Gloria Stuart Sheekman; Hyams, *Bogie*, p. 160; Stephen Humphrey Bogart, *Bogart: In Search of My Father*, foreword by Lauren Bacall (New York, 1995), p. 219.

19. Michael, *Humphrey Bogart,* p. 20; Jeffrey Meyers, *D. H. Lawrence: A Biography* (New York, 1990), pp. 148–149; Hyams, *Bogart and Bacall*, p. 77; Ernest Hemingway, *To Have and Have Not* (New York, 1937), p. 177; Hyams, *Bogart and Bacall*, p. 76.

20. Howe, Oral History, p. 7; Stephen Bogart, *Bogart*, p. 224; Ezra Goodman, *The Fifty-Year Decline and Fall of Hollywood* (1961; New York, 1962), p. 251; Terence Pettigrew, *Bogart* (London, 1981), p. 11.

21. Thompson, *Bogie and Me*, pp. 18; 121; 5; 6; 4; Memos from Steve Trilling to Roy Obringer, March 11 and 17, 1946, Warner Archive; Thompson, *Bogie and*

Me, p. 140; Interviews with Verita Peterson Thompson; Benchley, *Humphrey Bogart*, p. 52.

5. PROFESSIONAL GANGSTER

1. Jonathan Kobal, *People Will Talk* (New York, 1986), pp. 549–550; Interview with Vincent Sherman, Malibu, California, March 7, 1996; Research Department memo to screenwriters, May 17, 1938, Warner Archive; *Louisville Courier-Journal*, April 2, 1938, 2:4.
2. Richard Brooks' *The Producer*, p. 124, makes the Bogart character, Steve Taggart, reject the very role that O'Brien had chosen for Cagney: "I don't mind dying at the end. But I'm not going to crawl. Not me. I'm not going to turn chicken. . . . The fans won't believe it. . . . Steve Taggart doesn't die like a coward. I never did before and I never will. My audience doesn't expect it of me."
3. Jaffe, "Oral History," pp. 193, 210; 211–212; 256; Interviews with Verita Peterson Thompson; Benchley, *Humphrey Bogart*, p. 148. Vincent Sherman said that Warner tried to fire Kay Francis after she had made several flops, but she hung on to her contract and remarked: "I'll sweep the stage, if necessary, to keep my salary."
4. Coe, *Humphrey Bogart*, pp. 42, 44; Michael Freedland, *James Cagney* (London, 1974), p. 116; *Cagney by Cagney* (1976; New York, 1977), pp. 99–100; "The Art of Mr. Bogart," *New York Times*, February 19, 1939, 9:4.
5. Louella Parsons, "Dr. Freud Gets Warners' Bid," *New York Journal-American*, July 22, 1938; Letter of August 1, 1938, *Dark Victory* file, Warner Archive; Memos from Bob Ross to T. C. Wright, November 7 and December 3, 1938, Warner Archive.
6. Stine, *Conversations with Bette Davis*, p. 136; Bette Davis, with Whitney Stine, *Mother Goddam* (1974; New York, 1975), p. 109; D. H. Lawrence, "*St. Mawr*" and "*The Man Who Died*" (1925; New York, 1960), p. 17; Joseph Conrad, *Victory* (1915; Garden City, N.Y., 1957), p. 242; Casey Robinson, *Dark Victory*, ed. Bernard Dick (Madison, Wisc., 1981), pp. 164, 166–167.
7. John McCarty, "Bogey," *Hollywood Gangland* (New York, 1993), p. 50; Letter from James Farrell to his agent, December 21, 1939, Warner Archive; Memo from Jack Warner to Bryan Foy, May 25, 1939, Warner Archive; Coe, *Humphrey Bogart*, p. 54.
8. Bob Thomas, *Clown Prince of Hollywood: The Antic Life and Times of Jack L. Warner* (New York, 1990), p. 124; Thompson, *Bogie and Me*, p. 63; Interview with Gloria Romanoff, Carlsbad, California, March 24, 1996; Johnson, *Letters*, p. 84; Goodman, *Bogey*, p. 49. Romanoff closed his restaurant in 1962, and died rich and respectable in 1971.
9. Memos from Frank Mattison to T. C. Wright, December 16, 1939 and December 9, 1939, Warner Archive; Leo Rosten, *Hollywood: The Movie Colony, The Movie Makers* (New York, 1941), p. 11.

10. Raoul Walsh, *Each Man in His Time* (New York, 1974), p. 302; Behlmer, *Inside Warner Bros.*, p. 143; Vincent Sherman, Oral History, p. 78, American Film Institute, Los Angeles; Rudy Behlmer, *Behind the Scenes* (1982; Hollywood, 1990), p.140; Behlmer, *Inside Warner Bros.*, p. 144.

11. Frank, *Humphrey Bogart*, p. 22; Niven, *Bring On the Empty Horses*, p. 214. Many of those parts were dreadful, but he was also a radio station manager, test pilot, crusading D.A., film producer, wrestling promoter, prison official, radio contact man, horse trainer, trucker, carnival owner, private detective and anti-Nazi fighter.

12. Gehman, *Bogart*, p. 68; Shipman, *Great Movie Stars*, p. 72; "Bogey Boom," *Newsweek*, 66 (November 1, 1965), 95; Brooks, *The Producer*, p. 205.

13. Goodman, *Bogey*, p. 23; Howard Greenberger, *Bogey's Baby: A Biography of Lauren Bacall* (New York, 1976), p. 67; Thompson, *Bogie and Me*, p. 157; "The Art of Mr. Bogart," 9:4.

14. Goodman, *Bogey*, p. 32; "Humphrey Bogart," *Current Biography* (New York, 1942), p. 91; "The Art of Mr. Bogart," 9:4; Bogart, "Why Hollywood Hates Me," *Screen Book*, p. 69; Sklar, *City Boys*, p. 114.

15. Interview with Gloria Stuart Sheekman; Interviews with Verita Peterson Thompson; Interviews with Cynthia Lindsay. For Maud's obituary, see *Variety*, November 27, 1940.

6. John Huston and *The Maltese Falcon*

1. Axel Madsen, *John Huston* (Garden City, N.Y., 1978), p. 40; Interview with Arthur Miller, Roxbury, Connecticut, October 25, 1995; Capote, "John Huston," *Observations*, pp. 10–11.

2. Madsen, *John Huston*, p. 26; Telegram from Bogart to Huston, October 10, 1953, Herrick Library; Interviews with Evelyn Keyes, Los Angeles, September 11, 1995 and March 6, 1996; Madsen, *John Huston*, p. 141; Ruddy, *Bogey*, p. 156; Howard Thompson, "Humphrey Bogart Speaks Up on *The African Queen* and Future Screen Production," *New York Times*, March 2, 1952, 2:5.

3. Jaffe, "Oral History," p. 238; Behlmer, *Inside Warner Bros.*, p. 156; W. R. Burnett, in *Backstory*, p. 64; Behlmer, *Inside Warner Bros.*, p. 127; Behlmer, *Behind the Scenes*, pp. 138–139.

4. Behlmer, *Inside Warner Bros.*, p. 126; Memo from John Wexley to Hal Wallis, March 21, 1940, Warner Archive; W. R. Burnett, in *Backstory*, pp. 64, 81; W. R. Burnett, Oral History of the American Film Institute, Herrick Library.

5. Richard Schickel, "Humphrey Bogart: Gentleman Declassed," *Schickel on Film* (New York, 1989), p. 225; Richard Schickel, "Raoul Walsh," *The Men Who Made the Movies* (New York, 1975), p. 44; Interviews with Joan Leslie, Los Angeles, March 17 and March 23, 1996.

6. William Donati, *Ida Lupino: A Biography* (Lexington, Ky., 1996), p. 66; Kobal, *People Will Talk*, p. 542; Behlmer, *Inside Warner Bros.*, pp. 128–129; McCarty, *Hollywood Gangland*, p. 130; Thomas Schatz, *The Genius of the System: Hollywood Filmmaking in the Studio Era* (New York, 1988), p. 305.

7. John Huston and W. R. Burnett, *High Sierra,* ed. Douglas Gomery (Madison, Wisc., 1979), pp. 80; 76; 130; 181.

8. *Variety,* January 22, 1941; *Kansas City Star,* January 26, 1941, p. 12-D; Ferguson, *Film Criticism,* p. 339; Jeffrey Meyers, "Orwell as Film Critic," *Sight and Sound,* 48 (Autumn 1979), 256 (in Orwell's *Nineteen Eighty-Four,* New York, 1949, p. 271, the tyrannical O'Brien's image of the future is "a boot stamping on a human face—forever"); Letter from the Milwaukee Better Films Council to Warner Bros., March 7, 1941, Warner Archive.

9. Letter from Sam Jaffe to Jack Warner, May 12, 1939, Warner Archive; Benchley, *Humphrey Bogart,* p. 78.

10. Edmund Wilson, "The Boys in the Back Room," *Classics and Commercials* (1950; New York, 1962), p. 49n; Behlmer, *Behind the Scenes,* p. 136; "John Huston," *Interviews with Film Directors,* ed. Andrew Sarris (1967; New York, 1969), p. 255; Madsen, *John Huston,* p. 51.

11. Behlmer, *Inside Warner Bros.,* p. 151; Dashiell Hammett, *The Maltese Falcon* (1930; New York, 1972), p. 108; Mary Astor, *A Life on Film* (New York, 1971), p. 160.

12. Grobel, *The Hustons,* p. 218; *Voices of Film Experience: From 1894 to the Present,* ed. Jay Leyda (New York, 1977), p. 278; Mary Astor, "Bogie Was For Reel," *New York Times,* April 23, 1967, 2:21; Astor, *A Life on Film,* p. 166.

13. Behlmer, *Inside Warner Bros.,* p. 151; Wallis, *Starmaker,* pp. 110–111; Meta Carpenter and Orin Borsten, *A Loving Gentleman* (1976; New York, 1977), pp. 262–263.

14. John Huston, *The Maltese Falcon,* ed. Richard Anobile (New York, 1974), pp. 8; 79; 108; 118; 92; 68; 227; 145; 210; Grobel, *The Hustons,* p. 219.

15. Huston, *The Maltese Falcon,* pp. 172; 185; 233; 242; 245–247; 253; Grobel, *The Hustons,* p. 222. All critics, from Virginia Wexman, "*The Maltese Falcon* from Fiction to Film," *Library Quarterly,* 45 (January 1975), 50 to James Naremore, "John Huston and *The Maltese Falcon,*" *Reflections in a Male Eye: John Huston and the American Experience,* ed. Gaylyn Studler and David Desser (Washington, D.C., 1993), p. 134, have also missed the allusion to Shakespeare.

16. William Nolan, *John Huston: King Rebel* (Los Angeles, 1965), p. 42; Coe, *Humphrey Bogart,* p. 74; "101st Changes Mind on Rarity of Falcons," *New York Times,* September 28, 1941, p. 41.

The Maltese Falcon begins with a shot of San Francisco. Brigid stays at the "St. Mark Hotel," a fictional composite of the real St. Francis and Mark Hopkins hotels, and the city has paid tribute to both the novel and the film. John's Grill, at 63 Ellis Street, mentioned at the end of the novel, has a Maltese Falcon Room on the second floor of the restaurant—complete with photographs, memorabilia and statue of the bird. On the southwest corner of the intersection of Bush and Burritt, near Stockton Street and diagonally across from Dashiell Hammett Street, a plaque states: "On approximately this spot, Miles Archer, partner of Sam Spade, was done in by Brigid O'Shaughnessy."

In September 1974 one of the falcons made for the film was stolen from an exhibition at the Los Angeles County Museum. The *Herald-Examiner* called for a new Sam Spade to find it, but also suspected the theft was a publicity stunt.

7. War Movies and *Casablanca*

1. Memo from Jack Warner to Lewis Seiler, May 4, 1942, Warner Archive; Doug McClelland, *Forties Film Talk: Oral Histories of Hollywood* (Jefferson, N.C., 1992), p. 127; Interview with Irene Manning, San Carlos, California, March 21, 1996.

2. Kobal, *People Will Talk,* p. 556; Sherman, Oral History, pp. 139–140; Interview with Vincent Sherman; Sherman, Oral History, p. 139.

3. Astor, "Bogie Was For Reel," 2:2; Astor, *A Life on Film,* p. 168; John Huston, *An Open Book* (1980; New York, 1990), pp. 87–88; Interview with Vincent Sherman; Madsen, *John Huston,* p. 60.

4. John Brosnan, *Movie Magic* (New York, 1974), p. 51; Marcel Dalio, *Mes Années folles* (Paris, 1976), p. 177, my translation; Behlmer, *Inside Warner Bros.,* p. 214; Paul Henreid, with Julius Fast, *Ladies' Man: An Autobiography* (New York, 1984), p. 128; Julius Epstein, Philip Epstein and Howard Koch, *Casablanca,* ed. Richard Anobile (New York, 1974), p. 6; Francisco, *You Must Remember This,* p. 193.

5. Behlmer, *Behind the Scenes,* p. 157; Frank Miller, *"Casablanca": As Time Goes By: 50th Anniversary Commemorative* (London, 1993), p 134; Behlmer, *Behind the Scenes,* p. 164.

6. Laurence Leamer, *As Time Goes By: The Life of Ingrid Bergman* (New York, 1986), p. 88; Benchley, *Humphrey Bogart,* p. 112; Harmetz, *Round Up the Usual Suspects,* p. 97; Epsteins and Koch, *Casablanca,* p. 6; Pauline Kael, *Kiss Kiss Bang Bang* (1968; New York, 1969), p. 303.

7. Howard Koch, *Casablanca: Script and Legend* (Woodstock, N.Y., 1973), pp. 20, 25; 41; 47; 31 and 137; 38 and 83; 47.

8. Koch, *Casablanca,* p. 53; Bacall, *By Myself,* p. 132; Koch, *Casablanca,* p. 68; George Orwell, *Homage to Catalonia,* introduction by Lionel Trilling (1938; New York, 1959), p. 232; Koch, *Casablanca,* p. 77.

9. Koch, *Casablanca,* p. 86; Albert Camus, *Between Hell and Reason: Essays from the Resistance Newspaper "Combat," 1944–1947,* ed. and trans. Alexandre de Gramont (Hanover, N.H., 1991), p. 42; Koch, *Casablanca,* pp. 91; 115; 124; 130; 133; 136–138.

10. Julius Epstein, *Remembering "Casablanca"* (Los Angeles: Imprenta Glorias, 1994), pp. 13; 26; 28, courtesy of Gloria Stuart (Epstein forgot that Sam Warner had died in 1927); Irving Lazar, with Annette Taper, *Swifty* (New York, 1995), p. 170; Memo from Hal Wallis to Michael Curtiz, May 21, 1942, Warner Archive.

11. Koch, *Casablanca,* pp. 155–156; Kobal, *People Will Talk,* p. 470; Harlan Lebo, *"Casablanca": Behind the Scenes* (New York, 1992), p. 148.

12. Wallis, *Starmaker,* p. 209; Koch, *Casablanca,* pp. 160; 161; Wallis, *Starmaker,* p. 212.

13. Julius Epstein, in *Backstory*, pp. 171, 185; Evan William Cameron, ed., *Sound and the Cinema: The Coming of Sound to American Film* (Pleasantville, N.Y., 1980), p. 105; Koch, *Casablanca*, pp. 127; 155–156; 42; 91–92.

14. Wallis, *Starmaker*, p. 90; Koch, *Casablanca*, pp. 10; 109; Clayton Koppes and Gregory Black, *Hollywood Goes to War: How Politics, Profits and Propaganda Shaped World War II Movies* (1987; London, 1988), p. 290; Richard Raskin, "*Casablanca* and United States Foreign Policy," *Film History*, 4 (1990), 160.

15. Koch, *Casablanca*, p. 82; Umberto Eco, "*Casablanca*: Cult Movies and Intertextual Collage," *Sub-Stance*, 47 (1985), 3, 7, 10; Robert Sherwood, *Roosevelt and Hopkins* (New York, 1948), p. 655.

16. Lebo, *Casablanca*, p. 193; Letter from Charles Einfeld to Martin Weiser of Warner Bros. in Kansas City, July 17, 1940, Warner Archive. According to Powdermaker, *Hollywood: The Dream Factory*, p. 209, the other top movie salaries in 1946 were: "Bette Davis $328,000; Bing Crosby $325,000; Deanna Durbin $325,477; Betty Grable $299,333; Ann Sheridan $269,345; Robert Montgomery $250,000; Errol Flynn $199,999; Rosalind Russell $190,104; Ronald Reagan $169,750; Rita Hayworth $94,916."

17. *The Groucho Letters: Letters from and to Groucho Marx*, ed. Arthur Sheekman (1967; New York, 1994), p. 14; Gordon, *My Side*, p. 410; Raymond Massey, *A Hundred Different Lives* (Boston, 1979), p. 283; Koppes and Black, *Hollywood Goes to War*, p. 119.

18. Telegram from Bogart to Jack Warner, April 6, 1943, Warner Archive; James Agee, *Agee on Film* (1958; Boston, 1964), 1:53; Ruddy, *Bogey*, p. 14.

19. Sklar, *City Boys*, p. 166; Shipman, *Movie Talk*, p. 18; Todd Rainsberger, *James Wong Howe: Cinematographer* (San Diego, 1981), p. 199.

20. Mayo Methot Bogart, "Bogie—Over There," *Photoplay*, May 1944, p. 28; "'Hollywood Battlefield' (Word From the Front), 1944–1945," *The Hollywood Reporter: The Golden Years*, ed. Tichi Wilkerson and Marcia Borie (New York, 1984), p. 165.

21. Mayo Bogart, "Bogie—Over There," p. 87; Huston, *An Open Book*, p. 114.

8. Warner, Bacall and Howard Hawks

1. The repetitive titles of Bogart's films, both early and late, suggest how the industry capitalized on successful pictures and repeatedly used the same plots and themes: *A Devil with Women* (1930) and *Beat the Devil* (1954); *Big City Blues* (1932), *The Big Shot* (1942) and *The Big Sleep* (1946); *Two Against the World* (1936) and *The Two Mrs. Carrolls* (1947); *Kid Galahad* (1937) and *The Oklahoma Kid* (1939); *Dead End* (1937) and *Dead Reckoning* (1947); *The Amazing Dr. Clitterhouse* (1938) and *The Return of Doctor X* (1939); *Angels with Dirty Faces* (1938) and *We're No Angels* (1955); *Dark Victory* (1939) and *Dark Passage* (1947); *They Drive By Night* (1940), *The Wagons Roll at Night* (1941) and *All Through the Night* (1942); *High Sierra* (1941) and *The Treasure of the Sierra Madre* (1948); *Across the Pacific* (1942) and *Action in the North Atlantic* (1943); *Casablanca* (1943), *Sahara* (1943) and *Sirocco* (1951).

2. Shipman, *Movie Talk,* p. 211; Kobal, *People Will Talk,* p. 421; Behlmer, *Inside Warner Bros.,* pp. 228–233.

3. Telegram from Bogart to Warner, May 26, 1944, Warner Archive; Interview with Malvin Wald, Sherman Oaks, California, March 3, 1996; Hedda Hopper Papers, Herrick Library; Bacall, *By Myself,* p. 101; Brooks, *Lulu in Hollywood,* pp. 67–68.

4. Stephen Bogart, *Bogart,* p. 231; Hyams, *Bogie,* p. 84; Humphrey Bogart, as told to Jack Holland, "What Do I Owe My Wife?," *Movieland,* March 1950, p. 54.

5. Bacall, *By Myself,* p. 104; Ernest Hemingway, *A Moveable Feast* (1964; New York, 1967), p. 208; *Hawks on Hawks,* ed. Joseph McBride (Berkeley, 1982), p. 102; Bacall, *By Myself,* pp. 114–119.

6. Bogart, "What Do I Owe My Wife?" *Movieland,* p. 53; Bacall, *By Myself,* pp. 133; 106. Methot returned to Portland after their divorce in May 1945 and lived with her mother. On June 9, 1951, while Bogart was making *The African Queen,* she died alone in a Portland motel room at the age of forty-seven, of alcoholism and complications following surgery for cancer. She had spent most of her divorce settlement, and left $1,400 in cash and an estate of $50,000. Her obituary appeared in the *New York Times* on June 10, 1951, p. 93. When he emerged from the African jungle and learned of her death, Bogart said: "Too bad. Such a waste. . . . She had had real talent, she had just thrown her life away" (Bacall, *By Myself,* p. 209).

7. Raymond Chandler, *Selected Letters,* ed. Frank MacShane (New York, 1987), p. 30; William Wellman, Jr., "Howard Hawks: The Distance Runner," *Focus on Howard Hawks,* ed. Joseph McBride (Englewood Cliffs, N.J., 1972), p. 8; Niven Busch, in *Backstory,* p. 94; Bacall, *By Myself,* pp. 107–108.

8. *Hawks on Hawks,* p. 95; Hemingway, *To Have and Have Not,* pp. 9, 225; Behlmer, *Inside Warner Bros.,* p. 236.

9. Jules Furthman and William Faulkner, *To Have and Have Not,* ed. Bruce Kawin (Madison, Wisc., 1980), pp. 190; 215; Bogart to Gladys Hall, May 9, 1946, Herrick Library.

10. Furthman and Faulkner, *To Have and Have Not,* pp. 217; 96; 222; "Interview with Howard Hawks," *Focus on Howard Hawks,* p. 20; Peter Bogdanovich, *The Cinema of Howard Hawks* (New York, 1962), p. 24; Lauren Bacall, *Now* (New York, 1994), pp. 109–110.

11. Bacall, *By Myself,* p. 104; Furthman and Faulkner, *To Have and Have Not,* p. 157; Gerald Mast, *Howard Hawks, Storyteller* (New York, 1982), p. 243; Bacall, *Now,* p. 107; Furthman and Faulkner, *To Have and Have Not,* p. 115.

12. Bacall, *By Myself,* p. 417; Kobal, *People Will Talk,* p. 488; Furthman and Faulkner, *To Have and Have Not,* pp. 85; 89; 118; 209; 198; "Interview with Howard Hawks," *Focus on Howard Hawks,* p. 21.

13. Bogdanovich, *Pieces of Time,* p. 162; Stine, *Conversations with Bette Davis,* p. 136; Agee, *On Film,* 1:354, 121; Bacall, *By Myself,* p. 142. Bacall, Veronica Lake and Lizabeth Scott had the same elegant figure, husky voice and curtain of silky blond hair. Lake, born in 1919, made her film debut with RKO in

1939. Scott (born in 1922, film debut 1945), who had also been a New York model and played small parts on Broadway, was shorter and had a gentler personality. She became Paramount's equivalent to Lake and Bacall, "almost parodying Betty's gestures, voice, hair-do, clothes, even to wearing a checked suit and black beret" (Greenberger, *Bogey's Baby*, p. 88).

14. Memos from Eric Stacey to T. C. Wright, November 24, 1944 and December 22, 1944, Warner Archive; Behlmer, *Inside Warner Bros.*, pp. 244–245; Bacall, *By Myself*, pp. 134; 142. Bogart's drunkenness continued well after his marriage to Bacall. On October 11, 1948, for example, an employee told Jack Warner that Bogart had called the studio, "talked as though he was quite 'drunk' and when he used some foul language he was cut off. Our operator explained that the Telephone Company will cut people off who use foul language" (Warner Archive).

15. Chandler, *The Big Sleep*, p. 213; William Faulkner, Leigh Brackett and Jules Furthman, "*The Big Sleep,*" *Film Scripts One*, ed. George Garrett, O. B. Hardison, Jr., and Jane Gelfman (New York, 1989), pp. 193–195; 308 (this early version of the screenplay differs in many ways from the film); *Hawks on Hawks*, ed. McBride, p. 148; Mast, *Howard Hawks, Storyteller*, p. 276; *Raymond Chandler Speaking*, ed. Dorothy Gardiner and Kathrine Walker (Boston, 1962), p. 221.

16. Faulkner, Brackett and Furthman, *The Big Sleep*, p. 185; McClelland, *Forties Film Talk*, p. 325; Behlmer, *Inside Warner Bros.*, pp. 248–249; Mast, *Howard Hawks, Storyteller*, p. 286.

17. Letter from the Breen Office to Warner Bros., August 10, 1948, Herrick Library; John Houseman, "What Makes American Movies Tough?," *Vogue*, January 15, 1947, p. 125; *Hawks on Hawks*, ed. McBride, p. 102; Chandler, *Selected Letters*, p. 75; Leigh Brackett, in *Backstory Two: Interviews with Screenwriters of the 1940s and 1950s*, ed. Pat McGilligan (Berkeley, 1991), p. 18.

18. Ernest Hemingway, *A Farewell to Arms* (1929; New York, 1957), p. 185; Faulkner, Brackett and Furthman, *The Big Sleep*, pp. 315; 293.

9. FOURTH MARRIAGE

1. Ruddy, *Bogey*, p. 87; Bacall, *By Myself*, pp. 139; 156; 153.

2. Interviews with Verita Peterson Thompson; Interview with Sylvia Sheekman Thompson, Idlewild, California, September 6, 1995; Interview with Dorris Johnson.

3. Greenberger, *Bogey's Baby*, p. 130; Howard Hawks, Oral History, p. 12, Columbia University.

4. Gladys Hall, "I Think It's Fine," Herrick Library; Lazar, *Swifty*, p. 170; Bacall, *By Myself*, p. 242.

5. Interview with Sylvia Sheekman Thompson; Interview with Billy Wilder; Interviews with Warren Stevens, Los Angeles, September 23, 1995, and March 8, 1996; Stephen Bogart, *Bogart*, pp. 217, 8; Interview with Dorris Johnson.

6. Brooks, *The Producer,* p. 237; Bacall, *By Myself,* pp. 192, 215; Bogart, "What Do I Owe My Wife?" *Movieland,* p. 53.

7. Jim Bishop, *The Mark Hellinger Story* (New York, 1952), p. 309; Gladys Hall, "I Think It's Fine," Herrick Library; Astor, "Bogie Was For Reel," *New York Times,* 2:21.

8. Goodman, *Bogey,* p. 25; "Bogart on Hollywood," *Look,* p. 101; Hyams, *Bogart and Bacall,* p. 107.

9. Bacall, *By Myself,* p. 138; Benchley, *Humphrey Bogart,* p. 176; Hyams, *Bogie,* p. 96.

10. Interviews with Verita Peterson Thompson; Interview with Ted Eden (the present owner of the *Santana*), San Francisco, September 20, 1995; Shipp, "The Adventures of Humphrey Bogart," p. 33; Interview with Gloria Stuart Sheekman.

11. Humphrey Bogart, "The Most Unforgivable Character I've Met," *Photoplay,* July 1949, p. 48; Bacall, *By Myself,* p. 183.

12. Bacall, *By Myself,* p. 188; Art Linkletter, *Women Are My Favorite People* (Garden City, N.Y., 1974), p. 69; Stephen Bogart, *Bogart,* p. 17; Benchley, *Humphrey Bogart,* p. 169.

13. Goodman, *Bogey,* p. 60; Jaffe, Oral History, p. 209; Interviews with Verita Peterson Thompson.

10. A CELEBRITY IN POLITICS

1. House of Representatives, 76th Congress, Hearings Before a Special Committee of Un-American Activities, *Investigation of Un-American Propaganda Activities in the United States* (1940), Volume 3, Executive Hearings, pp. 1382, 1385; 1376–1378.

2. Ronald Brownstein, *The Power and the Glitter: The Hollywood-Washington Connection* (1991; New York, 1992), p. 101; Humphrey Bogart, "I Stuck My Neck Out," *Saturday Evening Post,* 217 (February 10, 1945), 19, 87–88.

3. Bioff and Browne turned up in the West Street jail in 1943 when Robert Lowell was serving time as a conscientious objector. "Hairy, muscular, suburban, / wearing chocolate double-breasted suits," the "Hollywood pimps" blew their tops when a pacificist vegetarian tried to convert them to his diet and "beat him black and blue" (Robert Lowell, "Memories of West Street and Lepke," *Life Studies,* 1964; New York, 1967, p. 86). In 1955 Bioff was blown up in Phoenix, Arizona by a booby trap that was planted in his car.

4. David Caute, *The Great Fear: The Anti-Communist Purge Under Truman and Eisenhower* (New York, 1978), p. 488; Higham, *Warner Brothers,* p. 180; Sklar, *Movie-Made America,* p. 258.

5. Stephen Ambrose, *Nixon: The Education of a Politician, 1913–1962* (New York, 1987), p. 150; Philip Dunne, *Take Two: A Life in Movies and Politics* (1980; New York, 1992), p. 196; Huston, *An Open Book,* p. 131; Larry Ceplair and Steven Englund, *The Inquisition in Hollywood: Politics in the Film Community, 1930–1960* (Garden City, N.Y., 1980), p. 275. The Holly-

wood Ten were the producer Adrian Scott, the directors Edward Dmytryk and Herbert Biberman, and the writers Alvah Bessie, Lester Cole, Ring Lardner, Jr., John Howard Lawson, Albert Maltz, Samuel Ornitz and Dalton Trumbo.

6. Goodman, *Bogey,* p. 201; Bacall, *By Myself,* p. 175; Sklar, *City Boys,* p. 195.

7. Interview with Marsha Hunt, Los Angeles, September 16, 1995; Robert Carr, "The Hollywood Hearings," *The House Committee on Un-American Activities* (Ithaca, N.Y., 1952), p. 55; Ceplair and Englund, *Inquisition in Hollywood,* p. 281.

8. Nancy Schwartz, *The Hollywood Writers' Wars* (New York, 1982), p. 254; Behlmer, *Inside Warner Bros.,* p. 288; Ceplair and Englund, *Inquisition in Hollywood,* p. 280; Grobel, *The Hustons,* p. 302.

9. Dunne, *Take Two,* p. 199; Ceplair and Englund, *Inquisition in Hollywood,* p. 283; Schwartz, *Hollywood Writers' Wars,* p. 272.

10. Dunne, *Take Two,* p. 199; Ian Hamilton, *Writers in Hollywood, 1915–1951* (New York, 1990), p. 293; Victor Navasky, *Naming Names* (1980; New York, 1981), p. 83; Hamilton, *Writers in Hollywood,* p. 290.

11. Carr, *The House Committee on Un-American Activities,* p. 55; Madsen, *John Huston,* p. 92; Henreid, *Ladies' Man,* p. 183; Gehman, *Bogart,* p. 71; Navasky, *Naming Names,* p. 83.

12. Goodman, *Bogey,* p. 91; Henreid, *Ladies' Man,* p. 185; "Hollywood Fights Back," ABC radio broadcast, November 2, 1947, courtesy of Marsha Hunt, who was one of the actresses on the CFA flight to Washington; Humphrey Bogart, "I'm No Communist," *Photoplay,* March 1948, p. 86; Sklar, *City Boys,* p. 196.

13. George Eells, *Hedda and Louella* (1972; New York, 1973), p. 17; Louella Parsons, radio script, November 9, 1947, Warner Archive; Jaffe, Oral History, pp. 256–257; Letter from Malvin Wald to Jeffrey Meyers, November 19, 1995.

14. John Cogley, *Report on Blacklisting,* in Mast, ed., *Movies in Our Midst,* p. 579; Hamilton, *Writers in Hollywood,* p. 293.

15. Navasky, *Naming Names,* p. 153; "The Bogarts Regret," *Newsweek,* December 15, 1947, p. 23; Bogart, "I'm No Communist," *Photoplay,* pp. 53, 86–87.

16. Lillian Ross, "Onward and Upward with the Arts," *New Yorker,* February 21, 1948, pp. 40–41. David Caute, *The Great Fear,* p. 502, points out that in 1952, before releasing *Moulin Rouge,* Huston also had to bend the knee: "Ray Brewer, labor boss of IATSE, negotiated [Huston's] repentance, confession and final clearance."

17. Lester Cole, *Hollywood Red* (Palo Alto, Calif., 1981), p. 289; Alvah Bessie, *Inquisition in Eden* (New York, 1965), p. 223; Gary Giddons, *Faces in the Crowd* (New York, 1992), p. 130.

18. Interviews with Evelyn Keyes; Interview with Marsha Hunt; Stephen Bogart, *Bogart,* p. 147.

19. Dunne, *Take Two,* p. 202; Studler and Desser, eds., *Reflections in a Male Eye,* p. 223; Letter from Ring Lardner, Jr., to Jeffrey Meyers, July 23, 1995; Interview with Arthur Miller.

20. Schwartz, *Hollywood Writers' Wars,* p. 281; Brooks, *The Producer,* pp. 238, 333; Interview with Edward Dmytryk, Encino, California, September 2, 1995; Edward Dmytryk in *Hollywood on Trial,* documentary film, written by Arnie Reisman, directed by David Helpern, narrated by John Huston, 1988.
21. Arthur Laurents, in *Backstory Two,* p. 130; *Conversations with Losey,* ed. Michel Ciment (London, 1985), p. 71.
22. "Bogart Defends Actors' Right on Political Stump," *Daily Variety,* November 6, 1950; see also "Inalienable Right," *New York Times,* November 12, 1950, 2:5; ALERT, August 1951, Herrick Library; Eric Bentley, ed., *Thirty Years of Treason: Excerpts from Hearings before the House Un-American Activities Committee, 1938–1968* (New York, 1971), p. 345.
23. House of Representatives, 82nd Congress, *Committee on Un-American Activities, Communist Infiltration of the Hollywood Motion-Picture Industry* (July 6, 1951), Part 1, p. 145; Huston, *Open Book,* p. 137; Sterling Hayden, *Wanderer* (1963; New York, 1964), p. 366.

11. MEXICO AND THE FLORIDA KEYS

1. Brooks, *The Producer,* pp. 64–65; Benchley, *Humphrey Bogart,* p. 158.
2. Coe, *Humphrey Bogart,* p. 112; Lizabeth Scott, Oral History, pp. 50–51; 53, Southern Methodist University; Interview with Lizabeth Scott, Los Angeles, March 7, 1996; Letter from Jerry Wald to Jack Warner, July 22, 1946, *Dark Passage* file, Warner Archive.
3. Letter from "Charlie" to Henry Blanke, May 2, 1947, *The Treasure of the Sierra Madre* file, Warner Archive; Evelyn Keyes, *Scarlett O'Hara's Younger Sister* (Secaucus, N.J., 1977), p. 112.
4. William Hawkins, "Bogart Made Possible Director's Venture," no citation, [1947–48], Herrick Library; Coe, *Humphrey Bogart,* p. 121; Humphrey Bogart, "Locationing in Mexico" (September 1947), *The Hollywood Reporter: The Golden Years,* p. 206; John Huston, publicity release, *Sierra Madre* file, Warner Archive.
5. Letter from Bogart to Steve Trilling, April 25, 1947, *Sierra Madre* file, Warner Archive; Huston, *An Open Book,* p. 147. Evelyn Keyes confirmed this incident.
6. John Huston, *The Treasure of the Sierra Madre,* ed. James Naremore (Madison, Wisc., 1979), p. 54; Grobel, *The Hustons,* p. 290; John Huston, *The Treasure of the Sierra Madre,* pp. 170; 193–194.
7. Behlmer, *Inside Warner Bros.,* pp. 282–283; John Huston, *The Treasure of the Sierra Madre,* pp, 62–64; Agee, *On Film,* 1:291–293; Will Whiteside, "Crew Really Sweats It Out in Producing Jet Fighter Film," *Richmond News-Leader,* July 18, 1949.
8. Bacall, *By Myself,* p. 180; Interviews with Verita Peterson Thompson; Brosnan, *Movie Magic,* p. 108.
9. Edward G. Robinson, with Leonard Spigelglass, *All My Yesterdays* (New York, 1973), p. 181; Pettigrew, *Bogart,* pp. 9–10; Huston, *An Open Book,* p. 151.

10. Letter from Collier Young to Jerry Wald, December 10, 1947, *Key Largo* file, Warner Archive; Letter from Jerry Wald, March 6, 1948, Warner Archive; John Huston, statement on *Key Largo,* July 29, 1948, Warner Archive; *Time,* 52 (August 2, 1948), 74; Agee, *On Film,* 1:328.

11. Huston, *An Open Book,* p. 352; Sam Jaffe, Oral History, p. 241; Interview with Jess Morgan; Sam Jaffe, Oral History, p. 214; Bacall, *By Myself,* p. 136.

12. "Bogart's Moroccan Campaign," *Newsweek,* October 10, 1949, p. 22; "Bogie the Playboy," *Los Angeles Evening-Herald,* November 10, 1949, p. A-11; Goodman, *Bogey,* p. 37; Earl Wilson, *Daily News,* September 28, 1949; Letter from Warner Bros. to Humphrey Bogart, April 27, 1950, Warner Archive.

13. Otis Guernsey, Jr., *New York Herald-Tribune,* February 20, 1950; Dana Polan, *In a Lonely Place* (London, 1993), pp. 56–57; Brooks, *Lulu in Hollywood,* pp. 62–63; Polan, *In a Lonely Place,* p. 12; Ray, *I Was Interrupted,* p. 105.

14. Polan, *In a Lonely Place,* pp. 61, 64; Geoff Andrew, *The Films of Nicholas Ray* (London, 1991), p. 61; Howard Thompson, "Humphrey Bogart Speaks Up on *The African Queen* and Future Screen Production," *New York Times,* March 2, 1952, 2:5; Benchley, *Humphrey Bogart,* p. 188; Interview with Billy Wilder; Interviews with Joe Hyams, Burbank, California, March 23 and 26, 1996.

12. AFRICA AND THE ACADEMY AWARD

1. Telegram from Mort Blumenstock of the East Coast office to Jack Warner, Oct. 16, 1950, Warner Archive; Lillian Ross, *Picture* (1952; New York, 1984), p. 127. Bogart first wore his trademark trench coat in *Across the Pacific* (1942).

2. *Conversations with Losey,* p. 102; Louella Parsons, "Dies Holding Bogart Baby," *Los Angeles Examiner,* March 13, 1951; Louella Parsons, "Bogie Man," *Cosmopolitan,* 139 (November 5, 1955), 95.

3. Katharine Hepburn, *The Making of "The African Queen"* (New York, 1987), p. 34; Greenberger, *Bogey's Baby,* p. 126; Ruddy, *Bogey,* p. 152; *Sunday News* (Los Angeles), December 2, 1951.

4. Interview with Angela Allen, London, July 22, 1996; Joseph Conrad, *"Heart of Darkness," Three Great Tales* (New York, [1960]), p. 248; Hepburn, *The Making of "The African Queen",* p. 23; John Huston, *"The African Queen:* Behind-the-Scenes Story," *Theatre Arts,* 36 (Fall 1952), 92; Huston, *An Open Book,* p. 204.

5. Ruddy, *Bogey,* pp. 151–152; Hepburn, *The Making of "The African Queen",* p. 118; Ruddy, *Bogey,* p. 151.

6. Greenberger, *Bogey's Baby,* p. 115; Humphrey Bogart, "Humphrey Bogart Tells the Truth about Hepburn," *Coronet,* 31 (April 1952), 144; Wilkerson and Borie, *Hollywood Reporter: The Golden Years,* p. 246; Bogart, "Bogart Tells the Truth about Hepburn," *Coronet,* p. 146; Nolan, *John Huston: King Rebel,* p. 104.

7. Peter Viertel, *White Hunter, Black Heart* (London, 1954), pp. 70; 282; 72; 284; 282.

8. Huston, *An Open Book,* p. 198; Hepburn, *The Making of "The African Queen,"* p. 69; Brosnan, *Movie Magic,* p. 93.

9. "Mr. Huston Makes a Comic Epic," *Daily Telegraph,* January 7, 1952; Grobel, *The Hustons,* p. 363; Hepburn, *The Making of "The African Queen",* p. 110; Theodore Bikel, *Theo: An Autobiography* (New York, 1994), p. 113; Bogart, "Bogart Tells the Truth about Hepburn," *Coronet,* p. 146.

10. Interview with Jack Cardiff, Saffron Walden, England, July 18, 1996; Jack Cardiff, *Magic Hour: The Life of a Cameraman* (London, 1996), p. 148; James Agee [and John Huston], *"The African Queen," Agee on Film* (1960; New York, 1969), 2:180; 199–200; 197; 235; 253. There is no marriage ceremony in the printed screenplay.

11. Grobel, *The Hustons,* p. 377; Ruddy, *Bogey,* pp. 176, 181; Bogart, "The Oscar Myth," *Cosmopolitan,* pp. 31, 165; Brooks, *The Producer,* p. 332.

12. Interview with John Strauss, Los Angeles, September 5, 1995; Bogart, "The Oscar Myth," *Cosmopolitan,* p. 31; Interview with Dorris Johnson.

13. McClelland, *Forties Film Talk,* p. 183; Bacall, *By Myself,* p. 216; Anthony Holden, *Behind the Oscar: The Secret History of the Academy Awards* (1993; New York, 1994), p. 55; Bogart, "The Oscar Myth," *Cosmopolitan,* p. 165.

14. Gehman, *Bogart,* pp. 41; 28; Thompson, *Bogie and Me,* p. 154; Hedda Hopper, "Bogart Clears Way for *Battle Circus,*" *Los Angeles Times,* May 19, 1952, 3:10.

15. Brownstein, *The Power and the Glitter,* pp. 129–130; Lauren Bacall, "I Hate Young Men," *Look,* November 3, 1953, pp. 36–37; Brownstein, *The Power and the Glitter,* p. 126; Bacall, *By Myself,* p. 235; Johnson, *Flashback,* p. 218.

16. Johnson, *Letters,* p. 205; Noel Coward, *Diaries,* ed. Graham Payn and Sheridan Morley (London, 1982), pp. 273, 298; Lazar, *Swifty,* p. 165; Mary Hemingway, *How It Was* (1976; New York, 1977), p. 590.

17. Joan Peyser, *The Memory of All That: The Life of George Gershwin* (New York, 1993), p. 271; "Bogart's Venture," *Newsweek,* 37 (April 9, 1951), 48; *Variety,* September 8, 1954.

18. Linkletter, *Women Are My Favorite People,* p. 68; Ruddy, *Bogey,* p. 177; Gehman, *Bogart,* p. 53; "Neighbors Ask Law Muffle Bogart's Three Barking Boxers," *Los Angeles Times,* April 7, 1953, 2:1.

19. Interviews with Warren Stevens; Interview with Kim Hunter, New York, October 27, 1995. For more on Brooks, see Patrick Brion, *Richard Brooks* (Paris: Chêne, 1986).

20. Jeanine Basinger, *The World War II Combat Film: Anatomy of a Genre* (New York, 1986), p. 269; "Survivor," *Time,* 63 (June 7, 1954), 72; André Bazin, "The Death of Humphrey Bogart," *Cahiers du Cinéma: The 1950s,* ed. Jim Hillier (Cambridge, Mass., 1985), p. 99. Bogart's transition from the typecast gangster of the Thirties to more complex roles in the Forties and Fifties is reflected in the names of the characters he played. He moved from the slangy Mug, Duke, Bugs, Haps, Turkey, Red, Baby Face, Rocks, Whip, Chips, Rip, Mad Dog and Gloves to the more refined Valentine, Sherry, Douglas, Marshall, Geoffrey, Vincent, Dixon and Linus.

21. Sam Jaffe, Oral History, p. 242; Hedda Hopper, *Los Angeles Times,* May 19,

1952, 3:10; Letter from Roy Obringer to Bogart, July 7, 1952, Warner Archive; Richard Brooks, in *Backstory Two*, p. 69.

13. A VERSATILE ACTOR

1. Telegram from Bogart to Huston, September 28, 1951, Herrick Library; Ross, *Picture*, p. 127; Grobel, *The Hustons*, pp. 396–397 (Grobel does not print the last 21 words of Bogart's letter and the first 27 words of Huston's letter, now in the Herrick Library).

2. Huston, *An Open Book*, p. 246; Hyams, *Bogie*, p. 134; Unidentified clipping on *Beat the Devil*, USC Library; James Bacon, "My Friend Bogie," *Made in Hollywood* (New York, 1978), p. 90; *Casablanca*, ed. Richard Anobile (New York, 1974), p. 7.

3. Peter Viertel, *Dangerous Friends: At Large with Huston and Hemingway in the Fifties* (New York, 1992), p. 175; Bacall, *By Myself*, p. 231; Gerald Clarke, *Capote: A Biography* (1988; New York, 1989), p. 239.

4. "Truman Capote," *Writers at Work: The "Paris Review" Interviews*, ed. Malcolm Cowley (1959; New York, 1964), p. 294; Huston, *An Open Book*, p. 246; Ruddy, *Bogey*, p. 170; Clarke, *Capote*, p. 238; Telegram from Robert Morley to John Woolf, Woolf Papers, London; Letter from Bogart to John Woolf, July 15, 1953, Woolf Papers.

5. Letter from Huston to Bogart, November 19, 1952, Herrick Library; W. R. Burnett, in *Backstory*, p. 65; Interview with Dorris Johnson; Shipman, *Movie Talk*, p. 129; Madsen, *John Huston*, p. 139.

6. Letter from Joseph Breen to Jess Morgan, December 1, 1952, Herrick Library; Goodman, *Bogey*, p. 36; Grobel, *The Hustons*, p. 412; Huston, *An Open Book*, p. 248; Gerald Pratley, *The Cinema of John Huston* (South Brunswick, N.J., 1977), p. 101.

7. Gene and Marjorie Fowler, Oral History, p. 46, Herrick Library; Viertel, *Dangerous Friends*, p. 176; Ted Sennett, *The Masters of Menace: Greenstreet and Lorre* (New York, 1979), p. 177. For more on Lorre, see Beyer Friedemann, *Peter Lorre: Seine Filme, sein Leben* (München, 1988).

8. Frank, *Bogart*, p. 67; John McCarten, "Mediterranean Lark," *New Yorker*, 30 (March 20, 1954), 118; Interview with Jess Morgan; Goodman, *Bogey*, p. 111.

9. Interview with Edward Dmytryk; Stanley Kramer, in *The Humphrey Bogart Legend*, HBO documentary, 1979; Jaffe, Oral History, p. 249.

10. Donald Spoto, *Stanley Kramer: Filmmaker* (New York, 1978), p. 173; Rudyard Kipling, "Tommy," *A Choice of Kipling's Verse*, ed. T. S. Eliot (1941; Garden City, N.Y., 1962), p. 181; Letter from Huston to Bogart, June 10, 1953, Herrick Library; Roffman and Purdy, *The Hollywood Social Problem Film*, p. 294.

11. Hyams, *Bogie*, p. 139; Quoted in a letter from Huston to Bogart, September 6, 1953, Herrick Library; Jack Moffit, *Hollywood Reporter*, July 9, 1954; Interviews with Warren Stevens.

12. Dmytryk, *It's a Hell of a Life but Not a Bad Living*, p. 178; Interview with Billy

Wilder; Interview with Ernest Lehman, Los Angeles, August 29, 1995; Bob Thomas, *Golden Boy: The Untold Story of William Holden* (New York, 1983), p. 85.

13. Charles Higham, *Audrey: The Life of Audrey Hepburn* (New York, 1984), p. 64; Stephen Bogart, *Bogart*, p. 180.

14. Interview with Billy Wilder; Maurice Zolotow, *Billy Wilder in Hollywood* (New York, 1977), p. 252; Goodman, *The Fifty-Year Decline and Fall of Hollywood*, p. 258; Goodman, *Bogey*, p. 113.

15. Coe, *Humphrey Bogart*, p. 176; Hyams, *Bogie*, p. 140; Benchley, *Humphrey Bogart*, p. 142; Coe, *Humphrey Bogart*, p. 173.

16. Gehman, *Bogart*, p. 58. The Holden-Hepburn affair was mentioned in Thomas, *Golden Boy*, p. 86; James Spada, *Grace* (Garden City, N.Y., 1987), p. 86; Hellmuth Karasek, *Billy Wilder: Eine Nahaufnahme* (Hamburg, 1992), p. 383; Alexander Walker, *Audrey: Her Real Story* (New York, 1995), p. 89; Stephen Bogart, *Bogart*, p. 181; and in my interview with Ernest Lehman.

14. THE DESPERATE HOURS

1. Interviews with Warren Stevens; Kenneth Geist, *Pictures Will Talk: The Life and Films of Joseph L. Mankiewicz* (New York, 1978), p. 251; David Hanna, *Bogart* (New York, 1976), p. 155; Geist, *Pictures Will Talk*, p. 251.

2. Interviews with Verita Peterson Thompson; Bill Adler, *Sinatra: The Man and the Myth* (New York, 1987), p. 115; Ava Gardner, *Ava: My Story* (New York, 1990), p. 196.

3. Interview with Ernest Lehman; Thompson, *Bogie and Me*, pp. 102, 114; 159; 197, 179; Interviews with Warren Stevens; Interviews with Verita Peterson Thompson; Wilson, *The Show Business That Nobody Knows*, p. 262.

4. Reader's report, Paramount Archive, Herrick Library; Peter Ustinov, *Dear Me* (1977; London, 1978), p. 250; Interview with Sir Peter Ustinov, London, July 5, 1996; Joan Bennett and Lois Kibbee, *The Bennett Playbill* (New York, 1970), p. 307.

5. Memo from Darryl Zanuck to William Bacher, March 22, 1954, p.1, Fox Archive, UCLA; Interview with Edward Dmytryk; Sklar, *City Boys*, pp. 249–250; Pettigrew, *Bogart*, pp. 134–135; Gene Tierney, with Mickey Herskowitz, *Self-Portrait* (New York, 1979), pp. 191–192.

6. Paul Newman, Oral History, p. 43, Columbia University; Interview with Delbert Mann; Harry Sosnick, Oral History, p. 138, Columbia University; Don Marlowe, "The Man, Bogie," *Classic Film Collector*, 30 (1971), 31.

7. *Variety*, September 14, 1955; Gehman, *Bogart*, p. 112; Henry Fonda and Howard Teichman, *Fonda: My Life* (1981; New York, 1982), p. 253.

8. Lewis Yablonsky, *George Raft* (1974; New York, 1975), pp. 38–39; Philip Yordan, in *Backstory Two*, p. 375; Rod Steiger, in *Humphrey Bogart: Behind the Legend*, Television documentary, 1995.

9. Frank, *Humphrey Bogart*, p. 74; Benchley, *Humphrey Bogart*, p. 140; Nunnally

Johnson, Oral History, p. 4, Columbia University; Stephen Bogart, *Bogart*, p. 178.

10. Rod Steiger, Oral History, pp. 36, 42, 41, 55, Columbia University; Jerry Wald, Oral History, p. 6, Columbia University.

15. A RESPECTABLE DISEASE

1. Interview with Amanda Dunne, Malibu, California, March 16, 1996; Bacall, *By Myself*, p. 253; Thompson, *Bogie and Me*, p. 224; Hyams, *Bogie*, p. 151.
2. Interview with Dr. Michael Flynn, Rancho Santa Fe, California, March 6, 1996; Letter from Dr. Mario Papagni to Jeffrey Meyers, February 3, 1996. Benchley, a friend of the Bogarts, used poetic license when describing the operation: "They went in from his back [i.e., from his front], opening him like a side of beef, and cut away his esophagus, around which the cancer had wrapped itself [i.e., in which the cancer had grown]" (*Humphrey Bogart*, p. 228).

   Richard Meade, *A History of Thoracic Surgery* (Springfield, Ill., 1961), p. 704, gives a precise and accurate description: "A cervical incision was made to expose the cervical esophagus and to start the tunneling under the sternum from above with the finger. The esophagus was mobilized and divided, and the lower end sutured and invaginated [folded back within itself], and dropped into the chest. The jejunum was then brought up and sutured to the cervical esophagus. A gastrostomy was then done. The patient was given only intravenous feedings for three days, and then gastrostomy feedings were started. Clear fluids by mouth were started after the second week, and solid foods after the third week."
3. Hyams, *Bogart and Bacall*, p. 217; Bacall, *Now*, p. 42; Letter from John Huston to Ernst Scheidegger in Zurich, April 3, 1956, Herrick Library.
4. Bob Thomas, *King Cohn* (1967; New York, 1968), p. 280; Matthew Bernstein, *Walter Wanger: Hollywood Independent* (Berkeley, 1994), p. 313; Sam Jaffe, Oral History, p. 245.
5. Ray, *I Was Interrupted*, p. 159; Interview with Sylvia Sheekman Thompson; Interviews with Warren Stevens.
6. Bacall, *By Myself*, pp. 268; 280; Interviews with Verita Peterson Thompson; Grobel, *The Hustons*, p. 444.
7. Bacall, *By Myself*, pp. 274–275; John O'Hara, *Selected Letters*, ed. Matthew Bruccoli (New York, 1978), p. 262; Bernard Eisenschitz, *Nicholas Ray: An American Journey*, trans. Tom Milne (London, 1993), p. 192.
8. Interview with Dorris Johnson; Interview with Billy Wilder; Bogdanovich, *Pieces of Time*, pp. 38; 97.
9. Coe, *Humphrey Bogart*, pp. 189–190; Bacall, *Now*, p. 170; Bacall, *By Myself*, p. 239.
10. Adler, *Sinatra*, p. 65; Earl Wilson, *Sinatra* (1976; New York, 1977), p. 130; Gehman, *Bogart*, p. 64; Bacall, *By Myself*, pp. 266, 307.

11. Niven, *The Moon's a Balloon*, pp. 304–305; Melvyn Bragg, *Rich: The Life of Richard Burton* (1988; London, 1989), pp. 515–516; Coward, *Diaries*, p. 301.

12. Wilson, *Sinatra*, p. 134; Greenberger, *Bogey's Baby*, p. 160.

13. Ray, *I Was Interrupted*, p. 159; Confidential interview; Interview with Verita Peterson Thompson; Kitty Kelly, *His Way: The Unauthorized Biography of Frank Sinatra* (1986; New York, 1987), p. 263.

14. John Huston, "A Friend Pays Tribute to a Unique and Beloved Man," *Photoplay*, April 1957, p. 26; Huston, *An Open Book*, p. 249; Lazar, *Swifty*, p. 174; Kitty Harrison, "Down to 80 Pounds, Bogart Fights for Life against Throat Cancer," New York *Daily News*, January 3, 1957; Interview with Gloria Stuart Sheekman.

15. Bacall, *By Myself*, pp. 281–282; Meyers, *D. H. Lawrence*, p. 380; Benchley, *Humphrey Bogart*, p. 232. Bogart died at the same age as I am as I write these words.

16. Nunnally Johnson, Oral History, p. 5, Columbia University; Tynan, *Profiles*, p. 203; Interview with Dorris Johnson; Hanna, *Bogart*, p. 22.

17. Nunnally Johnson, *Letters*, pp. 147–148; Huston, "A Friend Pays Tribute," pp. 24, 26.

EPILOGUE: THE BOGART CULT

1. Like Hemingway, he has inspired memorabilia-filled watering-holes from the Casablanca restaurant in Cambridge to John's Grill and Bogie's Pizza in San Francisco, Bogart's Café in Santa Barbara and Bogart's restaurant in San Mateo, California.

2. "Bogey Worship," *Time*, 83 (February 7, 1964), 81; François Truffaut, *Correspondence, 1945–1984*, ed. Gilles Jacob and Claude de Givray, trans. Gilbert Adair (New York, 1990), p. 401.

3. Robert Sacchi and Robert Fisher's play *Bogart* was produced in 1955, Sacchi's *Bogey's Back* in 1985. Sacchi played the title role in *The Man With Bogart's Face*.

4. Mignon McLaughlin, "The Woman Who Dreamed about Humphrey Bogart," *Good Housekeeping*, 125 (October 1947), 169, 171; John Berryman, *The Dream Songs* (New York, 1969), p. 11; V. S. Naipaul, "Bogart," *Miguel Street* (1959; New York, 1984), pp. 9, 13–14; Robert Coover, "You Must Remember This," *A Night at the Movies* (New York, 1987), pp. 178, 171.

5. See Adolf Heinzlmeier, *Das Humphrey Bogart Fan-Buch* (Hamburg, 1984), Wolfgang Fuchs, *Humphrey Bogart, Cult Star: A Documentation* (Berlin: TACQ, 1987), and the comic books by Jean-Philippe and Patrick Lesueur, *Bogey* (Paris: Dargand, 1984) and John Wagner and Alan Grant, *The Bogie Man* (London: John Brown, 1991). Five poems on Bogart, *Casablanca* and *The Big Sleep* appeared in *The Faber Book of Movie Verse* in 1993. Two years later publishers, capitalizing on the actor's name and criminal roles, brought out George Baxt's *The Humphrey Bogart Murder Case*, Lawrence Block's *The*

Burglar Who Thought He Was Bogart and Stephen Bogart's mystery, *Play It Again.*

6. Haskel Frankel, "Tough Guy and Jet Set," *Saturday Review,* 49 (September 24, 1966), 33; Greenberger, *Bogey's Baby,* p. 205; Bacall, *By Myself,* p. 372; Barry Norman, *The Hollywood Greats* (New York, 1980), p. 150; Interview with Dorris Johnson.

7. Schickel, *On Film,* p. 243; Capote, "Humphrey Bogart," *The Dogs Bark,* p. 374.

Bogart's Plays and Films

PLAYS

Drifting, by John Colton and D. H. Andrews, January 22, 1922, producer: William Brady, director: John Cromwell, with Alice Brady and Robert Warwick, 63 performances.

Swifty, by John Peter Toohey and W. C. Percival, October 16, 1922, producer: William Brady, director: John Cromwell, 24 performances.

Meet the Wife, by Lynn Starling, November 26, 1923, with Mary Boland and Clifton Webb, 232 performances.

Nerves, by John Farrar and Stephen Vincent Benét, September 1, 1924, producer: William Brady, director: William Brady, Jr., with Mary Philips and Kenneth MacKenna, 16 performances.

Hell's Bells, by Barry Connors, January 26, 1925, with Shirley Booth, 120 performances.

Cradle Snatchers, by Russel Medcraft and Norma Mitchell, September 7, 1925, with Mary Boland, 332 performances.

Baby Mine, by Margaret Mayo, June 9, 1927, with Fatty Arbuckle and Lee Patrick, 12 performances.

Saturday's Children, by Maxwell Anderson, April 9, 1928, director: Guthrie McClintic, with Ruth Gordon, 310 performances.

Skyrocket, by Mark Reed, January 11, 1929, producer and director: Guthrie McClintic, with Mary Philips, 11 performances.

It's a Wise Child, by Laurence Johnson, August 6, 1929, producer and director: David Belasco, 378 performances.

After All, by John Van Druten, December 3, 1931, 20 performances.

Mad Hopes, by Romney Brent, May 1932, with Billie Burke, 12 performances.

I Loved You Wednesday, by Molly Ricardel and William Du Bois, October 11, 1932, with Henry Fonda in a non-speaking role, 63 performances.

Chrysalis, by Rose Albert Porter, November 15, 1932, director: Theresa Helburn, with Margaret Sullavan, Elisha Cook, Jr. and Elia Kazan, 23 performances.

Our Wife, by Lynn Mearson and Lilian Day, March 2, 1933, 20 performances.

The Mask and the Face, by Luigi Chiarelli, translated by Somerset Maugham, May 8, 1933, with Shirley Booth, Judith Anderson and Leo G. Carroll, 40 performances.

Invitation to a Murder, by Rufus King, May 17, 1934, 37 performances.

The Petrified Forest, by Robert Sherwood, January 7, 1935, director: Arthur Hopkins, with Leslie Howard and Peggy Conklin, 181 performances.

The Stag at Bay, by Beverly Nichols, July 1935, Skowhegan, Maine.

Ceiling Zero, by Frank Wead, summer 1935, Skowhegan, Maine.

Rain, by Somerset Maugham, August 1935, Skowhegan, Maine, 20 performances.

FILMS

I. BEST FILMS: *The Maltese Falcon* (1941), *Casablanca* (1943), *To Have and Have Not* (1945), *The Big Sleep* (1946), *The Treasure of the Sierra Madre* (1948), *The African Queen* (1951)

II. IMPORTANT FILMS: *The Petrified Forest* (1936), *Stand-In* (1937), *High Sierra* (1941), *Dead Reckoning* (1947), *Key Largo* (1948), *In a Lonely Place* (1950), *The Enforcer* (1951), *Beat the Devil* (1954), *The Caine Mutiny* (1954), *Sabrina* (1954), *The Harder They Fall* (1956)

III. GOOD FILMS: *Marked Woman* (1937), *Kid Galahad* (1937), *Dead End* (1937), *The Amazing Dr. Clitterhouse* (1938), *Dark Victory* (1939), *The Roaring Twenties* (1939), *The Return of Doctor X* (1939), *All Through the Night* (1942), *Across the Pacific* (1942), *Conflict* (1945), *Dark Passage* (1947), *Deadline — U.S.A.* (1952), *The Barefoot Contessa* (1954), *The Desperate Hours* (1955)

IV. POOR FILMS: *A Devil with Women* (1930), *Up the River* (1930), *Body and Soul* (1931), *Bad Sister* (1931), *Women of All Nations* (1931), *A Holy Terror* (1931), *Love Affair* (1932), *Big City Blues* (1932), *Three on a Match* (1932), *Midnight* (1934), *Bullets or Ballots* (1936), *Two Against the World* (1936), *China Clipper* (1936), *Isle of Fury* (1936), *Black Legion* (1937), *The Great O'Malley* (1937), *San Quentin* (1937), *Swing Your Lady* (1938), *Crime School* (1938), *Men Are Such Fools* (1938), *Racket Busters* (1938), *Angels with Dirty Faces* (1938), *King of the Underworld* (1939), *The Oklahoma Kid* (1939), *You Can't Get Away with Murder* (1939), *Invisible Stripes* (1939), *Virginia City* (1940), *It All Came True* (1940), *Brother Orchid* (1940), *They Drive By Night* (1940), *The Wagons Roll by Night* (1941), *The Big Shot* (1942), *Action in the North Atlantic* (1943), *Sahara* (1943), *Passage to Marseilles* (1944), *The Two Mrs. Carrolls* (1947), *Knock on Any Door* (1949), *Tokyo Joe* (1949), *Chain Lightning* (1950), *Sirocco* (1951), *Battle Circus* (1953), *We're No Angels* (1955), *The Left Hand of God* (1955)

Bibliography

I. BY HUMPHREY BOGART *(or published under his name)*

"Why Hollywood Hates Me," *Screen Book,* 22 (January 1940), 66, 68–69.

"Censorship," *Hollywood Reporter,* October 31, 1941. Reprinted in *The Hollywood Reporter: The Golden Years.* Ed. Tichi Wilkerson and Marcia Borie. New York: Coward-McCann, 1984. Pp. 140–141.

As told to Kay Proctor, "Women I'd Like to Bump Off," *Screen Guide,* 1942.

"Bogart: Neuroses: Methot," *Herald Express,* c. 1942.

As told to Sara Hamilton, "Things I Don't Like About Myself," *Photoplay,* c. 1942.

As told to Dorothy Haas, "Sister Annie," *Silver Screen,* 13 (March 1943), 26–27, 64–65.

As told to Jack Holland, "How to Keep Your Marriage Alive," *Silver Screen,* 14 (November 1943), 30–31, 68–70.

"The Romance I Can't Forget," *Photoplay,* 24 (March 1944), 55.

"I Stuck My Neck Out," *Saturday Evening Post,* 217 (February 10, 1945), 19, 87–88.

As told to Gladys Hall, "Listen, Kreep," *Silver Screen,* 15 (June 1945), 22, 68–69.

"In Defense of My Wife," *Photoplay,* June 1946, pp. 38–39, 99–100.

"The Role I Liked Best," *Saturday Evening Post,* 219 (December 14, 1946), 136.

"Locationing in Mexico," *Hollywood Reporter,* September 1947. Reprinted in Wilkerson, pp. 205–206.

"I'm No Communist," *Photoplay,* March 1948, pp. 52–53, 86–87.

"Bogart Balks at Bogey," *New York Times,* November 28, 1948, 2:5.

"Imagine Me a Father!," *Silver Screen,* 19 (May 1949), pp. 24–25, 55.

"Safety Pin Expert Tells of His Diaper Troubles," *News* (LA), June 21, 1949.

"The Most Unforgivable Character I've Met," *Photoplay,* July 1949, pp. 48–49, 94.

As told to Kate Holliday, "My Mother: I Never Really Loved Her" (July 1949), *McCall's,* 103 (April 1976), 41–42.

"The Keys to the Keelson," *News* (LA), August 16, 1949.

"Listen to Me, Kid," *Photoplay,* September 1949, pp. 34–35, 83–84.

"The *Santana* and I." *Hollywood in the 1940s: The Stars' Own Stories.* Ed. Ivy Wilson. New York: Ungar, 1980. Pp. 33–37.

Bibliography

As told to Jack Holland, "What Do I Owe My Wife?," *Movieland*, March 1950, pp. 52–55, 94.

"The Oscar Myth," *Cosmopolitan*, March 1950, pp. 31, 165.

"Love Begins at 40," *Los Angeles Times: This Week*, October 7, 1951, pp. 10, 19.

"Humphrey Bogart Tells the Truth about Hepburn," *Coronet*, 31 (April 1952), 139–140, 142, 144, 146, 148, 150.

"African Adventure," *American Weekly* (NY), August 31, 1952, p. 11.

"Beat the Devil," Look, 17 (September 22, 1953), 128–129, 131, 133.

As told to Joe Hyams, "Movie Making Beats the Devil," *Cue*, 22 (November 28, 1953), 14–15.

"Around the World in 80 Reels," *Los Angeles Times: This Week*, March 21, 1954, pp. 14–15.

"Bogart on Hollywood," *Look*, 20 (August 21, 1956), 96–98, 100–101.

II. On Bogart

Astor, Mary, "Bogie Was For Reel," *New York Times*, April 23, 1967, 2:21.

Bacall, Lauren. *By Myself*. New York: Knopf, 1978.

———. *Now*. New York: Knopf, 1994.

Bazin, André. "The Death of Humphrey Bogart." *Cahiers du Cinéma: The 1950s*. Ed. Jim Hillier. Cambridge, Mass.: Harvard University Press, 1985. Pp. 98–101.

Benchley, Nathaniel. *Humphrey Bogart*. Boston: Little, Brown, 1975.

Bogart, Mayo Methot, "Bogie — Over There," *Photoplay*, May 1944, pp. 28–29, 86–88.

Bogart, Stephen Humphrey. *Bogart: In Search of My Father*. Foreword by Lauren Bacall. New York: Dutton, 1995.

Bogart's Face. New York: Random House, 1970.

Bogdanovich, Peter. "Bogie in Excelsis." *Pieces of Time*. New York: Arbor House, 1973. Pp. 82–99.

Brooks, Louise. "Humphrey and Bogey." *Lulu in Hollywood*. New York: Knopf, 1982. Pp. 57–69.

Brooks, Richard. *The Producer: A Novel*. New York: Simon & Schuster, 1951.

Capote, Truman. "Humphrey Bogart." *The Dogs Bark*. New York: Random House, 1950. Pp. 373–374.

Coe, Jonathan. *Humphrey Bogart: Take It and Like It*. New York: Grove Weidenfeld, 1991.

Cooke, Alistair. "Humphrey Bogart: Epitaph for a Tough Guy" (1957). *Six Men*. London: Penguin, 1978. Pp. 125–146.

Gehman, Richard. *Bogart*. Greenwich, Conn.: Fawcett, 1965.

Goodman, Eric. *Bogey: The Good-Bad Guy*. New York: Lyle Stuart, 1965.

Greenberger, Howard. *Bogey's Baby: A Biography of Lauren Bacall*. New York: St. Martin's, 1976.

Hanna, David. *Bogart*. New York: Leisure Books, 1976.

Hyams, Joe. *Bogie: The Biography of Humphrey Bogart*. Introduction by Lauren Bacall. New York: New American Library, 1973.

Bibliography

———. *Bogart and Bacall.* New York: Warner, 1976.

Niven, David. "Bogie." *Bring On the Empty Horses.* New York: Putnam, 1975. Pp. 211–230.

Ruddy, Jonah and Jonathan Hill. *Bogey: The Man, the Actor, the Legend.* New York: Tower, 1965.

Talty, Stephen, "Young Bogart," *American Film,* 16 (April 1991), 40–45.

Thompson, Verita, with Donald Shepherd. *Bogie and Me.* New York: St. Martin's, 1982.

Tynan, Kenneth. "Humphrey Bogart" (1966). *Profiles.* Ed. Kathleen Tynan and Ernie Eban. London: Hern, 1989. Pp. 196–203.

III. Screenplays

Agee, James and John Huston. "*The African Queen.*" *Agee on Film: Volume Two: Five Film Scripts.* Foreword by John Huston. New York: Grosset and Dunlap, 1969. Pp. 151–259.

Epstein, Julius, Philip Epstein and Howard Koch. In Howard Koch. "*Casablanca*": *Script and Legend.* Woodstock, N.Y.: Overlook, 1973. Pp. 19–161.

———. *Casablanca.* Ed. Richard Anobile. New York: Universe, 1974.

Faulkner, William, Leigh Brackett and Jules Furthman. "*The Big Sleep.*" *Film Scripts One.* Ed. George Garrett, O. B. Hardison, Jr., and Jane Gelfman. New York: Irvington, 1969. Pp. 137–329.

Furthman, Jules and William Faulkner. *To Have and Have Not.* Ed. Bruce Kawin. Madison, Wisc., 1980.

Huston, John. *The Maltese Falcon.* Ed. Richard Anobile. New York: Universe, 1974.

———. *The Treasure of the Sierra Madre.* Ed. James Naremore. Madison, Wisc., 1979.

Huston, John and W. R. Burnett. *High Sierra.* Ed. Douglas Gomery. Madison, Wisc., 1979.

Robinson, Casey. *Dark Victory.* Ed. Bernard Dick. Madison, Wisc., 1981.

IV. On the Films

Barbour, Alan. *Humphrey Bogart.* New York: Galahad, 1973.

Behlmer, Rudy. *Behind the Scenes.* Hollywood: Samuel French, 1990.

———, ed. *Inside Warner Bros. (1935–1951).* New York: Simon & Schuster, 1985.

Cahill, Marie. *Casablanca.* New York: Smithmark, 1991.

———. *The Maltese Falcon.* New York: Smithmark, 1991.

Carlinsky, Dan. *The Great Bogart Trivia Book.* New York: Fawcett, 1980.

Eco, Umberto, "*Casablanca:* Cult Movies and Intertextual Collage," *Sub-Stance,* 47 (1985), 3–12.

Eisenschitz, Bernard. *Humphrey Bogart.* Paris: Terrain Vague, 1967.

Bibliography

Eyles, Allen. *Bogart.* New York: Doubleday, 1975.

Francisco, Charles. *You Must Remember This: The Filming of "Casablanca."* Englewood Cliffs, N.J.: Prentice-Hall, 1980.

Frank, Alan. *Humphrey Bogart.* New York: Exeter, 1982.

Grobel, Lawrence. *The Hustons.* New York: Avon, 1989.

Harmetz, Aljean. *Round Up the Usual Suspects: The Making of "Casablanca": Bogart, Bergman and World War II.* London: Weidenfeld & Nicolson, 1993.

Hepburn, Katharine. *The Making of "The African Queen."* New York: Knopf, 1987.

Lebo, Harlan. *"Casablanca": Behind the Scenes.* New York: Simon & Schuster, 1992.

McCarty, Clifford. *Bogey: The Films of Humphrey Bogart.* New York: Citadel, 1965.

Michael, Paul. *Humphrey Bogart: The Man and His Films.* Indianapolis: Bobbs-Merrill, 1965.

Miller, Frank. *"Casablanca": As Time Goes By: 50th Anniversary Commemorative.* London: Virgin, 1993.

Pettigrew, Terence. *Bogart.* London: Proteus, 1981.

Schickel, Richard. "Humphrey Bogart: Gentleman Declassed." *Schickel on Film.* New York: Morrow, 1989. Pp. 213–243.

Sklar, Robert. *City Boys: Cagney, Bogart, Garfield.* Princeton: Princeton University Press, 1992.

Truffaut, François. "A Portrait of Humphrey Bogart" (1958). *The Films in My Life.* Trans. Leonard Mayhew. New York: Simon & Schuster, 1978. Pp. 292–295.

V. Political Background

Bessie, Alvah. *Inquisition in Eden.* New York: Macmillan, 1985.

Brownstein, Ronald. *The Power and the Glitter: Hollywood and the Washington Connection.* New York: Pantheon, 1990.

Carr, Robert. "The Hollywood Hearings." *The House Committee on Un-American Activities, 1945–1950.* Garden City, N.Y.: Doubleday, 1980.

Caute, David. "Hollywood." *The Great Fear: The Anti-Communist Purge Under Truman and Eisenhower.* New York: Simon & Schuster, 1978. Pp. 487–520.

Ceplair, Larry and Steven Englund. *The Inquisition in Hollywood: Politics and the Film Community, 1920–1960.* Garden City, N.Y.: Doubleday, 1980.

Dick, Bernard. *Radical Innocence: A Critical Study of the Hollywood Ten.* Lexington, Ky.: University Press of Kentucky, 1989.

Goodman, Walter. *The Committee.* Baltimore: Penguin, 1969.

House of Representatives, 76th Congress, Hearings Before a Special Committee of Un-American Activities, *Investigation of Un-American Propaganda Activities in the United States* (1940), Volume 3, Executive Hearings, pp. 1375–1378, 1381–1385.

Kahn, Gordon. *Hollywood on Trial: The Story of the Ten Who Were Indicted.* Foreword by Thomas Mann. New York: Boni & Gaer, 1948.

Bibliography

Kanfer, Stefan. *A Journal of the Plague Years.* New York: Atheneum, 1973.

Lardner, Ring, Jr. *The Lardners: My Family Remembered.* New York: Harper & Row, 1978.

Mast, Gerald, ed. "The War Abroad, the War at Home (1941–1952)." *The Movies in Our Midst: Documents in the Cultural History of Film in America.* Chicago: University of Chicago Press, 1982. Pp. 476–588.

Navasky, Victor. *Naming Names.* New York; Penguin, 1981.

Trumbo, Dalton. *The Time of the Toad: A Study of the Inquisition in America by One of the Hollywood Ten.* Hollywood: Hollywood Ten, 1950.

VI. DOCUMENTARIES

Edward R. Murrow, *Person to Person,* CBS-TV, September 3, 1954, 14 minutes.

The Man Called Bogart, in "Hollywood and the Stars," narrated by Joseph Cotten, produced by David Wolper, United Artists TV, September 11, 1963, 30 minutes.

Bogart, with interviews and film clips, directed by Martin Flamm, ABC-TV, April 22, 1967.

The Best of Bogart, narrated by Edward G. Robinson, with clips from his best films, Warner Bros., 1971, 12 minutes.

Tribute to Bogart, BBC-TV Omnibus, January 1972.

The Humphrey Bogart Legend, narrated by Richard Basehart, interviews with Stanley Kramer and Joe Hyams, HBO, 1979, 25 minutes.

Bogie: The Last Hero, made-for-television dramatization of his life, with Kevin O'Connor and Kathryn Harrold, based on Joe Hyams' biography, written by Daniel Taradash, directed by Vincent Sherman, March 4, 1980.

Hollywood on Trial, written by Arnie Reisman, directed by David Helpern, narrated by John Huston, with Zero Mostel, Otto Preminger, Ronald Reagan and Martin Ritt, 1988, 90 minutes.

Bacall on Bogart, on his film career rather than personal life, narrated by Bacall, interviews with Ingrid Bergman, Peter Bogdanovich, Richard Brooks, Alistair Cooke, Julius Epstein, Katharine Hepburn, John Huston, Van Johnson and Budd Schulberg, A&E documentary, PBS, March 11, 1988, 90 minutes.

Bogart: The Man Behind the Myth, directed by Mike Omansky, Ciné Production, 1991.

Humphrey Bogart: Behind the Legend, interviews with Bacall, Theodore Bikel, Cooke, Epstein, Hepburn, Huston, Hyams and Rod Steiger, "Biography A-to-Z" series, September 1995, 45 minutes.

Black List: Hollywood on Trial, written and directed by Chris Koch, AMC, 1995, 85 minutes.

Index

Adler, Buddy, 295
Adler, Larry, 203, 213
Agate, James, 64
Agee, James, 67, 154, 177, 229–230, 234, 254
Algiers, 137
All About Eve, 289
Alleborn, Al, 138
Allen, Angela, 257–258
Allen, Woody, *Play It Again, Sam,* 319–320
Allyson, June, 74, 267
Altman, Robert, *M*A*S*H,* 267
Anderson, Judith, 45
Anderson, Lindsay, 41
Anderson, Maxwell, 37, 230
Antheil, George, 236
Arbuckle, Fatty, 31
Ardrey, Robert, 203
Astor, Mary, 59, 92, 104, 125–126, 128, 134–135, 136, 190, 221
Avedon, Richard, 88
Axelrod, George, 263

Bacall, Lauren, 2, 34, 53, 92, 104, 203, 212–213, 231, 268, 286, 340–341 n13; affairs: Bogart, 164–170, 177–179, Sinatra, 310–313; after Bogart's death, 322, marriage to Bogart, 184–195, 239, 241, 247–248, 249, 260–265, 269, 270–271, 291–292, 305; "I Hate Young Men," 262; *The Big Sleep,* 177–179, 181, *Dark Passage,* 223–224, *Key Largo,* 232, 233, *The Petrified Forest,* 298–299, *To*

Have and Have Not, 172, 173–177, 220
Bacon, Lloyd, 67, 105
Baker, Mary, 78, 92, 99
Baker, Mel, 140
Barnard, Ivor, 273, 275
Barnes, Howard, 121, 219
Barrymore, Ethel, 266
Barrymore, John, 26, 125, 138
Barrymore, Lionel, 232, 233
Bazin, André, 268
Belmondo, Jean-Paul, 319
Benchley, Nathaniel, 94, 123
Benchley, Robert, 76
Bennett, Joan, 99, 293–294
Benny, Jack, 264
Bergen, Edgar, 123
Bergman, Ingrid, 2, 92, 104, 137, 138–139, 140, 146, 272
Bernstein, Leonard, 310
Berryman, John, "Dream Song 9," 321
Bessie, Alvah, 213
Bible: Numbers, 154, Ruth, 143, Job, 71
Bikel, Theodore, 255
Bioff, William, 59, 200, 342 n3
The Birth of a Nation, 67
Black, Lesley, 114
Blanke, Henry, 114, 126
Blondell, Joan, 40, 41, 72, 111
Bogart, Belmont DeForest (father), 1, 5–6, 8–19, 21, 22, 26, 34, 35–36, 38, 46, death, 48
Bogart, Catherine "Kay" (sister), 8–9, 46

Bogart, Frances "Pat" (sister), 8–9, 33, 46–47, 78, 113
BOGART, HUMPHREY DEFOREST
LIFE:
accused as Communist, 198–199
ancestry, 1–5
birth, 1, 8, 328 n2
cancer, 304–314, 349 n2
car accident, 271–272
Coast Guard service, 132
death, 314
education, 11–19, 328 n8
family background, 1–2, 5–11, 34–35, 48, 85–86
first trip to Hollywood, 36, 38–41, second trip to Hollywood, 43
friendships: 81–82, 88, 166, 307, 309, Brooks, 230–231, Hellinger, 28, 235–236, Katharine Hepburn, 248, 255, Huston, 114, 115, 225–227, 270, Jaffe, 99, "Rat Pack," 263–264, Romanoff, 106–107, Sinatra, 310–311
funeral, 315–317
hormone treatments, 194, 224–225
lip injury, 21, 38
love affairs: Lauren Bacall, 154, 164–170, 177–179, Verita Peterson, 93–94, 184, 191–192, 291–292
marriages, 2, Lauren Bacall, 2, 184–195, 239, 241, 247–248, 249, 260–265, 269, 270–271, 291–292, 298–299, 305, Helen Menken, 33–35, 79, Mayo Methot, 73, 78–81, 88, 90–93, 118, 134, 154, 156–158, 166–167, 169–170, 177–179, 241, Mary Philips, 37, 51, 73–74
navy service, 19–22
panda incident, 238–239
papal audience, 248
poses for Maud, 8, 12–13, 22
posthumous cult, 4, 318–323, 350 n2, 350–351 n3
residences: Benedict Canyon, 186, 187, Garden of Allah, 51, 185–186, Holmby Hills, 260–261, Horn Avenue, 80–81, Kings Road, 186, Shoreham Drive, 80
Santana Pictures, 230, 235–236, 243, 270, 277, 306

travels: Africa, 247, Italy, 248, 271–272, 287, London, 248, Paris, 248
USO tour, 156–158
will, 314–315
ACTING CAREER:
advertising, 42, 122, 264, 321
agents, 99
appearance, 1, 9, 15, 28, 31, 38, 63, 256, 268
awards: Golden Lion, 281, Oscar, 258–260
contracts, Columbia, 43–44, Fox, 38, Warner Bros., 51, 54–55, 69, 151, 218, 268
diction, 21, 29, 39, 62
early film work, 23–24, 36, 38–39
earnings, 38, 42, 51, 54, 68, 74, 97, 108, 109, 122, 151, 218, 224, 247, 264, 267, 294, 295
public image, 1, 2, 34, 75–77, 80, 86, 111, 158, 185, 199, 209–210, 238–239, 264, 268
range, 40–41, 55, 111–112, 132, 270, 336 n11, 346–347 n20, comedy, 72–73, 129, 158, 181, 294, detective, 128–130, 179–183, 220–222, gangsters, 4, 43–46, 59–60, 61–63, 65, 69, 95, 96–97, 104, 111, 117, 119–122, 132–133, horror, 104–105, nautical, 193, 233–234, 280, realism, 286, 290–291, 302, rebellious hero, 141, romantic, 103–104, 139, 140, 151, 176, 281, war hero, 152–154, 158, westerns, 100–101, 108
relationship with Warners, 51, 54–55, 74–77, 86, 93, 94, 95, 99, 101, 105, 109–113, 132, 151, 159–164, 185, 222–223, 246, 268–269
reviews, 27, 29, 30, 38, 41, 51, 72, 121–122, 229–230, 239–240, 281, 296, 299
screen personality, 1, 4, 49, 64–65, 69, 242, 268
stage work, 25–31, 39, 43, 44–45, 48–51
style, 22, 60, 240, 323
technique, 62–64, 69, 126, 129, 136, 148–149, 173–175, 182–183, 222, 255, 283, 289, ad-libs, 96, manner-

Index

isms, 2, 21, 29, 63, 70, 104, 158, 176, 219, 245, psychological disintegration, 154–155, 241–242, 280–281

typecast, 95, 106, 109–113, 151, 222, 346–347 n20

voice, 49, 63

work habits, 40, 56, 63–64, 220, 242–243, 255, 283, 288

CHARACTER:

argumentative, 82, 88, 90–93

attitude to acting, 61, 86, 94, 109, 159–164, 191, 220, 255

attitude to children, 194–195, 297

attitude to Hollywood, 85, 86–87, 192–193, 199, 258, 316

complainer, 109–113, 118, 225, 226–227, 250–251

conversation, 82

courageous, 309, 313

cynical, 36, 61, 75

dogs, 186–187, 265–266

domestic habits, 107, 187–188, 190–191

drinking habits, 2, 82, 87–88, 189, 251, 252, 282, 299, 307, 341 n14

embittered, 42–43

generous, 137, 255, 293, 296, 298

guarded, 155

integrity, 75

hobbies: chess, 28, 42, 107, reading, 81–82, sailing, 2–3, 11, 22, 80, 226–227, *Santana*, 192–193

kindness, 94, 118, 240

mockery of Oscars, 258

modest, 85, 303

needling, 2, 22, 34, 88–90, 126, 283–284, 292, 301, 309

outspoken, 85, 284

polite, 31, 37, 48,

political views, 85, 196, 198–200, campaigns, 216, 217, 261–262, CFA activities, 203, 205–215

pugnacious, 55, 265

quarrelsome, 80

sense of humor, 186,

smoking, 87, 288, 295, 307

FILMS:

Across the Pacific, 3, 22, 66, 134–136, 237, 319, 345 n1

Action in the North Atlantic, 151–153, 201, 208

The African Queen, 158, 247, 249–258, 323

All Through the Night, 3, 133–134, 142

The Amazing Dr. Clitterhouse, 66, 96–97

Angels with Dirty Faces, 97–98

Bad Sister, 41

The Barefoot Contessa, 4, 287–291

Battle Circus, 231, 267

Beat the Devil, 243, 270–277, 287

The Big Shot, 132–133

The Big Sleep, 104, 158, 164, 170, 177, 179–183, 218

Black Legion, 58, 66–67, 236

Broadway's Like That, 40

Brother Orchid, 60, 112

Bullets or Ballots, 65–66, 97, 135

The Caine Mutiny, 19, 22, 154, 270, 277–281, 287, 323

Casablanca, 4, 93, 104, 137–152, 323, cult, 318–320, 321, imitated, 153, 156, 172–173, 237, 244

Chain Lightning, 239–240

China Clipper, 239

Conflict, 154–155, 159–163

Crime School, 59, 96

Dark Passage, 191, 222–224, 320

Dark Victory, 53, 100, 101–104, 112

Dead End, 59, 66, 69–72, 116, 120

Deadline—U.S.A., 231, 266–267

Dead Reckoning, 219–222

The Desperate Hours, 111, 297–298

A Devil with Women, 41

The Enforcer, 244–246

The Harder They Fall, 58, 287, 299–302, 319

High Sierra, 41, 111, 112, 114, 116, 117–122, 133, 237, 321

A Holy Terror, 240

In a Lonely Place, 154, 224, 240–243, 287

Invisible Stripes, 105–106

It All Came True, 116

Key Largo, 67, 191, 230–234

Kid Galahad, 68–69, 97

King of the Underworld, 100

Knock on Any Door, 236–237, 243

Index

Bogart, Humphrey Deforest (*cont.*)
  The Left Hand of God, 293, 294–295
  The Maltese Falcon, 30, 104, 112,
    116, 123–131, 135, 139, 179, 221,
    323, 337–338 n16, parody, 274
  Marked Woman, 66, 67–68, 77, 79
  Midnight, 45–46, 62, 112, 331 n20
  The Oklahoma Kid, 100–101
  Passage to Marseilles, 53, 155–156,
    161–162, 164
  The Petrified Forest, 60–63, 111, 120–
    121, 287
  Racket Busters, 97
  The Return of Doctor X, 100, 104–
    105, 112
  The Roaring Twenties, 41, 100, 104,
    133, 235
  Sabrina, 270, 281–286, 287
  Sahara, 153–154
  Sirocco, 243, 244, 246
  Stand-In, 66, 72–73, 77, 285
  Swing Your Lady, 95
  They Drive By Night, 108–109, 118,
    119
  Three on a Match, 43–44, 62
  To Have and Have Not, 4, 104, 167,
    170–177, 220
  Tokyo Joe, 236, 237–238, 243
  The Treasure of the Sierra Madre, 154,
    224–230
  The Two Mrs. Carrolls, 218, 219, 224,
    236
  Up the River, 41, 287
  Virginia City, 108
  We're No Angels, 287, 292–294
  RADIO WORK: 42
  The African Queen, 123
  Bold Venture, 4, 264
  Bullets or Ballots, 123
  Edgar Bergen Show, 123
  A Farewell to Arms, 4
  Louella Parsons Show, 123
  The Maltese Falcon, 264
  To Have and Have Not, 219, 264
  The Treasure of the Sierra Madre, 123
  STAGE PLAYS:
  After All, 43
  Baby Mine, 30–31
  Chrysalis, 44–45
  Cradle Snatchers, 29–30, 33

  Drifting, 26, 31
  Invitation to a Murder, 49
  It's a Wise Child, 37–38
  The Mask and the Face, 45, 62
  Meet the Wife, 26, 28
  Nerves, 26, 29, 37
  The Petrified Forest, 26, 48–51, 54,
    62
  A Ruined Lady, 25
  Saturday's Children, 36, 37
  Skyrocket, 37
  Swifty, 26, 29
  TELEVISION:
  Ed Sullivan Show, 307
  Edward R. Murrow, 264–265
  Jack Benny Show, 264
  The Petrified Forest, 298–299
  ARTICLES:
  "I'm No Communist," 212
  "I Stuck My Neck Out," 199–200
  "My Mother: I Never Really Loved
    Her," 2, 42, 330 n13
  "The Oscar Myth," 259
  "Things I Don't Like About Myself,"
    191
  "Why Hollywood Hates Me," 42
  INTERVIEWS: 86, 101, 212–213, 216
  LETTERS: 14, 82–85, 166–169, 211,
    270–271, 272, 274, 333 n7
  SPEECHES: 199–200, "Hollywood Fights
    Back," 202–203, 209
Bogart, Leslie (Schiffman) (daughter),
  194, 322
Bogart, Maud Humphrey (mother), 1–
  2, 6–10, 12–13, 18, 19, 21–22, 27,
  33, 34, 35–36, 80, 165, death, 113;
  *Treasury of Stories, Jingles and
  Rhymes*, 7
Bogart, Stephen (son), 19, 194–195,
  248, 311, 314, 322
Bogdanovich, Peter, 176
Boland, Mary, 28, 30, 33
Bolster, Anita, 219
Bond, Ward, 126
Brackett, Leigh, 182
Brady, Alice, 24, 26, 33
Brady, Bill, Jr., 9, 24, 29, 33
Brady, William A., 11, 23, 26, 27; *Show-
  man*, 24
Brando, Marlon, 236, 259, 281

Index

Brandsma, Maynard, 304, 305, 308, 309
Brazzi, Rossano, 289
Brecht, Bertolt, 202
Breen, Joseph, 276
Brennan, Walter, 176
Brent, George, 97, 101, 102, 192
Bromfield, Louis, 50, 81, 185, 186, 262; *It All Came True,* 116
Brooks, Geraldine, 203
Brooks, Louise, 21, 29, 31, 55, 76, 81, 165
Brooks, Richard, 47, 74, 81, 85, 88, 166, 230–231, 266, 309, 315; *The Producer,* 34, 36, 111, 167, 189, 214, 218, 258, 320, 335 n2
Brosnan, John, 231
Brown, Lyman, 34
Browne, George, 59, 200, 342 n3
Browning, Robert, "My Last Duchess," 219
Bruce, Nigel, 219
Brute Force, 164
Bryan, Jane, 68, 105
Buck, Jules, 203
Bukowski, Charles, "Bogart in the World of the Dead," 321
Burnett, W. R., 275; *High Sierra,* 116
Burton, Richard, 311–312
Busch, Niven, 170
Bushman, Francis X., 285
Butterworth, Charles, 76
Byron, George Gordon, Lord, "Hebrew Melodies," 135

The Cabinet of Dr. Caligari, 142
Cagney, James, 8, 38, 54, 60, 64, 75, 95, 111, 116, 151, 159, 198, on Bogart, 101; *Angels with Dirty Faces,* 97–98, *The Oklahoma Kid,* 100–101, *The Roaring Twenties,* 104
Cain, James M., *The Postman Always Rings Twice,* 73
The Caine Mutiny Court Martial, 280
Camus, Albert, 143, 319
Capa, Robert, 272
Capote, Truman, 12, 87, 115, 272–274, 275, 323
Cardiff, Jack, 251, 255–256
Carmichael, Hoagy, 172
Carnera, Primo, 299–300

Carpenter, Meta, 127
Carr, Robert, 207
Carroll, Leo G., 45
Carter, Ann, 219
Ceplair, Larry, *The Inquisition in Hollywood,* 202, 204
Chandler, Raymond, 221, *The Big Sleep,* 3–4, 170, 179, 180–183
Chasen, Dave, 88, 111
Chaucer, Geoffrey, "The Pardoner's Tale," 229
Cheyenne, 164
Ciannelli, Eduardo, 68
Clarke, Fred, 186
Cleary, Frederic, 259
Cobb, Lee J., 99, 244, 246, 294, 295, 296
Cockburn, Claud, *Beat the Devil,* 270, 272
Cogley, John, *Report on Blacklisting,* 210
Cohn, Harry, 153, 306–307, 315
Cole, Lawrence, 12
Cole, Lester, 213, 215
Columbia Pictures, 43, 153, 236, 247, 306
Committee for the First Amendment (CFA), 201–203, 205–215
Conrad, Joseph, *Heart of Darkness,* 179, 250, *Lord Jim,* 179, 252, *Victory,* 103
Conte, Richard, 203
Cook, Elisha, Jr., 45, 128, 129
Cooke, Alistair, 22, 262
Cooper, Gary, 79, 204, 315, 323
Coover, Robert, "You Must Remember This," 321
Coward, Noel, 8, 89, 263–264, 312
Cromwell, John, 26, 220
Cukor, George, 309–310
Cummings, Don, 108, 157
Curtiz, Michael, 68, 98, 137, 138, 146, 148, 150, 155, 163

Dalio, Marcel, 137, 166, 172, 285
Daves, Delmer, 222–223
Davis, Bette, 41, 59, 95, 111, 151, 162, and Warner, 54, 75, 102, on Bogart, 64, 102, 159, 176; *Dark Victory,* 101–104, *Marked Woman,* 67–68, *The Petrified Forest,* 60–61, 63, 64
Dead End Kids, 69, 70, 96, 97

Index

DeCorsia, Ted, 245
de Havilland, Olivia, 54, 136
Delineator, 7–8
Derek, John, 237
Deutsch, Armand, 89–90
Devlin, J. J., 98
Dewey, Thomas E., 67, 97, 199
Dies, Martin, 196–197, 198–199, 204
Dillinger, John, 59–60, 61, 119
Disney, Walt, 204
Dmytryk, Edward, 90, 205, 215, 218, 244, 277, 278, 279, 281, 294
Dominguín, Luis Miguel, 288
Dos Passos, John, 2
Douglas, Helen Gahagan, 216
Douglas, Melvyn, 198, 216
Douglas, Paul, 89
Dunne, Amanda, 304
Dunne, Philip, 201, 205–206, 208, 214, 217
Dvorak, Ann, 44

Eco, Umberto, 150
Einfeld, Charles, 151
Eliot, T. S., "The Hollow Men," 61
Englund, Steven, *The Inquisition in Hollywood*, 202, 204
Epstein, Julius, 137, 140, 145, 147, 293
Epstein, Philip, 137
Eyer, Richard, 297

Farrell, James, 104
Faulkner, William, 171, 172, 175, 182, 219, 230, 287, 294–295
Federal Theater Project, 204
Feldman, Charles, 181, 184, 263
Ferguson, Otis, 67, 69, 121
Ferrer, José, 278, 280
Finney, Albert, 320
Fitts, Buron, 198
Fitzgerald, F. Scott, *The Great Gatsby*, 282, *The Last Tycoon*, 73, 306, "May Day," 27, *Tender Is the Night*, 101, *This Side of Paradise*, 139
Fitzgerald, Zelda, 10
Flynn, Errol, 55, 95, 108, 111, 138, 151, 162, 315
Flynn, Michael, 305, 309
Fonda, Henry, 280, 298, 299

Fontaine, Joan, 4
Ford, John, 41, 218
Forester, C. S., *The African Queen*, 247, 254, *The Good Shepherd*, 306
Forman, Milos, *Taking Off*, 320
Fowler, Gene, 276
Fowler, Marjorie, 276
Fox Film Corporation, 36, 38, 41
Fox, Sidney, 46
Foy, Bryan, 57, 96
Francis, Kay, 100, 335 n3
Francis, Robert, 278
Freud, Sigmund, 101–102
Furthman, Jules, 171, 182

Gable, Clark, 38, 178, 315, 323
Gabler, Neal, 53
Gardner, Ava, 74, 288–289, 291
Garfield, John, 113, 116, 203
Garland, Judy, 263
Garson, Greer, 259, 304
Gellhorn, Martha, 2
George, Grace, 24, 35
Gershwin, Ira, 203, 217
Gershwin, Lee, 264
Gleason, Jackie, 134
Godard, Jean-Luc, *Breathless*, 319
God Is My Co-Pilot, 163–164
Goldwyn, Samuel, 26, 69, 74
Goodman, Ezra, 76
Gordon, Ruth, 37, 152
Graham, Sheilah, 75
Grahame, Gloria, 240, 241, 243, 312
Grant, Cary, 74, 281
Grapewin, Charley, 61
Greene, Graham, 67, 72
Greenstreet, Sydney, 135–136, 137, 138, 154–155, 156; *The Maltese Falcon*, 124–125, 127, 128–130, 131
Grobel, Lawrence, 130
Guernsey, Otis, Jr., 239–240
Gumshoe, 320

Hall, Gladys, 36
Hamilton, Ian, 210
Hamilton, Patrick, *Hangover Square*, 162
Hamlin, Frank, 10–11, 35
Hammett, Dashiell, 221, 230; *The Maltese Falcon*, 123–124

Hanna, David, 288
Hartley, Alyce, 248
Hatch, Eric, 81, 82–84
Havoc, June, 203
Hawks, Howard, 2, 91, 158, 165, 168, 170–171, 173–174, 175, 184, 191; on Bogart, 188; *The Big Sleep*, 177–179, 180, 182–183
Hawks, Nancy "Slim," 165, 170–171
Hayakawa, Sessue, 237
Hayden, Sterling, 203, 216–217
Hayes, Joseph, *The Desperate Hours*, 297
Hayward, Leland, 99, 170, 315, 316
Hellinger, Mark, 28, 76, 81, 116, 164, 165, 190, 210, 230, 235–236; *Manpower*, 109, *The Roaring Twenties*, 104
Hellman, Lillian, 69, 230
Hemingway, Clarence, 1
Hemingway, Ernest, 1–4, 65, 79, 230; code of honor, 130; *A Farewell to Arms*, 4, 183, *For Whom the Bell Tolls*, 228, "The Gambler, the Nun, and the Radio," 3, "The Killers," 3, 96, *A Moveable Feast*, 166–167, *The Old Man and the Sea*, 4, "The Snows of Kilimanjaro," 236, "Soldier's Home," 2, *The Sun Also Rises*, 289–290, *To Have and Have Not*, 92, 171, 172, 232
Hemingway, Grace, 1–2
Henley, W. E., "Invictus," 141
Henreid, Paul, 137, 138, 140, 148, 203, 207, 208
Hepburn, Audrey, 281–286
Hepburn, Katharine, 247, 248–249, 250–253, 255–256, 257, 309, 315
Hitchcock, Alfred, 8; *Rebecca*, 219, *The Thirty-Nine Steps*, 133
Hobart, Rose, 43, 154
Holden, William, 105, 106, 282–283, 284–286
Hollywood Ten, 202, 205–208, 342–343 n5
Holt, Tim, 228
Hopkins, Arthur, 49, 50
Hopkins, David, 203
Hopkins, Miriam, 108
Hopper, Hedda, 75, 165, 209, 261

Houseman, John, 182
House Un-American Activities Committee (HUAC), 196–199, 201–217
Howard, Cy, 265–266
Howard, Frances, 26
Howard, Leslie, 50, 60, 61–62, 63, 72, 73, 165
Howe, James Wong, 155
Hughes, Dorothy, *In a Lonely Place*, 240, 241
Hughes, Howard, 239, 249
Hunt, Marsha, 203
Hunter, Kim, 266
Hupfield, Herman, "As Time Goes By," 137
Huston, John, 2, 54, 81, 82, 194, 262, 306, 307, 309, and CFA, 201, 203, 205, 206, 208, 217, 235, as director, 115, 116, 125, 126–127, 131, 135–136, 158, 218, as screenwriter, 96, 97, 115, 117, 123–124, 130, 230–231, 234, 254, 279, FBI clearance, 343 n16, life, 114, on Bogart, 119, 158, 213, 214, 308, 313, 316–317; *An Open Book*, 135; *The African Queen*, 247, 249–258, *Beat the Devil*, 270–277, *The Treasure of the Sierra Madre*, 224–230
Huston, Walter, 74, 114, 125, 129, 225, 228, 230
Hyams, Joe, 76, 308

Inge, William, *Come Back, Little Sheba*, 268

Jaffe, Mildred, 313
Jaffe, Sam, 82, 89, 90, 99, 116, 166, 178, 195, 210, 236, 240, 268, 282, 307
Jenkins, Alan, 307
Johnson, Dorris, 79, 309, 314, 322
Johnson, Nunnally, 30, 64, 81, 88, 107, 259, 262, 263, 276, 301, 309, 314, 315, 316
Johnson, Van, 278, 280
Johnston, Eric, 200, 205
Jones, Jennifer, 99, 271, 273, 275–276, 315
Jones, John, 305
Joyce, James, 79, *Ulysses*, 52

Index

Kael, Pauline, 140–141
Kaufman, George S., 125, 165
Kaye, Danny, 203, 213, 214, 315
Kazan, Elia, 45
Keaton, Diane, 320
Kelly, Gene, 203, 213
Kelly, Kitty, 312
Keyes, Evelyn, 115, 203, 207, 214, 225
Kilgallen, Dorothy, 307–308
Kingsley, Sidney, *Dead End,* 69
Kipling, Rudyard, 166; "The Man Who Would Be King," 306, "Tommy," 279
Koch, Howard, 137
Kramer, Stanley, 277, 278

Lacy, Jerry, 319
Laemmle, Carl, Jr., 41
Lake, Veronica, 340–341 n13
Lancaster, Burt, 268
Lane, Mike, 300
Lane, Priscilla, 104
Lane, Rosemary, 100, 105
Lardner, Ring, Jr., 207, 214, 215
Laughton, Charles, 8
Laurents, Arthur, 215
Lawes, Lewis E., 105
Lawrence, D. H., 91, 314, *Lady Chatterley's Lover,* 289–290, *St. Mawr,* 103
Lawrence, Frieda, 91, 314
Lawson, John Howard, 206–207, 208
Lazar, Irving "Swifty," 145, 166, 188, 263, 264, 282, 309, 313, 315, 316
LeBeau, Madeleine, 137
Lederer, Charles, 263
Leech, John L., 198–199
Lehman, Ernest, 281, 283, 285, 291
Leslie, Amy, 30
Leslie, Joan, 118
Lewis, Sinclair, *It Can't Happen Here,* 209
Life, 24
Linkletter, Art, 195, 265
Little Caesar, 3, 60
Logan, Joshua, 45
Lollobrigida, Gina, 273, 275–276
Longfellow, Henry Wadsworth, "Paul Revere's Ride," 84
Lord, Robert, 66, 236
Loren, Sophia, 275
Lorre, Peter, 91, 92, 125, 126, 128–

129, 137, 138, 156, 166, 307; and Warner, 159; *Beat the Devil,* 271, 273, 275, 277
Losey, Joseph, 215, 247
Lowell, Robert, "Memories of West Street and Lepke," 342 n3
Luciano, Charles "Lucky," 67, 232
Luft, Sid, 89, 263
Lukas, Paul, 150
Lupino, Ida, 59, 109, 110, 111, 118–121

MacKenna, Kenneth, 33, 36, 74
MacMurray, Fred, 278, 280
Main, Marjorie, 71
Malone, Dorothy, 181
Mankiewicz, Joseph, 287–288, 289
Mann, Delbert, 53, 298
Manning, Irene, 132–133
Mansfield, Katherine, 91
The Man with Bogart's Face, 320
March, Fredric, 99, 198, 244, 297
Maree, Morgan, 74, 210, 235, 236, 270, 308
Marquand, John, *Melville Goodwin, USA,* 306
Martin, Dewey, 297
Martin, John Barlow, 262
Marx, Groucho, *A Night in Casablanca,* 151–152
Massey, Raymond, 152, 239
Maugham, W. Somerset, 245, 260
Mayer, Louis B., 204, 207
Mayo, Archie, 62
McCarten, John, 277
McCrea, Joel, 69, 71, 72
McLaughlin, Mignon, "The Woman Who Dreamed About Humphrey Bogart," 320
Menjou, Adolphe, 204
Menken, Helen, 27, 31–33, 158, 165, 179, marriage to Bogart, 33–35, 79
Methot, Mayo, death, 340 n6, divorce, 177–179, marriage to Bogart, 2, 73, 78–81, 88, 90–93, 118, 134, 156–158, 166–167, 169–170; *Marked Woman,* 67–68, *Mr. Deeds Goes to Town,* 79
Middleton, Robert, 297
Milland, Ray, 192

Miller, Arthur, 214, *The Misfits,* 115
Mission to Moscow, 201
Mitchum, Robert, 87
Monogram, 171
Monroe, Marilyn, 263
Montgomery, Robert, 204
Moorehead, Agnes, 223
Morgan, Dennis, 164
Morgan, Jess, 74, 87, 276
Morgan, Michele, 155
Morley, Robert, 256, 271, 273, 274
Morris, Wayne, 69, 105
Mostel, Zero, 99, 244, 245, 246
Motion Picture Association, 200, 205
Motley, Willard, *Knock on Any Door,* 236–237
Movie-making: "A" and "B" movies, 57, 96, blacklist, 215, 217, casting of actresses, 58–59, censorship, 58, 67, 122, 146, 149–150, 156, 171, 181–182, 197, 200, 201, 204–205, 276, *film noir,* 123, gangster genre, 59, Production Code, 58, 62, 98, 117, 176, script formulas, 112, 156, 222, 237, 339 n1, scripts, 57–58, 101, 103, 171–172, 295, special effects, 56–57, 152, 231–232, 253–254, studio system, 38–39, 54–55, 151, 235, working conditions, 39–40, 56–57, 63
Muni, Paul, 100, 116
Murphy, George, 204
Murrow, Edward R., *Person to Person,* 264–265

Nagel, Conrad, 41
Naipaul, V. S., *Miguel Street,* 321
Navasky, Victor, 206–207, 208
Nazimova, Alla, 51
Newman, Paul, 298
Niven, David, 88, 89, 110, 263, 309, 311–312, 314, 315, 316
Nixon, Richard, 197, 200–201, 204, 216
Nolan, Lloyd, 280
Norris, Frank, *McTeague,* 229

O'Brien, Edmond, 288
O'Brien, Pat, 98
Obringer, Roy, 94, 177, 268
O'Hara, John, 309
Orlova, Gay, 233

Orwell, George, 122, 337 n8, *Homage to Catalonia,* 143
Out of the Fog, 113

Page, Joy, 137
Paramount Pictures, 44
Parker, Eleanor, 239–240
Parks, Larry, 216
Parsons, Louella, 75, 207, 209–210, 248, 312–313
Patrick, Lee, 30
Peerless Film Studios, 24
Petersen, Carl, 193
Peterson, Verita, 18, 36, 195, 218, 282, 305, 308, 312, affair with Bogart, 93–94, 184, 287, 291–292, on Bogart, 81
Philips, Mary, 29, 36, 165, 179; marriage to Bogart, 37, 51, 73–74
Porter, Whitworth, *History of the Knights of Malta,* 127
Powell, Anthony, 54
Powell, Dick, 74, 192
Public Enemy, 3, 60, 98

Raft, George, 60, 69, 95, 105, 108–110, 111, 116–117, 124, 133
Rains, Claude, 137, 138, 156
Rapper, Irving, 64
Raskin, Richard, 149
Ray, Aldo, 293, 294
Ray, Nicholas, 88, 236, 240, 241–243, 307, 309, 312
Reagan, Ronald, 204, 315
Rebecca, 219
Redwing, Roderic, 231
Report from the Front, 158
Richardson, Cliff, 253–254
RKO, 44
Robards, Jason, 322
Roberts, Robin, 238–239
Robinson, Casey, 53
Robinson, Edward G., 60, 95, 109, 111, 112, 116, on Bogart, 47, 202, 212–213; *The Amazing Dr. Clitterhouse,* 96–97, *Brother Orchid,* 112, *Bullets or Ballots,* 65, *Key Largo,* 232–234, *Kid Galahad,* 68–69, *Little Caesar,* 65–66
Robson, Flora, 105

Index

Romanoff, Mike, 82, 88, 106–107, 166, 208, 240, 263, 315, 316
Romulus Films, 247
Roosevelt, Eleanor, 297
Roosevelt, Franklin, 150, 199, 201
Rose, Stuart, 21, 33, 37, 38, 47
Rosenbloom, Maxie, 91, 96
Ross, Lillian, 246
Rossellini, Roberto, 2, 272
Ruddy, Jonathan, 76

Sakall, S. Z. "Cuddles," 123, 137
Salazar, Aurelio, 186
Sanders, George, 272, 289
Satan Met a Lady, 123–124
Schickel, Richard, 323
Schlesinger, Arthur, Jr., 65, 261–262
Schulberg, Budd, *The Harder They Fall,* 300
Scott, Adrian, 205
Scott, Lizabeth, 219–222, 340–341 n13
Seberg, Jean, 319
Seiler, Lewis, 96, 132
Selznick, David, 74, 138, 207, 272, 315
Selznick, Irene, 74
Selznick, Myron, 54, 99
Seymour, Dan, 138, 172
Shakespeare, William, *The Tempest,* 130–131
Shaw, Irwin, *Gentle People,* 112–113
Shaw, James, 278
Sheekman, Arthur, 91
Sheridan, Ann, 93, 109, 111, 159, 228
Sherman, Vincent, 85, 96, 105, 110, 133–134, 136, 335 n3
Sherwood, Robert, 81, 150, 262, *The Petrified Forest,* 49–51
Sidney, Sylvia, 69–70, 71, 72
Siegel, Benjamin "Bugsy," 105
Silver Heels, Jay, 231
Silvers, Phil, 13
Sinatra, Frank, 213, 263, 288, 291, 299, 309, 310–313
Siodmak, Curt, 28
Sistrom, Joseph, 203
Sklar, Robert, 54
Slater, Peggy, 80
Sloan, Kathy, 186, 315
Sloane, Everett, 245, 246
Smith, Alexis, 154–155, 219

Smith, Art, 240, 244
Smith, May, 186
Sokolsky, George, 209, 210
Solt, Andrew, 240
Sosnick, Harry, 299
Spiegel, Sam, 247, 249, 254
Stacey, Eric, 177, 178
Stallion Road, 164
Stanwyck, Barbara, 74, 219
A Star Is Born, 269
Stearns, Alfred, 13, 14, 15–16, 19–20
Steiger, Rod, 300–302
Steinbeck, John, *Of Mice and Men,* 112
Steiner, Herman, 28, 107
Steiner, Max, 279
Sterling, Jan, 89
Stevens, Warren, 189, 266, 288, 289, 292, 307
Stevenson, Adlai, 261–263, 271, 310
Strauss, John, 259
Street Scene, 24
Stroheim, Erich von, 42, *Greed,* 229
Stuart, Gloria (Sheekman), 90, 91, 313–314
Sullavan, Margaret, 45
Sullivan, Ed, 209
Sweet, Blanche, 50

Taylor, Robert, 204
Taylor, Samuel, *Sabrina Fair,* 281
Thank Your Lucky Stars, 123
The Third Man, 289
The Thirteen, 153
Thomas, J. Parnell, 201, 204, 205, 207, 215
Thompson, Sylvia, 88–89
Thurber, James, 80, 81, 113
Tierney, Gene, 295, 296
Toland, Gregg, 70
Tone, Franchot, 198
Toren, Marta, 246
Tracy, Spencer, 4, 38, 41, 64, 249, 252, 281, 297, 309
Traven, B., *The Treasure of the Sierra Madre,* 227–230
Trevor, Claire, 59, 70–71, 96, 232–233, 234, 259
Trilling, Steve, 94, 110, 116, 226
Trintignant, Jean-Louis, 275
Truffaut, François, 318

Index

Truman, Harry, 165, 207, 220
Trumbo, Dalton, 206, 207
Tulli, Marco, 273
Twentieth Century–Fox, 162, 266, 294
Tynan, Kenneth, 65

Underdown, Edward, 273
Universal Studios, 36
Ustinov, Peter, 293, 294
The Usual Suspects, 320

Van Druten, John, *After All,* 43
Van Heusen, Jimmy, 263
Veblen, Thorsten, *The Theory of the Leisure Class,* 8
Veidt, Conrad, 134, 137, 138
Veiller, Anthony, 272
Verne, Kaaren, 134, 275
Vickers, Martha, 181
Viertel, Peter, 2, 250, 272, 277, *White Hunter, Black Heart,* 252–253
Vitaphone, 40
Vreeland, Diana, 165

Wald, Jerry, 222, 233, 302
Wald, Malvin, 210
Wallis, Hal, 53, 55, 57, 96, 101–102, 108, 116, 119, 126, 137, 138, 146, 150, 163
Walsh, Raoul, 41, 109, 116
Wanger, Walter, 293–294, 307
Warner Bros., 36, 43, 51–55, 59, 66, 67, 69, 76, 93, 94, 95, 101–102, 109–113, 123, 132, 151–152, 171, 218, 247, 268
Warner, Jack, 51–54, 96, 99, 138, 150–151, 181, 246, and Bogart, 55, 74–75, 86, 93, 95, 99, 105, 112–113,
116, 118–119, 123, 142, 159–164, 185, 222–223, 268–269, 315, and HUAC, 200, 204–205, 207, 293–294, concern for efficiency, 104–106, 108, 132, 136, 145, 231
Warshow, Robert, 59
Warwick, Robert, 240
Watch on the Rhine, 150
Webb, Clifton, 28, 31, 89
Weinstein, Charles, 238
Welles, Orson, 272
Welsh, Mary, 2
West, Nathanael, *The Day of the Locust,* 73
Westmore, Percy, 94
Wexley, John, 117
The White Sister, 38
Whittier, John Greenleaf, "Barbara Fritchie," 84
Wilder, Billy, 53, 218, 243, 281–283, 285–286, 315
Wilson, Dooley, 137
Wilson, Earl, 292, 311
Wilson, Edmund, 27, 124
Winchell, Walter, 192
Woolf, John, 247, 274
Woollcott, Alexander, 27, 29
Wouk, Herman, *The Caine Mutiny,* 278, 280
Wright, T. C., 177, 178
Wyatt, Jane, 203
Wyler, William, 69, 70, 74, 201, 218, 276, 297, 315

Yordan, Philip, 300
Young, Roland, 73

Zanuck, Darryl, 53, 261, 295

compiled by Valerie Meyers